PATERNOSTER BIBLICAL MONOGRAPHS

Saint Paul as Spiritual Director

An Analysis of the Imitation of Paul with Implications and Applications to the Practice of Spiritual Direction

PATERNOSTER BIBLICAL MONOGRAPHS

A full listing of titles in this series and Paternoster Theological Monographs appears at the end of this book

PATERNOSTER BIBLICAL AND THEOLOGICAL MONOGRAPHS

Saint Paul as Spiritual Director

An Analysis of the Imitation of Paul with Implications and Applications to the Practice of Spiritual Direction

Victor A. Copan

WIPF & STOCK · Eugene, Oregon

Wipf and Stock Publishers
199 W 8th Ave, Suite 3
Eugene, OR 97401

Saint Paul as Spiritual Director
An Analysis of the Concept of the Imitation of Paul with Implications and Applications to the Practice of Spiritual Direction
By Copan, Victor A.

ISBN 13: 978-1-55635-661-2
ISBN 10: 1-55635-661-7
Publication date 1/8/2008

This Edition Published by Wipf and Stock Publishers by arrangement with Paternoster

Paternoster
9 Holdom Avenue
Bletchley
Milton Keyes, MK1 1QR
Great Britain

PATERNOSTER BIBLICAL MONOGRAPHS

Series Preface

One of the major objectives of Paternoster is to serve biblical scholarship by providing a channel for the publication of theses and other monographs of high quality at affordable prices. Paternoster stands within the broad evangelical tradition of Christianity. Our authors would describe themselves as Christians who recognise the authority of the Bible, maintain the centrality of the gospel message and assent to the classical credal statements of Christian belief. There is diversity within this constituency; advances in scholarship are possible only if there is freedom for frank debate on controversial issues and for the publication of new and sometimes provocative proposals. What is offered in this series is the best of writing by committed Christians who are concerned to develop well-founded biblical scholarship in a spirit of loyalty to the historic faith.

Series Editors

To my wonderful partner, Kathy, my constant source of encouragement and love. To Annaliesa, Andreas, and Benjamin, my constant source of joy and laughter. To Valery and Valtraut Copan, humble, loving, and godly role models, my constant source of inspiration.

Contents

Acknowledgements

To all those who aided me in many ways throughout the research and writing of this work:

Many thanks to Prof. Dr. Susanne Heine, who oversaw the project from beginning to end. She took on this dissertation in its confused beginnings and saw potential where I saw fog; she maintained the fine balance between giving wise counsel and allowing freedom to explore. It was a pleasure to interact with her throughout this time.

Thanks also to Mark Reasoner and Michael Holmes for their guidance early on in this project. Their conceptual insights helped tremendously in sharpening my focus.

Special thanks to my former weekly men's group in Vienna, Austria, Wolfgang Conrad, Werner Engel, Alex Hagmüller, Christian Hagmüller, Siegi Kröpfl, Harald Kruzik, Heiner Schmidt, Kaarlo Schörkl, and Patrick Todjeras, who rejoiced in my progress and stood by me in my frustration.

Also heartfelt thanks to my former colleagues, Fritz Neubacher, Rudie Matheuszik, Gerald Wakolbinger, Susanne Budaker, Mathilde Defner, who freed me from many responsibilities for the duration of the initial project. I sorely miss the close fellowship we enjoyed.

My sister, Helen Neubacher, was a perpetual source of joy and encouragement. She was the strong shoulder to lean on, especially for Kathy, through the ups and downs of this project.

I cannot say enough about the help and encouragement of my brother, Paul. He was ever willing to track down hard-to-get articles for me. Then, in preparation for publication, he volunteered to take on the meticulous task of proof-read the entire work. I couldn't ask for a better brother!

I thank Annaliesa, Andreas, and Benjamin for putting up with an absentee father while I was writing ("Is dad *still* in his office?" "Isn't he done *yet*?"). They mean more to me than words can express. Finally, and most importantly, I want to honor my wife, Kathy. She not only deserves my deepest gratitude but also a long vacation! She freed me up from responsibilities so that I could focus on writing, and she also willingly inflicted upon herself the task of proof-reading the rough draft of the dissertation. Words cannot express how grateful I am to her. This book is dedicated to her and our three children.

Abbreviations

The abbreviations used in this monograph for Latin terms, periodicals, reference works, and serials follow the *SBL Handbook of Style For Ancient Near Eastern, Biblical, and Early Christian Studies*, Patrick H. Alexander et al. (Peabody: Hendrickson, 1999), 68-152, 237-63. The names and titles of ancient authors not referenced in the *SBL Handbook* are taken from THESAURUS LINGUAE GRAECAE Version E on CD-ROM, University of California, Irving, Calif. (TLG-E). All other terms and titles have been either written out in full or are abbreviated as follows.

Latin Abbreviations:

ascet.	*Asceticus*
Beat.	*Beatitudines*
Bib.	*Bibliotheca*
Cant.	*Cantica*
cap.	*capita*
Cat.	*Catena(e)*
Coll.	*Collectio*
Decl.	*Declamationes*
Diss.	*Dissertationes/um*
dub.	*dubia*
Hymn.	*Hymnographus*
Interr.	*Interrogationes*
Matt.	*Matthaeum*
Mel.	*Melodus*
respons.	*responsiones*
Rom.	*Romanus*
Schol.	*Scholia*
Serm.	*Sermo, Sermones*
uirg.	*Uirginitate*
vet.	*vetera*
vig.	*viginti*

Ancient Works:

Andocides

Myst.	*De mysteriis*

Aristeas	
Phil.	*Epistula ad Philocratem*
Asterius Sophista	
Frag. Ps.	*Fragmenta in Psalmos*
Basil Scr. Eccl.	
Serm. xli	*Sermones xli*
Basil Theol.	
reg. Mor.	*regulae Morales*
Sebast.	*in quadraginta martyres Sebastenses*
Serm. 11	*Sermo 11 (sermo asceticus et exhortation de renuntiatione mundi)*
Spir.	*De Spiritu Sancto*
Cat. Matt.	*Catena in Matthaeum (catena integra)*
Choricius	
Op.	*Opera*
Damascenus, Joannes	
Comm. Paul.	*Commentarii in epistulas Pauli*
Diodorus Siculus	
Hist.	*Bibliotheca historica*
Ephraem Syrus	
Ascet.	*Sermo asceticus*
Beat.	*Beatitudines aliae, capita viginti*
Inter.	*Interrogationes ac responsiones*
Iud. comp.	*De iudicio et compunctione*
Uirg.	*Sermo de uirginitate*
Virt.	*Sermo de virtutibus et vitiis*
Epictetus	
Arriano	*Dissertationes ab Arriano digestae*
Galenus Med.	
Advers.	*Adversus ea quae a Juliano in Hippocratis aphorismos enuntiata sunt libellus*
Gregory Nyssenus	
Eunom.	*Contra Eunomium*
Greg.	*de vita Gregorii Thaumaturgi*
Melet.	*Oration funebris in Meletium episcopum*
Par.	*De paradise*
Perf.	*De perfectione christiana ad Olympium monachum*
Or. Meletium	*Oration funebris in Meletium episcopum*
Himerius	
Decl.	*Declamationes et orationes*
John Chrysostom	
Frag. Prov.	*Fragmenta in Proverbia (in catenis)*
Julianus, Flavius Claudius	
Caes.	*sive Caesares*
Ep.	*Epistulae*
Lysias	
Epitaph.	*Epitaphius*
Marcellinus	

Thuc.	*Vita Thucydidis*
Marcus Diaconus	
Porph.	*Vita Porphurii eposcopi Gazensis*
Numenius	
Frag.	*Fragmenta*
Photius	
Bib.	*Bibliotheka*
Pseudo Justin Martyr	
Diogn.	*Epistula ad Diognetum*
Pseudo Macarius Scr. Eccl.	
Hom. 7	*Homiliae 7 (collectio HA)*
Romanus Melodus	
Cant. dub.	*Cantica dubia*
Scholia Pindarum	*Scholia in Pindarum (scholia vetera)*
Stobaeus, John	
Anth.	*Anthologium*
Syncellus, George	
Ec. chron.	*Ecloga chronographica*
Theodoretus	
Epist.	*Epistulae: Collection Patmensis (epistulae 1-52)*

Other Works:

AfB	Archiv für Begriffsgeschichte
ANTS	Approaches to New Testament Study
AuG	*Amt und Gemeinde* (*Evangelische Kirche Österreich*)
B&C	*Books & Culture*
BECNT	Baker Exegetical Commentary on the New Testament
BHÖSH	Bensheimer Hefte Ökumenische Studienhefte
BWM	Bibelwissenschaftliche Monographien
BZNWKK	Beihefte zur Zeitschrift für die neutestamentliche Wissenschaft und die Kunde der älteren Kirche
CCR	Cambridge Companions to Religion
CCS	Cistercian Study Series
ChBib	The Church's Bible
ChCT	Challenges in Contemporary Theology
ChrEdJ	*Christian Education Journal*
ChrTod	*Christianity Today*
CoQoG	Christian Origins and the Question of God
CrCur	Cross-Currents
DCS	*Dictionary of Christian Spirituality*
DJ	*Discipleship Journal*
DNTB	*Dictionary of New Testament Backgrounds*
EBC	*Expositor's Bible Commentary*
ECBKNT	Edition C-Bibelkommentar zum Neuen Testament
ETSS	Evangelical Theological Society Studies

EWNT	*Exegetisches Wörterbuch zum Neuen Testament*
FilNeo	*Filologia Neotestamentaria*
FormSpir	*Formative Spirituality*
FT	*First Things*
HfT	Helps for Translators
IBR	Institute for Biblical Research
IVPNTCS	The Intervarsity Press New Testament Commentary Series
JETh	*Jahrbuch für Evangelikale Theologie*
JPC	*Journal of Psychology and Christianity*
JPCC	*Journal of Pastoral Care and Counseling*
JPT	*Journal of Psychology and Theology*
JRH	*Journal of Religion and Health*
JSHJ	*Journal for the Study of the Historical Jesus*
JVOG	*Jesus and the Victory of God*
LCBI	Literary Currents in Biblical Interpretation
Lead	*Leadership Magazine*
M&S	Monographien und Studienbücher
MCB	Mercer Commentary on the Bible
MNTS	McMaster New Testament Studies
NCBC	The New Cambridge Bible Commentary
NDT	*The New Dictionary of Theology*
NIVAC	The New International Version Application Commentary
NLCNT	The New London Commentary on the New Testament
NLitHist	*New Literary History*
NTC	New Testament Commentary
NTDER	Das Neue Testament Deutsch Ergänzungsreihe
NTPOG	*The New Testament and the People of God*
NTR	*New Theology Review*
NTTh	New Testament Theology
ÖTKNT	Ökumenischer Taschenbuchkommentar zum Neuen Testament
PastPsych	*Pastoral Psychology*
PhInt	Philosophical Introductions
PilNTC	Pillar New Testament Commentary
PM	Past Masters
RC	The Reader's Commentary
RBL	*Review of Biblical Literature*
RevMet	*Review of Metaphysics*
Rel	*Religion*
RelLit	*Religion and Literature*
SBLF	*Society of Biblical Literature Forum*
SNTW	Studies of the New Testament and its World
SNTSMS	Studiorum Novi Testamenti Societas Monograph Series
SS	Studies in Spirituality

SupJSJ	Supplements to the Journal for the Study of Judaism
TAK	Thornapple Commentaries
THNTC	Two Horizons New Testament Commentary
TLG-E	Thesaurus Linguae Graecae CD-Rom E
TNN	*Theology, News & Notes* (Fuller Theological Seminary)
Trans	*Transformation*
WesTJ	*Wesleyean Theological Journal*
WSB	Wuppertaler Studien Bibel
WWSup	Word and World Supplement Series
WycBC	Wycliffe Bible Commentary

Other:

JT	Jesus Tradition

Bible Translations:

ASV	American Standard Version
BBE	The Bible in Basic English
CSB	Holman Christian Standard Bible
DBY	The Darby Bible
DRA	The Douay-Rheims American Edition
EIN	Einheitsübersetzung der Heiligen Schrift
ELB	Elberfelder Bibel revidierte Fassung (1993)
ERV	English Revised Version (1885)
ESV	English Standard Version
GNV	Geneva Bible (1599)
GWN	God's Word to the Nations Translation
HRD	Herder Übersetzung der Heiligen Schrift des Alten und Neuen Bundes
KJV	King James Version
LUT	Revidierte Lutherbibel (1984)
LXE	English Translation of The Septuagint Version of the Old Testament by Sir Lancelot C. L. Brenton (1851)
NAB	New American Bible
NAS	New American Standard Bible (1977)
NAU	New American Standard Bible (1995)
NRS	New Revised Standard Version (1989)
NET	New English Translation
NIB	New International Version (British Version)
NIV	New International Version
NJB	New Jerusalem Bible
NKJ	New King James Version
NLT	New Living Translation (2004)
Phillips	J. B. Phillips Translation of the New Testament
RSV	Revised Standard Version (1952)

RWB	Revised Webster Bible (1995)
SCH	Die Heilige Schrift des Alten und Neuen Testaments nach dem Urtext Übersetzt von Franz Eugen Schlachter
TEV	Today's English Version
TNT	The Tyndale New Testament
WEB	The Webster Bible
YLT	Young's Literal Translation

Introduction

This book was birthed out of personal struggle. I was involved both in pastoral ministry as well as in ministry to theology students. As parishioners and students came to me with their spiritual questions, I found that the means and methods for spiritual growth that I had inherited from my religious subculture (broadly evangelical) were increasingly inadequate to effect genuine spiritual growth and change. This initiated a period of deep reflection in my life and ministry, and I began asking embarrassingly rudimentary questions: How do I define spiritual growth? What is the goal of spiritual growth? How do I help people in their journey toward spiritual growth?

With these questions banging around in my head, I began to search for answers. Since I had at that time been living in Austria, a predominantly Catholic country, I had developed friendships with Catholic priests and monks, who were well-versed in the art of spiritual direction. A new world opened up to me, with new ways of understanding "the spiritual life" and assisting those on their journey into this life. Yet the more I read in the literature, the more I discovered that spiritual direction was not monolithic. There was a wide divergence in intention, presuppositions, models, and methodologies. This initiated another set of questions: How do I choose between the various approaches? Are they all equally valid? Which are the most effective—and to what end are they effective?

The key question for me at this stage was the question of criteria: I needed an anchor, a measuring instrument by which I could evaluate the various approaches. This then led me to asking the question: How did spiritual direction happen in the New Testament? What did spiritual growth, as defined by the New Testament, look like? What were the goals and methodologies of spiritual direction the key players in the New Testament books? I realized that I was both begging the question, since I had not defined spiritual direction for myself, and was guilty of anachronism, since the term "spiritual direction" is nowhere to be found in the New Testament writings. But I had to start somewhere.

Realizing that tackling the whole of the New Testament would be a monumental undertaking, I decided that my course of action should be a case study approach, analyzing one key figure with respect to what I could learn about the definition and aims of spiritual growth as well as the means and methods this figure used to effect this growth. Because of my prior work in Pauline studies and because of the major role he played in the life of the early church, I was naturally drawn to him.

Again, I was confronted with methodological issues: How do I study these sets of questions in the life and ministry of Paul? This would be a mammoth undertaking. What I needed was a means of delimiting my study to make it on the one hand manageable while on the other hand producing results that would be solid enough to draw well-founded conclusions with respect to the practice of spiritual direction. I needed "keyholes" through which I could look that would allow me

- to understand how he understood the nature, the goals, and the ideal lifestyle of a Christian, and
- to discern his own methodology of spiritual direction.

But what could these keyholes be? I needed texts that would expose "the personal Paul in action"—where he revealed those aspects for which I was looking? As I was batting these issues around with my doctoral advisor, Dr. Susanne Heine, she suggested that I consider looking at the texts in which Paul either called the recipients of his letters to imitate him or noted with approval that they were doing such. Could these texts give insight into Paul's actual *modus operandi* for spiritual direction? This monograph is my exploration of these texts for that purpose.

In preparing this work for publication, I took the opportunity to review the literature on the imitation of Paul that had been published since I wrote my dissertation and incorporate it into this monograph.

CHAPTER 1

Introduction

1.1 The Research Topic

1.1.1 Purpose of this Study

My goal in this work is to analyze afresh the concept of the imitation of Paul as reflected in the uncontested Pauline epistles in order to determine its relevance to the practice of spiritual direction. In order to do this, it is necessary to understand Paul's use of imitation language within the context of its usage in antiquity. This concept of one person imitating another has, however, with the postmodern turn, come under sharp criticism as an illegitimate power play. Perhaps the strongest postmodern critique of Paul's call to imitation is by Elizabeth Castelli in her work *Imitating Paul: A Discourse of Power*. It is right and proper to be concerned with abuse of power and authority. Was the Apostle Paul guilty of the abuse of power as Elizabeth Castelli alleges? We shall need to examine her claims and the foundation for her arguments. The final goal of this work is to discuss the implications, applications, and limitations of our findings for the practice of spiritual direction today.

1.1.2 Approaching Spiritual Direction and Imitation

Spiritual direction, with its roots in the Catholic and Orthodox traditions, has become increasingly popular within the Protestant tradition in the last three decades. When one begins to look at the various models of spiritual direction, one notices a great degree of divergence both on the presuppositional and methodological levels. The plethora of approaches can be bewildering. How do we go about choosing which model of spiritual direction to practice? Does it matter? What are the criteria for deciding between approaches? What qualifications does a person need for practicing direction?

When one reads the contemporary literature on spiritual direction,[1] one factor that does not receive adequate discussion is the impact the total shape of the director's life has on the directee—that is, his personal life and praxis, work/ministry, emotional, intellectual life, and most of all the shape his

---

1 For an overview of the literature on this topic, see the discussion in chapter one.

spirituality. Technique is at the forefront of the discussions on spiritual direction, while the life of the director is given short shrift.

It is my contention—one that will be born out in the body of this work—that

- the total shape of the life of the director is a key factor—if not *the* key factor—in the success of spiritual direction;
- effectiveness in spiritual direction is not to be found primarily in technique, but in the character and lifestyle of the one providing the direction.

What we are describing builds on what the classical rhetoricians called ethos. It is a term used to describe the impact that the totality of the speaker's life has on the audience even before she opens her mouth. Ethos, in its written variation, is an author's appeal to her own moral character and other aspects of her life, which enhance her credibility—whether this is a conscious rhetorical strategy or not. It is "the relationship built up within the speech between the rhetor and the auditor which induces the auditor to believe the person speaking. Such a relationship is built up by means of identification between the rhetor and auditor, through participation in the world that exists between them."[2] Aristotle's discussion of ethos in *Rhetoric* is the first extant theoretical discussion of ethos as an artistic proof:

> Now the proofs furnished by the speech are of three kinds. The first depends upon the moral character [ἦθος] of the speaker. . . . The orator persuades by moral character when the speech is delivered in such a manner as to render them worthy of confidence, for we feel confidence in a greater degree and more readily in persons of worth in regard to everything in general. . . . For it is not the case, as some writers of rhetorical treatises lay down in their 'Art', that the worth of the orator in no way contributes to the orator's powers of persuasion; on the contrary, moral character, so to say, constitutes the most effective means of proof.[3]

It is this factor of ethos with respect to the life of St. Paul, which has special relevance for the practice of spiritual direction: The Apostle Paul sets himself up intentionally and boldly as a model for others; he functions as a model, a prototype for the 'directees'—the congregations that he birthed. It will be clear, I trust, in the analysis that follows, that it was the ethos of the Apostle Paul that made such a strong and life-changing impact on his followers.

It is in this point that we seek to make a contribution through this work: to rediscover the concept and role of imitation—properly understood—for the practice of spiritual direction today through the analysis of imitation in Paul.

---

2 John W. Marshall, "Paul's Ethical Appeal in Philippians," in *Rhetoric and the New Testament: Essays from the 1992 Heidelberg Conference* (ed. Stanley E. Porter and Thomas H. Olbricht; JSNTSup; Sheffield: JSOT Press, 1993), 360.

3 Aristotle, *Rhet.* 5.76 (Freese, LCL). (Noted in Marshall, "Paul's Ethical Appeal," 358.)

1.2 Methodology and Scope of Research

1.2.1 Rationale for Choosing Paul

The Apostle Paul was chosen because of his prominence in the canon and because of his more thorough treatment of how life is to be lived as a Christian—in combination with his use of "imitation" language throughout his writings, thus setting himself up as a model to be emulated and because he simultaneously functioned as a "spiritual director" to the fledgling communities.[4] The uncontested letters were chosen to limit the scope of this study to a manageable size and to work from a commonly accepted starting point for Pauline studies.

1.2.2 Limitations

There are a number of inherent limitations in this type of analysis. One limitation has to do with *the nature of these writings*. The uncontested Pauline letters are of an occasional nature and were intended to be neither systematic nor exhaustive treatments of this topic. Thus any analysis of Paul's letters must remain tentative, indicative, and partial. Another closely related limitation has to do with the *parameters we have set for our study*. Our sample texts, the uncontested writings of Paul, do not provide a full picture, but merely a starting point. For a full picture, all the texts of the Pauline corpus, the book of Acts and extracanonical references to Paul would have to be considered. This is not possible within the confines of a work of this nature.

1.2.3 Outline of Study

In the second chapter we survey the various terms in the semantic field "spiritual direction" and how leading practitioners in the English-speaking world define it. We look at the works of these practitioners to observe what weight they give to ethos and imitation of the spiritual director. Chapter three surveys imitation language outside the Pauline corpus in order to develop a nuanced, informed understanding of the concept of imitation in the Greco and Jewish world. The focus of chapters four through six is on analyzing the imitation of Paul—examining afresh the relevant imitation passages, seeking to understand the full breadth of the imitation of Paul; and then drawing interim conclusions and observations based on our discoveries. Chapter seven addresses the radical proposal of Elizabeth Castelli in her book *Imitation Paul: A Discourse of Power*[5] and critique her understanding of Pauline imitation. The

4 I am aware that I have not defined the term "spiritual direction" and am using it anachronistically. Chapter one deals with these matters of definition and anachronism.

5 Elizabeth A. Castelli, *Imitating Paul: A Discourse of Power* (LCBI; Louisville, Ky.: Westminster, 1991).

eighth chapter summarizes our findings from chapters four through seven. In the final chapter, we discuss some issues with respect to practicing the concept of imitation today and then turn to implications and applications of our findings to the practice of spiritual direction today.

A few concluding notes: We have taken as our standard Bible translation the New Revised Standard Version (NRS). Other versions will be identified if their reading is preferred. Unless otherwise noted, all translations of ancient and German texts are my own.

CHAPTER 2

Surveying and Clarifying Terminology Regarding Spiritual Direction

Introduction

Corresponding to the well-documented explosion of interest in spirituality in the English-speaking world in the past years, there has also been a parallel surge of written material on spiritual direction. Gordon Jeff, a pioneer in spiritual direction in England, notes: "If publishers' lists are anything to go by, spiritual direction is a fashionable growth industry."[1]

Along with this writing explosion there has also been an inflation of terminology orbiting around the concept of spiritual direction. In the literature, the following terms are often used interchangeably, at times imprecisely, and with only slight differences in meaning or emphasis: "spiritual guide," "spiritual friend," "spiritual companion," "soul friend," "discipler,"[2] "spiritual mentor," etc. An example of such imprecise use of terminology is found in the foreword of a book on mentoring:

> great *spiritual directors* are ones who understand that, as their *disciples* progress and mature, the *teacher-learner* relationship will evolve. . . . [The] best phrase is '*mutual mentoring.*' It is the proverbial "iron sharpening iron" principle . . . by which both *director* and *directee* become indistinguishable in their needs.[3]

Throughout the whole of Jones' book, the following terms are used interchangeably with virtually no differentiation in meaning: spiritual director, discipler, spiritual guide, spiritual friend, spiritual companion and mentor. What seems to be the common generative idea behind all these varying terms, to put it simplistically at this point, is helping others grow in their faith or developing

---

1 Gordon Jeff, *Spiritual Direction for Every Christian* (London: SPCK, 1987), 1. Virtually all of the books on spiritual direction referenced in this chapter note this upsurge in interest.

2 A term not found in standard dictionaries, but one that is often used in evangelical circles.

3 Timothy K. Jones, *Mentor and Friend: Building Friendships that Point to God* (Oxford: Lion, 1991), 11 (emphasis mine).

their spirituality.

However, at other times the understanding of spiritual direction of one author—both with respect to the definition of the term, the proposed methodology of direction, and the framework—clearly contradicts that of another author.

Therefore, a broad range of challenges confronts the person who attempts a more systematic examination of the concept of Christian spiritual direction. Four of them are germane to our study: (1) terminological confusion, imprecision, and contradiction noted above; (2) wide variance in the understanding of the practice of spiritual direction within the literature of the past twenty years; (3) no agreed upon methodological controls to determine the validity of a model of a spiritual direction that is truly Christian in nature; (4) finally, the more fundamental problem that the term "spiritual direction" is not found in Scripture, making the drawing of parallels and analogies to today's terminology and conceptual world prone toward subjective predilection.

Is there a way to deal with this set of problems? I would argue that there is. The solution, I would suggest, is to ask specific *generative* questions that can bridge the gap between Scripture and the contemporary understanding of the definition and method of spiritual direction and can find common ground between them.

The preliminary generative questions I would suggest for our understanding of spiritual direction, which I expand at the end of the chapter, are the following: What is the essential core of spiritual direction in contemporary definitions that allow us then to apply the term to parallel phenomena in the New Testament? Based on this core definition, is spiritual direction, in fact, occurring in the pages of the New Testament, even though the term and concept is not used by the authors of the New Testament? If so, what is the specific shape and practice of spiritual direction in the New Testament? Finally, how does Scripture, in turn, inform, correct, and critique modern approaches to spiritual direction?

It is this set of generative questions for which we seek to find answers in this monograph, especially as we apply them to the Apostle Paul in his function as a spiritual director.

I need, at this point, to insert—and assert—something that I only argue in chapters three (marginally) and four through six (primarily): the importance of the role that ethos and the concept of imitation plays in the spiritual growth of a person. Primarily with respect to the Apostle Paul, one of the key strategies for the development of the faith of members of the communities he founded was the appeal to examine his life and character and to follow his ways. This is not something original to Paul but was standard practice in the world of his day. Since this plays such a strong role in Paul's methodology of spiritual direction (which, again, remains to be argued), it would be more than a little interesting to see if and how contemporary practitioners of spiritual direction also focus on the concepts of ethos and imitation in our survey of them later in this chapter.

The remainder of this chapter will deal with four issues that will inform the structure of the remainder of the chapter: (1) a survey of which terms are used in the discussion and how various practitioners understand these terms and their trade; (2) a discussion of the interrelationship between spiritual direction and therapeutic approaches; (3) observations of how much weight contemporary published spiritual directors place on the concepts of ethos and imitation. (I shall limit my interaction to acknowledged authorities in the field of spiritual direction from the English-speaking world of the last thirty years); and finally, (4) a proposed a definition of spiritual direction, which allows us to understand and analyze Paul as spiritual director.

2.1 Surveying the Semantic Field of Spiritual Direction

2.1.1 Spiritual Director

Probably the term with the longest tradition attached to the art of aiding individuals in their spiritual journey is the term "spiritual director." Although it has had historically troublesome authoritarian connotations,[4] it still enjoys widespread usage even today.

Thomas Merton's little booklet *Spiritual Direction and Meditation* sparked renewed interest in the topic beyond the Catholic tradition. In it he defines the spiritual director as "one who helps another to recognize and to follow the inspirations of grace in his life, in order to arrive at the end to which God is leading him."[5] The spiritual director's task is to help the directee discern the "special vocation" to which he is called and to grow in his union with God.[6] Put in other words: the purpose of the director is to penetrate the façade of the directee's life in order to "bring out his inner spiritual freedom, his inmost truth, which is what we call the likeness of Christ in his soul."[7]

Kenneth Leech, a leading voices in the movement of spiritual direction in the English-speaking world, provides no original definition of spiritual direction. He simply adapts Thomas Merton's[8] and supplements it with Edward Carter's emphasis that the director's task is 'to assist in helping the person read the breathings of the Spirit.'[9] This combination of definitions functions as his working framework for understanding spiritual direction.

---

4 Gerald May, *Care of Mind/Care of Spirit: Psychiatric Dimensions of Spiritual Direction* (San Francisco: Harper & Row, 1982), 7.

5 Thomas Merton, *Spiritual Direction and Meditation* (Collegeville, Minn.: Liturgical Press, 1960), 17.

6 Merton, *Spiritual Direction*, 13.

7 Merton, *Spiritual Direction*, 16.

8 A director is "one who helps another to recognize and to follow the inspirations of grace in his life, in order to arrive at the end to which God is leading him" (Kenneth Leech, *Soul Friend: The Practice of Christian Spirituality* [San Francisco: Harper & Row, 1977], 89).

9 Leech, *Soul Friend*, 89.

However, Leech closely weds this definition of direction to five fundamental characteristics that a director should embody. A director (1) exudes closeness to God and holiness of life; (2) has experience in prayer and life; (3) is a person of learning, having been steeped in Scripture and the wisdom of the Fathers; (4) has discernment, perception and insight into life; (5) gives way to the leading of the Holy Spirit and helps others recognize the Spirit's leading.[10]

Barry and Connolly offer an extended definition of spiritual direction. They see it as

> help given by one Christian to another which enables that person to pay attention to God's personal communication to him or her, to respond to this personally communicating God, to grow in intimacy with this God, and to live out the consequences of the relationship. The *focus* of this type of spiritual direction is on experience, not ideas, and specifically on religious experience, i.e., any experience of the mysterious Other whom we call God. Moreover, this experience is viewed, not as an isolated event, but as an expression of the ongoing personal relationship God has established with each one of us.[11]

This definition highlights the experiential, communicative, and relational dimensions of direction and seeks to remain true to the traditional intent of spiritual direction throughout the centuries, which was seen as striving for "union with God."[12]

Gordon Jeff seeks to bring the tradition of spiritual direction as widely as possible into the local parish. He views the enterprise of spiritual direction primarily as assistance with respect to prayer and guidance for life's path:

> Direction, as I understand it, is two people sitting down together in an attitude of prayer to try to discern where the Holy Spirit is directing. The "director", from his or her experience of others, from insight or wisdom, may sometimes have suggestions to offer to the "directee"; but the whole exercise is one in which the potential of the directee is being helped to emerge, and not in any sense a pushing of directees into any one kind of path of prayer.[13]

Alan Jones, also a noted authority in the field of spiritual direction, provides a definition (albeit not intended to be a clinical one) of a perspective on spiritual direction that is so bland as to be unhelpful: "True spiritual direction is about the great unfixables in human life. It's about the mystery of moving through time. It's about mortality. It's about love. It's about things that can't be

---

10 Leech, *Soul Friend*, 88-89.

11 William A. Barry and William J. Connolly, *The Practice of Spiritual Direction* (San Francisco: HarperSanFrancisco, 1982), 8 (authors' emphasis).

12 Barry and Connolly, *Practice*, 8.

13 Jeff, *Spiritual Direction*, 10.

fixed."[14]

In his historical overview of spiritual direction, Gerald May notes that spiritual direction has been viewed primarily as formal relationship between two individuals that tended to focus on five basic areas over the years: (1) the deepest heart-journey possible (John of the Cross, Teresa of Avila), (2 & 3) grappling with matters of conscience and vocation (some developments after the Council of Trent), (4) discerning good and evil spirits (Ignatius of Loyola), and (5) involving psychological growth, individuation, and self-actualization (more modern approaches).[15] Although May welcomes newer terminology, he questions whether they do justice to the actual practice of aiding another in his growth as a Christian. For example, regarding *spiritual friendship*[16] he questions whether friendships, as we experience them today, can actually deliver what people seek with respect to direction. It is questionable to May whether a spiritual friendship will provide the proper framework for accountability, confrontation and/or definitiveness in discernment.[17] Regarding the term *spiritual guidance*, he observes that guidance occurs through many avenues such as friends, religious communities, Scripture, nature, art, etc., but when "spiritual guidance occurs in a formal, one-to-one relationship with another individual, it can be called *spiritual direction*."[18] The term *director* is then to be the preferred term, provided one sees the director not as one who gives orders, but rather "as one who points direction."[19]

Two organizations that have had a wide impact on the development of spiritual direction in the English-speaking world are the *Shalem Institute for Spiritual Formation* in Washington, D.C. and *Spiritual Directors International*.[20] Shalem Institute, which has had well over 1,200 participants complete its Spiritual Direction Program,[21] defines spiritual direction as an "on-going relationship in which one person (the directee), desirous of being attentive to his or her spiritual life, meets with another person (the director) on a regular basis . . . specifically for the purpose of becoming more attuned to God's Presence in order to respond more fully to that Presence in all of life."[22]

The director of Shalem Institute, Tilden Edwards, acknowledges that for

14 In his forward to Margaret Guenther, *Holy Listening: The Art of Spiritual Direction* (Boston: Cowley, 1992), x.

15 May, *Care of Mind*, 2.

16 See discussion on *spiritual friendship* below.

17 May, *Care of Mind*, 8.

18 May, *Care of Mind*, 7 (author's emphasis).

19 May, *Care of Mind*, 7.

20 Shalem Institute for Spiritual Formation, n.p. [cited 23 January 2001]. Online: http://www.shalem.org/.

21 Gerald May, email from author, 17 May 2001.

22 Shalem Institute for Spiritual Formation, "Spiritual Direction: An Online Verson [sic] of the Shalem Pamphlet on Spiritual Direction," n.p. [cited 19 May]. Online: http://www.shalem.org/sd.html.

some, the title 'spiritual direction' has authoritarian connotations and thus alongside it deliberately uses other terms that have also long tradition: spiritual friend or companion, soul friend, guide, spiritual father or mother, brother or sister.[23] In his most recent book, he shifts back more confidently to the term "director," since his understanding is that it is the Holy Spirit who is the true director.[24]

Jeffrey Gaines, former executive director of *Spiritual Directors International*,[25] defines spiritual direction as "the art of Christian listening carried out in the context of a one-to-one trusting relationship. It is when one Christian is trained to be a competent guide who then 'companions' another person, listening to that person's life story with an ear for the movement of the Holy, of the Divine."[26]

2.1.2 Spiritual Guide

One potential danger in the practice of spiritual direction is abuse of authority leading to coercion of the directee. Spiritual direction can and did imply unquestioning submission and obedience to a superior. This danger was manifest early within the Christian tradition. An example of this over-authoritarian understanding of direction is evident in Clement of Alexandria:

> It is of utmost necessity for you, who are pompous and powerful and rich, by all means to set over yourself some man of God as trainer and guide. Reverence and fear him, though he is but a man. Give attention to listening to him even though he speak with utmost forthrightness—using harshness together with healing. . . . Fear this man when he is angry, and be in pains at his grief, and reverence him when making his anger to cease; and be quick to entreat him when he is punishing you.[27]

Because of the abuse of power by authoritarian directors through the centuries, there has been a trend away from the term "direction" toward the

23 Tilden H. Edwards, *Spiritual Friend: Reclaiming the Gift of Spiritual Direction* (Mahwah, N.J.: Paulist Press, 1980), 2.

24 Tilden H. Edwards, *Spiritual Director, Spiritual Companion: Guide to Tending the Soul* (Mahwah, N.J.: Paulist Press, 2000), 2.

25 This is a network of over 3,500 spiritual directors world-wide begun in 1989. Jeffrey S. Gaines, "Connections: SDI Newsletter (June 2000)," n.p. [cited 17 May 2001]. Online: http://www.sdiworld.org/html/newsletr.html.

26 "Spiritual Direction as Choosing Life: Excerpts from an Interview with Jeffrey S. Gaines (Summer 1996)," n.p. [cited 12 April 2000]. Online: http://www.sdiworld.org/html/whatis.htm#distinct. For an extensive anthology of definitions of spiritual direction, see:http://sdiworld.org/index.pl/what_is_spiritual_ direction2.html.

27 Clement of Alexandria, *Quis div.* 41.1. Directed to this text by Alan W. Jones, *Exploring Spiritual Direction: An Essay on Christian Friendship* (San Francisco: HarperSanFrancisco, 1982), 3.

term "spiritual guidance." This terminological shift has intentionally sought to de-emphasize the controlling, authoritative dimension of the relationship and accentuate the *joint* search for spiritual help in one's life.

It is for this reason that John Yungblut prefers the term *spiritual guidance* to spiritual direction.[28] He views spiritual guidance not as a science, but as an art intended to help the "human psyche realize its inherent destiny, its still unrealized potential within the vast ongoing process of evolution, to find its way home to its own center, God, through a kind of unfolding incarnation."[29] It is, further,

> a matter of being an instrument by which the divine course can find its way in this other solitary individual so that the crucial inward journey of this child of God may become creatively aligned with the immense journey of evolution itself, moving through the human species to the unknown ultimate destination of fully raised consciousness. We do not and cannot see the distant scene. One step is enough for us: a step in the direction of Christ-consciousness, individuation, wholeness.[30]

Yungblut explicitly and with startling dogmatism has wed his understanding of spiritual direction to Carl Jung's myth of the psyche and to Teilhard de Chardin's understanding of evolution.[31] Although a former Episcopalian and presently a Quaker, he apparently owes most of his thought regarding the soul and its development not to the Christian tradition, but to modern science and psychology.

Carolyn Gratton also prefers the term "spiritual guide" over-against the more traditional term "spiritual director."[32] She differentiates slightly between "direction" and "guidance"—terms she does not further develop—seeing spiritual direction as normally involving adherence to a religious tradition, whereas spiritual guidance does not necessitate such a tradition (12). Although

---

28 "The term 'direction' is rejected because it has an "authoritarian ring which is inappropriate in our time. We are more aware than our predecessors of the besetting temptations that accompany all forms of 'direction' in the shape of hubris and inflation." John R. Yungblut, *The Gentle Art of Spiritual Guidance* (New York: Continuum, 1995), 86.

29 Yungblut, *Gentle Art,* 2.

30 Yungblut, *Gentle Art,* 3.

31 "I shall *insist* that spiritual guidance . . . must take into account the accumulating insights of modern depth psychology, especially those emerging from Carl Jung's myth of the psyche. It *must* also be in harmony with the laws operative in the universe as *revealed* by the natural sciences in the twentieth century. I shall argue that contemporary spiritual guidance *must be placed* in the context of continuing creation through evolution as discerned by Teilhard de Chardin in his myth of cosmogenesis . . . " Yungblut, *Gentle Art,* 1-2 (emphasis mine).

32 Carolyn Gratton, *The Art of Spiritual Guidance: A Contemporary Approach to Growing in the Spirit* (New York: Crossroad, 1992), 107.

she prefers the term guidance, she does use both. Her choice of the term "guide" communicates more relational closeness and identification: "The guide becomes the heart's companion, a co-discoverer. He or she is there to co-perceive the ways in which life events might contain directives that are calling forth that person's freedom and 'deep gladness'" (109). Her thoughts on guidance are a weaving of modern spirituality, Eastern and Western philosophy and psychology. Leaving classical Christian terminology and categories behind, she speaks more of the "ultimate Other," "the Sacred Presence," "the divine Someone else," "the Mystery," "Otherness," or "the Holy Other" more often than of "God" or "Jesus Christ"[33] Although coming from a Christian orientation, she attempts a universalizing approach to spiritual guidance. It is in the following way that she defines her approach to spiritual guidance: "the aim of spiritual guidance becomes that of helping persons get the various parts of their life in tune with the larger Mystery as it flows throughout the whole."[34] This guide helps the individual on his or her spiritual quest. Gratton reveals much, not only about her perspective on guidance, but also on her understanding of Christianity and other religions, when she writes:

> [T]he spiritual quest is about the relationship of the human person to what is not oneself—to what is ultimately Other, to a Sacred Presence, to, if you will, a divine Someone Else. We today sometimes turn spiritual guidance into concern for a merely interiorized process of growth and development. Thus, we can miss out on the energy available only when we see human life as a dynamic dialogue—as the possibility for an *encounter* between our partial selves and a larger mysterious whole.[35]

This description is so generalized as to fit accommodate virtually any religious system. It is questionable, however, whether a faithful practitioner of any religious faith would be comfortable with her abstract terminology and symbolic world.[36]

2.1.3 Spiritual Friend

Another term that is used with respect to aiding another in spiritual growth is "spiritual friend." The term is derived from the Celtic concept of *anamchara*, meaning "soul friend." This term was in use in the fifth century in Ireland, but its exact origins are unknown. Edward Sellner argues that its specifically

---

33 Gratton, *Spiritual Guidance*, 4, 5, 39, 52, 53.

34 Gratton, *Spiritual Guidance*, 5.

35 Gratton, *Spiritual Guidance*, 4.

36 For a critique of the illegitimacy of this type of universalizing of language and thinking, see George A. Lindbeck, *The Nature of Doctrine: Religion and Theology in a Postliberal Age* (Philadelphia: Westminster, 1984), 32-42.

Christian usage can be directly traced back to the Desert Fathers,[37] even though the term itself had non-Christian, Celtic origins.[38]

Alan Jones intentionally uses the term spiritual friendship interchangeably with the term *spiritual director*[39] to break down the overly authoritarian aspect of the term *director*, thereby accentuating the element of mutuality in the relationship. The use of the term *friend* returns the concept of spiritual direction to the sphere of every-day life, demystifies it, and allows this activity to take place within the context of any friendship between two Christians. Within this framework, Jones sees that the object of spiritual direction is to "help us keep in touch with Jesus as the key to true *companionship*, the bearer of meaning and value, and the power over sin and death. Spiritual direction seeks to guide us deeper into the double mystery of God and of ourselves by means of *companionship*."[40]

2.1.4 "Discipler"

Whereas the previous terms are more at home in the traditional churches (Catholic, Episcopalian, Orthodox), the next two terms, *discipler* (a term coined within the evangelical community) and *mentor* are of more recent vintage and are more frequently used in evangelical and charismatic churches. The term *discipler* and attendant terms *disciplee, disciplemaking, disciplemaker,* and *discipling*—none of while can be found in standard dictionaries—are common parlance in evangelical books and publications.[41]

However, the term *discipler* can boast a clear terminological link with the NT terms μαθητής (disciple) and μαθητεύω (make disciples). The *locus classicus* for many involved in the modern discipleship movement is the so-called "Great Commission" passage of Matt 28:19. The mandate to "make disciples" is viewed, in fact, as the *raison d'être* of many evangelical churches

37 "[W]hile no one knows precisely how or where anamchara relationships began, scholars are in agreement that the early desert Christians had a major influence on their development." Edward C. Sellner, "Soul Friendship in Early Celtic Monasticism--part I," *Aisling Magazine* 17 (Samhain 1995): n.p. [cited 2 May 2000]. Online: www.aislingmagazine.com/aislingmagazine/articles/TAM17/Friendship.html

38 Kenneth Leech writes: "Certainly, every Celtic chief had his counselor or druid at his court, and his ministry included incantations, fortune-telling and spells. . . . the Celtic church saints inherited much of the pastoral status and functions of these old druids." Leech, *Soul Friend*, 45-46.

39 Jones, *Exploring*, 3.

40 Jones, *Exploring*, 47 (emphasis mine).

41 A Google search for the term *discipler* registered over 11,000 hits on 30 June 2005.

and organizations.[42] A classic example of how this verse is used as the foundational task of the church is illustrated in Christopher Adsit's book *Personal Disciplemaking: A Step-by-Step Guide for Leading a Christian from New Birth to Maturity*:

> Making disciples was the pursuit that weighed so heavily on the heart of Jesus. It's what He asked us to do, just before He left. He didn't say, "Go therefore and make church buildings" . . . or, "Go therefore and get converts." All of those activities are terrific, in proper context. But when they become the focus of our ministry—when the means to the end becomes the end itself—we are no longer conforming to the final wishes of Jesus Christ.[43]

Adsit sees the object of a discipleship relationship, the *disciple* or *disciplee*, as "a person-in-process who is eager to learn and apply the truths that Jesus Christ teaches him, which will result in ever-deepening commitments to a Christ-like lifestyle."[44] The *disciplemaker* is viewed as the "primary agency through which God works to bring the disciple to maturity,"[45] whose main responsibility it is to provide an atmosphere wherein the growth process (which God causes) can occur. The characteristic of Adsit's book and other books on discipleship[46] is the emphasis on practicality and usability, though often short on theological reflection.

In a review article, which looks back on the modern discipleship movement, Stacey Rinehart notes three hallmarks of the movement: (1) They were designed to quickly train individuals in their walk with Christ and to evangelize others; (2) The focus was on "the basics and generics of the Christian life;" (3) Methodology (tools and programs) were seen as essential for success.[47] However, the over-emphasis on programming and individualism led to

---

42 Evangelical organizations such as the Navigators, Campus Crusade for Christ and Intervarsity, have made this their goal and have integrated it into their philosophy of ministry.

43 Christopher B. Adsit, *Personal Disciplemaking: A Step-by-step Guide for Leading a Christian from New Birth to Maturity* (San Bernardino, Calif.: Here's Life, 1988), 28.

44 Adsit, *Personal Disciplemaking*, 35.

45 Adsit, *Personal Disciplemaking*, 38.

46 A sampling of now classic, albeit simplistic, books on the process and content of discipleship are: Leroy Eims, *The Lost Art of Disciplemaking* (Colorado Springs, Colo.: NavPress, 1978); *Design for Discipleship* (Colorado Springs, Colo.: NavPress, 1980); Albert L. Kurz, *Disciplemaker: Practical Lessons for Maturing Believers (Workbook)* (Chicago: Moody, 1981); William R. Bright, *The Transferable Concepts* (San Bernardino, Calif.: Campus Crusade for Christ, 1972); William R. Bright, *Ten Basic Steps to Christian Maturity* (San Bernardino, Calif.: Here's Life, 1983).

47 Stacy Rinehart, "Discipleship: Looking Backward, Looking Forward," *DJ* 55 (1990): 8.

increased problems within the movement.[48] By focusing on "spiritual growth" alone, it truncated the New Testament concept of being a follower of Jesus.[49] As a whole, the approach was cognitive (as opposed to holistic), individualistic (as opposed to seeing it in the context of a local congregation) and exclusivist (as opposed to allowing a diversity of approaches as well as considering the factor of gifting and personality). The movement is maturing, growing in its theological reflection,[50] and recognizing some of its failures.[51]

2.1.5 Mentor

Perhaps due to some of the unhealthy features of the modern discipleship movement, there has, in evangelical and charismatic churches and organizations, been a shift away from *discipleship* terminology to more classical terms. There has been a shift back, on the one hand, to the traditional terms *spiritual direction* and *spiritual friendship* through the rediscovery of this Catholic/Orthodox tradition by Protestants. On the other hand, there has been a shift toward the more neutral term *mentoring* rooted in the classic Greek story, which has resurfaced recently in business and management publications.

While for many, "discipling" (also coined within the evangelical community) is virtually identical with mentoring, some seek to make a clear distinction between discipling and mentoring. Ted Engstrom, for example, sees discipling as a rough parallel to mentoring, but with a difference in focus. *Discipling* to Engstrom focuses on helping an understudy (1) exchange his will for the will of God, (2) live a life of spiritual sacrifice for Christ's glory, and (3) seek to be obedient to the commands of God,[52] whereas "a mentor . . . provides modeling, close supervision on special projects, individualized help in many

---

48 MacDonald describes a number of problems that have resulted in the movement. See Gordon MacDonald, "Disciple Abuse," *DJ* 30 (1985): 24-28.

49 "But by focusing only on spiritual growth . . . we have trivialized what it means to be a disciple. We have reduced discipleship to one small, spiritual compartment of life and let the secular culture set the agenda for our lives in all other areas." Tom Sine, "Right-Side-Up Values in an Upside-Down World: Whole-Life Discipleship in the '90s," *DJ* 55 (1990): 36.

50 See, for example the helpful set of essays and extensive bibliography in Richard N. Longenecker, ed., *Patterns of Discipleship on the New Testament* (ed. Richard N. Longenecker; Grand Rapids: Eerdmans, 1996). See also Michael J. Wilkins, *Concept of Disciple in Matthew's Gospel as Reflected in the Use of the Term μαθητής* (NovTSup 59; Leiden: Brill, 1988); Dallas Willard, *Spirit of the Disciplines: Understanding How God Changes Lives* (San Francisco: Harper & Row, 1988); Dallas Willard, "Spiritual Disciplines, Spiritual Formation, and the Restoration of the Soul," *JPT* 26 (1998): 101-09.

51 For critiques from within see especially Sine, "Right-Side-Up."

52 Ted W. Engstrom, *The Fine Art of Mentoring* (Brentwood, Tenn.: Wohlgemuth & Hyatt, 1989), 4.

areas – discipline, encouragement, correction, confrontation, and a calling to accountability."[53] Thus, discipling is seen as referring to the interior life, and mentoring to virtually identical to apprenticeship for the learning of physical tasks.

Similarly, Paul Stanley and Robert Clinton view mentoring as "relational empowerment"[54] and define it as

> a relational process, in which someone who knows something, the mentor, transfers that something (the power resources such as wisdom, advice, information, emotional support, protection, linking to resources, career guidance, status) to someone else, the mentoree, at a sensitive time so that it impacts development.[55]

This mentoring relationship is highly flexible: the mentor shares with the mentoree the God-given resources of "wisdom, experiences, patterns, habits of obedience, and principles . . . ."[56] This can take place in virtually any setting, over any timespan, face-to-face or long-distance, regular or occasional. They view mentoring as the general term under which the terms discipler, spiritual guide, coach, counselor, teacher, model, and sponsor are subsumed.[57]

The definition and description of mentoring by Stanley and Clinton and others[58] focus on clearly defined, concrete tasks that can be performed more effectively through interaction with one who is viewed as competent.

In stark contrast to Clinton and Stanley's view of mentoring stands Timothy K. Jones's, who describes mentoring as a relaxed extension of the work of spiritual direction. Leaning on the thoughts of Alan Jones and St. Basil, he writes:

> "God has so ordained things," wrote Alan Jones, "that we grow in the Spirit only through the frail instrumentality of one another." The fourth-century church leader

---

53 Engstrom, *Fine Art*, 4. For a parallel understanding of Engstrom's, see John E. Johnson, "The Prophetic Office as Paradigm for Pastoral Ministry," *TJ* n.s., 21 (2000): 36.

54 J. Robert Clinton and Richard W. Clinton, *The Mentor Handbook: Detailed Guidelines and Helps for Christian Mentors and Mentorees* (Altadena, Calif.: Barnabas, 1991), 2-5.

55 Clinton and Clinton, *Mentor Handbook*, 2-4.

56 Paul D. Stanley and J. Robert Clinton, *Connecting: The Mentoring Relationships You Need To Succeed in Life* (Colorado Springs, Colo.: NavPress, 1992), 33.

57 Stanley and Clinton, *Connecting*, 33.

58 See, for example Bob Biehl and Glen Urquhart, *Mentoring: How to Find a Mentor, How to Become One* (Laguna Niguel, Calif.: Masterplanning Group International, 1990); Howard Hendricks and William Hendricks, *As Iron Sharpens Iron: Building Character in a Mentoring Relationship* (Chicago: Moody, 1995); Engstrom, *Fine Art*; Ron Lee Davis, *Mentoring: The Strategy of the Master* (Nashville: Thomas Nelson, 1991).

> Basil told his readers to find someone "who may serve you as a very sure guide in the work of leading a holy life," one who "knows the straight road to God."[59]

Mentoring is, thus, for Jones something that occurs naturally within the spiritual direction and simply spills over into other areas of life and vocation.

What becomes clear from this survey of terms related to spiritual direction is that they have a high degree of elasticity and span a broad semantic range. This makes arriving at the core, common understanding of what spiritual direction should be challenging. Before we propose a core, unifying definition of spiritual direction, however, we will look at two further areas that bear upon the understanding of spiritual direction: (1) the interrelationship between spiritual direction, counseling and psychotherapy and (2) the concept of ethos in contemporary spiritual direction.

2.2 Interrelationship between Spiritual Direction, Counseling, and Psychotherapy

Within this discussion of terminology, it is important to survey the understanding of spiritual direction over against psychotherapy and counseling.[60] Is spiritual direction a form of therapy? Should therapy involve spiritual direction? How do they relate to one another? Morton Kelsey maintains that there "are few clear-cut differences" among these and allied helping professions,[61] which means that also here we enter a definitional jungle, with various therapists suggesting varying boundaries between the disciplines of psychotherapy/counseling and spiritual direction. Surveying the various options will hopefully clarify the specific focus of spiritual direction.

2.2.1 Surveying the Possible Options

2.2.1.1 Therapy and Direction are Identical

Whereas some see some see spiritual direction and therapy as being diametrically opposed, others seek to wed the psychological focus on self with the spiritual focus on God. For example, Yungblut writes that the goal of spiritual direction is for the individual to be brought to state of "fully raised consciousness." Not that this is fully possible, but "one step is enough for us: a step in the direction of Christ-consciousness, individuation, wholeness."[62] More explicitly he writes: "The objective of spiritual guidance . . . is to serve as a

---

59 Jones, *Mentor and Friend*, 23.

60 In the discussion that follows, I use the terms psychotherapy, counseling, psychology, therapeutic approaches, etc. as general synonyms.

61 Morton Kelsey, *Companions on the Inner Way: The Art of Spiritual Guidance* (New York: Crossroad, 1991), 172.

62 Yungblut, *Gentle Art*, 3.

means by which the consultee may be guided on his or her inward journey to the self and to the Self, God within, a process at once of individuation and of sanctification."[63] Thus, for Yungblut, finding the true self is identical with finding the god within and apparently both therapy and spiritual direction can help the individual achieve this.

Gratton, as does Yungblut, fuses the language games of psychology with biblical terminology in ways that indicate there is little distinction for her between therapy and direction. She "assumes that each person's life develops as an expression of his or her emerging foundational life form, or embodied soul."[64] In other words, "[w]e tend to develop a false self, a counterfeit of the deeply buried image of God (or Christ-form) that remains in the depths of our souls. Each of us grows up imprisoned in this false self."[65]

Of all the authorities on spiritual direction, Morton Kelsey is the most explicit in his claim that "the psychological and religious goals are similar: to bring the total personality, conscious and unconscious, into integration under the self or Holy Spirit."[66] In fact, he disparages those who have no place for psychotherapy in their work of spiritual direction.[67]

Although all these authors assume that it is possible to harmonize the "self" of psychology with New Testament view of the self, it seems to lie in the very essence of psychology to focus on the self in ways that run counter to the message of the New Testament. For example, Paul calls his readers to be wary of their inner motives and of their bent toward sin (Rom 3 and 7); he encourages them to live selflessly for the gospel (Phil 2:1-11) and for others (1 Cor 13), to deny oneself and one's achievements for the sake of the gospel (Phil 3:7-11;1 Cor 9:27), and to strive ultimately not for self-fulfillment but for the goal of knowing Christ (Phil 3:10). All these run directly counter to the focus on self-discovery and self-actualization by therapeutic approaches. Thus, the self of modern psychology tends to view God as orbiting around it—"using" God as a necessary factor for personal well-being, in contrast to the biblical view of God as the center around which all of the cosmos, including our selves, should orbit.

2.2.1.2 Therapy and Direction are Mutually Incompatible

There are also practitioners, both therapists as well as spiritual directors, which maintain that therapy and direction are mutually incompatible. This is due, in large part, to the understanding of the "self" within the psychotherapeutic movement, which goes hand-in-hand with other societal trends toward self-

63 Yungblut, *Gentle Art*, 81.

64 Gratton, *Spiritual Guidance*, 14.

65 Gratton, *Spiritual Guidance*, 67.

66 Kelsey, *Companions*, 167.

67 Kelsey, *Companions*, 164.

orientation and narcissism.[68] Paul Vitz has documented this trend of the secular mental health movement's worship of the "self" in his book with the telling title *Psychology as Religion: The Cult of Self-Worship.*[69] Jeffrey Boyd, former Jungian who studied at the C. G. Jung Institute in Switzerland and presently chair of Psychiatry and Ethics at Waterbury Hospital (a teaching hospital affiliated with Yale Medical School) concludes that the ultimate goals of modern psychotherapy are fundamentally at cross-purposes with the ultimate goals of life as the New Testament.

> I remain a skeptic about Carl Jung and the Jungian approach to the soul. Why? In the first place, because the ultimate goal and purpose of Jungian treatment is individuation and personal growth. I think the ultimate goal of life is different: serving and loving God, sometimes to the point of becoming less of a person, denying myself, and taking up my cross to follow Jesus (Matt 10:38; 16:24; Mark 8:34; Luke 9:23; 14:27).
>
> [The central goal of psychotherapy] is to promote autonomy, to maximize the potential and growth of the individual, to encourage the hidden aspirations of the person. That is why therapists ask, "How do you feel about that?" and never ask, "How does God feel about that?"[70]

2.2.1.3 Therapy and Direction have Differing Content and Intent

Other practitioners of spiritual direction view the relationship between therapy and direction in terms of each having differing "content" and "intent,"[71] each of which has its place, but must not be confused. Regarding *content*: psychotherapy tends to focus more on the mental and emotional dimensions of life whereas spiritual direction focuses on spiritual issues, such as prayer, religious experiences and one's relationship to God.[72] However, May cautions against psychotherapeutic approaches, which claim that all of life is spiritual, since these end up being less helpful to the individual. Such a stance results often in losing the focus on the spiritual dimension altogether. It is certainly true that "[a]ll human experience can be said to be spiritual in the largest sense,

---

68 Jeffrey Boyd comments on this: "But today, when psychotherapy is the central way of understanding the soul in America, everyone is out for his or her own self-interest, and there is rampant narcissism. American society is unraveling because the goals of 'growth' and 'self-fulfillment' do not motivate people to make sacrifices for the common good." Jeffrey H. Boyd, "An Insider's Effort to Blow Up Psychiatry," *TJ* n.s., 17 (1996): 228 n. 15.

69 Paul Vitz, *Psychology as Religion: The Cult of Self Worship* (2d ed.; Grand Rapids: Eerdmans, 1994).

70 Boyd, "Insider's Effort," 226, 230-31.

71 Gerald May makes this helpful distinction. May, *Care of Mind*, 12. Edwards follows May closely at this point. Edwards, *Spiritual Friend*, 129-30; Edwards, *Spiritual Director*, 24.

72 May, *Care of Mind*, 13.

but spiritual direction should deal primarily with those qualities that seem most clearly and specifically spiritual, those that reveal the presence or leadings of God, or evidence of grace . . ."[73]

Regarding *intent*: The goals of psychotherapy tend to shift, based on the culture's current reigning values, such as gratifying needs, self expression, self-liberation, self-autonomy etc. The intention of spiritual direction is often the reverse of the prevailing culture's values.[74] Thus, the goals of psychotherapy and spiritual direction could in certain instances be polar opposites. It is for reasons of diverging content and intent that May argues that they are "fundamentally different undertakings."[75]

Tilden Edwards maintains that the content and intent of psychology, at its root, is 'pathology driven' and needs to be complemented by the ministry of spiritual direction.[76] It is true that each school of psychology has the goal of the health of the patient in mind, but the understanding of what health actually is is based often on the implicit values of the individual therapist.[77]

Although one can observe a loosening of strictly humanistic categories in psychology, thus narrowing the gap between various psychologists/schools of psychology and spiritual direction, Edwards still maintains that fundamentally, they address two different foci: Counseling is focused on "hang-ups" and problems and how to function well in daily living. Direction is focused on the spiritual dimension of life, our relationship to God, and healing our separation from God in all of life.[78]

Merton also sees the difference between these fields being in their areas of focus: spiritual direction is not focused on ethics or guidance in the realm of the social or psychological; rather the focus is solely spiritual.[79]

2.2.1.4 Therapy is Subordinate to Spiritual Direction

The majority of authors writing on spiritual direction see therapy as subordinate to spiritual direction. Alan Jones rightly claims that it is impossible to draw a clear line between the psychological and the spiritual, for the tasks virtually

73 May, *Care of Mind*, 14.

74 "In contrast, spiritual direction – at least in its more mature forms – seeks liberation from attachment and a self-giving surrender to the discerned power and will of God." May, *Care of Mind*, 15.

75 May, *Care of Mind*, 12.

76 Edwards, *Spiritual Friend*, 29. See also Edwards, *Spiritual Director*, 23.

77 "Since the values [of the psychological school] rarely are made explicit and open for deepening in the training of therapists, they may well be hidden even to him or her. This exposes therapist and patient alike to hidden values and more than likely to unconscious cultural mirroring." Edwards, *Spiritual Friend*, 30.

78 Edwards, *Spiritual Director*, 24.

79 Merton, *Spiritual Direction*, 14, 49.

overlap "in the common concern for integrity, harmony and radiance."[80] Thus there is a strong alliance between them. However, psychology cannot tell us the direction in which we should go, since that is the role of spiritual direction. But psychology can give us hope to show us that growth and change are possible.[81] Although they are clearly allies, Jones subordinates psychology to the task of direction.[82]

In the same way that Jones cannot divide clearly between the psychological and the spiritual, so Barry and Connolly also cannot. "For us, the relationship between God and a human person cannot be parceled out into natural and supernatural elements."[83] Although one can borrow from the insights of psychotherapy, they are and must remain distinct from one another. The explicit task of direction is to "help people relate personally to God, to let God relate personally to them, and to enable them to live the consequences of that relationship."[84] In concert with Alan Jones's thinking, they hold that psychology is subordinated to spiritual direction and is only used insofar as it aids this task.

Carolyn Gratton also sees the relationship of psychology to spiritual guidance as a subservient one, since "methods of psychological observation cannot by themselves yield understanding of someone who is seeking spiritual guidance."[85] Although they have much to teach and one can draw on the models and techniques of psychology, they need to be complemented by "a much more intuitive perception of how a particular person is living in relation to the larger Whole."[86] She makes a clear distinction between what she calls "formative counseling" and "formative spiritual direction." Counseling deals with the issues of "growth and development that belong to the sociohistorical, vital, functional, and transcendent dimensions of human life" whereas direction seeks to awaken the person's heart "to the larger life of participation in Mystery."[87]

The Shalem Institute also clearly draws a distinction between therapy and

---

80 Jones, *Exploring*, 33. See also p. 38, where he describes how the tasks of therapist and spiritual director converge.

81 Jones, *Exploring*, 47.

82 "Psychology shows that psychology is not enough, that it is only a means and not an end. . . . [A psychiatrist] can get [people] going, but he cannot tell them which road to take." Jones, *Exploring*, 47.

83 Barry and Connolly, *Practice*, 136.

84 Barry and Connolly, *Practice*, 136.

85 Gratton, *Spiritual Guidance*, 11.

86 Gratton, *Spiritual Guidance*, 11.

87 Gratton, *Spiritual Guidance*, 13. Gratton makes the astute observation that the various psychologies only offer their "slice of reality"—the Freudian, Adlerian, Jungian, Rogerian etc. slice (12). These "slices" have been taken up by various spiritual directors and integrated into their understanding of spiritual direction. Although insights into human psyche can be gained by them, they are insufficient in themselves.

direction and indicates that direction takes priority over therapy. Whereas therapy and counseling focus more on problem areas of an individual's life, seeking to restore them to health, direction focuses on "finding and responding to God (in the midst of pain or disorder as well as in the rest of life). Problem/issue resolving is not the primary focus of direction."[88] Similarly Spiritual Directors International sees a strong difference in these two tasks. "While it may be appropriate at times to discuss personal and relational struggles in the context of spiritual direction, a spiritual director is not a psychotherapist, nor does the spiritual director provide such services."[89]

2.2.1.5 Other Views on the Relationship between Therapy and Spiritual Direction

Whereas the practitioners we have looked at to this point have a (more or less) thought-through articulation of the relationship between spiritual direction and psychotherapy, others have either not clearly defined the relationship between these two fields or posit various ways they to relate to each other that do not fall into neat categories. Gary Moon has surveyed a number of psychotherapists who seek to integrate various techniques of spiritual direction into their therapeutic praxis and observes that they have not delineated a clear relationship between these two approaches.[90] An example of this indefinite relationship is Guenther, who writes: "Spiritual direction is not psychotherapy nor is it an inexpensive substitute, although the disciplines are compatible and frequently share raw material. Spiritual direction is not pastoral counseling."[91] Other practitioners view the fields of spiritual direction and psychotherapy on a continuum with areas of congruence, areas of tension and areas of synthesis.[92] Then there are those practitioners, who do not even acknowledge the existence of therapy, thus by default seeing it as of secondary importance.[93]

---

88 Shalem Institute for Spiritual Formation, "Spiritual Direction: An Online Verson [sic] of the Shalem Pamphlet on Spiritual Direction," n.p. [cited 19 May 2001]. Online: http://www.shalem.org/sd.html.

89 Spiritual Directors International, "What Is Spiritual Direction?" n.p. [cited 19 May 2001]. Online: http://www.sdiworld.org/index.pl/what_is_spiritual_direction2.html.

90 Gary W. Moon et al., "Self-Reported Use of Christian Spiritual Guidance Techniques by Christian Psychotherapists, Pastoral Counselors, and Spiritual Directors," *JPT* 12 (1993): 24-37.

91 Guenther, *Holy Listening*, 3.

92 Marilyn A. Ganje-Fling and Patricia R. McCarthy, "A Comparative Analysis of Spiritual Direction and Psychotherapy," *JPT* 19 (1991): 103-17. Laurel Artress Ulrich, "The Relationship between Psychotherapy and Spiritual Direction" (Ph.D., Andover Newton Theological School, 1986).

93 Jeff, *Spiritual Direction*; Keith R. Anderson and Randy D. Reese, *Spiritual Mentoring: A Guide for Seeking and Giving Direction* (Downers Grove: InterVarsity, 1999).

2.2.2 Reasons for No Common Understanding of the Relationship between Psychotherapy and Spiritual Direction

This survey reveals a startling spectrum of perspectives on the relationship of psychotherapy to spiritual direction. What are the reasons for the strong divergence? Although the reasons are certainly many, I would suggest three fundamental and interlocking factors. The first reason is simply the individual practitioner's personal understanding of the nature and purpose of psychology/psychotherapy—and conversely her understanding of the nature and purpose of spiritual direction. If the therapists understanding of psychology has no room for the spiritual domain, then spiritual direction will be dismissed out of hand.[94] Conversely, if the spiritual director sees little value in understanding the motives, emotions, and history of an individual, then psychotherapy will be dismissed or ignored.

A second factor has to do with the practitioner's worldview and specific understanding of the Christian story.[95] How an individual interprets the Christian story and how she understands its application to life will, in a multitude of conscious and subconscious ways, shape and inform the definition, role, and goal of psychotherapy over-against those of spiritual direction. If the biblical record is given more foundational status, then the psychological models will be subordinated to it. If a psychotherapeutic understanding is held as the ultimate interpretive framework, then the biblical record will be interpreted in light of it and scriptural truth will be adjusted to fit that framework. Between these two poles lies a broad spectrum of possibilities with respect to how therapy and spiritual direction can relate to each other.

A third key factor has to do with the differing "language games" that the fields of psychotherapy and spiritual direction play. It is methodologically problematic to import or export concepts from one field of meaning or symbolic world to another—in this case from psychology to religion or vice versa—since the terms have different meanings, significance, and roles in those respective worlds. For example, the concept of love in psychotherapy does not necessarily mean the same thing as love referred to in biblical texts. Terminological parallels may, in fact, mask radically divergent understandings. Referring to the terms "sin" and "wholeness," Chan writes:

> For example, Rogerian "incongruence" of personality is sometimes equated with the Christian idea of sin. If the phenomenological is equated with the theological, a psychological goal like personal integration may be identified with spiritual

---

94 As Morton Kelsey writes: "If the only psychology we know is one that has no place for the spiritual domain or even for a real psyche, then it is quite understandable why those interested in spiritual development believe that psychology has little to offer the art of spiritual companionship." Kelsey, *Companions*, 164.

95 Simon Chan, *Spiritual Theology: A Systematic Study of the Christian Life* (Downers Grove: InterVarsity, 1998), 229.

> maturity. Psychological wholeness may be *structurally* similar to spiritual wholeness but is *essentially* quite different. Spiritual direction cannot occur apart from the Christian story. The goal of direction is to learn to live in congruence with the Christian story, and therefore it cannot simply be identified with personal integration. . . . A psychologically well-adjusted person is not necessarily a saint.[96]

2.2.3 Conclusion

Although most of these practitioners of spiritual direction would concur that (1) spiritual direction focuses on the individual's life in relationship to God and that (2) there are no hard boundaries between direction, therapy and/or counseling, the relationship remains unclear with no established consensus. The diversity of approaches to spiritual direction and psychotherapies and their fundamental tasks makes it impossible to posit a relationship between them that would be satisfactory to the majority of practitioners of therapy and spiritual direction.

The framing of the question "What is the relationship between therapy and spiritual direction?" is in fact responsible for part of the confusion. The question masks the many variables implicit within it. The question should actually read: "What is the relationship between spiritual direction approach X to psychotherapy approach Y as practiced by therapist Y1 as understood by theologian Z—or vice versa?"[97]

In private correspondence, Gerald May openly admits to confusion between these fields and lays partial blame for this state on the frequently vacillating understanding by spiritual directors themselves of the essential nature of direction:

> There's been, in my opinion, far too much confusion between [spiritual] direction and psychological counseling, [spiritual directors] first creating it, then trying to clear it up. In the process, I believe the real charism of direction, the true appreciation of the Holy Spirit as director, has been terribly muddied—and the so-called "authorities" (including yours truly) are primarily responsible for this state of affairs.[98]

My personal understanding of the relationship is that the boundaries between these two fields are and must remain fluid since the nature of the human personality cannot be divided neatly into the isolated compartments of "the spiritual realm" and "the realm of the self." Both impinge strongly on each other. However, as we will discuss below in my proposed generative definition

---

96 Chan, *Spiritual Theology*, 228.

97 The question can naturally be inverted from the perspective of the psychotherapist.

98 May, email from author, 10 November 2000.

of spiritual direction, the focus in spiritual direction needs to remain on the development of the primary relationship between the individual and God. If spiritual direction focuses centrally on the self and places God on the periphery, then it is my conviction that the essential purpose of spiritual direction has been lost.

2.3 The Role of Ethos and Imitation in Contemporary Approaches to Spiritual Direction

The Apostle Paul, as we shall see in subsequent chapters, invited others to observe his life with intense scrutiny and intentionally called others to imitate him. As was mentioned in the introduction, the ethos of a communicator comprises the most effective form of proof of a message and is thus a strong element of persuasion. If the power of the character is such that evokes trust and confidence in the listener or follower, then it is more probable that the message of the communicator will have its intended effect.

The ethos of Paul had three roots: (1) the grace of God at work in his life (even before his birth), coming to expression in his calling into ministry (Gal 1:15-6); (2) life experiences and the integration/reflection on those experiences; (3) the various "spiritual disciplines," to use an anachronistic term, which were practiced in order to conform his life to Christ and the gospel (Phil 3:10). The first root we have no control over. The second root we have only partial control over (i.e., our response). The third root we have the most control over, and it is something in which we can actively engage.

Since Paul laid such a heavy emphasis on imitation of his life (ethos), it is of value to compare this emphasis with that of contemporary practitioners of spiritual direction.[99] We are asking the question here: "What emphasis do the acknowledged contemporary authorities of spiritual direction place on ethos and imitation?"

The following overview of ethos and imitation in contemporary approaches to spiritual direction needs to be prefaced by important clarifications and limitations. (1) When we speak of ethos in the following overview, we are focusing on the spiritual disciplines they mention that lead to the development of character, mastering the passions, and living in the presence of God. (2) The choice of the following individuals was made on the basis of their acknowledged role as leading figures in the renaissance of spiritual direction in the latter twentieth century.[100] (3) We do not intend to imply that both ethos and

---

99 We are presuming at this point something that we only discuss in chapters three through six—that one of the objects of imitation in Paul is what I call "holistic imitation," that is, referring to life in its totality.

100 However, one of these leading authorities, who asked not to be named, in a personal email to me, dated 22 January 2001, wrote in response to my question: "Who have been the 'top ten' authorities (published) on spiritual direction in the last forty

imitation are not important in the following approaches. We merely intend to indicate how and to what extent they are explicitly addressed. Thus, this is not to be understood as a critique of these conceptions of spiritual direction, but merely an observation of whether and how *they deal with ethos and imitation* in their published works. (4) One could counter that everything the following authors recommend that directors do for and suggest to their directees automatically implies that they should be doing them as well. This again lies on the implicit level. We are seeking what is *written* in these works about the lives of the directors, how they themselves developed their own character, mastered their passions and lived in the presence of God. (5) The observations below are based on their written works and not on their actual practice of spiritual direction. (6) It could be argued that the authors' books discussed below contain the ethos of the individual authors and were written that readers should imitate their praxis. This, in theory, is legitimate. However, as we shall observe, the comments and directives are, with only sporadic exceptions, phrased in general "how to" or "the spiritual director should" terminology and not in terms of the actual life and practice of the individual author.[101] (7) It can also legitimately be argued, that developing the ethos of the spiritual director was not the intention of the individual authors. Although this is certainly true, this very fact buttresses our thesis that ethos and imitation often play a subordinate role to technique and information-transfer in the contemporary practice of spiritual direction.

2.3.1 Thomas Merton

Thomas Merton dwells on the topic of ethos and imitation in the introduction to his insightful book on spiritual direction, noting that in the roots of spiritual direction in "primitive times" the work of direction implied much more than it does today. The spiritual director "was a spiritual father who 'begot' the perfect life in the soul of his disciple by his instructions first of all, but also by his prayer, his sanctity and his example."[102] He goes further into a description of how the early monastics performed their direction:

> In the early days of Christian monasticism the spiritual father did much more than instruct and advise. The neophyte lived in the same cell with him, day and night,

---

years?" He responds: "I'll deny it if you quote me, but in my opinion there really haven't been any significant authorities on spiritual direction published in the last 40 years. For real authorities I'd go back at least 400 years, to John of the Cross and Teresa of Avila . . . and to the great directors who preceded them."

101 Gratton and Guenther provide more glimpses into their lives and practice than do the others. Kelsey has one section where he is more autobiographical in his life and praxis. The section on journaling gives an insight how he actually performs it. For details, see Kelsey, *Companions*, 127-43.

102 Merton, *Spiritual Direction*, 17.

> and did what he saw his father doing. He made known to the father "all the thoughts that came into his heart" and was told, on the spot, how to react. In this way he learned the whole spiritual life in a concrete and experimental way. He literally absorbed and reproduced in his own life the life and spirit of his "father in Christ."[103]

Although he writes approvingly of these early monastics, noting the holistic approach to direction they lived out, he observes that in the development of the tradition of spiritual direction, power-hungry, spiritual autocrats have abused their authority, intentionally humiliating those who came to them, causing intense frustration, and beating them down physically and emotionally. This overly-authoritarian practice of spiritual direction resulted in "a procession of robot 'victim souls' moving jerkily from exercise to exercise in the spiritual life, secretly hating the whole business and praying for an early death . . ."[104] Because of this Merton shies away from *imitative* aspects of direction, preferring the approach of seventeenth century Dom Augustine Baker, whom he quotes approvingly: "The director is not to teach his own way, nor indeed any determinate way of prayer, but to instruct his disciples how they may themselves find out the way proper for them . . . . In a word he is only God's usher, and must lead souls in God's way, and not his own."[105]

Thus, although Merton begins approvingly to talk about imitation, he downplays it because of the abuse that so easily creeps in and because of the danger of a "meaningless pantomime of perfection"—performing the disciplines externally without full integration into the soul of the individual.[106] The concept of ethos is not explicit in the work.

2.3.2 Kenneth Leech

Kenneth Leech, as we have seen above, weds his understanding of spiritual direction closely to five characteristics that are integral to the task of direction. The way he discusses these five characteristics hints strongly that ethos and imitation are in play, but these (or similar) concepts are not explicit. In his survey of the origins and development of spiritual direction, he details how spiritual direction among the Desert Fathers was imitatory in nature and that the pilgrims were drawn to these fathers because of their knowledge, wisdom and supernatural ability which were the "fruits of asceticism and purity of heart."[107] He incorporates this theme of the Desert Fathers into the fundamental characteristics of a modern spiritual director. He sees the director as someone who first and foremost exudes the quality of "holiness of life, closeness to

---

103 Merton, *Spiritual Direction*, 17.

104 Merton, *Spiritual Direction*, 20.

105 Merton, *Spiritual Direction*, 20-21.

106 Merton, *Spiritual Direction*, 23.

107 Leech, *Soul Friend*, 43.

God."[108] This individual does not aid the disciple primarily in what he says, but "by their radiation of sanctity and inner peace."[109] These directors are individuals rich with experience in wrestling with their own passions and mastering them. They are perceived as "the most extraordinarily human members of the community."[110]

There is little more discussed in the early part of the book about the actual life and character of the director until his discussion on prayer. He relies heavily on spiritual directors of the past as models for learning how to pray,[111] Aside from the topic of prayer, little else is mentioned regarding either ethos or imitation.[112]

2.3.3 Alan Jones

Alan Jones' perspective on imitation is similar to that of Merton's. He sees that a "relationship of submission, while necessary at times, is fraught with danger."[113] He cites Clement of Alexandria as the antithesis of his style of direction.[114]

Jones admits that at the beginning of the spiritual journey, a "trainer" or "pilot," as Clement calls them, may be necessary, but the goal is to find true spiritual friendship in which spiritual direction is understood as "a relationship entered into with another under mutual obedience to the revelation of God in Christ."[115] With this type of an understanding, there is little emphasis on imitation necessary.

Jones goes on to illustrate further his understanding of spiritual direction with a formative encounter with a monk, who asked him to be his spiritual director. He retells the encounter in these telling words:

> Alan, I want you to be my spiritual director.
> (Laughing) But brother, I can't!

---

108 Leech, *Soul Friend*, 89.

109 Leech, *Soul Friend*, 89.

110 Leech is quoting Sheldon Kopp. Leech, *Soul Friend*, 89.

111 Especially the chapter on "the practice of the life of prayer." Leech, *Soul Friend*, 168-86.

112 Within the topic of prayer he makes passing reference to the need for the director to battle spiritual pride through the disciplines of self-examination, confession, humble service, learning to receive and to give as means to work against it, but it remains a reference without further explication or concretization. Leech, *Soul Friend*, 172.

113 Jones, *Exploring*, 4.

114 Jones, *Exploring*, 3.

115 Jones, *Exploring*, 4.

(with a twinkle in his eye) I know![116]

Jones goes on to note that through this encounter he came to realize three fundamental truths of the nature of spiritual direction, two of which are relevant here: (1) "my incompetence need not be an impediment as long as I didn't rely on my own limited resources;" (2) "the true director of us both was the Holy Spirit on whom we both waited expectantly."[117] While one need not quibble with these insights, there is a decided down-playing of the ethos as well as the role of the director as a person, which virtually mitigates against seeking to imitate him.[118] In his book *Soul Making*, Jones' self-deprecating opinion of himself—"I make no claim that mine is the right view or even the preferred one. I am simply looking for company in a world struggling to find its way"[119]—stands in stark contrast to the conviction of the Apostle Paul, who intentionally called people to imitate him.

The closest Jones gets to dealing with the ethos of the spiritual director is in his discussion of the three monastic virtues of poverty, chastity, and obedience[120] and his discussion on which qualities are desirable in a spiritual director Jones lists: love (i.e., "openness to accept another into ones heart"), discernment, patience, honesty, the embrace of solitude and developing detachment.[121] But these are dealt with generically with respect to what values a director should possess. The deeper issues of the shape of the director's own life are not discussed.

2.3.4 Morton Kelsey

In the writing of Morton Kelsey the concepts of ethos and imitation are also not explicit. There is no hint of imitation going on between spiritual director and the ones directed. In fact, "our task as spiritual companions is to encourage people in the development of their own values, not in accepting ours."[122]

Very little is said of the character qualities that a spiritual director (or a therapist, between which Kelsey sees little difference) should have—except for

116 Jones, *Exploring*, 8.

117 Jones, *Exploring*, 8.

118 We do not wish to minimize this understanding of spiritual direction. We merely wish to point out that ethos and imitation play a strongly subordinate role in his understanding of it.

119 Alan W. Jones, *Soul Making: The Desert Way of Spirituality* (San Fransisco: HarperSanFransisco, 1985), 5.

120 Jones, *Exploring*, 68-72.

121 Jones, *Exploring*, 77-80.

122 Kelsey, *Companions*, 203.

that of love,[123] about which he goes into a fair amount of detail, what he means by this term.[124] Yet, even in this discussion of the "thirteen pieces of the puzzle of love" the focus is on how one *ought* to be and not how one *comes to be* loving.[125] He gives an aside remark as to how love develops, but disparages any form of concrete advice: "No one needs to wear hair shirts or chains, cultivate lice, or live on cabbage leaves in order to pick up crosses and follow Jesus. All we have to do is come to God and ask that we be forged into adequate instruments of divine love."[126] There seems to be avoidance of concrete advice on how he as director has experienced this or how others can practice it. The beginning spiritual director is given general maxims but virtually no help in how one goes about inculcating these truths into her life.

2.3.5 William Barry and William Connolly

Barry and Connolly in their chapter on "Becoming a Spiritual Director" ask the question: "By what right does one do this work [of spiritual direction]?"[127] In answering, they reject formal criteria, such as an official office or even technical training, since some of the exceptional spiritual directors had none of these.[128] Barry and Connolly detail the crucial character qualities that make directors them trustworthy guides to follow.

(1) Exuding trust. The foundation for trust that one places in a spiritual director is based on his membership in the faith community.[129] This trust is further rooted in the trustworthiness of the director,[130] which is understood by

---

123 "When all is said and done, the heart of all the helping professions is providing an atmosphere of life in which people may be healed and then continue to grow." Kelsey, *Companions*, 197.

124 Kelsey, *Companions*, 197. Regarding spiritual direction and love, Kelsey remarks: "we perceive the goal of spiritual direction as an encounter with the healing, saving, restoring Divine Lover . . . [and we] see ourselves as instruments of that love. Seldom can we lead others to Love except by love" (198).

125 These thirteen pieces are: (1) place a conscious priority on being loving persons; (2) be disciplined; (3) accept and love ourselves; (4) learn to pray; (5) be humble when seeking help; (6) know the human psyche; (7) learn to listen intelligently; recognize and encourage individual differences; (8) deal with our hostilities; (9) love the family with whom we live; (10) create conditions in which others grow to their maximum potential; (11) be hospitable; welcome strangers; (12) do not ignore the misery of the world around us; (13) love even our enemies. Kelsey, *Companions*, 199-207.

126 Kelsey, *Companions*, 199.

127 Barry and Connolly, *Practice*, 121.

128 They mention Catherine of Siena and Ignatius of Loyola. Barry and Connolly, *Practice*, 121.

129 Barry and Connolly, *Practice*, 122.

130 Barry and Connolly, *Practice*, 122.

them as "developed" or "mature," and not necessarily as perfect individuals.[131] These individuals are

> optimistic, but not naïve, good-humored, but not glad-handers. They have suffered, but not been overcome by suffering. They have loved and been loved and know the struggle of trying to be a friend of another. They have friends for whom they care deeply. They have experienced failure and sinfulness—their own and others'—but seem at ease with themselves in a way that indicates an experience of being saved and freed by a power greater than the power of failure and sin. They are relatively unafraid of life with all its light and darkness, all its mystery.[132]

(2) Deep faith. This is faith in God's desire and ability to communicate with us, which is grounded in themselves having experienced God communicating with them. This leads to a contemplative attitude, which they have developed through prayer and receiving direction from others.[133]

(3) "Surplus of warmth (love)"—for dealing honestly with a variety of people "warts and moles and all."[134] This warmth is necessary for the difficult work of direction. But this warmth cannot be taught: "There are no books that teach one how to be warm, no training programs that develop warmth."[135] One must simply be a "warm, interested [person]."[136]

(4) Self-confidence. This self-confidence is not arrogance, but confidence that stems from "awe before the living God."[137]

(5) Patient listening. This listening is not clouded by self-interest; it guards itself against being unduly enmeshed in the cultural, social, political world around them; it does not depend on the directee for support and encouragement; it is unafraid of strong emotion and is tolerant of painful experience.[138]

Following this list of qualities a director should have, Barry and Connolly shift to discussing how these are qualities are to be attained: "These attitudes are not achievements to be arrived at by dint of hard work and diligent attention to responsibilities. Rather, they are gifts to be prayed for and to be grateful for. Moreover, they are not fixed and absolute realities that one must have, but ideals realistically to be hoped for."[139] They minimize concrete action and disciplines as a means to attain these qualities, and maximize praying for these

---

131 Barry and Connolly, *Practice*, 123.
132 Barry and Connolly, *Practice*, 124.
133 Barry and Connolly, *Practice*, 124-25.
134 Barry and Connolly, *Practice*, 126.
135 Barry and Connolly, *Practice*, 127.
136 Barry and Connolly, *Practice*, 128.
137 Barry and Connolly, *Practice*, 129.
138 Barry and Connolly, *Practice*, 129-30.
139 Barry and Connolly, *Practice*, 130.

qualities as gifts to be received.

Although they assume that "warmth" cannot be taught, they do insist that a spiritual director is made, not born. The "school" of spiritual direction is, according to Barry and Connolly, composed of broad life experience; a growing experience of "the Lord Jesus not just as personal savior, but also as one who calls us to decision and self-sacrifice";[140] continued study of the Bible (as a source of personal prayer); informed understanding of the faith and theology (without having to be a specialist in it); increased knowledge of the history of spirituality and psychology. This daunting list leads them to revise their initial downplaying of the role of formal preparation: "professional preparation should not be too easily dispensed with."[141]

Barry and Connolly go further than practitioners in their detail of the qualities (ethos) of a spiritual director and how they are to be attained, there is relatively little concrete instruction as to how this is done, and little hope that these qualities can be achieved "by dint of hard work and diligent attention."[142] The concept of imitation does not play any significant explicit role in their discussion.

2.3.6 Tilden Edwards

Tilden Edwards, head of the *Shalem Institute for Spiritual Formation*,[143] understands the task of spiritual direction as "the meeting of two or more people whose desire is to prayerfully listen for the movements of the Holy Spirit in all areas of a person's life . . . . It is a three-way relationship: among the *true* director who is the Holy Spirit (which in the Christian tradition is the Spirit of Christ who is present in and among us), and the human director (who listens for the *directions* of the Spirit with the directee), and the directee."[144] This ministry is shaped by the conception of the spiritual life developed in Scripture and the lives and writings of the saints throughout the centuries.[145]

In his book *Spiritual Friends* there are a number of personal references to Edwards, what he has experienced, and how he *does* direction throughout the book.[146] His tone is in the form of dialogue especially in the chapter "Seeking a Spiritual Friend." He gives extremely helpful advice both on the practice of spiritual direction as well as preparation for becoming a spiritual director. Yet,

140 Barry and Connolly, *Practice*, 131.

141 Barry and Connolly, *Practice*, 134.

142 Barry and Connolly, *Practice*, 130.

143 When Shalem began in 1979 there were only two other existing programs in the U.S. for spiritual direction and none (that Edwards is aware of) outside the U.S. By 1996, there were hundreds worldwide, mostly in North America. Edwards, *Spiritual Director*, 185.

144 Edwards, *Spiritual Director*, 2.

145 Edwards, *Spiritual Director*, 2.

146 P. 106-07, 162, 165, 171-72, 184-85, 188-89.

although the advice is helpful, one does not actually pierce through to the level of "this is how I do it." In addition, since his commitment is to let the Holy Spirit be the guide, there is virtually no emphasis on the concept of imitation. This is due, in large measure, to his understanding of the uniqueness of each individual.[147] References to personal experience, opinion and practice are even less than in his other book on direction.[148]

2.3.7 Gerald May

Gerald May's book on spiritual direction, *Care of Mind/Care of Spirit: Psychiatric Dimensions of Spiritual Direction*,[149] concentrates on, as the title indicates, how modern psychiatry and medicine impinge on the work of spiritual direction. There is virtually no reference to the qualifications and ethos of the spiritual director. The focus is on understanding the psychological dynamics at work within the direction sessions as well as in the life of the directee. Only passing reference is made to the director's own life and qualifications she brings into the setting of spiritual direction.[150] Speaking in the context of the dangers of inappropriate, distracting transference, May warns against seeing spiritual directors as "authority figures" in parental roles by the directees. There is a minimal amount of transference that is healthy, but this must be monitored closely.[151] This seems the closest May comes to the concept of imitation, and it comes with a strong warning attached.

2.3.8 Carolyn Gratton

Gratton's understanding of the human soul as a "unique, never-to-be-replicated image of the Mystery"[152] has implications for her understanding and use of ethos and imitation. Concrete imitation simply does not fit well within her framework. She notes that, as the guide seeks to help persons connect all the events and inner workings of their lives with their longing for God,[153] the guide will need to develop into a certain type of person—that is, "a person of prudence and of practical wisdom"—and will have also to "become a person of

---

147 Edwards, *Spiritual Friend*, 161, 172-73.

148 The personal references are vague and do not give insight into personal practice. See, for example, pages 48-9, 51-52, 137.

149 May, *Care of Mind*.

150 May mentions in passing the need for the "absolute necessity of [the director's] attention to [his] own prayer life and daily awareness of God, and of being in spiritual direction [himself]." May, *Care of Mind*, 95.

151 Although in early phases of transference "this may simply involve admiring the director as a channel of grace, it is very likely to progress to admiring the director more than the grace." May, *Care of Mind*, 106.

152 Gratton, *Spiritual Guidance*, 14.

153 Gratton, *Spiritual Guidance*, 20.

prayer" that attracts seekers to her on the basis of their holiness.[154] What this specifically means and how one attains it is not further developed.

Gratton gives sage advice for what the spiritual guide should look for and techniques of interaction with the seeker[155]—much of which is focused on problem-solving and psychological information/technique.[156] she laments the lack of clear requirements for directors,[157] and in chapter seven[158] of her book, she asks the question: "What are some qualities that make a guide 'trustable'. . . ?"[159] Even in this chapter, most of the focus is on what information one can pass on and techniques one can use with the directee. The eight qualities she lists that are important for the spiritual director to have are reduced to the acquiring of certain techniques. [160] Only one of these eight, "developing honesty and compassion," have to do with the ethos of the director. This list is not developed, and there are only scattered hints as to how one learns these.

Her discussion on "what guides must be ready to offer" is most telling for her understanding of ethos and imitation.[161] Experienced guides "try consistently not to impose anything on those who come to them" since this can easily become manipulation.[162] Indeed, one must "avoid expressing sentiments of praise or of blame, or enthusiasm or rejection of what the other thinks or says. Enthusiasm often turns out to be pleasure over something that conforms to our own preferred ways of thinking and acting."[163] What one thinks and feels is a bias that should be suppressed so that God's Spirit, "the true guide" can do

---

154 Gratton, *Spiritual Guidance*, 21.

155 See, for example, the suggestions for how to uncover the seekers "fascination with the Mystery" (37), developing attentive listening skills (39-40, 71), being sensitive to life patterns and their disruption (40-41), helping others understand change (46-47), as well as the helpful advice in the chapter on "Guiding the Human Spirit" (55-73).

156 See especially the chapter on "Challenges and Practices for Today's Spiritual Guides." Gratton, *Spiritual Guidance*, 74-91.

157 She quotes Thomas Dubay: "Almost anyone who is of a mind to can venture into the guidance not of mortal bodies, but of immortal souls." Gratton, *Spiritual Guidance*, 107.

158 "On being a wise fish," (107-21).

159 Gratton, *Spiritual Guidance*, 108.

160 (1) "Lived familiarity" with the God of Scripture, but also with the stories of the saints through the centuries; (2) avoidance of limiting our guidance based on our subjective perception; (3) avoidance of being an answer-giver and being rather a "relaxed co-listener"; (4) distance from our own as well as the seeker's hidden drives and passions; (5) quiet honesty and compassion; (6) avoidance of focusing on oneself in the interview; (7) nurturing skills in developing a "relaxed meditative atmosphere" for the interview; (8) cultivating the "gentle art of not getting in the way." Gratton, *Spiritual Guidance*, 116-17.

161 Gratton, *Spiritual Guidance*, 115-18.

162 Gratton, *Spiritual Guidance*, 116.

163 Gratton, *Spiritual Guidance*, 116.

his work.[164] In addition, the spiritual guide must not give in to becoming the "answer-giver" or "problem-solver" for the seeker. On the contrary, the "helpful guide tries to be a calm, relaxed co-listener for what the Spirit may be asking at this point in the other's sacred journey."[165] This stance of Gratton militates against picturing the guide as one to imitate. The act of imitation would not allow the directee the freedom to pursue their own unique path toward God.

2.3.9 Margaret Guenther

Guenther does refer to the concept of ethos of the spiritual director, in that she asks the (rhetorical?) question "What makes this person think that I am worthy of his trust?"[166] She does not, however, specify what a trustworthy person as spiritual director actually looks like. She does not mention imitation as a concept that is part of direction. In fact, imitation is not what spiritual direction is about; rather, the personhood of the director is *per definition* shut out of the process: ". . . the director has agreed to put himself aside so that his total attention can be focused on the person sitting in the other chair."[167] She does note that the Desert Fathers "taught by the example of their own lives,"[168] but does not develop this topic for our world today.

She notes that the major difference between direction and psychotherapy is that "the director must be willing to be known—not just by her credentials, affiliations, and titles, but known in her vulnerability and limitations as a child of God,"[169] but this thought, which carries the seed ideas of ethos and imitation, is not pursued further. What the director is to *do* (technique) is spelled-out, but what she is to *be* (character, lifestyle) is either assumed or only discussed in passing. Imitation is not thematized in her writing.

2.3.10 John Yungblut

John Yungblut's book, *Gentle Art of Spiritual Direction*, contains two sections devoted to developing the life and character of the director. He poses the question: "how does one go about devising an adequate program of cultivation?"[170] The framing of the question indicates that information transfer plays the major role in the development of a spiritual director. The most important component of Yungblut's program is a "disciplined, lifelong inward

164 Gratton, *Spiritual Guidance*, 111.
165 Gratton, *Spiritual Guidance*, 116.
166 Guenther, *Holy Listening*, 5.
167 Guenther, *Holy Listening*, 3.
168 Guenther, *Holy Listening*, 52.
169 Guenther, *Holy Listening*, 46.
170 Yungblut, *Gentle Art*, 87.

journey."[171] Further, it is important, he maintains, to develop the "mystical faculty" by means of extensive immersion into the writings of the "cultivated mystics."[172] This should be coupled with the practice of the classic disciplines of meditation, contemplation, fasting, scriptural reflection, journaling.[173] In addition, there should be "a sustained study of the psychology of C. G. Jung, and if possible some Jungian counseling, if not analysis."[174] There is a concluding comment regarding the need for a spiritual director to "tether himself" to his own spiritual director for confession and accountability,[175] and thus a reference to ethos is hinted at, but not developed.

Yungblut does, however, explain how (according to him) one should cultivate the inner life: "The disciplines of devotion for the spiritual guide will vary considerably with the individual. But there are certain constants which all guides would do well to accept as part of a way of life . . . ."[176] The "required" disciplines are: a time and place apart, Bible meditation, reading from the classics of devotion, meditative prayer, contemplative prayer, fasting and journaling.[177] The variable disciplines he suggests are: listening to great music, regular walks in nature, the faithful practice of yoga, and the pursuit of an art or craft (cabinet-making, weaving, sculpting, painting).[178]

The references to Yungblut's own practice cannot clearly be discerned in his suggestions. Instead he defers to the past masters of direction for instruction: "we must be prepared to follow in their train, that is, to have the humility to learn from the great masters so that we may become adequate [directors]."[179] The suggestions Yungblut makes as to the practice of these disciplines are a combination of advice from past masters but with only third person suggestions from him.[180] He rightly maintains that each director is an individual with her own style,[181] but nonetheless gives no comment that—or how—he himself practices these suggestions. It is ultimately a matter of individual choice: "In the end, having garnered what one could from any of the classic sources one must create ones own pattern while following the well-charted way."[182] In summary: the topic of ethos is more pronounced in Yungblut than in the other

171 Yungblut, *Gentle Art*, 88.
172 Yungblut, *Gentle Art*, 88.
173 Yungblut, *Gentle Art*, 88.
174 Yungblut, *Gentle Art*, 88.
175 Yungblut, *Gentle Art*, 92.
176 Yungblut, *Gentle Art*, 93.
177 Yungblut, *Gentle Art*, 94-111.
178 Yungblut, *Gentle Art*, 111-12.
179 Yungblut, *Gentle Art*, 94.
180 For example: "It would seem that this time [apart for meditation] ought to be of at least half an hour duration . . ." (95). "One may wish to have some symbols present . . ." (96). "It would probably take the form . . ." (98).
181 Yungblut, *Gentle Art*, 93.
182 Yungblut, *Gentle Art*, 94.

authors, but is still strongly muted, not truly giving insight into the private practice in his life. This also holds true for the concept of imitation in his work.

This brief survey highlights the fact that ethos and imitation do not play an explicit and key role in the description of spiritual direction as can be ascertained in these writings. The personal life of the author, his personal *praxis pietatis* as it reflects on his role as spiritual director cannot be extracted from the structure and content of these works.

2.4 A Methodology for Understanding Paul as Spiritual Director: Generative Questions and Working Definition of Spiritual Direction

As has been noted above, when using the modern category of "spiritual direction," we are in danger of imposing contemporary modes of thinking onto the biblical texts, thus potentially abusing, distorting and misunderstanding them, as well as reading into them our own agenda. Since spiritual direction terminology, as has been observed above, has such elasticity of usage, they cannot be used as a solid beginning point for understanding Paul as a spiritual director. What then would be an appropriate approach/methodology?

2.4.1 Generative Questions

The strategy, which we suggest, is to pose specific, generative questions to biblical texts, which can (1) avoid imposing illegitimate categories on the text,[183] (2) give us a "lens" by which to gain an understanding of how Paul functioned as a spiritual director, and (3) make possible comparison, contrast, analysis, and critique of modern conceptions of spiritual direction. Below is suggestive catalogue of such generative questions specifically applied to the Apostle Paul:

Paul as individual. Analyzing texts for descriptions of how Paul characterizes his life – how he lives and what his goals are.

- **Ethos:** What is it about the person of Paul that evokes persuasion? What elements of his character are explicit in the text?
- **Goals/Desires:** How does Paul express his desires for his own life? In what way? Is there a hierarchy of desires? What textual indications do we have for what motivated, inspired, and drove him on a personal level (as opposed to his role, but see discussion below under "Relationship Paul→Recipients: Role")? How do these relate to one another (Hierarchy of goals? Co-equal? In tension?)?
- **Lifestyle:** What are the textual indications of how Paul lives his life? In which activities does Paul engage that leads him to achieve the desires he expresses? What things in Paul's life should others imitate? This set of questions is asking,

183 Although care must be taken here, since the framing of the question is itself an imposition of categories that may or may not be in line with the shape of the text.

among other things, about what some in contemporary language would call "spiritual disciplines."

Relationship Paul → Recipients. Analyzing the relationship between Paul and the recipients.

- **Role:** (1) What are the specific roles that Paul plays with respect to the recipients? How does Paul define himself with respect to the recipients? (2) How does he understand and define these roles? (3) How does he describe the purpose or goal of the individual role?
- **Manner:** What is the manner in which Paul lives out his role and conducts himself with respect to the recipients? These are questions of how Paul positions himself with respect to the recipients – authoritative, subservient, kindly, direct etc.
- **Activity:** What does Paul concretely do for the recipients (either *indirectly* on their behalf or *directly* to/with them) with respect to their growth?
- **Interaction:** What are the methods of direct interaction he uses with them? We are asking here, what the means of spiritual direction are (for example, writing, speaking, visiting . . .).
- **Response:** (1) How does Paul respond to the concrete life-situations of the recipients that are discussed in the text? (2) What are the various concrete life-situations discussed? (3) How does Paul deal with them? (4) Which emotions emerge in relation to the various life-situations?
- **Other:** Is there other information that gives insight into the character of the relationship between Paul and the recipients of his letters (supporting or illuminating factors)?

These questions provide more transparent criteria, which would facilitate legitimate comparison and contrast between the conception of Pauline spiritual direction and that of other practitioners, but this is not possible given the limitations of this work. Nor is it possible to develop a full-scale comparison covering all of Paul's life and writings. Our intention with this question catalogue is to indicate the lines along which a transparent comparison could be made, thereby exposing the presuppositions and elucidating the methodology in a clearer way. Our intention is that these questions will guide our analysis of the Pauline imitation texts in chapters four through six.

2.4.2 Establishing a Working Definition of Spiritual Direction

This set of generative questions, however, needs to be grounded in a common understanding of what spiritual direction is. When we take the above definitions that various practitioners of spiritual direction have put forward and compare that with the roles that Paul plays in the lives of the individuals of the churches he founded, we can detect points of convergence between the Apostle Paul and modern spiritual directors. On the basis of these points of contact, I would suggest the following working definition of spiritual direction that would form a minimal understanding of the conception of (Christian) spiritual direction, whereby we could understand the Apostle Paul as spiritual director and compare him to contemporary directors:

> Spiritual direction is the (variegated) means by which one person intentionally influences another person or persons in the development of his life as a Christian with the goal of developing his relationship to God and His purposes for that person in the world.

We do not suggest this as *the* definitive definition. We propose it as a working definition, on which basis Paul can legitimately be understood to be classified as a spiritual director.[184]

Our goal in the subsequent chapters will be to focus on one underdeveloped, even neglected, concept in the modern practice of spiritual direction: the concept of imitation. We shall begin with an examination of the understanding of the concept of imitation in the Greco/Judaic world, which shall be followed by an analysis of the concept of Pauline imitation in the uncontested writings and then in the final chapter draw conclusions and implications regarding the role of imitation in the practice of spiritual direction today.

---

184 There have been surprisingly few scholarly works that look at the Apostle Paul as spiritual director. Tilden Edwards, from a spiritual director's perspective, gives the briefest of descriptions of the Apostle Paul as spiritual director (Edwards, *Spiritual Friend*, 42-3; Edwards, *Spiritual Director*, 10-11). F.W. Beare appears to be the only NT scholar who has written on the topic of Paul as spiritual director, and that in a brief article. He notes this role of Paul has been neglected in scholarly studies:

> I want to speak of a highly important aspect of [Paul's] work which we generally pass over in silence – his work as Spiritual Director; that is, the manner in which he sought to lead his converts onward and upward to new heights of spirituality, and to inspire and encourage them to enter into the fullness of the new life which was given to them in Christ. Francis Wright Beare, "St. Paul as Spiritual Director," in *Studia Evangelica II* (ed. Frank L. Cross; SE II; Berlin: Akademie Verlag, 1964), 304.

CHAPTER 3

Putting Pauline Imitation in Context: The Concept of Imitation in the Greco-Judaic World

Introduction

In the discipleship language of the Gospels, there is no direct command by Christ to imitate him, but there are numerous calls to follow him. When we come to the Pauline writings, the situation is reversed: there are calls to imitate Paul, but none urging people to "follow" him in the same way Jesus did. This state of affairs has caused some to conclude that the μαθητής ("disciple") of the Gospels is one and the same as the μιμητής ("imitator") of Paul.[1]

Why does Paul use the language of imitation? What is the background to his use of this concept? What is his intent in using this concept and what did it encompass? The answering of these questions is our intention in this and the next chapters.

Our particular goal, however, is not to restate what has already been said well and in detail in previously published books, monographs and articles on the concept of imitation.[2] Our intent is to look at the concept of imitation as

---

1 We will be discussing this unusual phenomonen toward the close of this chapter.

2 The major works on imitation are: Wilhelm Michaelis, "μιμέομαι, κτλ," *TWNT* 4:695-74; David M. Stanley, "'Become Imitators of Me': The Pauline Conception of Apostolic Tradition," *Bib* 40 (1959): 859-77; Ernest J. Tinsley, *The Imitation of God in Christ: Essays on the Biblical Basis of Christian Spirituality* (Philadelphia: Westminster, 1960); Willis P. de Boer, *The Imitation of Paul: An Exegetical Study* (Kampen: Kok, 1962); Anselm Schulz, *Nachfolgen und Nachahmen: Studien über das Verhältnis der neutestamentlichen Jüngerschaft zur urchristlichen Vorbildethik* (SANT 6; Munich: Kösel, 1962); Edvin Larsson, *Christus als Vorbild: Eine Untersuchung zu den paulinischen Tauf- und Eikontexten* (3rd ed.; ASNU 23; Uppsala: Gleerup Lund, 1962); D. M. Williams, "Imitation of Christ in Paul, With Special Reference to Paul as Teacher" (Ph. D. diss., Columbia University, 1967); Hans Dieter Betz, *Nachfolge und Nachahmung Jesu Christi im Neuen Testament* (BHT 37; Tübingen: Mohr Siebeck, 1967); Benjamin Fiore, *The Function of Personal Example in the Socratic and Pastoral Epistles* (AnBib 105; Rome: Biblical Institute Press, 1986); Castelli, *Imitating Paul*; Michael J. Wilkins, "Imitate, Imitators," n.p., *ABD on CD-ROM*. Version 3.0a. 2006; Stephen E. Fowl,

illustrated in Greco/Judaic understanding (present chapter), and then to look at the Pauline conception of imitation (chapters four through six) *in light of their relevance for spiritual direction.* Our analysis will thus have the question in the background (though not be driven by): "What relevance does the concept of imitation have in the work of spiritual direction?"

It will become clear in this and the next chapters that the shape of the life of any person in a position of influence is foundational for what they do. Yet the shape of the life of such a person is more than simply a foundation. With respect to a spiritual director, it provides a living example of how one can live as an earnest seeker after God. The spiritual director thus "teaches" long before she opens her mouth. The shape of her whole life should be an "imitable," living example of how a follower of Christ lives, thinks and acts as well as of what she values. This is not at all, as we shall see, a call to unreflective, superficial "aping," "mimicking," or "parroting" of the director by the spiritual directee. Imitation provides an individual, particularly at the formative stage of his development, with a living, close-up, full-orbed experience of another as he lives out his experience with God in Christ.

The concept of imitating a virtuous person was common in the ancient world.[3] As we shall see, numerous references to imitation in the Greco/Jewish literature prior to and contemporaneous with Paul's writings indicate that the

> use of models for imitation was an important element of classical and Hellenistic moral instruction. Examples served as demonstrations of the appropriate manner of life. Calls for imitation, both explicit and implicit, of personal example are among the most common means of ethical exhortation across a wide variety of writings throughout the Hellenistic period.[4]

We shall be looking at a number of references to imitation in ancient Greco and Judaic literature, which have direct bearing on how Paul uses imitation language. We shall begin with a look at proposed roots of imitation, followed by a discussion on the basic usages of the term μιμέομαι (imitate) and μιμητής and other terms that regularly surface with them. We shall then give an overview of the major uses of imitation, proposing our own categorization of it.

"Imitation," *DPL* 428-31; Manfred Dumm, "'Nachahmung'—Ein vergessenes Thema?" *JETh* 10 (1996): 33-86; Seyoon Kim, "Imitatio Christi (1 Cor 11:1)" (paper presented at the annual meeting of the IBR, Toronto, Canada, November 2002). Merk's review article provides a helpful overview of the various positions in Otto Merk, "Nachahmung Christi: Zu ethischen Perspektiven in der paulinischen Theologie," in *Neues Testament und Ethik: Für Rudolf Schnackenburg* (ed. Helmut Merklein; Freiburg: Herder, 1989), 172-206.

3 The foundational works on imitation noted above all comment on this phenomenon, as does Ben Witherington, *The Paul Quest: The Renewed Search for the Jew of Tarsus* (Downers Grove: InterVarsity, 1998), 86.

4 Jerry L. Sumney, "Imitation," *DLNT* 533.

The intention here is to place Paul's references to imitation within their historical backdrop. We shall then turn to the discussion of human imitation in its Greco and Judaic contexts, analyzing select texts. This shall be followed by a closer look at illustrative imitation texts. These will, on the one hand, have relevance for the various roles Paul embodied with reference to his congregations (primarily, "parent-child" kinship language, rabbi/teacher-disciple/pupil, and wise man/leader-people). On the other hand, they will have relevance for the concept of spiritual direction, which we will explore in the final chapter. We shall end the chapter with a summary and conclusions of our observations.[5]

3.1 Roots of Imitation: Greco-Roman, Jewish, Mystery Cults?

There is debate as to the genesis of imitation and the specific backdrop of the concept of imitation in Paul. The major proposals that have been put forth are Judaism, the mystery religions, and Greek philosophy.[6]

Tinsley is a fervent proponent of the Judaic roots of imitation in Paul,[7] claiming strong parallels between the concept of imitation and the OT phrase "the ways of the Lord." This concept, according to Tinsley, was taken over by Jesus and then adopted by Paul.[8] A strike against Tinsley's thesis is that there is simply no terminological parallel in the LXX and intertestamental literature to the concept of imitation in Judaism. In addition, the phrase "the ways of the Lord," is not explicitly linked with imitation in the letters of Paul.[9] However, there are two further arguments for seeing the source of imitation being found in Judaism: (1) the strong usage of μιμητής language in Philo and Josephus, which draws a clear link between "the ways of the forefathers"[10] and imitation terminology; (2) the general closeness of Paul to Judaism as exhibited through frequent quotation and allusion to the OT and its personalities, who function as examples, though not always explicitly.[11]

---

5 In the citing of passages, I follow the Loeb Classical Library (LCL) numbering system. For texts not found in the LCL, I follow the TLG-E numbering system.

6 So, Ernst Best, *Paul and His Converts* (Edinburgh: T&T Clark, 1988), 59. Best mentions also Gnosticism as a possible source. This option has not persuaded the majority of scholars.

7 Tinsley, *Imitation of God*, 30.

8 Tinsley, *Imitation of God*, 134-35.

9 But see our discussion under 1 Cor 4:15-17 of "my way of life in Christ" in chapter five.

10 See discussion below on this phrase.

11 See, for example, David (Rom 1:3; 4:6; 11:9), Abraham (Rom 4; Gal 3), Sarah, Hagar, Isaac, and Ishmael (Gal 4), Adam (Rom 5:14), Moses (1 Cor 10:2; 2 Cor 3:7,13-14) and the significant general reference to Paul's perspective in the OT in 1 Cor 10:6: "Now these things occurred as examples (τύποι), so that we may. . . ."

Although these observations are accurate, as far as they go, they still do not explain the totality of Paul's understanding of imitation and his call to imitate him—especially in light of the strong tradition of imitation in the Greco-Roman settings of teacher-student and leader-follower, which we shall analyze in detail below. That is not to say that the Judaic source had no influence in the understanding of imitation in Paul. Rather, it is simply to say that it is one contributing source, which dovetails with certain Hellenistic conceptions of imitation.

H. D. Betz is the most forceful proponent arguing that the proper source for Paul's concept of imitation is the mystery cults,[12] tracing its roots to the cult of Dionysius. Imitation in this sense is a symbolic enactment of actions performed by the gods. It is "the cultic realization (*Vergegenwärtigung*) and representation of a myth or mythic experience."[13] There are three major weaknesses to Betz's approach: (1) the choice of language Paul used, if clearly taken from the mystery cults, would have negatively impacted Paul's apologetic purposes and would probably have met with resistance from Jews; (2) the theory is also weakened by the fact that, although it explains imitation relationships to divine figures, it "offers no explanation as to why Paul would employ cultic terminology to the imitation of his own life."[14] (3) The cultic practices of imitation in ancient religions were not controlled by historic events, as was the case with the *imitatio Dei* in the Old and the New Testaments. Rather, the pattern in Scripture is that human imitation oriented itself around specific, defining events that gave it content and significance.[15]

The view that has persuaded most scholars, however, is that the ultimate source of Paul's conception of imitation is derived from the Greek world—specifically the teacher-pupil and leader-follower relationships. Willem de Boer's seminal work *The Imitation of Paul* remains a classic presentation of this position.[16] He maintains that in the Greek-speaking world, people

> recognized that under almost every circumstance the older, more experienced, and more advanced serve as a pattern for the younger, less experienced, and less advanced to follow . . . . However, there was no area where the influence of one

---

12 Betz, *Nachfolge*, 48-83.

13 Betz, *Nachfolge*, 86.

14 These weaknesses noted by James Agan, "The Pauline Epistles," (unpublished paper, n.d.), 5. In addition, Agan notes that, "by calling others to imitate not only Christ but also himself, Paul weakens the analogy with the mysteries" (5). Betz concedes this point when he writes, "the Pauline variations of the concept of imitation goes beyond the practice of known historical analogies" (Betz, *Nachfolge*, 187).

15 Tinsley, *Imitation of God*, 30.

16 de Boer, *Imitation*. The other decisive presentation of this view is Fiore, *Personal Example*.

person over others was more recognized and sought after than that of the teacher or wise man over his own pupils.[17]

Castelli comes to the same conclusion that the true backdrop for understanding Pauline imitation is the educational system of Greco-Roman antiquity, but she sees the concept functioning also in the ethical sphere in Judaism and pagan writers.[18] She does note, however, that "educational imitation and ethical imitation often collapsed into a single notion."[19]

Our analysis below indicates that attempts to isolate the one determinant source of Pauline imitation are inadequate. Although the concept of imitation—although highly visible in the Hellenistic philosophical tradition—is much more widespread within Greek culture, it is also has a strong tradition in other Mediterranean cultures. Attempts to find a sole and exclusive source of Paul's use of imitation are not in harmony with social realities of strong intercultural exchange of the Middle East of the first century. It is, therefore, more likely that a number of traditions flowed into Paul's conception of imitation.

This has also been observed by a number of scholars. Sanders makes the sane observation that "Paul's thought was not simply taken over from any one scheme pre-existing in the ancient world."[20] Lyons, following Sanders, writes, "It is difficult, if not impossible, to determine both the extent to which Judaism, even Palestinian Judaism, and Hellenism were culturally distinct during the syncretistic first century A.D., and the nature of the influence of these on Paul."[21] Hengel notes that although it may be illuminating to see a possible relationship between Paul and the mystery religions (contra Betz), it is not wise to exclude the influences of Judaism and the Hellenistic philosophical/ educational traditions.[22]

In light of this, we would hold to the multiple roots of imitation, primarily influenced by the Greek educational/moral tradition and shaped by the Judaic understanding of parenting and teaching.

---

17 de Boer, *Imitation*, 25.

18 "It is clear . . . that the imitation of a teacher or a model in the educational systems of Greco-Roman antiquity and in the ethical positions of both pagan and Jewish writers is a fundamental category. The disciple is understood to be an impressionable person to be molded . . . and the role of the teacher/model is one of authoritative example" (Castelli, *Imitating Paul*, 85).

19 Castelli, *Imitating Paul*, 84.

20 Edward P. Sanders, *Paul and Palestinian Judaism: A Comparison of Patterns of Religion* (Philadelphia: Fortress, 1977), 12.

21 George Lyons, *Pauline Autobiography: Toward a New Understanding* (SBLDS 73; Atlanta: Scholars Press, 1985), 4.

22 Martin Hengel, *Nachfolge und Charisma: Eine exegetisch-religionsgeschichtliche Studie zu Mt 8,21ff und Jesu Ruf in die Nachfolge* (BZNW 34; Berlin: Töpelmann, 1968), 69.

3.2 Basic Usages of the Term "Imitation" and Related Terminology

The terms μιμέομαι, μιμητής are used broadly in the literature from the sixth century BC onward.[23] There are two basic usages for these terms: (1) the intentional emulation of a person or thing, which functions as a model, pattern and example for another; (2) the correspondence of a person or thing to some other object. In the first usage, the imitation is volitional and intentional. In the second usage, there is a certain parallelism that a writer finds between one object and another. These imitation terms occur regularly with other terms that highlight the mimetic aspect—often being used interchangeably within these imitation contexts. The terms μιμέομαι in its various verbal forms, and μιμητής appear in the context of the disciple-teacher relationship (μαθηταὶ – ὁ διδάσκαλος).[24] These terms are used in conjunction with εἰκών (image), μανθάνω (learn),[25] δεῖγμα (example), παραδεῖγμα (pattern), τρόπος (manner), and τύπος (example) as parallel in meaning to μιμέομαι and cognates in those contexts.[26] In addition the terms ὅμοιος (like),[27] εἰμί (am),[28] and σχῆμα (form)[29] also occur in conjunction with μιμέομαι and cognates. That all these terms occur regularly in collocation with μιμητής terminology in broadly divergent genres of literature both in Greek and Judaic contexts, supports the conclusion that the concept of modeling based on a prototype/example was widespread in the cultures of both the Greco and Judaic worlds.

3.3 Overview of Usage

In this overview our intention is to survey the usage of the terms μιμέομαι and μιμητής and illustrate them from the various time periods in antiquity as well as diverse contexts. The examples in each category are placed in chronological order—(1) Greek usage in the centuries before Christ, (2) Jewish usage prior to and contemporary with the NT, and (3) usage in the first centuries after the establishment of the NT canon.

---

23 For example: (Classical) Herodotus, Euripides, Plato, Andocides, Xenophon, Plutarch, Aeschines, Pausanius, (Jewish) LXX, Josephus, Philo, and (early Christian writers) Ignatius of Antioch, Athanasius, Gregory of Nyssa, Theodoretus. For overviews of the terminology see: BDAG; Michaelis, *TWNT* 4:695-74; Wolfgang Bauder, "μιμέομαι, κτλ," *NIDNTT* 1:490-2. In the TLG-E there are 954 instances of the noun μιμητής alone given and the verb μιμέομαι registered well over 1,500 hits.

24 Philo, *Sacr.* 64-65; Philo, *Congr.* 69; Xenophon, *Mem.* 1.6.3.

25 Xenophon, *Mem.* 1.2.2; Philo, *Congr.* 69-73; Philo, *Abr.* 154.

26 Philo, *Praem.* 114; Philo, *Ebr.* 95; Philo, *Mos.* 1.158-59; Isocrates, *Nic.* 3.57; Demosthenes, *[4] Philip.* 10.19; Isocrates, *Archid.* 6.83; Xenophon, *Mem.* 3.10.4. We shall be referring to and quoting from some of these passages in full below.

27 Isocrates, *De pace* 8.36-37.

28 Isocrates, *Nic.* 3.57; Plato, *Soph.* 235A.1.

29 Aeschines, *Tim.* 1.23; Philo, *Aet.* 135; Philo, *Post.* 104.

3.3.1 Imitation as Correspondence between Objects[30]

Imitation can be used of one object, which in some way, in the mind of an individual author, corresponds to another. For example, a theater corresponds to the human ear,[31] sickness parallels how fire spreads,[32] pillars are made to represent palms.[33] Philo sees a correspondence between the way a woman is physically endowed with breasts to care for her children and the way the earth prepares food for those who live on her.[34] In short, the term can be used of any object that (1) in some way corresponds to another object (whether living or inanimate), (2) somehow represents it, or (3) conjures up a certain parallel between objects in the mind of an individual.

3.3.2 Intentional Imitation of Persons, Spiritual Beings, and Non-Human Objects

We also note in the literature that persons, spiritual beings and non-human objects were the focus of imitation. In contrast to the first category, where mere correspondence between objects was described as imitation, in this and the following category it is the volitional aspect of imitation that is significant.

3.3.2.1 Imitation of Living Persons

There are numerous examples of persons imitating other living persons. Xenophon notes how the leader Cyrus commands his satraps "to imitate him in everything that they see him do."[35] Xenophon also describes how Socrates as teacher was a living model causing many to desire virtue.[36] The book of Maccabees recounts a youth being martyred by pagan invaders for remaining true to the Jewish religion and calls his fellow countrymen to imitate his actions.[37] Josephus mentions how the people imitated David's courage and piety.[38] Philo retells the gruesome story of how Phinehas slaughtered a harlot

---

30 The reference to objects imitated has little relevance for our purposes but is briefly illustrated for the sake of completeness.

31 πρὸς [γὰρ] τὸ ὤτων σχῆμα ἄκρως ἡ θεάτρων κατασκευὴ μεμίμηται (Philo, *Post.* 104). The ear, Philo notes, becomes the model (παράδειγμα) for the architectural design of the theater.

32 Sickness imitates (μιμουμένη) the power of fire as it in similar fashion spreads throughout the body (Philo, *Spec.* 4.83).

33 στύλιοσί τε φοίνικας τὰ δένδρεα μεμιμημένοισι (Herodotus, *Hist.* 2.169).

34 ἀλλὰ γυνὴ γῆν μεμίμηται (Philo, *Opif.* 133).

35 ὅσα αὐτὸν ἑώρων ποιοῦντα, πάντα μιμεῖσθαι (Xenophon, *Cyr.* 8.6.10).

36 ἀλλ' ἔπαυσε μὲν τούτων πολλοὺς ἀρετῆς ποιήσας ἐπιθυμεῖν (Xenophon, *Mem.* 1.2.2). The phrase τούτων ποιήσας (this one doing) is functionally equivalent to the phrase ἑαυτῷ μιμουμένους ἐκεῖνον (he was imitating that one) at the end of the sentence.

37 Μιμήσασθέ με, ἀδελφοί (4 Macc 9:23).

38 μιμητὴν . . . ἀνδρείαν καὶ εὐσέβειαν (Josephus, *A.J.* 8.315).

and her lover because of their shameless dishonor. "When some [of the Israelites], who were zealous for self-control and godliness, saw his example, they . . . imitated it and massacred all their relatives and friends."[39] Flavius Julianus writes that king Apollon complained that he was not being imitated by his subjects in a proper manner.[40]

3.3.2.2 Imitation of Persons of Antiquity

There are also abundant examples recorded of persons imitating individuals no longer living. Andocides records a person on trial for his life, who begs his hearers to hold the same thoughts and feelings toward him as toward his ancestors "in order that he might have the opportunity to imitate them."[41] In his speech to Archidamos, Isocrates speaks of the need to imitate the forefathers in order to recover their honor and to redeem themselves from the present ills that have befallen them.[42] Lysias associates imitation with virtue and with following the model, which the ancestors left behind. He calls hearers to remember the earlier fathers of Greece who fought for truth and democracy urging them to "imitate afresh the ancient virtues of the ancestors.[43] In 4 Macc 13:9 it speaks of imitating the martyrdom of three in the fiery furnace for the cause of the Jewish religion. Josephus makes multiple references to imitating the virtuous or corrupt actions of the forefathers.[44] In an especially significant example, King Josiah is noted for imitating the good deeds of the forefathers,[45] and specifically for "practicing the good virtues of King David as a goal and standard for the whole of [his] life."[46] In similar manner, Marcus Diaconus calls his readers to imitate Elijah.[47]

3.3.2.3 Imitation of Groups

We also see illustrations of one individual or group imitating another group of people. Isocrates claims that "if we should all imitate the sloth and greed of the

39 τοῦτο θεασάμενοί τινες τὸ παράδειγμα τῶν τὴν ἐγκράτειαν καὶ θεοσέβειαν ἐζηλωκότων . . . ἐμιμήσαντο καὶ πάντας τούς . . . . (Philo, *Mos.* 1.303).

40 "for they do no all imitate me nor are there among those imitating me, who are true imitators" (ὅτι με μὴ πάντα μιμεῖται μηδε ἐν οἷς με μιμεῖται γίγνεταί μου μιμητὴς δίκαιος) (Flavius Claudius Julianus, *Caes.* 6).

41 περὶ ἐμοῦ τὴν αὐτὴν γνώμην ἔχειν, ἥνπερ καὶ περὶ τῶν ἐμῶν προγόνων, ἵνα κἀμοὶ ἐγγένηται ἐκείνους μιμήσασθαι (Andocides, *Myst.* 1.141).

42 καλὸν οὖν μιμήσασθαι τοὺς προγόνους (Isocrates, *Archid.* 6.82).

43 καινοῖς κινδύνοις τὴν παλαιὰν ἀρετὴν τῶν προγόνων μιμησάμενοι (Lysias, *Epitaph.* 61).

44 For example, Josephus, *A.J.* 9.243 and 9.37.

45 Οὗτος μιμησάμενος τὰ τοῦ πατρὸς ἔργα (Josephus, *A.J.* 10.47).

46 καὶ πρὸς ἀρετὴν εὖ γεγονὼς Δαυίδου τοῦ βασιλέως ἐπατηδευμάτων καὶ σκοπῷ καὶ κανόνι τῆς ὅλης περὶ τὸν βίον ἐπιτηδεύσεως ἐκείνῳ κεχρημένος (Josephus, *A.J.* 10.49).

47 Marcus Diaconus, *Porph.* 98.

Lacedaemonians, we should straightway perish."[48] Isocrates also describes the Triballians' lack of virtue, and calls those readers, who seek excellence, "not to imitate their example, but rather [to imitate] the power of wisdom and of justice and of the other virtues."[49] In the book of Wisdom there is mention of potters and smiths imitating one another's work.[50] Philo urges the readers to imitate a good runner in how they live.[51] Philo does not have a specific runner in mind. He has in mind the virtues and characteristics that runners in general embody, which one should imitate: not becoming weary, not growing remiss, but finishing the race of life without stumbling. Ephraem Syrus urges his readers to adopt the ἄσκησις of the early Christian fathers and to "be imitators of the perfected and spiritual fathers and follow their rule [of life]."[52]

3.3.2.4 Imitation of Spiritual Beings

We also see that all manner of spiritual beings were seen as legitimate objects of intentional imitation. Choricius commands his readers (using the same terminology as the letter to the Ephesians) to imitate the goddess Aphrodite.[53] The text *Scholia Pindarum* contains references to imitating the god Zeus.[54] Isocrates blends the imitation of ancestors with the imitation of the god Heracles.[55] Numenius and Eusebius speak of imitating the demiurge.[56] Philo speaks of God's "loyal children imitating their Father's nature."[57] Pseudo Justin Martyr tells his readers not to marvel that a man can imitate God.[58] There are multiple references in the writings of Aristeas to imitating God.[59] Ephraem Syrus urges his readers to imitate the angels in that they abstain from

---

48 εἰ μὲν γὰρ ἅπαντες μιμησαίμεθα τὴν Λακεδαιμονίων ἀργίαν καὶ πλεονεξίαν, εὐθὺς ἂν ἀπολοίμεθα (Isocrates, *Bus.* 11.20).

49 οὓς οὐ χρὴ μιμεῖσθαι τοὺς ἀρετῆς ἀντιποιουμένους, ἀλλὰ πολὺ μᾶλλον τὴν τῆς σοφίας καὶ τῆς δικαιοσύνης καὶ τῶν ἄλλων ἀρετῶν δύναμιν (Isocrates, *Panath.* 12.228).

50 Wis 15:9.

51 μιμησάμενος δὲ τοὺς ἀγαθοὺς δρομεῖς (Philo, *Migr.* 133).

52 Ἀλλὰ γενοῦ μιμητὴς τῶν τελείων καὶ πνευματικῶν πατέρων, καὶ τῷ κανόνι αὐτῶν ἐπακολουθῆσον (Ephraem Syrus, *Ascet.* 158).

53 μιμητὴς γίνου τῆς θέας (Choricius, *Op.* 29.2.38). Compare Eph 5:1: Γίνεσθε οὖν μιμηταὶ τοῦ θεοῦ.

54 *Scholia Pindarum* P4.518.

55 Isocrates, *Phil.* 113-14.

56 ʼανάλογον δὲ τούτῳ μὲν ὁ δημιουργὸς θεός, ὢν αὐτοῦ μιμητής (Numenius, *Fragmenta*, 16). Identical wording found in Eusebius, *Praep. ev.* 11.22.3.

57 δεόντως οὖν μιμούμενοι τὴν τοῦ πατρὸς φύσιν οἱ ὑπήκοοι παῖδες (Philo, *Sacr.* 68).

58 Καὶ μὴ θαυμάσῃς εἰ δύναται μιμητὴς ἄνθρωπος γενέσθαι θεοῦ (Pseudo-Justin Martyr, *Diogn.* 501A).

59 For example: μιμούμενος τὸ τοῦ θεοῦ διὰ παντὸς ἐπιεικές (Aristeas, *Phil.* 188; see also 210, 281).

marriage.[60] Basilius Magus warns against imitating the Devil and, instead, calls his readers to imitate Christ and God.[61]

3.3.2.5 Of Persons Imitating Non-Human Objects

There are also examples of persons intentionally imitating objects other than persons. Theodoretus calls the reader to "imitate the bees,"[62] who strain out that which is bitter and make honey from it. Philo remarks, "you men will do well to take some beasts for your models."[63]

3.3.3 Intentional Imitation of Specific Characteristics and Virtues

A closer look at why people imitated other persons, spiritual beings, and non-human objects will often reveal that these had specific characteristics and virtues that others desired to incorporate into their lives.

3.3.3.1 Imitation of Virtues or Personal Character Traits

One of the major objects of imitation was "the virtues" (ἀρεταί). Aristotle speaks of imitating "the good" or "the virtues."[64] Demosthenes calls the Athenians not only to marvel at their ancestors but also to strive to imitate their virtues.[65] Xenophon calls Agesalius "a virtuous man"[66] who should be imitated. Philo observes that whereas many have become imitators of the wickedness they had previously despised, so others, who were earlier wicked, now attempt to be "copiers" of the virtues they opposed.[67] Ephraem Syrus urges his readers to 'be eager to imitate the life and virtues of the holy fathers."[68] Gregory

---

60 Μακάριος ὃς γέγονεν ἐπὶ τῆς γῆς ὡς ἄγγελος οὐράνιος καὶ μιμητὴς τῶν Σεραφίμ, ἁγνοὺς ἔχων καθ' ἑκάστην τοὺς λογισμούς ("Blessed are those who are on the earth as the angels of heaven, and are imitators of the Seraphim, having holiness in all of their thoughts") (Ephraem Syrus, *Beat.* 3).

61 Ταπείνωσις, Χριστοῦ μίμησις ἔπαρσις δὲ καὶ παῤῥησία καὶ ἀναίδεια, τοῦ διαβόλου μίμημα. Γίνου μιμητὴς Χριστοῦ, καὶ μὴ ἀντίχριστου· Θεοῦ, καὶ μὴ ἀντιθέου (Basil Theol., *Serm. 11* 31.648).

62 καὶ μιμοῦνται τὴν μέλισσαν (Theodoretus, *Epist.* 4).

63 μιμηταὶ θηρίων ἐνίων, ἄνθρωποι, γίνεσθαι (Philo, *Decal.* 114).

64 τὰ βέλτιστα μιμεῖσθαι. τῆς ἀρετῆς ἄρα παντελῶς τοῦτ' ἐστίν, τὸ καλὸν προθέσθαι (Aristotle, [*Mag. mor.*] 1.19.1).

65 τοὺς προγόνους ὑμῶν οὐχ ἵνα θαυμάζητ' αὐτὰ θεωροῦντες, ἀλλ' ἵνα καὶ μιμῆσθε τὰς τῶν αναθέντων ἀρετάς (Demosthenes, *Rhod. lib.* 15.35).

66 καλὸν ἄν μοι δοκεῖ [εἶναι] ἡ 'Αγησιλάου ἀρετὴ παράδειγμα γενέσθαι . . . τίς γὰρ ἂν ἢ θεοσεβῆ μιμούμενος (Xenophon, *Ages.* 10.2).

67 πολλοὶ γὰρ ἤδη καὶ ἀντιπάλου κακίας ἐγένοντο μιμηταί, ὡς ἀρετῆς ἔμπαλιν ἕτεροι (Philo, *Migr.* 26).

68 Σπούδασον οὖν, ἀδελφέ, τοῦ γενέσθαι μιμητὴς βίου καὶ ἀρετῶν τῶν ὁσίων πατέρων (Ephraem Syrus, *Uirg.* 196).

Nyssanus mentions the apostle Paul as imitating Christ and leading a virtuous life.[69]

There are also many references to the imitation of specific virtues. Demosthenes reminds the Athenians that they should be justly proud of the example of their ancestor and emulate their wise judgment.[70] Aeschines praises a man who lived a pure life from his youth[71] and says that he is worthy to be imitated. He mentions the virtues of this man: goodness, wisdom, excellent in righteousness and self-control. Aeschines speaks of the need to "imitate the wisdom of our forefathers."[72] In the LXX, the reader is called to imitate the virtue of wisdom.[73] Josephus has numerous references to the specific virtues that were imitated, among them the boldness of Phineas[74] and the courage and piety of David.[75] Ephraem Syrus calls the readers to imitate the obedience of Christ.[76]

There are also references to the imitation of the flip-side of the virtues: specific vices. Isocrates warns against imitating the sloth and greed of the Lacedaemonians.[77] Diodorus describes Pausanias, who, rejecting his former manner of life, began to imitate the licentiousness and luxury of the Persians.[78] Josephus recounts how people in Israel feared that others would imitate the rudeness of Zimri[79] as well as how the nation was led astray by Rehoboam when they imitated his unrighteousness and godlessness.[80] Basilius Magus calls his readers to imitate the virtues of mercy and brotherly love.[81]

3.3.3.2 Imitation of Concrete Actions

Imitation of the virtues was, however, never held in isolation from concrete action. Rather, the virtues went hand-in-hand with the tangible practice of those

---

69 ὡς ἐποίει ὁ Παῦλος μιμητὴς τοῦ Χριστοῦ διὰ τοῦ κατ' ἀρετὴν βίου γινόμενος (Gregory Nyssenus, *Perf.* 8.1.196).

70 χρῆσθαι παραδείγμασι, καὶ τοὺς προγόνους, οὓς ἐπαινεῖτε δικαίως, ἔργω μιμεῖσθαι (Demosthenes, *Fals. leg.* 269).

71 Ταῦθ' ὁ γέρων ὁ ἐκ παιδὸς σεσωφρονηκὼς παρῄνεσε (Aeschines, *Tim.* 180-81).

72 μιμεῖσθαι μέντοι τὰς τῶν προγόνων εὐβουλίας (Aeschines, *Fals. leg.* 2.75).

73 Wis 4:2.

74 μιμηταὶ γενόμενοι τῆς Φινεέσσου τόλμης (Josephus, *A.J.* 4.154).

75 τοῦτον μιμητὴν Δαυίδου τοῦ προπάππου κατά τε ἀνδρείαν καὶ εὐσέβειαν̀ (Josephus, *A.J.* 8.315).

76 ὅτι ὁ τοιοῦτος μιμητής ἐστι τοῦ ἀγαθοῦ ἡμῶν Διδασκάλου, ὃς ὑπήκοος γέγονε μέχρι θανάτου (Ephraem Syrus, *Virt.* 16).

77 Εἰ μὲν γὰρ ἅπαντες μιμησαίμεθα τὴν Λακεδαιμονίων ἀργίαν καὶ πλεονεξίαν, εὐθὺς α'ν ἀπολοίμεθα (Isocrates, *Bus.* 20).

78 τὴν δὲ τῶν Περσῶν ἀκολασίαν καὶ τρυφὴν ἐμιμήσατο (Diodorus Siculus, *Hist.* 11.46.3).

79 τῶν λογῶν ἀσελγείας ἀυτοῦ μιμηταὶ (Josephus, *A.J.* 4.151).

80 εἰς ἀδίκους καὶ ἀσεβεῖς ἐξετράπη πράξεις (Josephus, *A.J.* 8.251).

81 ἐλεήμων, φιλάνθρωος (Basil Theol., *Serm. 11* 31.684).

virtues. Demosthenes describes how some willfully refused to imitate the admirable practices of others, chosing rather to do the contrary.[82] Dionysius of Halicarnassus writes of those who intentionally imitated the writing style of Thucydides: "I shall append some brief examples of successful imitation and then conclude my discussion."[83] In 4 Macc one who is to be martyred calls out to his Jewish brothers to imitate the way that he resisted the tyrant Antiochus.[84] 4 Macc also encourages the readers to die a martyr's death in the same manner as the three young men, who were thrown into the fiery furnace in the book of Daniel.[85] Philo accuses Gaius of multiple wrong-doings, and, with biting sarcasm, goes through a list of possible people and describes the specific actions (rooted in the virtues) these heros performed, upon which Gaius could have patterned his actions.[86] Josephus boasts of how "the multitude of mankind" (translate) desired to imitate the custom of resting on the seventh day as well as other Jewish practices.[87] Himerius comments on those who imitated the writing style of the poet Heraclea.[88]

3.3.3.3 Holistic or Global Imitation

Imitation can, in addition, refer to something more global and all-encompassing in nature: imitating another's total-lifestyle—in orientation, thought, and action. Xenophon describes how Cyrus commands the satraps "to imitate him in everything that they see him do."[89] Josephus portrays Asa imitating David.[90] Philo, in a moving passage of the effect of Moses' seeing God, writes:

> Thus [Moses] beheld what is hidden from the sight of mortal nature, and, in himself and his life displayed for all to see . . . a piece of work beautiful and godlike, a model for those who are willing to imitate it. Happy are they who imprint, or strive to imprint, that image in their souls.[91]

---

82 τοῦτ' οὐ μιμοῦνται, μᾶλλον δ' αὐτὸ τοὐναντίον ποιοῦσιν (Demosthenes, *Exord.* 35.3).

83 περὶ δὲ τῶν κατορθωσάντων ἐν τῇ μιμήσει μικρὰ προσθέντες (Dionysius of Halicarnassensis, *Thuc.* 52.15-16).

84 4 Macc 9:23.

85 4 Macc 13:9.

86 "Did you imitate the twin brothers [of Jupiter] in their brotherly love? (ἐμιμήσω τοὺς Διοσκούρους εἰς φιλάδελφιαν;) . . . Did you imitate Dionysus? (ἐμιμήσω Διόνυσον;) . . . Or did you imitate Heracles? (ἀλλὰ καὶ Ἡρακλέα?)" (Philo, *Leg.* 87-90).

87 Josephus, *C. Ap.* 2.280-83.

88 καὶ μιμεῖται μὲν παῤ ἄλλοις ποιηταῖς Ἡρακλέα (Himerius, *Decl.* 54.56-57).

89 ὅσα αὐτὸν ἑώρων ποιοῦντα, πάντα μιμεῖσθαι (Xenophon, *Cyr.* 8.6.10).

90 Josephus, *A.J.* 8.315.

91 Picking up the last half of the quotation: ἔστησε παράδειγμα τοῖς ἐθέλουσι μιμεῖσθαι. εὐδαίμονες δ' ὅσοι τὸν τύπον ταῖς ἑαυτῶν ψυχαῖς ἐναπεμάξαντο ἢ ἐσπούδασαν ἐναπομάξασθαι (Philo, *Mos.* 1.159).

Although we will return to this passage below, we note here, that Moses is viewed as an all-encompassing model for life. In another passage, Philo mentions how Joshua, the disciple of Moses, patterned himself after the ethos of his master, who has observed all aspects of his master's life and has patterned his life after it.[92] Similarly, Marcellinus speaks of many who imitated the ethos of Georgius of Leontus.[93] Ephraem Syrus urges his readers to imitate both the life and virtues of the fathers of the Christian faith.[94] The tenor in all of these illustrations is that imitation encompasses all of life, not just an isolated part of it.

3.3.4 Negative Use of Imitation: Imitation as "Mimicking"

We have thus far primarily observed imitation being viewed positively, in that the process of imitation caused one person to develop or strive for the characteristic of the one imitated. It can also have a negative usage, namely, of persons "aping" or "mimicking" others in superficial ways that are not truly integrated into their person. Plato uses μιμητὴς to describe artists, who, seeking to imitate the real, actually create a "phantom" of the real, thus deceiving people.[95] Plato also speaks of the sophist as one who imitates, but does not truly know.[96] This type of imitation for Plato is a "mimicking" without a deeper understanding of the true nature of things. Aristotle observes that some people attempt to imitate "great-souled men" without truly being like them.[97] Plutarch makes an intriguing reference to Peisistratus: "even those virtues which nature had denied him were imitated by him so successfully that he won more confidence than those who actually possessed them."[98] However, Plutarch notes that the statesman Solon was not duped by the duplicitous Peisistratus. Imitation, thus, can refer to something being fake, superficial, or done for ulterior or duplicitous motives, without true integration into the actual character of an individual.

---

92 ἐπειδὴ γὰρ ἀριστίνδην ὁ φοιτητὴς αὐτοῦ καὶ μιμητὴς τῶν ἀξιεράστων ἠθῶν. (Philo, *Virt.* 66).

93 ἠθῶν μιμητὴς καὶ ἄριστος διαγραφεύς (Marcellinus, *Thuc.* 51).

94 Σπούδασον οὖν . . . τοῦ γενέσθαι μιμητὴς βίου καὶ ἀρετῶν τῶν ὁσίων πατέρων (Ephraem Syrus, *Uirg.* 196).

95 πάντας τοὺς ποιητικοὺς μιμητὰς εἰδώλων ἀρετῆς εἶναι καὶ τῶν ἄλλων περὶ ὧν ποιοῦσιν, τῆς δὲ ἀληθείας οὐχ ἅπτεσθαι (Plato, *Resp.* 600E).

96 ὁ γὰρ σοφιστὴς οὐκ ἐν τοῖς εἰδόσιν ἦν ἀλλ' ἐν τοῖς μιμουμένοις δή (Plato, *Soph.* 267E).

97 μιμοῦνται γὰρ τὸν μεγαλόψυχον οὐχ ὅμοιοι ὄντες (Aristotle, *Eth. nic.* 1124B).

98 ἃ δὲ φύσει μὴ προσῆν αὐτῷ, καὶ ταῦτα μιμούμενος ἐπιστεύετο μᾶλλον τῶν ἐχόντων (Plutarch, *Sol.* 29.4).

3.3.5 Unintentional Imitation: Paralleling Reality[99]

Besides the intentional imitation of one person imitating another, there are instances of unintentional imitation in the sense of noting parallels between persons or phenomena. Two examples from Philo will suffice: Philo notes that as God creates people, so parents create children, thereby imitating His power.[100] He also notes that when a person performs acts of kindness, he is thereby imitating the nature of God, even though he is not consciously seeking to do so.[101]

3.3.6 Summary

In our overview, we have seen that the concept of human imitation is broad. Human imitation can refer to imitating living persons, persons of antiquity, groups of persons, supernatural beings (God, the gods, angels, the devil, and demons), and even non-human objects. It often has the more specific focus imitating the virtues or character traits of those people or object. The actual manifestation of these virtues or character traits—concrete human action—is also imitated. However, it also used in a more global sense of imitating the thought, character, action and lifestyle of another.

Imitation is generally seen in most contexts as something positive; in certain instances, the imitation is degraded to mimicking another without the internal appropriation of the purpose and essence of that which is imitated. There is also, especially in Philo, the use of the term imitation as a form of mirroring reality, where imitation is used to note a parallel between two objects, both living and not.

3.4 Human Imitation in its Greco/Judaic Settings

When we observe where the concept of imitation occurs in the Greco/Judaic worlds, we see that there are four primary relational settings: parent-child, teacher-student, sage-people, leader-group.

---

99 This also has no immediate relevance to Pauline imitation, but is briefly noted to round out the picture of the uses of imitation.

100 καὶ οὗτοι μιμούμενοι καθ' ὅσον οἷόν τε τὴν ἐκείνου δύναμιν τὸ γένος ἀθανατίζουσιν (Philo, *Spec.* 2.225).

101 "In no other action does man so much resemble God as in showing kindness, and what greater good can there be than that they should imitate God—they the created, he the eternal" (ὅτι παραπλήσιον οὐδὲν ἄνθρωποι θεῷ δρῶσιν η' χαριζόμενοι. τί δ' α'ν εἴη κρεῖττον ἀγαθὸν η' μιμεῖσθαι θεὸν γενητοῖς τὸν ἀίδιον) (Philo, *Spec.* 4.73).

3.4.1 Parent-Child

3.4.1.1 ACTUAL KINSHIP

It was expected in the ancient Greek and Jewish cultures that children imitate their parents, primarily the father. For example, the son, Demonicus, is advised to view his father, Hipponicus, as a model for behavior:

> For now, I have produced an example of the nature of Hipponicus, after whom it is necessary to pattern your own life, regarding as a law his manner, both imitating and striving to [emulate] your father's virtues. For it would be a shame when painters represent the beautiful among the animals, for children not to imitate the goodness/nobility of their parents.[102]

Isocrates, in the context of this passage, recalls to Demonicus's memory, in detail, the virtues and lifestyle of his father. Hipponicus was, in every aspect of his life, a model for his son. The use of the term "shame" (αἰσχρός) in a shame-honor-based culture[103] indicates that this parent-child imitation was the norm; to move away from the norm would bring shame on the family, ancestry, and citizens.[104] In another passage Isocrates writes: "Exhort the young to virtue not only by your precepts but by exemplifying in your conduct what good men ought to be."[105] This text indicates that parenting, modeling, and education were inextricably bound together.

---

102 δεῖγμα δὲ τῆς Ἱππονίκου φύσεως νῦν ἐξενηνόχαμεν, πρὸς ὃν δεῖ ζῆν σ' ὥσπερ πρὸς παράδειγμα, νόμον μὲν τὸν ἐκείνου τρόπον ἡγησάμενον, μιμητὴν δὲ καὶ ζηλωτὴν τῆς πατρῴας ἀρετῆς γιγνόμενον. αἰσχρὸν γὰρ τοὺς μὲν γραφεῖς ἀπεικάζειν τὰ καλὰ τῶν ζῴων, τοὺς δὲ παῖδας μὴ μιμεῖσθαι τοὺς σπουδαίους τῶν γονέων (Isocrates, *Demon.* 11.4-9).

103 Joubert notes that honor and shame are *the* core values of the Mediterranean world (Stephan J. Joubert, "Managing the Household: Paul as *Paterfamilias* of the Christian Household Group in Corinth," in *Modeling Early Christianity: Social-Scientific Studies of the New Testament in its Context* [ed. Philip F. Esler; London: Routledge, 1995], 214). For an extensive look at honor and shame in the Greco/Judaic cultures, see David A. de Silva, *Honor, Patronage, Kinship & Purity: Unlocking New Testament Culture* (Downers Grove: InterVarsity, 2000), 23-94.

104 "Honor and dishonor represent the primary means of social control in the ancient Mediteranean world" (David A. de Silva, "Honor and Shame," *DNTB* 529). Aristotle notes that honor and shame are linked to the family in which one is born and those with whom one associates. Thus, what an ancestor has done directly impacts the amount of honor or shame one has. Regarding shame, Aristotle writes, "Men also feel shame when they are connected with actions or things which entail disgrace, for which either they themselves, or their ancestors, or any others with whom they are closely connected are responsible" (Aristotle, *Rhet.* 2.6.25 [Freese, LCL]).

105 Προτρέπετε τοὺς νεωτέρους ἐπ' ἀρετὴν μὴ μόνον παραινοῦντες, ἀλλὰ καὶ περὶ τὰς πράξεις ὑποδεικνύοντες αὐτοῖς οἵους εἶναι χρὴ τοὺς ἄνδρας τοὺς ἀγαθοὺς (Isocrates, *Nic.* 3.57).

Euripides records an impassioned plea of a father to his daughter: "Grant me this favor, and imitate the character of a just father; for this is the fairest glory for children, when the child of a good father resembles its parents in character."[106] This early reference to imitation places it squarely within the framework of the family, where the imitation of the parents is all the more strongly encouraged, since it is expected. Pausanias mentions how Glaucus, the son of a king, "was content to imitate his father in all matters, both in the public and in his private spheres."[107] Josephus describes a steward imploring the son of the household in which he served to imitate the noble example of his father, being shocked that the son was acting so out of step with the character of his father.[108] Philo speaks of God's "obedient children imitating their Father's nature."[109] Philo also provides an insight into the relationship between imitation of parents and the concept of shame:

> Yet let no one think that good lineage is a perfect blessing and then neglect noble actions, but reflect that greater anger is due to one who, while his parentage is of the best, brings shame upon his parents by the wickedness of his ways. For having in his own household models of true excellence to copy, reproduces nothing that serves to direct his life aright and keep it sound and healthy.[110]

Guilt is called down upon the child who ignores the pattern the parents have laid down for them and goes his own way. He brings shame and guilt not only on himself, but also on the family line.

3.4.1.2 Extended Kinship

These father-son instances, which refer to those who share no common blood lineage, indicate that the individuals in these cultures saw themselves as part of various interlocking webs of relationships. This understanding is largely lost on us in our western world today. Individuals were not viewed as autonomous

---

106 καὶ μιμοῦ τρόπους πατρὸς δικαίου· παισὶ γὰρ κλέος τόδε κάλλιστον, ὅστις ἐκ πατρὸς χρηστοῦ γεγὼς ἐς ταὐτὸν ἦλθε τοῖς τεκοῦσι τοὺς τρόπους (Euripides, *Hel.* 940-43).

107 Γλαύκῳ δὲ τῷ Αἰπύτου βασιλεύσαντι μετὰ Αἴπυτον τὰ μὲν ἄλλα ἐξήρκεσε μιμήσασθαι τὸν πατέρα ἔν τε τοῖς κοινοῖς καὶ πρὸς τοὺς ἰδιώτας (Pausanias, *Descr.* 4.3.9).

108 καὶ μιμητὴν αὐτὸν ἠξίου γενέσθαι τοῦ γεγεννηκότος (Josephus, *A.J.* 12.203).

109 δεόντως οὖν μιμούμενοι τὴν τοῦ πατρὸς φύσιν οἱ ὑπήκοοι παῖδες (Philo, *Sacr.* 68).

110 μὴ μέντοι νομίσας τις ἀγαθὸν εἶναι τέλειον τὴν εὐγένειαν ὀλιγωρείτω καλῶν πράξεων, λογιζόμενος ὅτι μείζονος ὀργῆς ἄξιος τυγχάνειν ἐστὶν ὁ γεννηθεὶς μὲν ἐκ τῶν ἀρίστων, αἰσχύνην δ' ἐπιφέρων τοῖς γεννήσασι διὰ τὴν τῶν τρόπων κακίαν· ἔχων γὰρ οἰκεῖα παραδείγματα καλοκἀγαθίας ἃ μιμήσεται καὶ μηδὲν ἀποματτόμενος εἰς ὑγιαίνοντος βίου κατόρθωσιν ἐπίληπτος (Philo, *Spec.* 4.182).

units; who you were was dependent upon your family and blood-relations that preceded you.

In addition to the actual kinship bond, there was a strong sense of the fictive kinship[111] understanding of being in the "family" of the village, city, country to which a person belonged. Within these webs of relationships, the concept of imitation was fully alive and simply an extension of the concept of imitation within nuclear parent-child relationship. It is due to the Western world's value on individualism that a Westerner does not sense the importance and emotional weight of familial identification through the generations on the people in these ancient cultures. It is important for us to realize how closely these ancient cultures identified with their kin.

There was close identification with the forefathers—be they actual, cultural, political, or spiritual—with who they were and how they lived, thought, and acted. To the living, these forefathers were an ever-present reality in their daily lives. They were thought about, meditated upon, written and sung about, often quoted and honored through stories told of them. Through these means, they were a living reality for those who came after them. It is this sense of existential identification that is in large measure lost upon us today in the West. A few examples of this will suffice. Aeschines writes of the need to "imitate the wisdom of our forefathers."[112] Andocides longs to have the opportunity to imitate his ancestors.[113] In an intriguing dialogue, Xenophon records Pericles asking Socrates how the Athenians can regain their old virtue, to which Socrates responds:

> There is no mystery about it, as I think. If they find out the customs of their *ancestors* and *practice them* as well as they did, they will come to be as good as they were; or failing that, they need but to *imitate* those who now have the pre-eminence and to *practice* their *customs*, and if they are equally careful in observing them, they will be as good as they, and, if more careful, even better.[114]

Isocrates calls his hearers to practice virtue, to reject the depraved examples of those who cheat and delude, and to return to following the example of their

111 De Silva defines fictive kinship as the "application of the roles and ethos of family to people who are not related" (de Silva, *Honor, Patronage*, 195).

112 μιμεῖσθαι μέντοι τὰς τῶν προγόνων εὐβουλίας (Aeschines, *Fals. leg.* 2.75).

113 ἥνπερ καὶ περὶ τῶν ἐμῶν προγόνων, ἵνα κἀμοὶ ἐγγένηται ἐκείνους μιμὴσασθαι (Andocides, *Myst.* 1.141).

114 Οὐδὲν ἀπόκρυφον δοκεῖ μοι εἶναι, ἀλλ' εἰ μὲν ἐξευρόντες τὰ τῶν προγόνων ἐπιτηδεύματα μηδὲν χεῖρον ἐκείνων ἐπιτηδεύοιεν, οὐδὲν ἂν χείρους ἐκείνων γενέσθαι· εἰ δὲ μή, τούς γε νῦν πρωτεύοντας μιμούμενοι καὶ τούτοις τὰ αὐτὰ ἐπιτηδεύοντες, ὁμοίως μὲν τοῖς αὐτοῖς χρώμενοι οὐδὲν ἂν χείρους ἐκείνων εἶεν, εἰ δ'ἐπιμέλεστερον, καὶ βελτίους (Xenophon, *Mem.* 3.5.14; emphasis mine).

ancestors.[115] Josephus writes that Seth "was himself of an excellent character, so did he leave descendants behind him who imitated his virtues."[116]

In addition, the term "father" was used liberally beyond blood-relations in many fictive kinship settings in the Greco-Judaic societies.[117] It was employed in an honorary manner to a number of individuals in the ancient Greco-Roman and Jewish world. The term "father" was applied to older mentors,[118] or to any respected elder.[119] Young persons often addressed older persons respectfully as "father,"[120] and the term was also used as an honorary title for individuals of rank.[121]

We see this same usage of the term "father" in fictive kinship language in early Christian writings, but in these writings it is associated with "spiritual" fathers and forefathers. In these writings there is a close connection between these spiritual fathers and imitation. Basilius writes: "For whether [it is] the good company of the fathers, prophets or apostles, seek to be an imitator of them."[122] Ephraem Syrus calls his readers to "be imitators of the perfected and spiritual fathers and follow their rule [of life]."[123]

The ultimate fictive kinship relationship is when God is seen as a father, who is to be imitated. Thus in the passage in Eph 5:1 the church is called to imitate God as a loving father.[124] This same thought is evident in a fifth century catena, in which Christians are seen as adopted as sons and daughters of God: "it is necessary for everyone wishing to be worthy of adoption, according to their ability, to imitate God in doing good."[125]

3.4.2 Teacher-Student

When we observe the practice of education in the ancient Greco-Jewish culture, we see that many were involved in the process, but primarily parents, teachers,

115 ὡς χρὴ τοὺς προγόνους μιμεῖσθαι (Isocrates, *De pace* 8.36).

116 καὶ γενόμενος αὐτὸς ἄριστος μιμητὰς τῶν αὐτῶν τοὺς ἀπογόνους κατέλιπεν (Josephus, *A.J.* 1.68).

117 For a helpful overview of family and household in Greco-Roman and Jewish culture, which pointed me to some illuminating texts, see Craig S. Keener, "Family and Household," *DNTB* 356-57.

118 Homer, *Od.* 1.308.

119 Acts 7:2; 1 John 2:13; *4 Bar* 5:28.

120 Homer, *Il.* 9.607.

121 Diodorus Siculus, *Hist.* 21.12.5.

122 Εἴτε γὰρ Πατέρες, εἴτε προφῆται, εἴτε ὁ τῶν ἀποστόλων εὐκλεὴς χορὸς, σοῦ μιμητὴς τυγχάνων (Basil Scr. Eccl., *Serm. xli* 472).

123 ʼαλλὰ γενοῦ μιμητὴς τῶν τελείων καὶ πνευματικῶν πατέρων, καὶ τῷ κανόνι αὐτῶν ἐπακολούθησον (Ephraem Syrus, *Ascet.* 158, also 196).

124 Γίνεσθε οὖν μιμηταὶ τοῦ θεοῦ ὡς τέκνα ἀγαπητά.

125 Πάντας τοὺς θέλοντας υἱοθεσίας ἀξιωθῆναι, δεῖ κατὰ τὸ δυνατὸν μιμεῖσθαι Θεὸν, ἐν τῷ ἀδιακρίτως εὐεργετεῖν (*Cat. Matt.* 41).

rabbis, etc. In virtually every educational context in both Jewish and Greek cultures, "father-son" language is commonly used to denote the relationship between teachers, philosophers, and rabbis ("fathers") with their pupils, students, or disciples ("sons").[126]

In these teacher-student contexts, imitation played a key role. Xenophon comments that professors "try to make their pupils copy their teachers."[127] Xenophon also praises Socrates as an ideal teacher who through his example caused many to desire virtue. Within this student-teacher context, the concept of imitation naturally arises: "Certainly [Socrates] never maintained to be a teacher of this; but by manifesting himself to live this out, it was his hope that those who spent time with him would become imitators of him."[128] Philo observes that humans can "become apt disciples of the only wise Being (i.e. God)" whose first virtue "is to desire that their imperfection may imitate as far as possible the perfection of the teacher."[129] Philo also describes Joshua the pupil and imitator of Moses.[130] A sixth century Christian text speaks of being an imitator of Christ, "the good teacher."[131]

3.4.3 Leader-People

The third context in which imitation commonly occurs is in the relationship between a leader and his followers, be they political, civic, or religious. In his description of Cyrus, Xenophon notes that because of his stellar character and action, the Persians were moved to imitate him.[132] Xenophon then goes into a detailed narrative of the concrete practices of Cyrus and the imitative effect it had on his subjects: "by setting such an example, Cyrus secured at court great correctness of conduct on the part of his subordinates."[133] In Xenophon's description of Cyrus, he notes how Cyrus commands the satraps "to imitate him in everything that they see him do."[134] Josephus mentions how the people

---

126 Epictetus, *Diatr.* 3.22.82; 4 Bar 2:4, 6, 8; 5:5; 7:24; 2 Kings 2:12; Mat 23:9; 3 John 4. (Directed to some of these references by Keener, "Family," 357.)

127 οἱ διδάσκαλοι τοὺς μαθητὰς μιμητὰς ἑαυτῶν ἀποδεικνύουσιν (Xenophon, *Mem.* 1.6.3).

128 Xenophon, *Mem.* 1.2.3. We will be looking more closely at this text below.

129 οἱ δ' ἅτε τοῦ μόνου σοφοῦ μαθηταὶ γεγονότες . . . πρώτη δὲ τῶν εἰσαγομένων ἀρετὴ τὸ διδάσκαλον ὡς ἔνεστι τέλειον ἀτελεῖς μιμεῖσθαι γλίχεσθαι (Philo, *Sacr.* 64-65).

130 ὁ φοιτητὴς αὐτοῦ καὶ μιμητὴς (Philo, *Virt.* 66).

131 μιμητὴς ὑπάρχων τοῦ καλοῦ διδασκάλου (Romanus Melodia Hymnographus, *Cant. dub.* 73.6).

132 Xenophon, *Cyr.* 8.1.24.

133 Xenophon, *Cyr.* 8.1.33.

134 ὅσα αὐτὸν ἑώρων ποιοῦντα, πάντα μιμεῖσθαι (Xenophon, *Cyr.* 8.6.10). See also similar comments about King Agesilaus in Xenophon, *Ages.* 10.2.

imitated the Jewish kings Zimri, Rehoboam, Jehoram, and Jehoahaz.[135] In the NT, there is a direct connection made between leaders and imitation.[136]

A subset of this leader-people imitation is the concept of the sage (wise man, elder) being imitated by the populous in general. Persons advanced in years, who had much experience and virtue, were esteemed as models for everyone imitate. Aeschines makes note of the council of Elders—a group of men "who are known to have been wise from their youth" as being worthy of imitation.[137]

3.4.4 Paul as Parent, Teacher, Leader

As we shall see in more detail in the next chapters, when we come to Paul's uncontested letters, Paul also positions himself as parent, teacher, and leader. The fact that the Greco/Judaic cultures of his day used the terms *father* and *son* with reference to all three of these roles, made the convergence of these different roles easier.

With respect to Paul as parent: Paul makes heavy use of "family language" with reference to the relationship Christians have with one another.[138] In the uncontested Pauline letters, one of the metaphors that he uses to describe his relationship with the recipients of his letters is that of a father to his child.[139] In

135 Josephus, *A.J.* 4.151; 8.251; 9.99, 173.

136 Heb 13:7: 2 Thess 3:7-9.

137 Aeschines, *Tim.* 1.180.

138 This seems to be a *Grundmotif* describing the Christian's relationship to God in the NT. Beginning with the Gospels, the heavy use of kinship language (especially the terms "father" and "son," but also "brother," "sister," and "mother") indicates a fundamental spiritual image that Paul takes up and develops. These terms seem to point to understanding faith within the imagery of a new family structure, the head of which is "my father," or "my father in heaven" (Matt 6:9; Luke 11:2; Matt 10:33; 11:25-27; 18:10, 14, 19; Mark 11:25; John 1:14; 5:17-27). Jesus views God not only as "my father," as in the previous texts, but also as the father of his disciples (Matt 10:20, 29; Luke 6:36; 12:30; John 20:17). He views his followers as being in a kinship relationship with himself and God (Matt 12:50). The imagery of the kingdom overlaps with kinship imagery. Thus Jesus can speak of "the kingdom of their [the disciple's] father" (Matt 7:21; 13:43; 19:14; 25:34; Luke 22:29). Jesus even goes so far as to say that this new spiritual relationship with the father in heaven is to be their primary family (Matt 12:46-50; 23:9; Luke 12:53; 14:26), which takes precedence over the biological one (Mark 10:29; Luke 9:59). We conclude that the pervasive use of kinship terminology leads one to see this as a core theological motif of the Gospels, which finds its correspondence, continuation and expansion in the epistles (without implying having the written Gospels as a *Vorlage*).

139 Paul used a limited number of terms when referring to the recipients: ἀδελφοὶ (brothers/siblings) sixty-seven times; ἀγαπητοί (beloved) eleven times; τέκνα (children) six times; ἐκκλησία (church) five times, only in the formal address at the

two of the five cases where Paul uses "father-child" language with respect to his relationship with the recipients, there is close association with imitation language.[140] Joubert's sociological analysis of Paul's function within the Corinthian church also notes that the predominant language Paul uses is that of fictive kinship relationships, where God is the heavenly *paterfamilias* and Paul is the earthly one.[141] As *paterfamilias* Paul is viewed as taking over virtually all the functions of an actual father: correcting their (moral) behaviour, expressing familial affection, defining and clarifying domestic roles and their respective activities.[142]

With respect to Paul as teacher: Although Paul does not identify himself as a teacher, it was in fact one of the major functions he performed. 1 Cor 4:17 is instructive here: "For this reason I sent you Timothy, who is my beloved and faithful child in the Lord, to remind you of my ways in Christ Jesus, as I teach (διδάσκω) them everywhere in every church." Paul mentions four things relevant to our concerns here: (1) the spiritual kinship relationship between Paul and Timothy; (2) that Paul "teaches *everywhere* in *every* church" identifies teaching as a component in his ministry to the churches; (3) Paul's "way of life" (τὰς ὁδούς μου) is understood as an integral part of what he teaches in the churches; (4) Timothy is sent to the churches to remind them of how Paul lives so that they through him can imitate Paul.

Further indications of Paul fundamental role as teacher are supported by the following observations. (1) The nature and content of Paul's letters, with their ethical instructions and vice and virtue lists, functioned as instruction for the congregations.[143] (2) Paul's use of the term "received" (παραλαμβάνω) points

---

beginning of a letter; ἅγιοι (saints) four times, only in the formal address at the beginning of a letter.

140 The two texts are 1 Cor 4:14-16 and 1 Thess 2:10-12; the other references are 2 Cor 6:13, 12:14; Gal 4:19; Phil 2:22.

141 Joubert, "Managing the Household," 217. This, however, needs to be tempered by the observation of Sanders that Paul did not simply take over the thought and practice of the society around him, but always adapted it (Sanders, *Palestinian Judaism*, 12).

142 Joubert, "Managing the Household," 219-22.

143 The Pauline vice and virtue lists and ethical instruction have as their backdrop the ethical catalogs of the Hellenistic world. Charles notes that "the ethical list, by which the ethical life is organized, accented and stereotyped, standardizes a type of attitude or behavior and thus becomes a common feature in the paraenetic tradition." (J. Daryl Charles, "Vice and Virtue Lists," *DNTB* 1252). See also A. Vögtle, *Die Tugend- und Lasterkataloge im Neuen Testament* (NTAbh 16; Münster: Aschendorff, 1936); S. Wibbing, *Die Tugend- und Lasterkataloge im Neuen Testament und ihre Traditionsgeschichte unter besonderer Berücksichtigung der Qumran Texte* (BZNTW 25; Berlin: Töpelmann, 1959); E. Kamlah, *Die Form der katalogischen Paränese im Neuen Testament* (WUNT 7; Tübingen: Mohr Siebeck, 1964).

clearly to a teaching function.[144] (3) In the Phil 4:9 passage, the link between teaching and imitation is functionally present. (4) Joubert also sees that Paul's role as *paterfamilias* implied that he had a responsibility for their religious education, which further implied that he was their "perfect role-model."[145]

With respect to Paul as leader: Paul's specific function as a leader was transported through his role as an apostle. Paul's understanding of apostleship has close ties with both the concept of fathering and teaching. Apostleship for Paul is not only proclamation of a message, but is bound up with spiritual parentage as well. Apostleship as Paul understood it goes beyond verbal proclamation of the message to embodying the message in all of life. Thus Paul becomes a "living message" that leads, confronts, and draws others to accept the message. In this process they become his spiritual children. 1 Cor 9 is suggestive here, though the concept of spiritual parentage is not explicit.[146] Paul describes the Corinthians as the fruit of his apostolic work and the seal of his apostleship, which was evident in their acceptance of his message. Apostleship and spiritual parentage are also wedded together in 1 Thess 2:7-11. Paul is at one and the same time apostle (bringing the message, founding a church) and spiritual mother (giving birth to spiritual children and nursing them in their faith) and father (being an example, performing fatherly tasks).

Thus, since Paul in his person combined the roles of spiritual father, teacher, and founder of fledgling Christian communities, it would have been perceived by his Greco-Jewish culture as perfectly normal that he would function as a model to be imitated. Gaventa goes even so far as to claim that "[h]ad Paul avoided the use of example and imitation, he might have appeared to his contemporaries as a person who knew himself unfit as a teacher.[147]

3.5 Observations on Illustrative Imitation Texts

Since, as we shall see in the next three chapters, the concept of one person imitating another has been strongly questioned, it is important to look more closely at texts, which can illuminate the true nature of how imitation functioned. We can thereby clear up modern misconceptions of the notion, which will then aid us in better understanding Paul's references to imitation.

144 1 Cor 15:1, Gal 1:9, Phil 4:9, 1 Thess 4:1.

145 "As a person who gave them accesss to the benefactions of God, Paul considered himself to be the perfect role-model . . . . He . . . not only symbolized the social honour of the new household group as their *paterfamilias*, but also symbolized their ethical honour because he exemplified the contents of his own message" (Joubert, "Managing the Household," 219).

146 Specifically the verses 1-2, 11, 22.

147 Beverly Roberts Gaventa, *First and Second Thessalonians* (IBC; Louisville, Ky.: John Knox, 1998), 16.

3.5.1 Basic Purpose of Human Imitation Illustrated

There are a number of texts, which highlight the purpose of imitation, of which we selected a few for closer analysis. Aristophanes observes that "those things we have not [yet] acquired, we must seek after by imitation."[148] Although the context for this is a profane play, what is highlighted here is that the lack of virtue can be compensated for through patterning ourselves after a model.[149] We imitate the model of others when something is lacking in our lives.

Xenophon records a conversation between Antiphon and Socrates, in which Antiphon thinks Socrates a miserable wretch since he eats bad food, wears the poorest of clothes, and never wears shoes or a tunic. Leading such a life, surmises Antiphon, "would drive even a slave to desert his master."[150] If it is the goal of teachers that they be imitated by their students, then, says Antiphon to Socrates, "you must consider yourself a professor of unhappiness."[151] To this Socrates replies describing all the benefits of his ascetical discipline, which brings lasting rewards in comparison to the fleeting rewards of "slavery to the belly or to sleep and incontinence."[152] Socrates concludes: "Do you think then that out of all this thinking there comes anything so pleasant as the thought: 'I am growing in goodness and I am making better friends?' And that, I may say, is my constant thought."[153] The purpose of all Socrates' striving was to become a virtuous person who had virtuous friends. The satisfaction that emanated from Socrates' virtuous life drew students to desire to imitate him.

Philo, in a text discussing the relationship between Abraham and Lot, writes that Lot accompanied Abraham "not that he may imitate the man who is better than he and so gain improvement, but actually to create obstacles which pull him back."[154] Lot is cast here as unvirtuous because he threw away the opportunity to improve himself, highlighting the purpose of imitation as the improvement of one's character.

Philo, in another text, writes that the goal of life is to live a life of virtue and excellence:

> every day of the man of worth must leave nothing void or empty where sin can come in, but have every part and space in it filled up with virtuous and excellent living, for virtue and excellence are judged not by quantity

---

148 "Α δ' οὐ κεκτήμεθα, μίμησις ἤδη ταῦτα συνθηρεύεται (Aristophanes, *Thesm.* 155-56).

149 In the play's context referring to heroes and gods.

150 Xenophon, *Mem.* 1.6.2 (Marchant and Todd, LCL).

151 Xenophon, *Mem.* 1.6.3

152 Xenophon, *Mem.* 1.6.7

153 Xenophon, *Mem.* 1.6.9

154 Philo, *Migr.* 149.

> but by quality. Therefore he held that the wise man's single day rightly spent is worth a whole life-time.[155]

The concentration on living each day as virtuously as possible is seen by Philo to be a fundamental goal of life. It is worth expending every effort to live in this way. This type of virtuous person who lives her days excellently functions as a model to be imitated.[156] The outcome of this imitation is a life lived well.

3.5.2 How Imitation Functions

There are a few texts, which illuminate how imitation functions; that is, they give insight into "the mechanics," if you will, of the process of imitation.

Xenophon heaps praise on Socrates as an ideal teacher, who through his example caused many to desire his quality of life in hopes "that they through imitation of him would attain to such excellence."[157] There are two points, which are germane to how imitation functions: (1) imitation begins by awakening hope in the hearts of others and inspiring them through the power of the example; (2) Socrates, in the words of Xenophon, did not "undertake to teach this" but intended his life to speak for itself. This indicates the need for effective teaching to be "biographical" in order for life-transformation to occur. The concepts (teachings) need to be embodied in a life in order for them to be genuine.

Philo offers another dimension of the mechanics of imitation.

> For to gaze continuously upon noble models imprints their likeness in souls which are not entirely hardened and stony. And therefore those who would imitate these examples of good living so marvelous in their loveliness, are bidden not to despair of changing for the better or of a restoration of wisdom and virtue from the spiritual dispersion which badness has wrought.[158]

This text, along with further references in the context of this passage, is important for understanding Philo's concept of imitation and how he conceives imitation to work. Six points stand out: (1) Philo sees that the virtues are worth imitating. But these are not virtues as abstract concepts; rather these virtues that are actively expressed through "virtuous and excellent living" (καλοκἀγαθιά).

---

155 Philo, *Praem.* 112.

156 Philo, *Praem.* 114.

157 Xenophon, *Mem.* 1.2.3. This text is quoted in full below.

158 αἱ γὰρ συνεχεῖς τῶν καλῶν παραδειγμάτων φαντασίαι παραπλησίας εἰκόνας ἐγχαράττουσι ταῖς μὴ πάνυ σκληραῖς καί ἀποκρότοις ψυχαῖς. ὅθεν εἴρηται πρὸς τοὺς ἐθέλοντας μιμεῖσθαι τὰ σπουδαῖα καὶ θαυμαστὰ κάλλη μὴ ἀπογινώσκειν τὴν ἀμείνω μεταβολὴν μηδὲ τὴν ὥσπερ ἐκ διασπορᾶς ψυχικῆς ἣν εἰργάσατο κακία πρὸς ἀρετὴν καὶ σοφίαν ἐπάνοδον (Philo, *Praem.* 114-16).

(2) The goal is to live life excellently (καλῷ βίῳ). (3) It is such virtuous individuals, who function as models (παράδειγμα) and who are worthy of our imitation (μιμεῖσθαι). (4) Imitation begins with "gazing continuously upon a noble pattern" (αἱ συνεχεῖς τῶν καλῶν παραδειγμάτων φαντασίαι). There is a concentration on the model, using the powers of the imagination and fantasy by means of an imaginative leap that transfers the lifestyle of another to oneself. This imagination allows one to picture within the mind how these character qualities and actions would look in one's own situation. (5) This type of gazing engraves the image into the soul (εἰκόνας ἐγχαράττουσι . . . ψυχαῖς). The result of this intentional reflection is that this image becomes engraved in the soul. The soul, then, begins to be formed and transformed by this reflection. (6) That Philo tells the imitator not to despair indicates that imitation is a process over time and implies a struggle against the negative habits or vices (εἰργάσατο κακία) that have for so long formed the lifestyle of the person.

This same conception is borne out in a text from *Scholia in Aelium Aristidem*: "gazing at the model, he became an imitator [of it]."[159] This compact text indicates how imitation works. Presupposed in the text are the first three steps: (1) initially seeing a model leads to (2) being attracted to it, which then leads to (3) wanting to be like it; (4) further gazing at it (i.e., intentionally studying the model) finally results in (5) "performing the model," that is, replicating the model in one's own life.

3.5.3 Descriptive Imitation Texts

The following texts highlight various aspects of imitation, which (1) provide a backdrop for the passages on Pauline imitation, (2) describe the scope, intent and/or content of imitation, or (3) provide a narrative framework, within which imitation can be observed and analyzed.

(1) **Socrates.** Xenophon in the context of this reference to imitation gives an extended, gripping description of Socrates' life, manner, thought, and action. There are a number of themes, which we shall later see, parallel Pauline imitation (parallels italicized):[160]

> In the first place, apart from what I have said, in *control of his own passions and appetites*[161] he was the strictest of men; further, in *endurance of cold and heat and every kind of toil*[162] he was most resolute; and besides, his needs were so *schooled*

---

159 εἰς παράδειγμα βλέπων μιμητὴς γενόμενος (*Scholia Aelium Aristidem* 175.1, reading B).

160 Xenophon, *Mem.* 1.2.1-8 (Marchant and Todd, LCL). There is not always terminological correlation between Xenophon's description and Paul's writings, but the themes and concepts are parallel.

161 Cf. Gal 5:23; 1 Cor 9:25.

162 Cf. 2 Cor 11:27.

> *to moderation* that *having very little he was yet very content.*[163] Such was his own *character*: how then can he have led others into *impiety, crime, gluttony, lust, or sloth?*[164] On the contrary, he cured these vices in many, by *putting into them a desire for goodness*, and by giving them confidence that *self-discipline* would make them gentlemen. To be sure he never professed to teach this; but, *by letting his own light shine, he led his disciples to hope that they through imitation of him would attain to such excellence.* Furthermore, he himself *never neglected the body*,[165] and reproved such neglect in others. Thus over-eating followed by over-exertion he disapproved. But he approved of taking as much hard *exercise as is agreeable to the soul*; for the habit not only insured good health, but did not hamper the *care of the soul.* On the other hand, he *disliked foppery and pretentiousness in the fashion of clothes or shoes or in behavior.*[166] Nor, again, did he encourage *love of money*[167] in his companions. For while he checked their other desires, he would *not make money himself out of their desire for his companionship.*[168] Socrates . . . was confident that those of his companions who *adopted his principles of conduct* would throughout life be good friends to him and to one another.

Contained within this text are key concepts with reference to imitation that, we shall later see, parallel Pauline imitation. The following observations are relevant for our purposes. (1) Socrates functioned as a teacher. (2) Imitation is regarded as simply occurring within the framework of this teacher-student relationship. (3) The lifestyle of the teacher was a "light" to his disciples, and played a vital role in the pedagogy of Socrates. (4) Xenophon offers a global description of all that the disciples of Socrates could imitate. This encompassed his demeanor, his private life, his thoughts, his perspectives on others' behavior, etc. (5) The concept of self-denial, endurance, and contentment are themes of this imitation. (6) Socrates' hope/intention is that his pupils would "adopt the principles of his conduct."

(2) **Athenians**. In an intriguing dialogue, Xenophon records Pericles asking Socrates how the Athenians can regain their old virtue, to which Socrates responds:

> There is no mystery about it, as I think. If they find out the customs of their *ancestors* (τῶν προγόνων) and *practice them* (ἐξευρόντες) as well as they did, they will come to be as good as they were; or failing that, they need but to *imitate* (μιμούμενοι) those who now have the pre-eminence and to *practice* (ἐπιτηδεύοντες) their *customs* (χρώμενοι), and if they are equally

163 Cf. Phil 4:12.

164 Cf. Rom 1:18; 13:14; 2 Cor 12:20. See also the vice lists of Paul in 1 Cor 6:9-10; Gal 5:19-21.

165 Cf. 1 Cor 9:27.

166 Cf. Gal 2:6.

167 Cf. 2 Cor 11:9; 12:14.

168 Cf. Phil. 1:17; 1 Thess 2:1-9.

> careful in observing them, they will be as good as they, and, if more careful, even better.[169]

Relevant for our purposes here are four points: (1) In the actual practicing of the customs, the character is formed and transformed. (2) It is the actual concrete practice of the virtues that shapes a person into being virtuous. (3) A virtuous person is not simply born, but is made and formed through doing virtuous things. (4) The practice of imitation has the power to transform the person.

(3) **Agesilaus**. In the description of Agesilaus, whom Xenophon praises him as "the perfect embodiment of goodness," we read:

> I think that the *virtue* of Agesilaus may well stand as a noble *example for those to follow who wish to* make *moral goodness a habit*. For who that *imitates* a pious, a just, a sober, a self-controlled man, can come to be unrighteous, unjust, violent, wanton? In point of fact, Agesilaus *prided himself less in reigning over others than on ruling himself*, less on leading the people against their enemies *than on guiding them to all virtue*.[170]

A number of points should be noted: (1) Agesilaus is a man of such virtue (ἀρετὴ) that he is (2) acknowledged by others, through the strength of his character to be (3) an example (παράδειγμα) for others. Agesilaus provides an orientation for them in their training. They can learn virtue through studying his life and imitating him. He is, however, an example for those persons of character (ἀνδραγαθίαν) who are willing to (4) commit to training (ἀσκεῖν) themselves to living virtuously. When someone commits to (5) imitating another who is virtuous (here, just, sober, self-controlled), it is not possible to end up becoming the opposite of these virtues. One becomes what one does. The practice of the virtues shapes the character, thought, and emotions of the one performing the virtues. Further, (6) Agesilaus puts a primary focus on "ruling himself" (ἐπὶ τῷ ἑαυτοῦ ἄρχειν) rather than ruling (βασιλεύειν) others. The virtuous life that he lives is the basis of his leadership as king. He knows that if his *private life* (we would say today) is not in order, then his authority to lead others in the *public sphere* would be based on his positional power rather than on the power of an authentic, virtuous life. Thus, he sees the need to concentrate on developing a virtuous life as his ultimate concern. Finally, (7) Xenophon recounts that Agesilaus' goal is not to lead and be victorious in battle, but to shape and guide his subjects into becoming people of virtue (πρὸς πᾶσαν ἀρετὴν ἡγεῖσθαι τοῖς πολίταις). His primary concern is not "cheap victories," but the development of people's character.

(4) **Hipponicus.** The description of Hipponicus by Isocrates reveals a number of aspects of imitation.

---

169 Xenophon, *Mem.* 3.5.14. (emphasis mine)

170 Xenophon, *Ages.* 10.2 (Marchant and Todd, LCL; emphasis mine).

> I have produced an example (δεῖγμα) of the nature (φύσεως) of Hipponicus, after whom it is necessary that your life would be based on this pattern (παράδειγμα). You should consider his manner (τρόπον) of life as a law for you. You should become an imitator and striver for the virtues of your father. For it would be a shame when painters portray the beauty of living creatures, for children not to imitate (μιμεῖσθαι) the goodness [or, nobility] of their parents.[171]

This text reveals a number of aspects of imitation that are highly instructive. (a) The terms δεῖγμα, παράδειγμα, τρόπον, μιμητὴν, μιμεῖσθαι are closely related, all of which having the same intention: the close inspection of a model for the purpose of patterning one's life on this model. (b) That which is imitated is the nature (φύσεως) of a person, his life (ζῆν), and his manner (τρόπον). (c) Isocrates encouraged Demonicus to look at the life of Hipponicus as a law (νόμον) upon which he should base his own conduct. This reflects a high level of seriousness and intentionality in the process of imitation. (d) That which Demonicus should imitate is his father's character, i.e., his virtues (ἀρετῆς), or the noble behavior (σπουδαίους) of his parents. (e) The realm of this imitation took place within a familial context—between father (πατρὸς, γονέων) and son (παῖδας).

(5) **Heracles.** Isocrates provides us with another text that gives us insight into the breadth of the concept of imitation.

> Now, while all who are blessed with understanding ought to set before themselves the greatest of men as their model, and strive to become like him, it behooves you above all to do so. For since you have no need to follow alien examples (παραδείγμασιν) but have before you one from your own house, have we not then the right to expect that you will be spurred on by this and inspired by the ambition to make yourself like the ancestor of your race? I do not mean that you will be able to imitate (μιμήσασθαι) Heracles in all his exploits (πράξεις); for even among the gods there are some who could not do that; but in the qualities (ἦθος) of the spirit, in devotion to humanity, and in the good will which he cherished toward the Hellenes, you can come close to his purposes.[172]

This text blends a number of important objects of imitation together: "the greatest of men," "ancestor of your race," and "the gods." All three of these categories are united in Heracles. This phrase "the greatest of men" is recorded in an off-the-hand way indicating that it was a commonly held assumption between Isocrates and his readers that all "great men" would be considered valid subjects of imitation. No further argumentation was needed to prove this.

This text implies, further, that one could have imitated the concrete exploits (πράξεις) of Heracles—if one were mighty enough to do so. But since even the other gods were unable, being limited by strength, humans could not either. The

171 Isocrates, *Demon.* 1.11.

172 Isocrates, *Phil.* 113-14 (Norlin, LCL).

specific items that one can imitate of Heracles are his ethos, his loving devotion to humanity, and his good will (ἦθος . . . φιλανθρωπίαν . . . εὔνοιαν).

An additional observation is relevant for our purposes: The conception of imitation here is bound up with the tradition of Heracles *as the Greeks had preserved it*, along with the attributes that were associated with Heracles that were exemplified in the stories about him. It was the community-held recollection of him and his character qualities—preserved in their living memory—that could be imitated. Thus a woodenness of imitation was not being called for by Isocrates, but an act of creative, imaginative association in which the imitator takes a living image along with its associated attributes as displayed in a specific context and imaginatively transfers that which they have "seen" into their specific context.

(6) **Jacob.** Philo provides us also with insight into his conception of imitation in his reflections on Jacob:

> For it is a characteristic mark of the learner that he listens to a voice and to words, since by these only is he taught; whereas he who acquires the good through practice, and not through teaching, fixes his attention not on what is said, but on those who say it, and imitates their life as shown in the blamelessness of their successive actions. Thus we read in the case of Jacob, when he was sent to marry into his mother's family. "Jacob heard his father and mother, and went to Mesopotamia" (Gen 28.7). "Heard them," it says, not their voice or words, for the practicer must be the imitator of a life, not the hearer of words, since the latter is the characteristic mark of the recipient of teaching, and the former of the strenuous self-exerciser. Thus, this text too is meant as a lesson to us that we may realize the difference between a learner and a practicer, how the course of one is determined by what a person says, the other by the person himself.[173]

This text makes a disjunction between teaching/learning and imitation. The learner (μανθάνοντος) listens to words since it is these that teach him. The actual acquisition of the good (ἀσκήσει τὸ καλὸν), however, is not through words (διδασκαλίᾳ) , but by fixing one's attention on the life of the speaker and imitating her life (μιμούμενος τὸν ἐκείνων βίον) as manifest in the blameless way she practices it (κατὰ μέρος ἀνεπιλήπτοις πράξεσι). The example of Jacob hearing—not the words of his parents, but hearing *them* directly—points to him imitating their life (βίου μιμητὴν). Philo makes a strong distinction here between a learner (μανθάνοντος) and a practicer (ἀσκητοῦ). This disjunction is between the learning of theories/words and the learning of life, the latter of which is the proper sphere of imitation.

(7) **Moses**. Philo also gives a description of Moses that contains insights into the workings of imitation.

---

173 Philo, *Congr.* 69-70.

> Thus, he beheld what is hidden from the sight of mortal nature, and, in himself and his life (τὸν ἑαυτοῦ βίον), which was displayed for all to see, he has set before us, like some well-crafted picture, a piece of work beautiful and godlike, a model (παράδειγμα) for those who are willing to copy it (τοῖς ἐθέλουσι μιμεῖσθαι). Happy are they who imprint (ἐναπομάξασθαι), or strive to imprint, that image (τύπον) in their souls.[174]

This text points out a number of aspects of imitation that relate to our concerns: (1) Philo describes Moses "seeing" (κατανοῶν) the invisible God, with the sense of studying, examining and reflecting upon. (2) Moses' life, in turn, becomes a reflection of this divine nature, which he saw. (3) Moses' life then becomes a model (παράδειγμα) on display for all to imitate (μιμεῖσθαι). (4) Finally, this model functions as an image (τύπος) that can become imprinted on the soul.

Aside: Relationship between Imitation and Discipleship

Although it is not in the purview of this work to explore the relationship between the terms disciple (μαθητής) and imitator (μιμητής), such a comparison would reveal insights into Paul's use of imitation language that would be fruitful for our study. In the article, "Μαθητής and Μιμητής: Exploring an Entangled Relationship" (*BBR*, 17 [2007]: 313-23), I do just this by analyzing texts from the Common Era where both of these terms occur. Based on my analysis there, I offer six findings: (1) It is clear that the term μαθητής in many contexts is a technical designation for a pupil of a teacher or a designation for someone who has proclaimed loyalty to a religious figure. (2) From the analyzed texts, there is no case in which μιμητής was used in a parallel sense to μαθητής. The term is never understood either as an equivalent to or replacing the term μαθητής. (3) Whenever the term μιμητής is elaborated upon, it is descriptive of (a) how one person has modelled, or should model, themselves on the pattern established by the exemplar, or (b) of specific virtues or characteristics that one should emulate. (4) The many references where μαθητής and μιμητής (and cognates) occur together in the texts from the second to the ninth century C.E. reveal that the term "imitator" continues to stand in disjunction to the term "disciple," never fusing with it or becoming a substitute for it. (5) Imitation is understood to be subsumed under discipleship, but not in an exclusive way; that is, imitation is not restricted to discipleship, since it occurs in many different relational contexts. (6) It would be incorrect to say that imitation is subordinate to discipleship. This would be a confusion of categories. The relationship between the terms is not understood in terms of positions over against each other. Rather, the relationship between the terms is seen as the one concept (imitation) occurring within the sphere of the other (discipleship).

---

174 Philo, *Mos*. 1.158.

3.6 Summary and Concluding Observations on Imitation in the Greco-Judaic World

We are now in a position to summarize our findings and offer some observations on the nature of imitation in the Greco-Judaic world.

(1) In the Greek literature there are numerous references (well over 2,000) to imitation (the term μιμητής and its cognates), with respect to emulation of human beings, things, or concepts.

(2) There are five general categories which are imitated by human beings: (a) other living persons, (b) persons of antiquity, (c) people groups, (d) the God of the Jews and Christians, the gods, angels and the devil, (e) animals (i.e., their characteristic traits).

(3) When we look more closely at what human beings specifically imitate in these five categories, we notice three major emphases of imitation: (a) the classical virtues (ἀρετή), for example, bravery, honesty, goodness, friendliness, wisdom, prudence, etc.; (b) concrete actions of another individual, commonly associated with the virtues; (c) "global imitation," which refers to the totality of another person—his lifestyle, character and manner of life.

(4) The concept of imitation is at home in three general relational spheres: (a) parent-child relations, (b) teacher-student relations, (c) leader-people relations. Kinship language is heavily used in all these settings, with the physical parent/teacher/leader often being referred to fictively as "father," and the physical child/student/people-group being referred to fictively as "child" or "children." It is assumed in these contexts that imitation would be occurring.

(5) Paul, in his person, united all these roles in which imitation was a natural component: parent, teacher, and leader. It would be expected by the people, who belonged to the voluntary association of the Christian ἐκκλησία, that they would imitate him as their spiritual father, teacher, and leader. Thus, Paul was not saying anything unusual when he encouraged members of this association to imitate him; it simply "went with the territory" of Paul's role.

(6) There are, further, abundant references to the imitation of ancestors, be they actual or fictive. The arenas in which these regularly occur are the political, civil, familial, and religious realms. The fictive kinship language of "father" and "forefather" also regularly accompany these references.

(7) These many references to imitation, both of living persons and ancestry indicate a high level of intergenerational identification, which is foreign to modern Western individualism. The ancestors were to be imitated through the medium of remembrance: they were thought about, written and sung about; they were recited, and stories were told of them. It is through these means that they seemed virtually present in the daily lives of the descendents. The virtues of the "fathers" were expected to be present in their living relatives.

(8) The concept of "shame" and "honor" were vital realities in the daily lives of Greek and Jewish people. What the individual did and said reflected on the immediate family, ancestors, city, nation or civil and religious association.

What one said or did brought either honor or shame/dishonor on the family, ancestors, city, etc. This concept of shame and honor was a key social concept for ensuring the individual's (a) conforming and adhering to the values of the family or group as well as (b) identifying with their respective family and group.

(9) The basic purpose of imitation was the improvement of the character of an individual based on a virtuous model. Based on this model, one could observe with all the senses how a virtuous person lived and thus have a pattern for one's own life.

(10) The process of voluntary imitation, which, we suggest, was operative in most contexts but is most explicit in the writings of Philo, is as follows: (a) initial contact with a model; (b) attraction to the model; (c) desire to be like the model; (d) intentional scrutiny of the model (using the thoughts and φαντασία); (e) "performing the model"—that is, attempting to replicate/adapt the model in ones own life.

(11) This process, when done authentically, was not a wooden, thoughtless act of mimicry. It required a "metaphorical leap" from the life situation of the model's to one's own life situation. Since no two personal contexts are alike, this metaphorical leap is imperative and implies, even demands, a thorough knowledge of the model's lifestyle, intentions, and goals. This knowledge is not based on theoretical knowledge, but rather intimate personal knowledge of and identification with the model—which Philo described as "imprinting the image [of the model] on one's soul."

These observations set the stage and provide the background for analyzing Paul's references to imitation, to which we now turn.

CHAPTER 4

Imitation of Paul, Part I: Imitation in the Thessalonian Correspondence

Introduction to Chapters 4-6

In this and the next two chapters, we look at the texts in the uncontested Pauline Epistles, which refer to the imitation of Paul. Our starting point is exegesis of these passages, but we are driven by the goal of determining how imitation is configured in these contexts. We seek to discern the scope of imitation in each context and interact with how other scholars understand imitation in these passages. We take some exegetical detours along the way in order to deal with issues relevant to the understanding of imitation in Paul's writings. We synthesize the findings of these three exegetical chapters as well as our discussion of Castelli's *Imitating Paul* in chapter eight. In chapter nine we look at issues surrounding the practice of imitation and discuss the relevance of our findings with respect to spiritual direction.

A further goal in these chapters is to look more closely at what the texts reveal explicitly or implicitly about Paul, the person, and about the shape of his relationship with the recipients. This, we contend, has relevance to the ministry of spiritual direction. Our working assumption is that these texts reveal to us something of the Paul behind the texts—his character, values, intentions, modes of interaction, etc. As Royce Gordon Gruenler, reflecting on Wittgenstein's concept of *language games*, says, "all the form-making activity of language is a reality in which persons define and extend themselves. Language is inseparable from the person who uses it."[1] Thus, language is a form of self-disclosure. Wittgenstein himself writes:

> Why do I want to tell him about an intention too, as well as telling him what I did? – Not because the intention was also something which was going on at that

1 Royce Gordon Gruenler, *New Approaches to Jesus and the Gospels: A Phenomenological and Exegetical Study of Synoptic Christology* (Grand Rapids: Baker, 1982), 20.

> time. But because I want to tell him something about *myself*, which goes beyond what happened at that time.[2]

Any written text includes two aspects of authorial self-disclosure: the intentional and the unintentional. The unintentional self-disclosure may further be broken down into (a) commonly held assumptions, which the author assumes the reader will acknowledge, and (b) details of the author's life that are below the radar screen of the author, which may or may not reveal fruitful insight into her way of thinking and operating. It is not always possible to determine whether a word, phrase, or discourse an author uses is intended to reveal a specific aspect of her person or not. In our analysis, where it seems important to determine intentionality and to distinguish between intentional and unintentional, we will do so, acknowledging the tentativeness of our observations. Our guiding question in the discussion of the texts below is: "what specifically does Paul want the recipients to imitate, and what do these imitation texts reveal to us about Paul that carries relevance for the practice of spiritual direction?"

Elizabeth Castelli has undertaken an analysis of the imitation of Paul from a radically different vantage point.[3] Basing her *de*construction of Paul on the writings of Michel Foucault and Jacques Derrida, she contends that Paul needs to be understood in terms of power relations. Since her approach is exemplary of some postmodern approaches to texts, which carry radical implications for the study of biblical texts, we will seek to critique her approach and exegesis. This we will undertake in chapter seven.

We will be taking the imitation texts in the generally accepted order of the time of writing: 1 Thessalonians ca. 50-52 C.E., 1 Corinthians ca. 54-57 C.E., and Philippians ca. 53-62 C.E.[4]

1 Thessalonians 1:5-7

4.1 General Introductory Comments

By wide consensus, 1 Thessalonians is considered among the earliest NT

---

2 Ludwig Wittgenstein, *Philosophical Investigations* (Oxford: Oxford University Press, 1953), par. 656. Cited in Gruenler, *New Approaches*, 23 (emphasis mine).

3 Castelli, *Imitating Paul*.

4 Werner Georg Kümmel, *Introduction to the New Testament* (Revised ed.; Nashville: Abingdon, 1975), 257-62, 278-79, 324-32; Carl R. Holladay, *Critical Introduction to the New Testament: Interpreting the Message and Meaning of Jesus Christ* (Nashville: Abingdon, 2005), 279; Raymond E. Brown, *An Introduction to the New Testament* (ABRL; New York: Doubleday, 1997), 428; D. A. Carson and Douglas J. Moo, *An Introduction to the New Testament* (2nd ed.; Grand Rapids: Zondervan, 2005), 543, 448, 506.

writings,[5] and in 1:6 we find a clear statement of imitation: καὶ ὑμεῖς μιμηταὶ ἡμῶν ἐγενήθητε καὶ τοῦ κυρίου (and you became imitators of us and the Lord). This text, in contrast to other passages discussed below, frames imitation as a *fait accompli*, not as a command to be imitators. A full discussion of the background and occasion for the writing of 1 Thessalonians is not germane to our understanding of imitation here. We note, however, the following aspects as relevant to the concept of imitation of Paul.

1 Thessalonians 1:1 positions Paul, Silvanus, and Timothy as joint authors, with Paul placed in the primary position. This immediately raises questions: Who truly was the author of the letter, and how should one understand the use of first person singular and plural in this letter?[6] Was Paul the true author, who just happened to mention his traveling companions? Or is there a sense in which all three are authors?[7]

When we look at the usage of the first person singular in 1 Thessalonians,[8] we note that specific activities of Paul are mentioned.[9] The use of the first person singular in these instances, along with Paul being placed in the primary position of writer in 1:1, provides strong indication that it was Paul who was the principal author—a point virtually undisputed in scholarship.[10] A closer

---

5 The date of writing is fairly certain, since it falls within Paul's period at Corinth. Scholars date it around the year 50 or 51, based on the reference in Acts 18 to the proconsul Gallio, who is mentioned on an inscription at Delphi. Kümmel, *Introduction*, 257; Brown, *Introduction*, 428; Holladay, *Critical Introduction*, 276; Carson and Moo, *Introduction*, 543.

6 Lyons has done an extensive study of the Pauline singular and plural and comes to the conclusion (following Karl Dick) that no set rules apply to Paul's use of first person singular or plural references. The Pauline "we," as an autobiographical comparison with Cicero and Josephus show, can refer to Paul alone or to a group. It is ultimately the exegesis of each text and not grammatical rules that has the last word. In addition, the alternation of "we" and "you"—both singular and plural—does not determine if the "we" references are exclusive, as a closer look at Gal 4:21-31 bears out. Lyons, *Pauline Autobiography*, 11 n. 37; 15-16.

7 Paul's earliest epistles reveal the highest percentage of plurals, i.e., 1 Thess 97.6% (2 Thess 93.8%). Llewellyn notes a strong contrast between Thessalonians and Philippians: "Philippians, though the opening greetings are by Paul and Timothy, must be considered the most individual of Paul's letters. All plurals with the exception of one (Phil.3:17) must be classed as literary plurals. Paul and Timothy never (apart from the introduction) address the Philippians together." S. R. Llewelyn, "Ammonius to Appolonios (*P.Oxy.* XLII 3057): The Earliest Christian Letter on Papyrus?" *NewDocs* 171-72.

8 1 Thess 2:18; 3:5 (2x); 5:27.

9 Llewelyn, "Ammonius," 171-72.

10 Krentz argues that Paul's "viewpoint is consistently preeminent" and that "there is nothing to suggest that either Sylvanus or Timothy participated in the writing." Edgar M. Krentz, "First and Second Epistles to the Thessalonians," n.p., *ABD on*

look at the second person plural indicates its usage, however, is not simply a literary formality,[11] behind which Paul the true author is hidden. Rather, it plays an important part in the strategy of the letter. This is especially evident in 1:5 as well as the extended description of the apostolic band's stay with the Thessalonians in 2:1-12. In both texts the interrelational nature of this threesome's presentation of the gospel is thereby underscored. The regular inclusion of the first person plural throughout the letter indicates that "all three missionaries stand together in the encouragement, instruction, and commands given to the Thessalonian congregation."[12]

There is little evidence in this letter either of polemicism or of theological problems standing at the core of why this letter was written. The warm style, along with the topics developed in the letter, has led some scholars to the conclusion that this letter is "confirmatory": Paul's basic intention is to confirm or solidify the faith of the Thessalonians in light of pressure from outside the congregation to revert to their former way of life.[13] Although this is plausible, it does not go far enough, for there are concerns mentioned, which go beyond consolidation: issues of moral purity (4:3-7), questions of the *parousia* and living in light of it (4:13-15:10), as well as various matters relating to their life together (5:12-22). Further, Holmes indicates that Paul wrote this letter to deal with two concerns: (1) the need to solidify the faith of this fledgling congregation in light of external pressure; (2) explaining his behavior to them, which they seem to have misunderstood.[14] Yet this too does not entirely encompass the themes and topics addressed in the book.

Paul's external motivation for writing the letter stems from the news that he received through Timothy on how the Thessalonians were faring. There are two pressing concerns he has for writing, and he takes the occasion to address

---

CD-ROM. Version 3.0a. 2006. He notes further that "scholars universally affirm that Paul is the actual writer of the letter" (515).

It is possible that Timothy may have delivered the letter (3:2, 5). Some have suggested that Silvanus was the amanuensis of Paul, but that is indeterminable (Michael W. Holmes, *1 & 2 Thessalonians* [NIVAC; Grand Rapids: Zondervan, 1998], 24). For Silvanus plausibly being the amanuensis, see the arguments of Ernst Best, *A Commentary on the First and Second Epistles to the Thessalonians* (BNTC; London: Black, 1972), 23-29; Edward Gordon Selwyn, *The First Epistle of St. Peter: The Greek Text with Introduction, Notes, and Essays* (TAC; Grand Rapids: Baker, 1981), 9-17.

11 Contrast this with Philippians, which includes Timothy in the prescript, but switches to the regular use of the first person singular from that point onward.

12 Holmes, *Thessalonians*, 23-24.

13 Gaventa, *Thessalonians*, 7. She follows Thomas H. Olbricht, "An Aristotelian Rhetorical Analysis of 1 Thessalonians," in *Greeks, Romans, and Christians: Essays in Honor of Abraham J. Malherbe* (ed. David L. Balch, et al.; Minneapolis: Fortress, 1990), 216-36.

14 Holmes, *Thessalonians*, 22.

additional items that he heard through Timothy. The first concern is to express his joy that they are still in the faith and that they are progressing in it. He wishes to encourage them to solidify ("consolidate") this fledgling faith (3:6-8). The second concern is to deal with questions about Paul's motives and character that had arisen after his abrupt exit from Thessalonica (2:1-12).

In addition to these concerns, he addresses other topics that are crucial to the Thessalonians: (1) answering nagging questions regarding persecution and suffering—both Paul's suffering as well as theirs (1:6; 2:2; 2:14-16; esp. 3:3-5; 3:7); (2) dealing with how to "be blameless and holy in the presence of our God and Father when our Lord Jesus comes with all his holy ones" (3:13). This verse seems to function as an introduction to the multiple concerns in the final two chapters, which are largely parenetic in style. Paul, in these final chapters, senses a need to instruct them about how to live as Christians in the time before the *parousia* and deals with several issues in light of it. He (1) calls them to live a life of sexual purity (4:3-8), and he (2) exhorts them to live a winsome life before outsiders (4:11-12); he (3) corrects misconceptions of the *parousia* (4:13-5:3), and (4) instructs them on how to live during this interim time (5:4-11); he (5) concludes with a community-specific list of instructions on how they should conduct their lives corporately and individually (5:12-22).

4.2 Exegetical Notes Bearing on the Concept of Imitation

The reference to imitation appears at the beginning of the body of the letter in the "thanksgiving" section, where Paul focuses on his thankfulness for the recipients' effort on behalf of the gospel.[15] The structure of this pericope up to our text formally begins in v. 2 with εὐχαριστοῦμεν (we give thanks) concludes in 2:1 when it shifts to another topic by means of the transitional phrase Αὐτοὶ γὰρ οἴδατε (for you know).

Paul's expression of thanksgiving (vv. 2-4) encompasses three elements, all expressed in the form of parallel participles: (1) his prayer for them (ποιούμενοι . . . προσευχῶν, v. 2); (2) the remembrance of three specific qualities evident in them (μνημονεύοντες, v. 3); (3) and his acknowledgement (εἰδότες) of their being seen as chosen by God as he recalls what he knows about them (v. 4).

Their calling is then expanded upon in verses 5-7. Their election relates integrally to how the gospel came to them (v. 5) and how they received it (v. 6). Their reception of it had an impact on others (v. 7), who heard about their conversion. Graphically, the structure of verses 2-7, which we will analyze below, is as follows:

---

15 It is difficulty to determine where the body exactly begins. It seems the body is assimilated into the thanksgiving or emerges out of it without clear grammatical or linguistic demarcation. Peter T. O'Brien, "Letters, Letter Forms," *DPL* 552.

Praying for you

Remembering our work of faith, labor of love, endurance of hope

Knowing your election/calling

For the gospel came to you

not merely with words

But also in power, in the Holy Spirit and in much conviction

just as you know what sort of people we were among your for your sake

And you became imitators of us and Jesus

Receiving the word in difficulty and much joy in the Holy Spirit

And so you also became models to other believers.

The basic thrust of this text is to describe how the gospel was first presented to and received by the Thessalonians. It is cast as going beyond mere rhetorical presentation (οὐκ . . . ἐν λόγῳ μόνον) and including demonstrations of power and deeply held personal convictions (ἀλλὰ καὶ ἐν δυνάμει καὶ ἐν πνεύματι ἁγίῳ καὶ [ἐν] πληροφορίᾳ πολλῇ).[16] Instead of reading these three prepositional phrases beginning with ἐν as a triad, this should be seen as a dyad in epexegetical relationship, where the second compound phrase qualifies the first: "the gospel came to you . . . with power, that is, with the Holy Spirit and full conviction."[17]

To what do the elements of this phrase refer? There seem to be three options: (1) to Paul's preaching directly, (2) to supernatural manifestations that attended the preaching, or (3) the conversion of the Thessalonians.[18]

It seems strained to play these options against each other, since all are highlighted in the epistle.[19] Nevertheless, the main thrust in 1:5 seems to be the effective presentation of the gospel attested by a number of experiential factors as opposed to mere rhetorical persuasiveness.

---

16 A textual variant here bears on the understanding of the passage. The final ἐν seems most likely a scribal insertion. The ἐν before πληροφορίᾳ is missing in ℵ B 33 lat. It is easy to understand how a scribe would insert it, since just prior to it καὶ ἐν occurs twice, linking the first two terms in coordinate conjunction. The scribe, thinking that the third term must also be in the series, since it is preceded by καὶ, assumed that the ἐν must have been inadvertently dropped and reinserted it. Trying to argue the reverse, that the ἐν was dropped intentionally, is more difficult. Gordon D. Fee, *God's Empowering Presence: The Holy Spirit in the Letters of Paul* (Peabody, Mass.: Hendrickson, 1994), 40 n. 5. Similarly Raymond F. Collins, *Studies on the First Letter to the Thessalonians* (BETL 66; Leuven: Leuven University Press, 1984), 192 n. 95; Robert L. Thomas, "1 Thessalonians," in *EBC*, vol. 11 (Grand Rapids: Zondervan), 224.

17 For a similar conclusion, see Fee, *Empowering*, 40-41.

18 Fee, *Empowering*, 43.

19 Paul's message of the gospel, as seen in 1 Thess 2:13-16, points to the effectiveness of the preaching. The juxtaposition of "not in word only" with "but in power . . ." points in the direction of supernatural manifestations, as in Rom 15:19. Witness to the powerful and effective conversion of the Thessalonians (1:3, 8, 9; 2:13) can also be seen in the text.

The phrase καθὼς οἴδατε οἷοι ἐγενήθημεν [ἐν] ὑμῖν δι' ὑμᾶς (just as you know what sort of people we were in your midst because of you) is relevant to the understanding of imitation in that it directs the recipients to examine the shape of the life of Paul and his companions as they experienced them during their stay in their midst. The term οἷοι (of what sort) points to the ethical credibility of this team. They had a proven character that could undergo closest scrutiny. Their conduct was stellar, above reproach.

This καθὼς (just as) phrase is global in scope: the lives of this Pauline band embodied the gospel message as it was spoken and lived out with and in front of the Thessalonians. They could touch, feel, observe, interact with, and experience the gospel through their encounter with Paul and his companions.

From a rhetorical standpoint, the use of οἴδατε (you know) has dual significance. On the one hand, it calls—virtually challenges—the Thessalonians to analyze the lives of Paul and his companions.[20] The Thessalonians are to recollect their encounter with Paul[21] and his companions in order to verify their integrity. The result of this recalling and testing that is implicit in Paul's rhetoric is that the Thessalonians would conclude: "Yes, they did present the gospel in this convincing manner and with integrity." This then would lead to a reconfirmation of both the validity of the gospel and the credibility of the message-bearers.[22]

On the other hand, οἴδατε has significance for Paul's method of interaction with them. It seems to imply intentionality on the part of Paul as to how he lived with them. Paul was aware that he was on public display with every move he made. Although the mimetic aspect is not explicit in this verse, what is explicit is that he intentionally calls the Thessalonians to look closely to examine his life, and that he saw his life as exemplary.[23]

It is important, as mentioned above, to note the use of the first plural form. Paul includes Silas and Timothy as persons to be imitated—not Paul alone. Paul thus, does not exalt himself as the sole role model here, but includes

---

20 The lengthy discussion in chapter 2:1-12 has bearing on the understanding of 1:4-7 since Paul there also is challenging them to scrutinize his life and action. This apologetic description of Paul's person, character, and activity amounts to a sustained justification of Paul and his companions' lives, motives, and actions against actual and potential accusers. The most likely reason for this is Paul's highly unusual departure from Thessalonica—slinking off in the middle of the night (Acts 17:1-9). This action would surely have raised questions and doubts in the minds of some about the intentions and character of Paul.

21 For the sake of ease of reading, I will at times refer primarily to Paul as the author, even though in the address Silas and Timothy are included.

22 This is rhetorically significant because of Paul's discussion in chapter two, where he mentions others who speak with empty words and used flattery as a mask for greed (2:4-6).

23 This is not to say, that this was foremost in his mind all the time he was with them. Rather, this was something that he expected to happen.

himself as one of several. This relativizes any claim to binding the Thessalonians to him alone in an exclusive manner.

The use of the verb γίνομαι in vv. 5, 6, and 7 also has strong relevance to the concept of imitation and plays a significant role in how we understand this text. Unfortunately, its use here is not given any treatment in the commentaries. This verb occurs four times within the space of three verses:

v. 5a	τὸ εὐαγγέλιον ἡμῶν οὐκ *ἐγενήθη* εἰς ὑμᾶς	aorist passive
v. 5b	καθὼς οἴδατε οἷοι ἐγενήθημε ν [ἐν] ὑμῖν	aorist passive
v. 6	Καὶ ὑμεῖς μιμηταὶ ἡμῶν ἐγενήθητε	aorist passive
v. 7	ὥστε γενέσθαι ὑμᾶς τύπον πᾶσιν τοῖς . . .	aorist infinitive

That Paul chooses this verb, which carries the nuance of "being" and "manner of being," and rejects the use of the static verb εἰμί (be), seems deliberate and significant.[24] Paul, it seems, is not interested in simply reporting naked facts. Rather, he wants to highlight the *manner in which* the Thessalonians have experienced the gospel and the apostolic band.

Although most translations, with some justification, opt to translate the first use of this verb in v. 5a with some form of the verb "come" ("the gospel *came* to you"), three older translations opt for a translation that seeks to capture the nuance of manner that this term carries: "were . . . with you" (DBY), "hath . . . been unto you" (DRA), and "was . . . unto you" (GNV). From this phrase alone, it is impossible to determine how to translate it. Note, however, that in this first chapter, there is no other indication of the gospel "coming" to them. Then, when there is indication of something "coming," the verb εἴσοδον is used (1:9; 2:1). In addition, if the focus were on the simple fact of "coming," the verb ἔρχομαι would have been the obvious choice.

Further, the decision of how to translate this first instance of γίνομαι must to take into consideration how the other instances of the term are used in these verses. The thrust of the second reference to γίνομαι (v. 5b), "what kind of persons we were (ἐγενήθημεν) among you," clearly accentuates the *manner in which* Paul in community with Silvanus and Timothy lived among the Thessalonians.

The third instance of this verb comes a mere nine words after the second instance: "you became (ἐγενήθητε) imitators of us" (v. 6). It would seem natural that the way these verbs would be understood would be equivalent. Thus, it seems that the Thessalonians were imitators of Paul and his companions in the same manner that they had experienced them. Again, the choice of this term and avoidance of εἰμί seems intentional.

The fourth instance of this term comes in v. 7: "so that you were/became examples (γενέσθαι . . . τύπον). Again, Paul opts for γίνομαι and not the static εἰμί. The translations are split in how they render this. The ASV, BBE, DBY,

24 BDAG, 197.

ESV, NAB, NAS, NET, NJB, NRS, RSV, YLT have "became an ensample/example/models," indicating the simple fact of what occurred. The DRA, GNV, KJV, PNT, RWB, TNT, WEB render this "you were examples/as ensamples/made a pattern," with the nuance of manner possibly present. From the nature of this chain reaction of imitation, it seems that the Thessalonians manner of life was what influenced the other believers to follow their example.

Since it seems the case that these last three instances of the verb γίνομαι indicate the focus being *manner in which*, it would follow that the first instance in v. 5a would also indicate a focus on how the Thessalonians experienced the gospel and not the mere fact of it "coming" to them.

Whereas imitation in verse 5 may be implicit, when we come to verse 6, imitation language becomes explicit: Καὶ ὑμεῖς μιμηταὶ ἡμῶν ἐγενήθητε (and you became imitators of us). The fact that imitation is not commanded but identified as having occurred is highly suggestive—if, in fact, active imitation is intended. Fiore, following Michaelis, sees this mention of imitation as "simple comparison. No deliberate imitation is meant."[25] This conclusion is warranted for three reasons: (1) As has been argued in chapter three, imitation would have been a culturally expected response for the Thessalonians given the roles Paul played with respect to the recipients: spiritual parent, teacher, leader, and apostle. Within these roles, imitation would have been assumed and expected. (2) The dynamics of the text indicate that it was deliberate: Paul had lived an exemplary life before them and had suffered persecution at the hands of the citizens of Thessalonica (2:1-12). Paul knew and banked on the Thessalonians observing him in all details of his life.[26] In light of this, they had observed a pattern of life in this context for how they themselves should live and respond to the difficulties that they faced. (3) The close juxtaposition of v. 5b (just as you know how we lived among you) immediately followed by Paul noting their imitation of him seems Paul was intending this to happen. So, rather than Fiore's term "simple" to describe the type of imitation noted here, a more accurate phrase that captures the dynamic would be "natural response imitation"—similar to younger children who naturally imitate those who are more mature than they.[27] Thus, Paul notes this natural response and commends them for it.

---

25 Fiore, *Personal Example*, 184. So also Merk, "Nachahmung Christi," 193; Traugott Holtz, *Der erste Brief an die Thessalonicher* (EKKNT 13; Zurich: Benzinger, 1986), 49.

26 That Paul assumed and encouraged them to observe his life is borne out in the following references in 1 Thessalonians: "You know how we were with you" (1:5); "you know" (2:1); "as you know" (2:2, 5, 11); "for you remember" (2:9); "you are witnesses" (2:10). In addition, there are other references to Paul's life: 3:4; 4:1-2, 6, 11; 5:1-2 (See also Andrew D. Clarke, "'Be Imitators of Me': Paul's Model of Leadership," *TynBul* 49 [1998]: 339 n. 32).

27 That Paul is not binding them exclusively to himself is indicated by the "imitated us . . . and the Lord."

To what does this imitation specifically refer? It is not immediately apparent if it refers to (1) how they received the word, (2) that they received the word in much affliction, (3) that they received it with joy, (4) whether imitation refers to a combination of 1-4 above, or (5) if it refers more generally to Paul and his companion's overall lifestyle. In order to decide how to understand imitation, we need to take a closer look at the thought-flow of the text.

The thought-flow points to a close connection between v. 6 with the content of v. 5. The editors of the Nestle-Aland Greek text have made an interpretive judgment that seems to run counter to Paul's flow of thought when they insert a mid-paragraph break between verses 5 and 6 and place a full-stop before the καὶ (and) at the beginning of verse 6. The *Novae Vulgatae Bibliorum Sacrorum* goes one step further and makes a paragraph division in the same place. A closer analysis of the development of the thought units seems to call for the καὶ to be understood as a coordinate conjunction, continuing the previous thought, and not as a case of Semitic parataxis.[28] Thus the basic flow of thought of vs. 4-7 would be:[29]

v. 4 knowing . . . your salvation,
  v. 5a for[30] our gospel came to you . . . with power and . . .
    v. 5b just as[31] you know[32] what sort of people we were in your midst

28 Fee notes that Semitic parataxis is unusual for Paul: "In most cases [Paul's use of καὶ] can be shown to be intentionally linking sentences that are coordinate in some way." Fee, *Empowering*, 45 n. 30.

29 Modifying and advancing Fee's suggestion. Fee, *Empowering*, 46.

30 It is not immediately apparent to what this ὅτι (for) is connected. Does it refer (1) to the previous participle, εἰδότες (knowing)? (2) To all three previous participles? (3) Does it refer back to εὐχαριστοῦμεν (we give thanks)? The first option seems to make most sense of the context, since the term ἐκλογὴν (choice) refers to their salvation. It would be natural for Paul, after mentioning their salvation, to lead into a description of how that salvation came to them. This reading would call for taking the ὅτι as explanatory ("for")—calling them to remember how the gospel actually was presented to them. In other words, they can be sure of their salvation when they reflect on how the gospel came to them and how they received it. The sense of causality, as some translations have it, may be present, but it is not in the forefront.

31 The term καθὼς is somewhat cryptic, not being immediately apparent how it is to be understood. The term is untranslated in the NIV and RSV ("You know"); the NJB carries some sense of being a coordinate conjunction ("And you observed"). The bulk of the versions take it as a comparative: the ASV takes it as a strengthened comparative ("even as"), the NAU and NRS as a straight comparative ("just as"), and the KJV as a weak or simple comparative ("as").

Of the possible ways to understand καθὼς, it seems to make most sense as a comparative conjunction translated "just as." What, then, is specifically being compared? It seems the readers are to compare how they experienced Paul ("you know what kind of people we were") with the content of the preceding ἐν phrases: "not with word only" but with "power, spirit and certainty." Clarke seems correct in

v. 6a and you became imitators of us . . .
v. 6b receiving the word in difficulty . . .
v. 7 so that[33] you became an example[34] to all . . .

Through the coordinating καὶ of v. 6, the reference to imitation maintains strong ties to the preceding verse. But μιμηταὶ also has strong ties to the participial phrase that immediately follows ("receiving the word . . ."). These two links are at the crux of the debate of how to understand the content of imitation here. A further ingredient that we need to factor into our understanding of imitation in this context is the phrase καὶ τοῦ κυρίου (and the Lord).

There have been multiple options and accentual shadings put forward as to how one resolves the understanding of imitation in this context in light of the exegetical factors noted above. Dobschütz and Michaelis see imitation as focusing solely on the acceptance of the gospel.[35] Holtz rejects this and says that the content of imitation refers to accepting the gospel *in difficulty and joy of the Holy Spirit.*[36] Both Frame and Lightfoot see the entire participial phrase as encompassing the content of imitation.[37] Similarly Neil sees the Thessalonians imitating Paul through the "distinctive temper and tone" the

---

observing that καθὼς "is an important conjunction which expressly links Paul's work of evangelization with his conduct among the Thessalonians." Clarke, "Be Imitators," 337. This is in contrast to Fee, who claims that the phrase is "somewhat parenthetical." Fee, *Empowering*, 45.

32 Every English translation puts some sort of break before the καθὼς clause (new sentence: NIV, RSV, NJB; semicolon: KJV, NRS, NAU, ASV). This full stop seems unjustified, since the idea of the previous sentence is being extended. It is an understandable move on behalf of the translators to insert a break for the sake of clarity, but it unfortunately separates thoughts that belong together.

33 This is an inferential conjunction, which expresses actual results, so that or with the result that. The sense of the text seems to indicate that their becoming an example simply occurred in the natural course of events. Just as it occurred between Paul and the Thessalonians, so now the chain is extended. The Thessalonians have now become a model for others.

34 The term τύπος (example) occurs regularly in Greek literature alongside μιμητής and cognates to refer to a moral exemplar or pattern. The conjunction of these terms occurs twice in the NT, here and in Phil 3:17.

35 Ernst von Dobschütz, *Die Thessalonicher-Briefe* (KEK; Göttingen: Vandenhoeck & Ruprecht, 1909), 73; Michaelis, *TWNT* 4:673.

36 Holtz, *Thessalonicher*, 49. So also Helmut Köster, "Apostel und Gemeinde in den Briefen an die Thessalonicher," in *Kirche: Festschrift für Günther Bornkamm zum 75. Geburtstag* (ed. Dieter Lührmann and Georg Strecker; Tübingen: Mohr Siebeck, 1980), 289.

37 James Everett Frame, *The Epistles of St. Paul to the Thessalonians* (ICC; Edinburgh: T&T Clark, 1912), 82; J. B. Lightfoot, *Notes on the Epistles of St. Paul* (Grand Rapids: Zondervan, 1957), 14.

converts had in "welcoming the word, though it brought you heavy trouble, with a joy inspired by the Holy Spirit." The imitation of Christ does not refer to the reception of the gospel, but "by displaying the same victorious mastery over outward circumstances as He did."[38] Best sees that imitation refers to *how* they received the word—that is "with much tribulation," and not *on the fact of* reception.[39] Dunn concentrates on the willing reception of the word.[40] Fee sees the content of the imitation as referring to "receiving the word in great affliction with joy," with the accent being joy.[41] Similarly, de Boer, Holmes, and Richard see the participial phrase as attendant circumstance (affliction) and manner (with joy) in which the imitation focuses on the joyful response.[42] Richard goes one step further and says that it is exclusively "joy" that is the content of imitation.[43] Stanley, Wanamaker, and Dumm see both parts of the participial phrase as significantly related to imitation.[44] Agan, with little argumentation, asserts the point of imitation as being "the *active* moral response to faithfulness despite persecution."[45] Thomas, taking his cue not from contextual factors, but basing his argument not on exegesis but rather on "conceivability," maintains that imitation here refers to the lifestyle of Paul. He simply cannot imagine that imitation be reduced to just one aspect here. He then imports the broader range of meanings that imitation has in the other Pauline passages.[46]

---

38 William Neil, *The Epistle of Paul to the Thessalonians* (MNTC; London: Hodder & Stoughton, 1948), 19 (author's emphasis).

39 Best, *Thessalonians*, 77-78. Best cannot reconcile the additional phrase "and of the Lord" with this interpretation and concludes it must refer to the "central features of the Christ event" rather than the daily life of Paul and Christ. "We would expect the use of 'Jesus' rather than of Lord if the historical example of his suffering and death were in mind" (77). See also Best, *Converts*, 63.

40 James D. G. Dunn, *The Theology of Paul's Letter to the Galatians* (NTTh; Cambridge: Cambridge University Press, 1993), 77.

41 Fee, *Empowering*, 46.

42 de Boer, *Imitation*, 114; Holmes, *Thessalonians*, 50 n. 9. Richard writes: "We conclude that it is not the joy of resisting 'persecution,' . . . which is Paul's concern but rather the divinely given joy which makes the new converts imitators of the missionaries and of the Lord . . . ." (Earl J. Richard, *First and Second Thessalonians* [SP 11; Collegeville, Minn.: Glazier, 1995], 67).

43 Richard, *Thessalonians*, 67. Richard's argumentation is unconvincing. On pp. 68-69 he seeks to develop a series of parallels between vv. 4-5 and 6-7, which require a number of explanatory moves that strain credulity.

44 Stanley, "Become Imitators," 865; Charles A. Wanamaker, *The Epistles to the Thessalonians: A Commentary on the Greek Text* (NIGTC; Grand Rapids: Eerdmans, 1990), 80-81; Dumm, "Nachahmung," 41.

45 James Agan, "The Christological Context of Luke-Acts: Moral Imitation in Early Christian Literature," (unpublished paper, n.d.), 2.

46 "Doubtless the Thessalonians' cordial reception of the message . . . was part of their imitation . . . but this could not exhaust it . . . ." (Thomas, "1 Thessalonians," 246).

The major options for how to understand this reference to imitation can be grouped into four general groups. Imitation refers to: (1) the reception of the word, (2) the joyful reception of the word, (3) the joyful reception of the word in the midst of tribulation, and, more broadly, (4) to the lifestyle of the messengers.[47]

(1) The main arguments for seeing imitation as referring to *the reception of the word* are:[48] (a) The term δεξάμενοι (receiving) is understood more broadly than simply referring to the initial reception of the gospel, and implies standing firm in the gospel as well. (b) The reference to imitating "the Lord" is understood as without formal content here.[49] (c) The participial construction focuses on the Thessalonians and not necessarily on those who were imitated. (d) The conscious imitation of the Pauline team and the Lord is questionable in this text.

The major problems of this position are: (a) It does not take seriously the aspect of reception that the term δεξάμενοι implies and seeks to extend it to holding on to the word.[50] (b) Seeing the reference to imitating "the Lord" as without content is not in line with how Paul normally refers to Christ. (c) There are strong textual indicators (as argued below under position 4) that conscious imitation was going on.

(2) For imitation referring to *the joyful reception of the word*, the following arguments can be marshaled: (a) the ἐν θλίψει (affliction, tribulation)[51] merely describes the circumstances of their joyful reception and is thus not necessarily envisioned by Paul; (b) there are no other NT references to Christ's *joy* in suffering; (c) the concept of Christ "receiving the word" is strained, illogical, and has no NT support.

(3) The following arguments for understanding imitation as referring to the *joyful reception of the word in the midst of tribulation* can be set forth. (a) The phrase "receive the word in affliction and joy" follows immediately the mention of imitation. (b) The flow of thought through vv. 6-8 suggests the focus on affliction: (i) the hint of affliction through the word "endurance" (v. 2), (ii) the description of how the gospel came to them (v. 5), (iii) the reference to Paul and Christ, who are noted examples of receiving a word from God and experiencing suffering and joy (vv. 6-7), and (iv) how the Thessalonians

47 The decision, whether one sees this as active imitation or "simple comparison," hinges on which option one chooses below. The decision to follow variant one or two leads to the conclusion that it was simple comparison. Variant three leads to the conclusion that it was active, or better, "natural" imitation. See discussion below.

48 This is the argumentation of Michaelis, *TWNT* 4:673.

49 Michaelis, *TWNT* 4:672.

50 von Dobschütz, *Thessalonicher-Briefe*, 73.

51 The term can either refer to troubles, difficulties of various kinds or to persecution.

became examples to others (v. 8).[52] (c) Paul refers to his suffering for the faith in 2:1-2. (d) Paul explicitly links imitation and suffering in 2:14, this time referring to the Thessalonians being imitated by others in how they suffered. (e) Paul makes reference to the suffering of Jesus in 2:15. (f) The theme of suffering recurs throughout the book.[53] (g) Many English and some of the German translations interpret it as relating to imitation in this way.[54]

The strongest argument for positions (2) and (3) above is the fact that (a) in both imitation references in 1 Thessalonians (1:6 and 2:14) there is explicit mention of receiving the word with suffering, coupled with (b) the explicit linkage in 2:14 of imitation with suffering. However, despite these parallels, the immediate context in both 1:6 and 2:14 must be the determining factor for how imitation is understood in both places. Two points are of special note. First, these parallels still do nothing to resolve the crucial problem in 1:6 of how the Thessalonians could become imitators of the Lord by "receiving the word," since there are no exegetical grounds for speaking of Christ "receiving the word" either "with joy" or "with joy in tribulation." Second, the reference to 2:14 does not seem to be active imitation, but rather is "simple comparison."[55] In contrast, it can be argued that in 1:6 there is an active element to the imitation, since the linkage with the preceding καθὼς phrase frames the mention of imitation, spotlighting "how Paul and his team were with them." These two factors lead us away from reading the meaning of 2:14 into 1:6 and lead us to seeing imitation in 1:6 as referring to a fourth option.

(4) Arguments for *seeing imitation more broadly as referring to the lifestyle of the messenger* and not just how the message was received are numerous. (a) There is no mention of the affliction of Paul or Christ directly in this passage.[56] (b) It is strained to talk about Christ either as "receiving the message with affliction," much less "receiving the message."[57] (c) The same argumentation of "b" applies also to Paul, since his receiving the message was not immediately

52 Would there even have been mention of this if it has not been for the affliction they suffered as a result of receiving the word and standing firm in it in the midst of affliction?

53 1:6; 2:2, 14-15, 18; 3:3-4, 7.

54 English: KJV, ASV, NAU, RSV, NRS, NJB ; German: ELB, SCH.

55 So, Fiore, *Personal Example*, 184. Although it must be admitted that we simply are not supplied information by Paul to make a definitive judgment (Holmes, *Thessalonians*, 82). Wanamaker notes that this "should not be taken in an active sense as though the Thessalonian Christians had intentionally sought to imitate the Judean Christians in suffering for their faith. Rather they had through circumstances been made imitators of the Judean Christians" (Wanamaker, *Thessalonians*, 112).

56 Although we know from Acts 17 that Paul encountered severe opposition while he was in Philippi, and that there is reference to Christ's suffering in 2:15, it is not brought into the discussion here.

57 Best, *Thessalonians*, 78; Dunn, *Theology of Galatians*, 78; Holmes, *Thessalonians*, 50 n. 9.

associated either with joy. (d) If opposition is the thrust of the term θλίψει, then imitation cannot refer to Paul, since there was no immediate opposition at his conversion.[58] (e) The other references to Pauline imitation do not reduce the imitation only to suffering. (f) There is a close association with the subordinate clause in v. 5b, which draws attention to Paul and his companions' lifestyle while he was with them. This clause indicates, as we have noted above, that intentional observation of the lives of the apostolic band was occurring. (g) The numerous references in 1 Thessalonians to how Paul and his team acted when he was with them strengthens this point. (h) Finally, as we have argued, implicit within the role Paul played with respect to this fledgling congregation—of apostle (leader), teacher, and spiritual father—was the concept of imitation, broadly understood. The Thessalonians would have assumed that a person like Paul (and his team) would be imitated.[59]

On balance, the fourth option seems to do best justice to the context, integrating best with the preceding verses. This would then lead to the following conclusions: (a) the preceding καθὼς phrase is understood as tying in how Paul and his companions lived before them—with persuasive conviction and power. This provides a direct parallel with Christ's own ministry that was also characterized with conviction and power. (b) This focus on "being" in the immediately preceding context leads one away from associating imitation with the simple entrance of the gospel, to paralleling how Paul and his companions "were" with how the Thessalonians "became." (c) This interpretation has the strength that it deals with two problems that other positions have constantly faced: (i) the problem of how to relate "receiving the word (with joy)" with the imitation of the Lord, and (ii) the corollary problem of how to understand Paul "receiving the word (with joy) in the midst of tribulation." (d) This reading also is strengthened by the sustained argument of chapter 2:1-11, where the focus is also on how Paul and his companions "were among" the Thessalonians (v. 7 ἐγενήθημεν . . . ἐν μέσῳ ὑμῶν). This is a situation in which close scrutiny of Paul and his companions is actually called for, indeed invited. (e) The resolution of the interpretation of the participle δεξάμενοι is easily understood as a description of the *circumstances* in which they found themselves, but which are not the focus of the imitation.[60]

---

58 In addition, as Dunn (following Tannehill) notes: if it is conscious imitation, then suffering is not something that can be imitated, since it is "inflicted at the whim of others" (Dunn, *Theology of Galatians*, 78).

59 As Gaventa argues, it would have been expected by the Thessalonians that Paul, being a teacher, would have been imitated. It would have been strange if this were not the case (Gaventa, *Thessalonians*, 16).

60 Although we tend toward this last reading, reading three has much to commend it. In essence, these two readings are not mutually exclusive, but complementary. From the many personal references to Paul and the team's ministry as well as the call for the Thessalonians to examine their lives and credibility—as well as the implicit assumption in society that teachers are to be imitated—it seems that

It is to this conclusion that Getty, Dunn, and Clarke also come.[61] Clarke notes that immediately after Paul emphasizes his ministry among the Thessalonians through the remark, "just as you know what sort of persons we were when we were among you," he refers to how they imitated Paul and his companions and Jesus:

> [I]t may be arguable, then, that it is their imitation of the *lifestyle* of these people, rather than, in a narrower sense, simply the suffering of persecution or the joy inspired by the Holy Spirit which Paul has in mind. If this is so, then the Thessalonians had become imitators by responding to the gospel in a way which reflected and was consistent with both Paul's and the Lord's conduct in living and proclaiming the message.[62]

A final issue that we have bracketed until now is the reference to imitating both Paul *and* the Lord. Some see this as an after-thought of Paul,[63] or Paul being self-effacing,[64] or Paul correcting himself,[65] but others see it as intentional.[66] It is somewhat clear how the Thessalonians could have imitated Paul, but it is not clear how they also could imitate the Lord, whom they had not experienced. There is considerable debate about whom Paul is referring to

---

imitation is in fact going on. If the third reading is the content of imitation, then Paul is simply lifting up one example of how they were imitating him—how they received the message (i.e., "his and Christ's joy"). This does not mean that they were not imitating him in other areas, but simply that he was highlighting one specific example of imitation that is specifically relevant for one of the themes of his letter. Thus, we concur with Fee who writes: "It should be noted that the concept of becoming 'imitators' means far more than this for Paul" (Fee, *Empowering*, 46).

61 Getty does not deal in detail exegetically with 1:6 but observes a general pattern in the book, which focuses on "Paul's own manner of acting when he was among them" (Mary Ann Getty, "The Imitation of Paul in the Letters to the Thessalonians," in *The Thessalonian Correspondence* [ed. Raymond F. Collins and Norbert Baumert; BETL; Leuven: Leuven University Press, 1990], 279). Dunn writes: "Yet just as some principles of behaviour may be a guide to them, so even more can the example of a Christian life. Paul points more often to himself as example than he does to Christ, for his own example is more readily available . . . . The spirit of the Christian life is seen embodied better in a Christian life than in a code of instruction" (Dunn, *Theology of Galatians*, 78-79). For a similar perspective, see Clarke, "Be Imitators," 337.

62 Clarke, "Be Imitators," 337.

63 Michaelis, *TWNT* 4:672; Stanley, "Become Imitators," 866.

64 Dobschütz uses the term "Bescheidenheit" (von Dobschütz, *Thessalonicher-Briefe*, 72).

65 Dobschütz claims that Paul is correcting himself (von Dobschütz, *Thessalonicher-Briefe*, 72). Similarly Martin Dibelius, *An die Thessalonicher I-II; an die Philipper* (2d ed.; HNT 11; Tübingen: Mohr Siebeck, 1925), 5.

66 Holtz, *Thessalonicher*, 48 n. 107.

here. Does he have in mind the "Jesus of history" or the "risen Lord"?[67] Since this issue impinges on not only the reference in 1 Thess, but also other references (especially 1 Cor 11:1), and since it has ramifications more generally for how we perceive Paul's use of the Jesus Tradition, we will deal separately with this issue in the following excursus.

Excursus: Imitation of the Jesus of History or the Risen Lord

A. The Problem and Positions

The observation that there are relatively few direct references to the life, activity, and teaching of Christ has led a number of scholars to posit that Paul had little interest in the historical life of Jesus and instead focused on the risen Christ.[68] Two examples will suffice for our purposes. H.D. Betz concludes that: "The call to *mimesis* is in no way oriented on the ethical and moral exemplary nature (Vorbildlichkeit) of the historic or a preexistent Christ figure or of Paul; rather it is oriented toward the Christ myth (Christus Mythos)."[69] W. Schrage argues similarly: "It is noteworthy that already instead of speaking of the imitation of *Jesus*, Paul speaks of the imitation of *Christ*."[70] Further he writes of the reference to the imitation of Christ in 1 Cor 11:1 that "this example is here also not the earthly Jesus."[71] He goes so far as to condemn as non-Pauline any attempt to orient oneself to imitating the historical life of Christ.[72] Dibelius,

---

67 Merk is quite clear that it can only refer to the risen Christ: "Not imitation of the 'earthly Lord' but rather the now-made-possible orientation toward the risen Kurios is meant" (Merk, "Nachahmung Christi," 193). So also Betz: "The μιμητής does not see himself connected with the life and action (*wirkenden*) of Jesus, but rather with the *presently* active Christ, who clearly is none other than the crucified Jesus" Betz, *Nachfolge*, 144 n. 18). Holz seems uncertain (Holtz, *Thessalonicher*, 50, especially n. 119). Others, on the contrary, see this as referring to Christ in his earthly ministry (Clarke, "Be Imitators," 337; de Boer, *Imitation*, 122).

68 From scriptural indications, Paul did not have direct contact with Jesus when he was here on earth. His only contact with Christ that Scripture expressly states is through supernatural encounters with him on the Damascus road (Acts 9:1-6) and other revelations of Christ: Gal 1:11-16 (which may refer to the Damascus road encounter), and possibly 2 Cor 12:1-6 (though the content of this revelation is not given, the reference to ἐν Χριστῷ strongly suggests this included an encounter with Christ).

69 Betz, *Nachfolge*, 168. Hengel is, however, critical of Betz's approach since he does not sufficiently consider Jewish roots as an adequate source of Paul's thought (Hengel, *Nachfolge*, 94 n. 2).

70 Wolfgang Schrage, *Ethik des Neuen Testaments* (NTDER 4; Göttingen: Vandenhoeck & Ruprecht, 1989), 214 (author's emphasis).

71 Schrage, *Ethik*, 214.

72 "Every attempt to copy or imitate the life of Jesus of those who see Jesus as a model is not Pauline" (Schrage, *Ethik*, 215).

Michaelis, Lohse, Schrage, Merk, and others hold a similar perspective.[73]

But is it in fact the case that Paul was not interested in the historical life of Christ? This thesis has been challenged by others who hold argue that Paul did have the historical Jesus as the object of Paul's call to imitation,[74] rejecting the caricature of the position that, for example, Käsemann and Martin present.[75] Williams, for example, concludes his study on imitation with a strong statement on Paul's orientation to the earthly Jesus:

> We have found that tradition on ethical, apocalyptic, sacramental, and kerygmatic matters reflecting the teaching of the earthly Jesus, actual sayings of the Lord, and quoted blocks of material is passed on to Paul's churches and lived out in Paul's life. He taught his converts by verbal instruction on basic matters and included appeal to his own example and that of the earthly Jesus who is now the exalted Lord.[76]

In a similar vein, Kümmel sees that the explicit paralleling of Christ as model and Paul as model in 1 Cor 11:1 as well as 1 Thess 1:6 presupposes "without a doubt the orientation on the earthly Jesus."[77]

---

73 Martin Dibelius, "Nachfolge Christi: I. im NT," *RGG*[2] 4:395; Michaelis, *TWNT* 4:672; Ernst Käsemann, "Kritische Analyse von Phil 2:5-11," *ZTK* 47 (1950); Eduard Lohse, "Nachfolge Christi: I. im NT," *RGG*[3] 4:1287; Wolfgang Schrage, *Die konkreten Einzelgebote in der paulinischen Paränese. Ein Beitrag zur neutestamentlichen Ethik* (Gütersloh: Gütersloher, 1961), 140; Schulz, *Nachfolgen*, 284-5; Schrage, *Ethik*, 198-202; Siegfried Schulz, *Neutestamentliche Ethik* (Zürich: Theologischer Verlag, 1987), 303; Ralph P. Martin, *Hymn of Christ: Philippians 2:5-11 in Recent Interpretation & in the Setting of Early Christian Worship* (1st ed.; Downers Grove: InterVarsity, 1997), 89-93. Merk seems to wrestle with the topic, for a time entertaining Christ as an "ethical example," but ultimately concludes his discussion adopting Betz's position (Merk, "Nachahmung Christi," 176, 203).

74 For example, de Boer, *Imitation*, 58; Larsson, *Vorbild*, 26-28; Ernest J. Tinsley, "The Imitation of Christ," in *Dictionary of Christian Spirituality* (ed. Gordon S. Wakefield; DCS; London: SCM Press, 1983), 208-09; Larry Hurtado, "Jesus as Lordly Example in Philippians 2:5-11," in *From Jesus to Paul: Studies in Honour of Francis Wright Beare* (ed. Peter Richardson and John Coolidge Hurd; Waterloo: Wilfred Laurier University Press, 1984), 125; Best, *Converts*, 59-60; Gordon D. Fee, *Paul's Letter to the Philippians* (NICNT; Grand Rapids: Zondervan, 1995), 191-201, 227-28; James D. G. Dunn, *The Theology of Paul the Apostle* (Grand Rapids: Eerdmans, 1998), 182-206; Kim, "Imitatio Christi" (paper presented at the annual meeting of the IBR, Toronto, Canada, November 2002), 33.

75 Fowl writes, "One might well question whether anyone actually ever held the view that Käsemann ridicules" (Stephen E. Fowl, *The Story of Christ in the Ethics of Paul: An Analysis of the Function of the Hymnic Material in the Pauline Corpus* [JSOTSup 36; Sheffield: JSOT Press, 1990], 79 n. 4).

76 Williams, "Imitation of Christ in Paul", 504.

77 Werner Georg Kümmel, "Jesus und Paulus," in *Heilsgeschehen und Geschichte: Gesammelte Aufsätze 1933-1964 von Werner Georg Kümmel* (ed. Erich Grässer;

B. UNDERSTANDING 2 CORINTHIANS 5:16

How is one to decide between these diametrically opposed options? One passage that has played a significant role in this debate 2 Cor 5:16, a passage in which a number of scholars note a strict differentiation between the Jesus of history and the Christ of faith.[78] The major issue in this passage, with reference to this differentiation, is whether κατὰ σάρκα (according to the flesh) modifies the noun, Christ, or whether it refers to the verb that describes a particular way of knowing? If it is modifying Christ, it could lead one to conclude that Paul does make a distinction between Jesus' life on earth and the eternal Christ.[79] If it modifies the verb ἐγνώκαμεν (we have known), it would then point to the participial phrase as indicating a specific way of knowing—that is, "knowing from a worldly perspective."[80]

The following textual observations lead to the conclusion that the phrase κατὰ σάρκα modifies knowledge (knowledge according to the flesh) and not Christ in the flesh.[81] (1) Paul's word-order in this passage strongly leans in the direction of modifying knowledge. (2) Paul's other use of κατὰ σάρκα in contradistinction to κατὰ πνεῦμα (explicitly, Rom 8:4-5, 12-13; Gal 4:29) is in harmony with taking it to refer to a human's way of thinking and living. (3) There is no clear evidence in this letter that indicates a Christological dispute about Christ's nature. (4) The verbs in the context indicate that Paul and the recipients (first plural "we," 5:1-14, 16) were the focus of Paul's attention—more specifically, the focus is on how they were to live and think in a way that

Marburg: Elwert, 1965), 439. His concluding statement is direct and pointed: "Therefore it is inaccurate to say that it is not the concrete person of Jesus, but rather the mere existence of him, that is important for Paul" (440).

78 Other passages used to maintain this distinction are Phil 2:6-11; 2 Cor 8:9 and Rom 15:3, 7.

79 For an extended study of Paul's use of "the spirit and the flesh" and the way interpreters have understood this, see Daniel Boyarin, *A Radical Jew: Paul and the Politics of Identity* (Contraversions 1; Berkeley, Calif.: University of California Press, 1994), 57-85.

80 "What Paul is rejecting is not knowledge of or interest in 'Christ-after-the-flesh' (viz., the historical Jesus) but a κατὰ σάρκα outlook on Christ" (Murray J. Harris, "2 Corinthians," in *EBC*, vol. 10 [Grand Rapids: Zondervan], 355 n. 16). For further discussions and support of this view, see J. Louis Martyn, "Epistemology at the Turn of the Ages: 2 Corinthians 5:16," in *Christian History and Interpretation: Studies Presented to John Knox* (ed. William R. Farmer, et al.; Cambridge: Cambridge University Press, 1967), 285-87; Victor Furnish, *Theology and Ethics in Paul* (Nashville: Abingdon, 1968), 312, 320-32; John W. Fraser, "Paul's Knowledge of Jesus: 2 Corinthians v:16 Once More," *NTS* 17 (1971): 293-313; Dunn, *Theology of Paul*, 184-85. Thus Tinsley concludes: "It is very unlikely that this passage implies that St Paul in any way denied the relevance for Christian thought and spirituality of the historical Jesus" (Tinsley, *Imitation of God*, 141).

81 Some of these observations are noted by Fee, *Empowering*, 331.

pleases Christ (v. 9) and the mindset they were to have of service (vv. 11-14) based on what Christ did (vv. 14-15). It was their mindset that Paul was trying to influence, so that it would be more in line with the gospel. (5) The reference to καινὴ κτίσις (new creation) in v. 17 refers also to the changed perspective and status of the Corinthians as a result of the death and resurrection of Christ. (6) The flow of the argument of the passage leads to interpreting κατὰ σάρκα as a way of thinking: vv. 14-15 is a description of the transformation which occurred through the resurrection, which then leads to the results of this transformation in v. 16—a new way of knowing, which then, in turn, leads in v. 17 to a further explanation of that transformation, defining them as a truly καινὴ κτίσις.[82]

C. Distinction Based on Terminological Grounds: "Jesus" versus "Christ"?

Nor can a distinction between the "historical Jesus" and the "Christ of faith" be maintained on terminological grounds. This type of "compartmentalized thinking"—seeking to make a neat division between references to the historical Jesus and the exalted Christ is a modern imposition onto the thinking of Paul, which would have been foreign to him.[83] To Paul, Christ was one and the same, whether on earth or in his exalted state. That is not to say, that these categories do not exist for Paul. There are references both to his earthly as well his exalted state. It is only to say that Paul's writings about Jesus Christ do not reflect a programmatic intention to distinguish neatly between these states.[84]

This conclusion is borne out in an analysis of how Paul uses the terms "Jesus" and "Christ." Normally the terms "Jesus Christ" or "Christ Jesus" occur together, appearing often in tandem with "Lord," and can refer to both his time on earth or his heavenly state.[85] At times the terms appear individually and are

---

82 In other words, the ἀπὸ τοῦ νῦν refers to the previous discussion of the death and resurrection of Christ in v. 14. It is because the Corinthians had, in Christ, experienced his death and resurrection that they can no longer look at Christ from the perspective of κατὰ σάρκα, since they are now living from the perspective of κατὰ πνεῦμα (Fee, *Empowering*, 331).

83 "There were not for St Paul three absolutely separate dimensions of time, that of the historical Jesus in the past, that of the Christian Church in the present, and that of the Coming of the Lord, but basically the one life of the eternal Christ in his Church" (Tinsley, *Imitation of God*, 141).

84 Whether Merk is correct "when Paul uses the phrase 'imitation of Christ,' he has the post-Easter situation in view, and imitation is for him in no other way relevant except in relation to the Christ-event" remains to be seen (Merk, "Nachahmung Christi," 204).

85 Cf. for a sampling: (referring to his time on earth) Rom 6:3; 8:34; 1 Cor 2:2; Gal 3:1; (referring to his eternal state) Rom 2:16; 1 Cor 1:7-8; 2 Cor 13:5; Phil 1:6; 1 Thess 5:23. Thus, Thompson can justifiably write: "Paul's use of Ἰησους and Χριστος reveals that he did not make a neat distinction between the Jesus of history

used interchangeably. For example, in Rom 8:11 Paul writes: τὸ πνεῦμα τοῦ ἐγείραντος τὸν Ἰησοῦν ἐκ νεκρῶν . . . , ὁ ἐγείρας Χριστὸν ἐκ νεκρῶν. Here Paul uses the terms "Jesus" and "Christ" in parallelism to refer to the resurrection from the dead.[86] There are, in addition, references to Jesus alone that seem to refer to his eternal state,[87] as well as others that refer to his earthly state.[88] In 1 Thess 4:14 the term "Jesus" is used with reference to both his earthly as well as to his eternal state. In most cases, where Paul uses the phrase "Jesus Christ" or "Christ Jesus," it is difficult, if not impossible, to determine if Paul is referring to Jesus in his historical or exalted state. Therefore, to divide the earthly Jesus from the exalted Christ based on the usage of these terms alone cannot be done and must be deemed exegetically tenuous.[89]

D. Why the Reluctance to Refer to Specific Events and Teaching of Christ?

It is for these and other reasons that scholars have rejected this dichotomy of Christ into "earthly" and "eternal" from this passage. The problem, however, of Paul's seeming reluctance to refer to specific events and teachings of Christ still remains. What is the explanation for this?

i. Comparison to How Other Early Christian Authors Refer to the Jesus Tradition

It is important at the outset to place Paul's writings alongside his contemporaries. Thus we ask: How do other NT and early Christian writers use the Jesus Tradition (JT)? Thompson has sought to answer this question in an important monograph.[90] In his survey of the use of the JT by NT authors and early Christian authors, he finds that they too (1) shy away from direct

---

and the risen Christ of faith" (Michael Thompson, *Clothed with Christ: The Example and Teaching of Jesus in Romans 12:1-15.13* [JSNTSup 59; Sheffield: JSOT Press, 1991], 26).

86 See also 2 Cor 11:3-4; Gal 6:17-18.

87 Rom 3:26(?); 10:9(?); 1 Cor 12:3; 2 Cor 4:10; Phil 2:10; 1 Thess 1:10.

88 Rom 8:11; Gal 6:17.

89 This neat delineation between the historical Jesus and the Christ of faith is especially pronounced in Schrage who, commenting that Paul does not orient his ethic on the person of Christ, takes the Christ-Hymn as an example: "This holds true, for example, for the Christ-Hymn (Phil 2:5ff), that certainly does not praise (*besingen*) the actions of the earthly Jesus nor his self-abasement of *having become* man; rather it simply illustrates (*veranschaulicht*) the process of him *becoming* man" (Schrage, *Ethik*, 24; author's emphasis). He rejects those who argue in this way as "clever," but it is exactly this differentiation between "having become" (*gewordenen*) and becoming (*werdenden*) that one cannot sustain either in the Christ-hymn as it functions in Philippians or in other Pauline texts, as we shall see below.

90 Thompson, *Clothed With Christ*, especially pp. 37-76.

quotation of Jesus, (3) mention infrequently stories from the life of Christ and (3) virtually the only specific story to which they make specific reference is the Passion of Christ. From these observations, it seems there is a decided strategy in the letters and early Christian writings not to reference events of the Gospels. There is a tantalizing passage in the Didache 15:3-4, which shows this avoidance of the Jesus Tradition clearly:

> And reprove one another not in wrath but in peace as you find in the Gospel, and let none speak with any who has done a wrong to his neighbour, nor let him hear a word from you until he repents. But your prayers and alms and all your acts perform *as ye find in the Gospel of our Lord.*[91]

This passage indicates that the Gospel Tradition of the life and sayings of Jesus was known and used. This fact that it is a passing reference to this tradition strengthens the case that a thorough knowledge of Jesus' life and teachings existed. Further, it seems that this tradition was clearly used for instruction. In addition, this text indicates that it was not the *Didache's* purpose to comment on this tradition, and thus only makes allusion to these teachings, which the readers of the *Didache* would be able to ascertain. The *Didache* works on the assumption of the JT and takes it at its starting point but focuses on issues and problems the communities are facing today.[92]

This is the identical pattern as found in Paul. Summarizing his survey of the NT writers outside of the Pauline Epistles and the Gospels and the Apostolic Fathers, Thompson notes that "only 2 Peter, Ignatius, *Barnabas*, and possibly Hebrews refer to pre-Passion events in Jesus' life; only *Barnabas* mentions Jesus' signs and wonders, none of which are specified."[93] From his analysis, he comes to five conclusions as to what one could expect in the Pauline corpus based on how the other NT writings and the Apostolic Fathers use the JT:

> 1. It is unrealistic to expect more than a few explicit references to Jesus' teachings in Paul. The important question that emerges from this survey is not why the tradition is absent, but why a writer uses it when he does. What causes him to break the "normal" pattern of relative silence?
> 2. It is unrealistic to expect exact or lengthy citations or echoes of Synoptic logia in Paul.
> 3. We might expect echoes particularly from the SM [Synoptic Material], but nothing of Jesus' parables, except perhaps the parables of the Thief and the Sower.
> 4. It is unrealistic to expect Paul to refer to events in Jesus' life prior to the Passion, especially to particular miracles.

91 Did 15:3-4 (Lake, LCL; emphasis mine).

92 This would be similar to a teacher of advanced math assuming knowledge of basic math and needing only to make passing reference or allusion to it, takes it for granted that they understand to what the teacher is referring.

93 Thompson, *Clothed With Christ*, 61.

> 5. We might expect a few references to the example of Jesus in Paul, but primarily to characteristics seen in his Passion. Specifically we could expect to find something about Jesus' love expressed in his suffering for others, his endurance, humility, obedience, submission and gentleness . . . .[94]

He concludes that Paul's task in writing his epistles was intentionally not the handing down of the JT since that was the task of others.[95] Thus, the argument, "since Paul refers infrequently to the life and teaching of Christ, he therefore is not interested in the earthly Jesus," does not hold weight in light of this comparison. Infrequent mention does not "prove ignorance or lack of interest."[96]

ii. Echoes and Allusions as Indications of Knowledge of the Jesus Tradition

There are a number of scholars who argue that the Pauline Epistles are heavily indebted to the JT from the foundational narrative discernable in the letters[97] to explicit references, echoes and allusions to the life and teachings of Jesus. Although much has been written on this in recent years,[98] we note the line of reasoning a few scholars have used to discern the JT in Paul's letters.

Kümmel argues that Paul clearly orients his teaching based on the earthly Jesus:

> In addition, the warning given "by the meekness and gentleness of Christ" (2 Cor 10:2) and the basis of the warning to be selfless through the reference to Christ, who did not please himself but endured shame (Rom 12:2-3), can only be understood as pointing to the earthly behavior (*Verhalten*) of Jesus. But next to these texts are also found references to the self-abasement of the pre-existent one

---

94 Thompson, *Clothed With Christ*, 61-62.

95 Thompson, *Clothed With Christ*, 62. He follows Stuhlmacher who claims that the "detailed or even complete reproduction of the Jesus Tradition was not the task or intent of the epistolary communication" (Peter Stuhlmacher, "Zum Thema: Das Evangelium und die Evangelien," in *Das Evangelium und die Evangelien: Vorträge vom Tübinger Symposium 1982* [ed. Peter Stuhlmacher; WUNT; Tübingen: J. C. B. Mohr, 1982], 19).

96 Thompson, *Clothed With Christ*, 63.

97 See especially Richard B. Hays, *The Faith of Jesus Christ: the Narrative Substructure of Galatians 3:1-4:11* (2nd ed.; Grand Rapids: Eerdmans, 2002); Ben Witherington, *Paul's Narrative Thought World: The Tapestry of Tragedy and Triumph* (Louisville, Ky.: Westminster John Knox, 1994), 131-68; Bruce W. Longenecker, ed., *Narrative Dynamics in Paul: A Critical Assessment* (Louisville, Ky.: Westminster John Knox, 2002).

98 See the thorough studies of Dunn, *Theology of Paul*, 183-206, 649-58. See also the succinct, but well argued discussion in Udo Schnelle, *Apostle Paul: His Life and Theology* (Grand Rapids: Baker Academic, 2005), 103-08.

as the norm for ethical behavior (2 Cor 8:9; 5:15; Rom 15:7-8), and it reveals itself also here, that Paul sees the earthly Jesus and the exalted Lord as a unity.[99]

Tinsley also observes numerous suggestive parallels in Paul, which indicate a strong dependence on the JT.[100] Using two textual catenae, he notes that they parallel closely the teaching and life of Christ,[101] whose themes form the core of Jesus' own life and ministry. This suggests "that the apostle was making use of a tradition about the manner of life of the Lord which had already achieved normative influence in the church."[102] It is for this reason that W. D. Davies claims that Jesus' words and lifestyle become the new Torah for Paul.[103]

Thompson's strategy in discerning references to the JT is to analyze the "echoes" of it in early Christian writings, which he then specifically applies to Rom 12-15. When one looks for echoes of Jesus' teaching in all the writings of Paul,[104] a more nuanced picture begins to develop. One can discern a deep and thorough influence of the life and teaching of the historical Jesus on the writings of Paul, making it, for Stanley, "impossible to deny Paul's interest in Jesus' earthly life and its force as an example."[105]

Richard Hays argues that Paul's ethical teaching is grounded in the life and teaching of Christ—which encompasses his death, but also extends beyond that

99 Kümmel, "Jesus und Paulus," 439-40. See also David Wenham, *Paul: Follower of Jesus or Founder of Christianity?* (Grand Rapids: Eerdmans, 1995), especially 407; Thompson, *Clothed With Christ*, 214.

100 Tinsley cites, for example: 1 Cor 4:17; Phil 2:5-7; 3:21; Rom 8:15; 15:1-3, 7; Gal 4:5-6. Note the parallel themes and similar terminology: humility as the way to exaltation (2 Cor 11:7; Phil 2:8; Rom 12:16—Luk 14:11; 18:14; Mat 23:12); blessing those who persecute (Rom 12:14, 17; 1 Cor 4:12-13—Luk 6:27); living at peace with one another (1 Thess 5:13; Rom 12:18—Mar 9:50); rejoicing always (1 Thess 5:16; Rom 12:12; Phil 3:1; 4:4—Luk 6:23); not judging (Rom 14:10, 13—Mat 7:1); not causing another to stumble (Rom 14:13—Mar 7:15; 9:42); be innocent in evil (1 Cor 14:20—Mat 10:16), in Tinsley, *Imitation of God*, 43-50. For additional parallels, see Agan, "Christological Context," 12-13; Best, *Converts*, 59-60.

101 For example, Tinsley claims that the "antithetical parallelism" of Christian existence in 2 Cor 4:8-11 intentionally echoes "the paradoxical life of humiliation and glory of the Lord himself" (Tinsley, *Imitation of God*, 142). Then he sees the description of Paul's life in 2 Cor 6:4-10 elsewhere in the NT clearly as reflected in the life of Christ himself (143).

102 Tinsley, *Imitation of God*, 142.

103 W. D. Davies, *Paul and Rabinnic Judaism: Some Rabbinic Elements in Pauline Theology* (London: SPCK, 1962), 148. Noted in Tinsley, *Imitation of God*, 150.

104 Thompson provides detailed criteria for detecting allusions and echoes of the Jesus Tradition in *Clothed With Christ*, 28-36.

105 Stanley, "Become Imitators," 862.

and cites numerous texts where he discern these echoes and allusions.[106]

Seyoon Kim presents a tightly reasoned argument on the sayings of Jesus in Paul, noting that Paul had specific knowledge of the JT, as evidenced through the six explicit "words of the Lord,"[107] and through the numerous allusions to teachings of and events in the life of Jesus. He argues that since the death and resurrection of Christ was the center of his theology, it would be natural that his letters would concentrate on this event and its implications.[108] Based on the work of Birger Gerhardsson,[109] Kim observes that the gospel tradition was "transmitted separately as a unique tradition within the early church,"[110] and because of this direct quotation was avoided, and allusion and paraphrase were preferred, thus lining up with the conclusions of Thomson above.

Agan, in his overview of the Pauline imitation passages, draws two conclusions regarding the concept of the imitation of Christ, which indicate that it is not only the eternal Christ that is the proper object of imitation: (1) Paul's appeal to Christ's character traits of faithfulness despite persecution (1 Thess 1:6; Phil 2:8), his acceptance and forgiveness (Rom 15:7), and his humble, self-sacrificial service and love (1 Cor 11:1; 2 Cor 8:9; Rom 15:3 Phil 2:5-11). These passages indicate that the "*imitatio Christi* motif . . . is to encourage the kind of love, service, and self-denial [evident] in Christ's ministry—and especially the cross."[111] (2) The imitation texts refer to various phases of Christ's ministry: his incarnation (2 Cor 8:9; Phil 2:6-7), his Passion and crucifixion (1 Thess 1:6; 1 Cor 11:1; 2 Cor 8:9; Rom 15:3; Phil 2:8), his earthly

106 Richard B. Hays, *Moral Vision of the New Testament: A Contemporary Introduction to New Testament Ethics* (San Francisco: Harper, 1996), 31. The following texts Hays cites bear this out: Rom 6:1-14; 8:17, 29-30; 15:1-7; 1 Cor 10:23-11:1; 2 Cor 4:7-15; 12:9-10; Gal 2:19-20; 5:24; 6:14. Hays rejects the Käsemann/Martin understanding of Phil 2:5-11, that it does not have ethical implications, but see below in the discussion under imitation in Phil 3:17-18. See also Richard B. Hays, "Christology and Ethics in Galatians: The Law of Christ," *CBQ* 49 (1987): 273-83.

107 1 Cor 7:10-11; 9:14; 11:23-25; 14:37; 2 Cor 12:9; 1 Thess 4:15-17 (Seyoon Kim, "Jesus, Sayings of," *DPL*, 475). He notes that some minimalists discount all but two of these.

108 Kim, "Jesus,", 486. He follows Thompson here who states: "Why should Paul point to an act of love, humility, or compassion during Jesus' ministry when he could cite his example of total commitment on the cross? Why should he cite a healing act of power, when he could refer to the resurrection? Everything Jesus said and did before his death and vindication paled in significance by comparison to the Christ-Event" (Thompson, *Clothed With Christ*, 73). Although plausible, whether this is, in fact, the case may be questioned based on the next sections below.

109 Birger Gerhardsson, "Der Weg der Evangelientradition," in *Das Evangelium und die Evangelien: Vorträge vom Tübinger Symposium 1982* (ed. Peter Stuhlmacher; WUNT; Tübingen: J. C. B. Mohr, 1982), 79-102.

110 Kim, "Jesus," 489; Gerhardsson, "Der Weg," 81-83, 98-102.

111 Agan, "Christological Context," 12-13.

ministry as a whole (Rom 15:3; 1 Thess 1:6(?), 1 Cor 11:1), and his work of reconciliation, both past and present (Rom 15:7). In addition, the generalized references that believers should live according to the law of Christ (Gal 6:2), should live κατὰ Χριστὸν Ἰησοῦν (according to Christ Jesus) (Rom 15:5), and according to "the meekness and gentleness of Christ" (2 Cor 10:1), indicate that the historical Jesus is in focus here.

iii. The Importance of Orality in the Passing on of the Jesus Tradition. The Studies of Dunn and Bailey

The observations by Tinsley, Hays, Kim, Agan and others, that Paul did know the JT, but intentionally avoided "officially" writing about it, has recently been given corroborative support (with necessary correction!) through recent research into orality and the living traditioning process in Middle Eastern culture. Dunn provides the most sustained argumentation about why Paul and other early Christian authors shy away from direct quotation of the sayings and events of the life of Jesus. Dunn has masterfully demonstrated in recent publications[112] that there has been a "repeated failure to take seriously the fact that in the initial stages of the traditioning process the tradition must have been *oral* tradition."[113] It is in this period of "oral memory" before a fixed, written record of Jesus' works and words were published, that Paul produced his letters. Observers of oral cultures have seen that in the passing on of a tradition, there are certain core constants that are passed on in a fixed form and there are other elements that can be passed on with varying degrees of flexibility and fluidity. The rationale for determining which elements are constant and which are flexible is based on the self-understanding and identity of the community. Dunn, drawing on the works of Gerhardsson, Werner Kelber, A. B. Lord, and Kenneth Bailey, writes that there is

> widespread recognition among specialists in orality of the character of oral transmission, as a mix of constant themes and flexibility, of fixed and variable elements in oral retelling . . . . Where stories or teaching was important for the community's identity and life there would be a concern to maintain the core or

112 Dunn, *Theology of Paul*, 183-206; Dunn, "Jesus in Oral Memory: The Initial Stages of the Jesus Tradition," n.p. [cited 20 June 2006]. Online: www.ntgateway.com/Jesus/dunn.rtf; Dunn, *Jesus Remembered* (Christianity in the Making 1; Grand Rapids: Eerdmans, 2003), 173-254; Dunn, *New Perspective on Jesus: What the Quest for the Historical Jesus Missed* (Grand Rapids: Baker Academic, 2005).

113 Dunn, *Jesus Remembered*, 192-205. He is not saying that the topic of oral transmission has not been raised; it has rather, been sidetracked by other questions. He lauds Bultmann and Gerhardsson for their insights, but notes that Bultmann's initial insights into oral tradition were too soon swallowed up in his understanding of the written tradition and that Gerhardsson's and Riesenfeld's approaches are too rigid, presupposing that the Gospel writers used a rigid traditioning process.

key features, however varied other details (less important to the story's or teaching's point) in successive retellings [were].[114]

Dunn's reliance on Bailey's pioneering work among the oral culture of the Bedouins of today is evident. Bailey has analyzed the traditioning process of present day Bedouin village life, which forms the closest modern parallel to the oral cultures of biblical times.[115] Bailey's social analysis reveals significant features of oral culture that have implications not only for understanding the nature of the Synoptic Gospels but also for understanding why Paul's letters shy away from direct quotation of Jesus.[116] Bailey critiques as inaccurate both Bultmann's hypothesis that the oral tradition was "informal and uncontrolled"[117] as well as Riesenfeld-Gerhardsson's thesis of the oral tradition being "formal and controlled."[118] He argues for a middle position between these extremes of an "informal and controlled" oral traditioning process.[119]

Bailey notes three levels of flexibility in oral transmission, which are controlled by the community: (1) no flexibility—with poems and proverbs; (2) some flexibility—with parables and the recollection "of historical people and events important to the identity of the community . . . [in which] the central threads of the story cannot be changed, but flexibility in detail is allowed"; (3) total flexibility—with the telling of jokes and casual news. This last category contains material that "*is irrelevant to the identity of the community* and is not judged *wise* or *valuable*. It floats and dies in a state of total instability."[120]

In addition to the levels of flexibility with regard to the various *topoi* of oral

---

114 Dunn, "Oral Memory."

115 "These villages have retained their identity over many generations, so that, arguably their oral culture is as close as we will ever be able to find to the village culture of first-century Galilee" (Dunn, *Jesus Remembered*, 206).

116 Kenneth E. Bailey, "Informal Controlled Oral Tradition and the Synoptic Gospels," *Them* 20, no. 2 (1995): 4-11. Article originally published in the *Asia Journal of Theology* 5, (1991): 34-54. But see Ted Weeden's strong critique of 6 September 2001 at http://groups.yahoo.com/group/crosstalk2/message/8301 and the ensuing exchange about the veracity of Bailey's recollection of the oral tradition surrounding John Hogg, the founder of an extended Christian Bedouin community. In *Jesus Remembered*, Dunn cites personal correspondence with Bailey, who, though overstating his case, stands by his experience of the oral traditioning process of the gathered community (Dunn, *Jesus Remembered*, 207 n. 182).

117 Rudolf Bultmann, *Jesus and the World* (New York: Scribners, 1921), 8-14.

118 Harald Riesenfeld, "The Gospel Tradition and Its Beginning," in *The Gospel Tradition* (Philadelphia: Fortress, 1970), 1-29; Birger Gerhardsson, *Memory and Manuscript: Oral Tradition and Written Transmission in Rabbinic Judaism and Early Christianity* (Lund: Gleerup, 1961); Birger Gerhardsson, *Tradition and Transmission in Early Christianity* (Lund: Gleerup, 1964); Birger Gerhardsson, *The Origins of the Gospel Traditions* (Philadelphia: Fortress, 1979).

119 Bailey, "Informal Controlled," 5.

120 Bailey, "Informal Controlled," 7-8 (author's emphasis).

transmission, there is also the *element of control* that can be observed in the passing on of the tradition, which protects the tradition against distortion. The *control* element of the traditioning process can be detected in Luke 1:2 where the author refers to οἱ ἀπ' ἀρχῆς αὐτόπται καὶ ὑπηρέται γενόμενοι τοῦ λόγου (those eyewitnesses from the beginning and servants of the word). The single definite article indicates that the ὑπηρέται were also eyewitnesses.[121] The ὑπηρέτης was an official office. In Luke 4:20 a ὑπηρέτης was charged with care for the scrolls. Bailey argues that in the early Christian communities these individuals were accredited eyewitnesses to the core traditions of the community and had the role of officially passing on and preserving the tradition.[122] Only a valid eyewitness (αὐτόπτης) of the historical Jesus would be qualified to be a true ὑπηρέτης τοῦ λόγου.[123] Through such recognized, community-approved witnesses, the authentic tradition of Jesus could be controlled as it is passed on in the traditioning process.

It is for this reason, claims Bailey that Paul shied away from reciting the informal, controlled oral tradition.

> [Paul] cannot become a *huperetes tou logou*. Thus he does not try. He presumes only to make passing references to the specific Jesus sayings in the Synoptic tradition . . . . [He] knows "the pattern of events" of the Passion. His writings are brilliant theological interpretations of that pattern of events with reflections on the ethical implications that stem from it. The evangelists in turn rely on the reciters of the tradition and produce the gospels.[124]

Paul avoided direct quotation of the JT not due to lack of interest; it was simply a matter of him not being entitled to do so. Even as an apostle, his status was still not that of official eyewitness to those events. As a result, this necessarily influenced the nature of his letters and how he appealed to the JT.

While Paul avoided direct reference to the JT, we do see him make liberal use of and reference to the core events of the tradition. It is beyond dispute that the death and resurrection of Jesus forms the bedrock of all Paul's theological reflection.[125]

iv. Orality, Community, and Identity

The works of Dunn, Bailey, and others have refocused the importance for

---

121 For justification, see Bailey, "Informal Controlled," 10.

122 Bailey, "Informal Controlled," 6.

123 Bailey, "Informal Controlled," 10.

124 Bailey, "Informal Controlled," 10 (author's emphasis).

125 "As the crucified and risen one, Jesus Christ is for Paul the central figure of the end time. He completely determines the apostle's understanding of reality" (Schnelle, *Apostle Paul*, 434). Reference to and sustained reflection on the crucifixion and resurrection of Christ arise in all uncontested writings of Paul (Rom 5:6-10; 1 Cor 1:21-25; 15:1-19; 2 Cor 4:3-14; Gal 6:12-14; Phil 2:5-11; 3:7-11; 1 Thess 4:14).

oral communities of a "community defining narrative." It lies in the very nature of these communities that they live out of such narratives around which everything in the community revolves and takes as its point of departure. There would be a strong sense of identification with and interest in the life of the main figure in this community defining narrative—how they lived, what they did, how wise and powerful they were.[126] The multifaceted stories of and about the founder of the community would feed into and support the core narrative. These stories would then be told and retold when the community gathered, thus functioning as a means of preserving the existence of the community and reinforcing their identity.

v. Communication of the Jesus Tradition in Early Christian Communities

This picture of the nature of oral communities and their concern for the foundational narrative is reinforced in *The Gospels for All Christians: Rethinking the Gospel Audiences*.[127] In his contribution, Bauckham analyzes the dynamics among the early Christian communities as described in Acts, the Epistles, and the Apostolic Fathers. He concludes that these were "not a scattering of isolated, self-sufficient communities with little or no communication between them, but quite the opposite: a network of communities with constant, close communication among themselves."[128] The JT would have been transported easily via the frequent travel and visits between these communities.[129] When this observation is combined with the

---

126 See examples of how this works in Bailey, "Informal Controlled," 6-9. As Dunn astutely comments: "It would be astonishing indeed if a movement which focused so intensively on one known as Jesus Christ, which marked itself out by baptism in his name, and which took its own name form that same individual . . . was as uninterested in this Jesus as Paul's letters seem to imply" (Dunn, *Theology of Paul*, 185).

127 Richard Bauckham, ed., *The Gospels for All Christians: Rethinking the Gospel Audiences* (Edinburgh: T&T Clark, 1998).

128 Richard Bauckham, "For Whom Were Gospels Written?" in *The Gospels for All Christians: Rethinking the Gospel Audiences* (ed. Richard Bauckham; Edinburgh: T&T Clark, 1998), 30. Bauckham challenges the consensus, which sees the early Christian communities as "self-contained, self-sufficient, introverted group[s], having little contact with other Christian communities" (31).

129 Michael Thompson has graphically described the frequency and ease of travel at the time of the early church in "The Holy Internet: Communication Between Churches in the First Christian Generation," in *The Gospels for All Christians: Rethinking the Gospel Audiences* (ed. Richard Bauckham; Edinburgh: T&T Clark, 1998), 49-70. He notes on p. 56 that the Pauline churches, which met in households, were not mere meeting places, but also "communication centers" (Acts 16:14-15, 40; Rom 16:23), in which information and news was passed on (p. 55). The repeated calls to hospitality in the epistles (Rom 12:13; 16:23; Tit 1:7-8; Heb 13:2; 1 Pet 4:9, etc.) indicate that travel between these communities was common (p. 55). The reference to the Thessalonians "loving their brothers and sisters in Macedonia" (1 Thess 4:10)

observations on orality, it leads Dunn to remark "that church founding included the initial communication of foundation tradition; and that Paul *could assume common tradition*, including knowledge of Jesus Tradition, even in a church which he had never previously visited (Rome)."[130]

We are in a position now to summarize our arguments regarding the "Jesus of History" and the "Risen Christ:" On a closer reading of the Pauline texts, a clean division between the Jesus of history and the Christ of faith cannot be maintained. Neither 2 Cor 5:16, nor an analysis of the terms "Jesus" and "Christ," nor the paucity of direct reference to Jesus' words and works implies that Paul had no interest in the historical Jesus. The contributions of Bailey, Dunn, Bauckham give a more solidly-argued rationale for positing that knowledge of the historical Jesus was, in fact, foundational to the existence of the newly formed Christian communities.[131] In light of this, the contention that the historical Jesus could not have been the referent for imitation in Paul cannot be sustained.

Thus we would agree with Waetjen when he writes:

> this modern distinction between the Jesus of history and the Christ of faith was unknown to Paul. For the Apostle there was only one Christ, one Son of God; and he was to be identified with the earthly Jesus. What is more, it was this Jesus Christ who was to be imitated.[132]

E. Imitating Jesus Against the Backdrop of Imitation in Antiquity

When we ask the question, "How would Paul's readers have reacted to the notion of imitating Jesus?" we observe from the texts themselves no apologetic exertion on behalf of Paul to convince them to imitate Christ. That no additional argumentation was needed is strong indication that Paul and the readers operated on assumptions they held in common that an appeal to imitating Christ would not be considered unusual.

This observation is in harmony with our analysis of the Greco-Judaic imitation texts discussed in the previous chapter, where we noted that people in

---

indicates they were in communication with them. Paul's frequent stays in the homes of various Christians (cf. Phm 22; 1 Cor 16:6-7) were mirrored by others (cf. Rom 16:1-2; 1 Cor 16:11; 2 Cor 7:15).

130 Dunn, "Oral Memory." This dovetails with Thompson's conclusion that "the readers' knowledge of JT *was assumed as fundamental* to their Christian instruction" (Thompson, *Clothed With Christ*, 63; emphasis mine).

131 N. T. Wright is also persuaded by Bailey's proposal and concludes: "Until it is shown that the process Bailey envisages is historically impossible, I propose that it be taken as a working model" (N. T. Wright, *Jesus and the Victory of God* [Minneapolis: Fortress, 1992], 136).

132 Herman C. Waetjen, "Is the 'Imitation of Christ' Biblical?" *Di* 2 (1963): 122. Similarly Schnelle, *Apostle Paul*, 104.

the Hellenistic and Judaic worlds had no theoretical difficulty with the conception either of imitation of God, the gods, of recently deceased ancestors, or those having died centuries before. These were looked upon as a present reality to be imitated in the daily lives of their descendents. These ancestors, "being dead, yet spoke." Both the supernatural entities and the historical ones were proper objects of imitation.

Regarding the imitation of the forefathers, their ancestors could only be encountered through the medium of the writings and oral tradition which the family or group kept alive. Through the stories of this tradition, an image had been preserved that could be imitated. In an analogous way, for Paul and the members of the churches he founded, Jesus was unknown to them as a physical, living person. Rather, it was through the encounter with Paul and other tradition-bearers and what these revealed to them and embodied about Jesus and the tradition surrounding him, that they could come to know Christ and then could imitate him—whether it was what they knew of him during his time on the earth or whether it spoke of him in his exalted state. It was this historically and eternally re-presented Jesus Christ, who could be imitated through the medium/messenger of Paul.

F. Conclusion

Based on our exploration here, there seem to be three mutually reinforcing reasons why Paul avoided reference to the JT. (1) Paul's role was not that of an official eyewitness to the events of Christ's life. (2) Paul's role as apostle was to proclaim the gospel, which focused on the central and defining event of the life of Christ—his death and resurrection. (3) This central event would have been placed within the assumed and shared framework of the JT, which apostle and fledgling community held in common.

4.3 Jesus of History, Christ of Faith and 1 Thessalonians 1:6

After this excursus, we turn back now to look again at the question: "How can the Thessalonians be imitators of the Lord when he is not present?" Based on our discussion above, we conclude that it is illegitimate as an apriori to assume that references to Christ in Paul (in particular, the imitation references) *must* refer to Christ in his ascended state. It simply *may* be the case. The crucial factor in deciding to what Paul was referring must be determined by contextual indicators.

Although Paul does refer explicitly to the resurrected Christ in 1 Thess 1:10, the other mentions of Christ in the introduction (v. 1) and thanksgiving (v. 3) are global references to him. Although it is theoretically possible that the resurrected Christ is to be seen as the object of imitation, the insurmountable difficulty is the intentional paralleling of imitating both Paul *and* Christ.[133] It seems contextually that the referent that is in view here is Christ in his earthly ministry. The three main reasons are: (1) Paul's remark immediately before the reference to imitation relates to "how they lived among them"—indicating, as we have argued above, that it was the lifestyle of Paul and his companions as it related to the gospel proclamation that was being focused on. (2) The close association between Paul and Christ that is seen here in the context of Paul's ministry to the Thessalonians—of bringing the gospel to them (v. 5). (3) The way Paul describes his ministry in v. 5—as proclaiming the word with power and the Holy Spirit—parallels closely Christ's own earthly ministry that was characterized by the presence of the Holy Spirit[134] and acts of power combined with persuasive proclamation.[135]

If this is the case, then how could the Thessalonians imitate a person they never met? There are two possible ways, which are mutually complementary:

(1) *Textually mediated imitation:* From our investigation of imitation in antiquity, the imitation of an absent person was never seen as an insurmountable problem, as the many references to imitating the forefathers show. The imitation of the Lord was a *mediated* imitation, parallel to how the ancients would imitate the forefathers by means of the oral narrative tradition that had been built up in the community, out of which a clearly identifiable picture (or, perhaps more accurately, a cinematic film) was painted that described who this individual was, how she lived, thought, acted and felt, etc. By means of a "metaphorical leap" the persons hearing heard the story, identified with this narrated character (the thoughts, actions, and perspectives, etc.), creatively interacted with the narrated picture of that person, and then sought to integrate that into their own context.

---

133 Thus, the conclusion that Merk draws about imitation in Paul is unwarranted, bordering on contradictory: "The imitation of Christ revolves around the crucifixion event (*Kreuzigungsgeschehen*)—nothing more and also nothing less. It has to do with that which is inimitable (*Unnachambare*), that is, the theologically and ethically unobtainable/repeatable (*nicht einholbar*); it is specifically for this reason that [the crucifixion event] remains the foundation of our salvation" (Merk, "Nachahmung Christi," 206). This conclusion—that the imitation to which Paul refers cannot be imitated—rests on a misunderstanding of how imitation functions and leads to a perspective that is logically contradictory. When we apply this to the context of 1 Thess, it becomes clear that this does not work. When Paul called his followers to imitate him *and* Christ, he must be referring to that which can be inimitable. Paul's coupling of his actions and attitudes with that of Christ's would lead the Thessalonians to think of Christ's life on earth. Even if one grants that Paul only had in mind the *Kreuzigungsgeschehen*, the point of contact still remains the "earthly" Jesus in his selfless giving of himself for others—just as Paul was doing.

134 Mat 4:1; 12:18; Mar 1:8-12 (Luk 3:16-22; Joh 1:32-33)

135 Mat 7:28-29 (Mar 1:21-22; Luk 4:32); Mat 8:27 (Mar 4:41; Luk 8:25); Mat 13:54 ("Where did this man get this wisdom and these miraculous powers?" cf. Mar 6:2)

(2) *Personally mediated imitation:* The second means by which the Thessalonians could have imitated the Lord was through the person of Paul and his team, who understood themselves to be imitators of Christ.[136] In addition, this also dovetails with our observations of our study of imitation in antiquity: Living persons can be seen as the embodiment of the lifestyle and ethos of another (i.e., a forefather). By orienting oneself to imitating the person (Paul and his team, in this case) who is a true embodiment of the person no longer living (the Lord, in this case), one can be also imitating both at once. Thus, through Paul and his team reflecting/mirroring the Lord in their lifestyle and teaching, the Thessalonians themselves can see the Lord in them and thus be imitators of Him and then in turn become an example (v. 7) for others.[137]

4.4 Summary of Imitation in 1 Thessalonians 1:6

Imitation in 1 Thess 1:6 is an active imitation of the lifestyle,[138] ethos, and message of Paul and his companions by the Thessalonian believers. This message is holistically understood to integrate both the embodiment of truth lived out before them as well as the verbal communication of truth. Paul observes here that this imitation is occurring and commends them for it. The numerous personal references to Paul and his team throughout this letter are fresh encouragements to the Thessalonian believers—through an act of internal "re-presentation" ("remembering")—to recall the ethos, lifestyle, and teaching

---

136 "The great example for Christians is that of Christ. If they imitate their teachers [i.e., Paul] it is in order that they may be brought to imitate Him more closely thereby." (Leon Morris, *The First and Second Epistles to the Thessalonians* [NLCNT; London: Marshall Morgan and Scott, 1959], 58). The reference to 1 Cor 11:1 is pivotal to our understanding here, where Paul says: "imitate me as I imitate Christ."

137 Fee, *Empowering*, 46 n. 35.

138 Not to be understood woodenly, but by a creative act of the imagination, that takes its center on the implications and outworkings of the gospel, which the Thessalonian believers could observe in Paul and his team.

of this team, and thus reinforce what they had initially learned through and from them.[139]

139 Although this emphasis is due, in part, to the need for Paul to justify his hasty departure and to quell questions about his character, this description of Paul's way of life with them would still function as example for them.

If, however, imitation refers to how they received the message—*with joy despite difficulties*, this does not negate our conclusions. Paul has simply highlighted one example of how they were imitating him—how they received the message (with joy in the midst of difficulty), and uses it to reinforce one of the themes of his letter. Thus, this one example stands *pars pro toto* for the broader imitation that was occurring.

Chapter 5

Imitation of Paul, Part II: Corinthian Correspondence

5.1 1 Corinthians 4:16

5.1.1 General Introductory Comments

The way in which Paul phrases the first reference to imitation in 1 Corinthians gives a strong indication of the type of letter it is and why he wrote it: "therefore, I urge you, be imitators of me" (4:16). In order for us to understand the import and content of this command, we need to (1) review salient aspects of the occasion of the letter, (2) trace Paul's argument up to 4:17, and (3) determine the purpose of the passage in which it is found.

A full discussion of the occasion for the writing of 1 Corinthians is not germane to our understanding of imitation here.[1] We simply note the following: Paul was the founder of the church in Corinth (Acts 18) after having had bruising encounters in Philippi, Thessalonica, and Athens (Acts 16-17). He came to Corinth "in fear and trembling" (1 Cor 2:3) and spent approximately a year and a half establishing the foundation of the church on Jesus Christ (3:11). After Paul left, a number of developments took place that caused severe strain both within the church and with their relationship to Paul. He hears about these through reports from members of Chloe's household (1:11) as well as from others (5:1; 11:18; 16:17). In addition, a letter had been written to him by the Corinthians, in which they posed specific questions to him, and in which the mounting problems may have been mentioned or hinted at (7:1).

The church was unhealthy in many ways. Factions had arisen that began dividing the church, with people picking their own authority figures: Paul, Apollos, Cephas, and Christ (1:10-17; 3:1-10).[2] In addition, Paul's ability, spirituality, and authority were being strongly challenged (9:1-27), especially in

---

1 With regard to the integrity of the letter, I am persuaded by the argument of Kümmel, Brown, Carson, and Morris, and Fee, all of whom conclude that the arguments for integrity outweigh those against. Kümmel, *Introduction*, 277; Gordon D. Fee, *The First Epistle to the Corinthians* (NICNT; Grand Rapids: Eerdmans, 1987), 15-16; Brown, *Introduction*, 515; Carson and Moo, *Introduction*, 443-44.

2 There are no indications that there were external opponents (Fee, *First Corinthians*, 8).

light of the Corinthians own supernatural abilities and wisdom (1:7; 4:6-13). Because of these things, they had become arrogant (4:18) and sat in judgment of Paul—misunderstanding his strategy of apostleship (9:1-23) and his intentional use of the "rhetorical weakness" he evidenced (1:18-25; 2:1-10). His person, and with him, his message was being eroded and undermined by their actions, their thinking, and their values.

In addition to the problems surrounding the authority of Paul, numerous issues had developed, which evoked rhetorically-loaded responses by Paul throughout the letter. The whole of 1:10-4:21 is, for example, peppered with biting irony, pointed rhetoric, and provocative sarcasm.[3] This type of rhetoric is also evident as Paul deals with the specific problems of immorality (5:1-13), lawsuits (6:1-11), abuse of the Lord's Table (11:17-22), and misunderstandings of the spiritual gifts (12:14-26). In short, Paul seems to be on the attack throughout the letter. He is grieved at how things have developed—their pride, the factionalism, moral problems, and detrimental behavior. As a response to all these diverse issues, he writes a letter of confrontation.[4] It is within this state of affairs that twice Paul appeals to them to imitate him.

5.1.2 Understandings of Imitation in This Context

There have been various proposals as to how to understand imitation in this passage. Before we look more closely at the structure and argumentation of Paul, we note as a backdrop the various positions scholars have taken regarding how to understand imitation in this context.[5] At the end of this overview, we will take a closer look at Linda Belleville's proposal since it understands imitation in light of the following chapters Paul has written and not the preceding ones.

(1) Imitation refers to following a general pattern of behavior[6] or to a manner of living[7] as opposed to a specific set of instructions. A variation of this view is Fee's, who notes that the immediate context of imitation is the preceding tribulation list (vv. 11-13), where the stress is on the "servant nature of discipleship." However, the additional comment in v. 17 expands this imitation to a broader scope: "the concern is now . . . being raised to the much

---

3 Fee, *First Corinthians*, 8 n. 22.

4 Fee goes so far as to call it an attack (10).

5 Linda Belleville provides a helpful summary of the various positions, which we expanded (Linda Belleville, "'Imitate Me, Just as I Imitate Christ': Discipleship in the Corinthian Correspondence," in *Patterns of Discipleship in the New Testament* [ed. Richard N. Longenecker; Grand Rapids: Eerdmans, 1996], 122-25). These positions are not to be seen in isolation from one another; rather, there are varying degrees of overlap among these positions.

6 Hans Lietzmann and Werner Georg Kümmel, *An die Korinther I-II* (4th ed.; HNT 9; Tübingen: J. C. B. Mohr, 1949), 21.

7 Bauder, *NIDNTT* 1:491.

broader level of their behavior in general, as it is reflected throughout the rest of the letter."[8]

(2) Orr concurs that it is a pattern, but argues, in contrast to Fee, that the additional phrase "my ways" moves it beyond a mere general pattern to something more specific, that is, "the range of Paul's practices: his policies as a missionary, his attitudes toward people, and his concern for the moral and spiritual welfare of his congregations."[9]

(3) Michaelis, followed by Wendland, sees imitation here as a call to obedience. It does not have personal standards so much in view as it does objective precepts.[10] Grounds for this can be seen in v. 17 where Paul states that "this is what I teach (διδάσκω) in all the churches"—indicating that what Paul taught here was a common Pauline standard everywhere he went.

(4) However, the repeated reference to Paul himself indicates that imitation has also to do with how Paul personally lived. The expressions "imitate *me*" and "he [Timothy] will remind you of *my* ways" indicate that Paul's life is to be looked at in terms of a moral standard that he embodied.[11]

(5) Imitation has to do with cultivating the specific qualities of humility and

---

8 Fee, *First Corinthians*, 186-87. Merklein can be seen in this general category as well, but for other reasons. Because he has rejected the concept of *Vorbildlichkeit* ("exemplarity"), he diffuses the concept of imitation into a vague generality: "Rather, it is important to believe in the death of Christ as a salvation event (*Heilsereignis*), . . . which then evidences itself—in contrast to the Corinthians' perspective—when the believer acknowledges the foolishness of the cross as godly wisdom . . . and allows himself in his existence to be molded (*prägen*) by the figure of the crucified one" (Helmut Merklein, *Der erste Brief an die Korinther* [*Kapitel 1-4*] [ÖTK 7/1; Gütersloh: Gütersloher, 1992], 327-28). The problem with this view is that Merklein does not explain sufficiently how his idea of imitation ties into the immediate context, specifically 4:1-13. We will argue below, that the preceding context focuses on Paul, his actions, and motivations and not on the "Heilsereignis."

9 William Orr and James Arthur Walther, *1 Corinthians* (AB; New York: Doubleday, 1976), 179.

10 Michaelis, *TWNT* 4:668-69. Also, Orr and Walther, *1 Corinthians*, 182. Wendland ties imitation closely to discipleship and rejects the thought of imitation being exemplary of conduct. Rather, imitation has to do with the "Christ Fellowship." He writes: "Therefore Paul can also dare to write the astonishing sentence, 'become my imitators.' The one who follows the apostle, follows Christ. This does not refer to being a moral example; rather it refers to the Christ Fellowship (*die Christus-Gemeinschaft*), in which Paul stands and lives, that incorporates the path of discipleship and obedience to Christ." (Hans-Dieter Wendland, *Die Briefe an die Korinther* [NTD 7; Göttingen: Vandenhoeck & Ruprecht, 1980], 41).

11 Thus, C. K. Barrett, *A Commentary on the First Epistle to the Corinthians* (BNTC; London: Black, 1968), 117; F. F. Bruce, *1 and 2 Corinthians* (NCBC; Grand Rapids: Eerdmans, 1980), 51.

self-sacrifice.[12] The justification for this is found in the immediately preceding context of vv. 11-13 in which Paul talks of the hardships he experienced for the gospel.

(6) Developing the relational qualities of peace, harmony, and unity in the church along with a corresponding rejection of selfishness.[13] For this view, justification is found in the general theme of 1 Cor 1-4, in which Paul responds to the divisions in the church, which Sanders sees as the major problem of the Corinthians.

(7) Imitation has to do with following a life of hardship and suffering.[14] Justification for this is also found in the previous context, specifically vv. 9-13 in which Paul describes the difficulties he encountered for the gospel.[15]

(8) Schrage sees the call to imitation to be directly connected to the preceding catalogue of actions, but sees this in conjunction with the background of life in conformity to the crucified Christ.[16]

(9) *The Proposal of Linda Belleville.* Linda Belleville argues that the Pauline concept of imitation is not to be linked with the previous chapters but with the

---

12 Archibald Robertson and Alfred Plummer, *A Critical and Exegetical Commentary on the First Epistle of St. Paul to the Corinthians* (ICC; New York,: C. Scribner's Sons, 1911), 90; Tinsley, *Imitation of God*, 139; de Boer, *Imitation*, 146.

13 Boykin Sanders, "Imitating Paul: 1 Cor 4:16," *HTR* 74 (1981): 361-63; Merklein, *Korinther (1-4)*, 328; Andreas Lindemann, *Der erste Korintherbrief* (HNT 9; Tübingen: Mohr Siebeck, 2000), 115. Although they add other nuances, Lang, Kremer, Wolff, and Betz also hold this position in Friedrich Lang, *Die Briefe an die Korinther* (2 ed.; NTD 7; Göttingen: Vandenhoeck & Ruprecht, 1994), 67; Christian Wolff, *Der erste Brief des Paulus an die Korinther* (TKNT 7; Leipzig: Evangelische Verlagsanstalt, 1996), 94; Betz, *Nachfolge*, 159; Jakob Kremer, *Der erste Brief an die Korinther* (RNT; Regensburg: Friedrich Pustet, 1997), 95.

14 Stanley, "Become Imitators," 873; Furnish, *Theology and Ethics*, 223; Fee, *First Corinthians*, 186; Hans-Josef Klauck, *1. Korintherbrief* (NEchtB 7; Würzburg: Echter, 1984), 40; William David Spencer, "The Power in Paul's Teaching (1 Cor 4:9-20)," *JETS* 32 (1989): 57; Fowl, "Imitation," 428; Clarke, "Be Imitators," 345.

15 Fowl follows Schütz, who writes: "To imitate the weakness and power of Christ is to become the recipient of God's power in ones own weakness" (John Howard Schütz, *Paul and the Anatomy of Apostolic Authority* [SNTSMS 26; Cambridge: University Press, 1976], 230. Noted in Fowl, "Imitation," 428). As we will argue below, this is confusing the *act* of selflessness with the *results* of selflessness that may or may not occur. This is evident in Spencer's article, in which he vigorously argues that suffering is that which is to be imitated, and then unwittingly shifts the emphasis when he writes: "we must incarnate our teachings in a life of service that may invite or at least will not avoid suffering for the faith" (Spencer, "Power," 61).

16 He writes: "The actual warning (*Mahnung*) to mimesis follows a direct line from the preceding peristasis catalogue. Paul is calling them concretely to live a life in conformity with the crucified one" (Wolfgang Schrage, *Der erste Brief an die Korinther, 1. Teilband 1 Kor 1,1-6,11* [EKKNT 7/1; Zurich: Benzinger, 1991], 358).

following ones. She understands Pauline imitation as referring to "a common core of ethical teachings and norms of Christian practice that were routinely passed along to new congregations."[17] Her argument is based on two points: (a) the introductory epistolary formula in 4:14 γράφω ταῦτα ("I write these things") signals the transition to the body of the letter, and (b) the recurring mention in the remainder of the letter of universal ethical practice in other congregations.[18]

Regarding the first argument, one needs to ask, is this always a signal for beginning the body of the letter? And is it usual to begin the body of a letter so far after the introduction? Belleville does not justify this. The phrase γράφω ταῦτα appears as a phrase only here in the NT. In 1 John 2:1 the inverted phrase ταῦτα γράφω is used, but not in the transition to the body, which occurs in chap. 1:4-5. The term γράφειν in its first person singular active form is not linked to the transition to the body of the letter in the other thirteen instances it appears in the NT. It does at times signal a topic under discussion.[19] At other times, it is used to reflect *back* over everything that was written in an epistle.[20] The use of ταῦτα by itself occurs 21 times in the uncontested Pauline letters and in every instance it is referring back to what was discussed previously.[21]

Regarding the second argument, Belleville rightly reasons that if the three other contexts deal with ethical norms, then it is a strong indication that it may mean that in this imitation context as well. This would be a strong argument were it not for the fact that there are significant factors in the immediate context that controvert this.

The following observations, however, indicate that Paul is referring to the previous chapters, not to subsequent ones: (a) Nowhere in the previous four chapters and in the six verses following the reference to imitation is Paul discussing ethics. He only signals a clear change in topic in 5:1 (ἀκούεται ἐν ὑμῖν). From this point on ethics becomes the focus of attention. (b) In the previous chapters, Paul gives ample autobiographical references to how he dealt with various concrete situations in actual practice. In the following chapters, there is virtually no reference that indicates *how* he acted in specific circumstances.[22] What we have in 1 Cor 5 and the subsequent chapters is Pauline *teaching* on various topics, about which he has heard (1 Cor 5:1) or about which were written to him (1 Cor 7:1). Imitation, when referring to

---

17 Belleville, "Imitate Me," 123.

18 Specifically 7:17 ("This is the rule I lay down in all the churches"), 11:16 ("We have no other practice, nor do the churches of God"), and 14:33 ("As in all the congregations of the saints").

19 E.g., 1 Cor 14:37; Gal 1:20.

20 E.g., 2 Cor 13:10.

21 Rom 8:31; 9:8; 1 Cor 4:6, 14; 6:11, 13; 9:8, 15; 10:6, 11; 12:11; 13:13; 2 Cor 2:16; 13:10; Gal 2:18; 5:17; Phil 3:7; 4:8, 9.

22 Unless one takes phrases like "I have already passed judgment on the one" (5:3), or "I wish all men were as I am" (7:7) to be such. But even in these cases, the focus is not on the *how* of doing, which is presupposed by the concept of imitation.

humans, has in focus *what they do* and *how they do it* and not merely teaching. This supports seeing 1 Cor 1-4 as the intended reference and not 1 Cor 5 and following chapters. (c) The previous verses are all looking back on the discussion in 1 Cor 1-4. "I am not writing this to shame you" (4:14) clearly looks back to what he has just written, about pride, boastfulness, glory-seeking intentions. The reference to guardians and fathers (4:15) also looks back on the previous discussion, where people take pride in following "leaders," putting one person above another. It is within this context of looking back that imitation is mentioned. (d) Belleville's argument assumes that the reader will think, "in light of all I am *about to say* . . . imitate me." This runs contrary to the direction of the thought of 4:14-15, as argued in the previous three points). Based on this, the natural reading would be, "in light of all I *have already said* . . . imitate me."[23] There are no verbal or temporal clues that would lead one to understand that Paul was anticipating his discussion on ethics that he begins in 1 Cor 5. (e) The topic of discussion that was begun in 1 Cor 1-4:13, the problem of pride, is continued in vv. 18-19 right after the reference to imitation. This seems to put the imitation clearly within this preceding context.[24]

In light of these contextual factors, it seems Belleville's proposal cannot be maintained that imitation refers to the subsequent chapters. For this reason, we need to look more closely at the prior chapters to discern the content of imitation.

There are four basic textual clues in vv. 14-16 that help us to narrow down the meaning of imitation: (1) It refers back to something he just wrote about (γράφω ταῦτα) in the previous context; (2) it relates to some aspect of Paul's life ("imitate *me*"), (3) more specifically, it refers to an aspect (or multiple aspects) of how he lives ("*my* way of life"), and that (4) it is informed and controlled by his lifestyle that is marked by being *in Christ.*

In order to determine which of the above (or other) proposals do justice to the context and the understanding of these four textual clues, we will need to place the call to imitation within the argument Paul has been developing up to this point.

5.1.3 Development of the Argument of 1 Corinthians 1-4:21

The letter begins with an introduction, in which Paul praises the Corinthians for their knowledge and their experiences of the spiritual gifts (1:1-9).[25] He then

---

23 Parallel to the sense of ταῦτα in 2 Cor 13:10.

24 The usage of the terms φυσιόω and καύχημα are also found in the following chapters (e.g., 5:2, 6) but have a different focus; these terms, however, point to a fundamental problem the Corinthians had with pride.

25 Paul uses the introduction as a means to foreshadowing the major topics he will discuss throughout the letter. For a discussion of this, see Peter T. O'Brien,

mentions the visit from those of Chloe's household and "launches" his first response to the reports that he heard (1:10-6:21). The first section of this (1:12-4:21) deals, broadly stated, with the issues of division and the nature of leadership (1:12-17); the true nature of wisdom (1:18-31); Paul's understanding and use of true wisdom (2:1-15); a revisiting of the problem of division and the nature of leadership brought into dialogue with wisdom and pride (3:1-23); and the working out of the implications of what he has written regarding how the Corinthians should perceive the apostolic band (4:1-21).

Before we look at the specific structure of 4:1-21, it is helpful to look at two interweaving threads that lead up to our text. The first thread has to do with how the Corinthians are portrayed. The second deals with how Paul portrays himself—functioning as a direct contrast to the actions and thinking of the Corinthians.

5.1.3.1 How are the Corinthians portrayed here with respect to how they lived and acted?

Chapter 1:10 begins a discussion surrounding disunity, quarreling, and dissention among the Corinthians as to who was the "best" leader—a way of thinking based on pride.[26] Paul's polemic against human wisdom (1:17) or worldly wisdom (1:20-29) shows that the Corinthians held much of eloquence and wisdom as the surrounding Corinthian society defined it. They had, it seems, accepted the reigning "plausibility structure"[27] of the Corinthian culture around them as to the *true* measure of what wisdom was. Paul speaks against "wise and persuasive words" (2:4) and "the wisdom of this age or the rulers of this age" (2:6), indicating thereby that they themselves were caught up in this way of thinking and as a consequence were looking down on Paul for his comparatively poor rhetoric. Paul simply did not measure up to the standard of wisdom that they had absorbed from their culture.

Since they were so thoroughly entrenched in this way of thinking, Paul had to descend to their level and treat them as immature (3:1). This immaturity evidenced itself in jealousy and quarreling that characterized their interaction (3:3)—all of this being a sign of their worldly/human (σαρκικοί) thinking (3:3). He tells them they are deceiving themselves if they pursue wisdom based on the standards "of this age" (3:18).

This description of how the Corinthians were thinking and behaving comes to a peak in 4:6-13, where Paul plainly states the core problem that is behind

---

Introductory Thanksgivings in the Letters of Paul (NovTSup 49; Leiden: Brill, 1976).

26 Whether the leaders themselves promoted this, seems not to be the case, since the language is focused on what the congregation of Corinth is doing. There is no textual evidence that the leaders were promoting this.

27 Peter Berger, *A Far Glory: The Quest for Faith in an Age of Credulity* (New York: Free Press, 1992), 3-24.

the factions and disunity in Corinth: pride (4:6). Verses 4:8-13 are a bluntly sarcastic, side-by-side portrayal of the fleshly thinking of the Corinthians contrasted with apostolic thinking and acting.

5.1.3.2 How is Paul portrayed here with respect to how he lived and acted—in contrast to the negative portrait of the Corinthians?

Paul intentionally did not come with eloquence or superior wisdom to the Corinthians (2:1), or with wise and persuasive words (2:4). He ignored the worldly concept of wisdom and focused on Jesus Christ and his crucifixion (2:2). He came in weakness, fear, and trembling (2:3) and his message was accompanied with a demonstration of the power of the Spirit, and not rhetorical polish (2:4). His message focused on the hidden wisdom of God (2:7) that the reigning epistemological standards of Corinthian society considered foolish. Paul built wisely on this foundation of Christ and his cross (3:10). In 1 Cor 4, after dealing with false thinking regarding wisdom that led to factions and conflict, Paul urges the Corinthians to see him as a public servant (ὡς ὑπηρέτας Χριστοῦ καὶ οἰκονόμους) of God, concerned solely with pleasing God and not caring how men judge him (4:1-5).

The juxtaposition of these two portraits of Paul and the Corinthians in 1:10-4:5, comes to its apex in 4:6-13. As mentioned above, Paul in v. 6b boils all the problems of destructive divisiveness down to being "puffed up in favor of one against another:" it is pride that was at the root of the specific problem in 1:11-4:21. As an antidote to this pride, Paul points to himself and Apollos in v. 6a as *examples* of right thinking and living. The terminology Paul uses, ἵνα ἐν ἡμῖν μάθητε ("in order that you may learn through us"),[28] is common imitation language and prepares his readers for the explicit reference to imitation in 4:16.

Paul never states the inversion of the phrase in v. 6 "so that none of you will be puffed up in favor of one against another." We are left to infer what they were to learn/imitate. Thankfully, we are aided in what we are to infer through the rhetorically charged, detailed, graphic, and deeply sarcastic contrast between these two ways of thinking that follow in 4:8-13. What these verses contain is a description of Paul's thought and action compared to the polar opposite description of the Corinthians, whose way of thinking and resulting lifestyle revolved around pride.[29] These verses (8-13) preceding Paul's call to

---

28 The addition of "Nothing beyond what is *written*" after "so that you may *learn*" does not take away from the fact that the learning was ἐν ἡμῖν ("in/through us"). The focus still remains on learning *from* or *through* the life of Paul, which is the focus of the quotation. The quotation in 4:6 has kept exegetes groping for answers, of which no reconstruction has thus far been persuasive. Thus Fee writes: "Here is a case where the apostle and his readers were on a wavelength that will probably be forever beyond our ability to pick up" (Fee, *First Corinthians*, 169).

29 This is the fatal flaw of the argumentation of Sanders, who sees the root problem of the Corinthians as divisiveness (Sanders, "Imitating Paul," 361-63). His reconstruction fails to take into account the deeper roots of the various problems in

imitation help us to narrow down the type of imitation Paul has in mind. The rhetorical development of these verses is pregnant with meaning and contains implications for the concept of imitation that could not be contained in a simple short description of what they are to imitate.

In summary, the general structure of the thought-flow of 1:1-6:21 (highlighting the more specific structure of 4:1-21, where the call to imitation occurs) can be outlined as follows:

- 1:1-9 Introduction
- 1:11-6:21 Response to report from members of Chloe's household
  - 1:11-4:21 Problem 1: The intertwining problems of division, authority, and a false understanding of wisdom rooted in the basic problem of pride
    - 1:11-3:23 Discussion of the problem of worldly wisdom that leads to disunity—contrasted with true, godly wisdom
    - 4:1-21 Conclusions and implications of this discussion for the Corinthians[30]
      - 4:1-5 They should view Paul as a servant of Christ
      - 4:6-7 "Learn from me . . . Don't take *pride* in one man over another"
      - 4:8-13 Juxtaposition of Corinthian pride and description of the way Paul and Apollos lived and thought, from which the Corinthians should learn[31]
      - 4:16-17 "Imitate me; Timothy will remind you of my way"
      - 4:18-21 Paul's call to change their ways, and warning of his coming to discipline them
  - 5:1-13 Problem 2: The immoral brother
  - 6:1-11 Problem 3: Lawsuits
  - 6:12-21 Problem 4: Sexual immorality

5.1.4 Exegetical Notes Bearing on the Concept of Imitation

Verse 14: In v. 14 Paul signals a transition through the term ταῦτα, which, as we have argued above, refers back specifically to 4:1-13, which functions as the conclusion of the argumentation begun in 1:10.[32] Paul expressly calls them

---

the Corinthian church. The root problems are summarized in 4:6-13, which Sanders seems to have overlooked.

30 The οὕτως ("thus," "in this way") of 4:1 brings the preceding discussion of 1:11-3:23 to a close and transitions to implications of the preceding discussion.

31 This juxtaposition is rhetorically sandwiched between two parallel calls to 'learn' (4:6) and 'imitate' (4:16).

32 Sanders sees this ταῦτα as referring specifically to "the description of Paul's and Apollos' role as servants according to 3:5-4:13" (Sanders, "Imitating Paul," 354). This, however, seems only to be one aspect of what Paul intended. We note the following reasons: (1) the clear delineation of 3:5-4:13 as a literary unit is lacking; (2) the discussion of Paul an Apollos in 3:5 actually began in the previous verse (3:4); and (3) the references to Paul and Apollos go back to 1:10. Fee notes of Sanders argumentation: "Sander's concern is the correct one; he is perhaps asking the pronoun to carry too much weight" (Fee, *First Corinthians*, 184 n. 8). Our

τέκνα μου ἀγαπητα ("my beloved children"). He frames his words with the intention not to shame, but to warn them that they are on a dangerous path.[33] Fee writes: "The very fact of this demurrer is evidence that he realized they should have been ashamed . . . but that was not the *reason* for what has preceded."[34]

Paul shifts here to the use of fictive kinship language evidenced through the terms "children" (τέκνα), "guardians" (παιδαγωγοὺς), "fathers" (πατέρας), "became your father" (ἐγέννησα . . .). As noted earlier, the concept of imitation occurred commonly in actual or fictive kinship contexts. Paul's intentional choice of parental language gives us insight into how Paul perceives his relationship with the Corinthians and the other communities he founded: as a result of birthing this community, he has *de facto* become their parent and has experienced the full range of corresponding parental emotions for them.[35] As their spiritual father, he could on the one side, express deep love for these communities (as in 1 Thessalonians), and he could also (as in 1 Corinthians), "claim the right to demand respect as well as obedience from them."[36] In fact,

---

observations concur with Fee, who follows Fiore in seeing this ταυτα as referring to 1:10-4:13 (Fee, *First Corinthians*, 184 n. 8; Benjamin Fiore, "'Covert Allusion' in 1 Corinthians 1-4," *CBQ* 47 [1985]: 97-98). Merk notes that this view has become common consensus (Merk, "Nachahmung Christi," 198). So also Dumm, "Nachahmung," 49; Robert L. Plummer, "Imitation of Paul and the Church's Missionary Role in 1 Corinthians," *JETS* 44 (2001): 230 n. 50. Plummer cites Conzelmann, Barrett, and Collins as holding this position.

33 Craig and Short see this as a bluff of Paul's: "Despite the disavowal in his words, Paul is definitely trying to shame his readers, as he explicitly affirms elsewhere in the letter (6:5; 15:34)" (Clarence Tucker Craig and John Short, *The First Epistle to the Corinthians* [IB 10; New York: Abingdon, 1953], 55-56. However, the fact that (1) Paul does make a distinction in this context between shame and warning, and (2) he clearly intends to shame them in the other context, does not support their case. Paul's point in 4:15 is that their thinking and acting is leading them into danger. Hence, a warning is appropriate. His intention is to describe for them the seriousness of the situation in which they find themselves.

34 Fee, *First Corinthians*, 184.

35 Not in terms of manipulative force, as Castelli argues (see chapter seven below), but in terms of benevolent parental care and concern.

36 Joubert, "Managing the Household," 219. Joubert, in analyzing how the *paterfamilias* would have been viewed in the Corinthian society, goes so far as to say: "As *paterfamilias* Paul was above criticism. The only legitimate options available to the Corinthians within this relationship were to trust him, to be proud of him, to imitate him and to obey him (4:21; 9:1-23; 10:31-11:1)" (220). For a similar perspective, see David John Williams, *Paul's Metaphors: Their Context and Character* (Peabody, Mass.: Hendrickson, 1999), 59. This would also mean that because of Paul's role as *paterfamilias*, culturally he had the right to "shame" them, as he does in 6:5 and 15:34. Yet, this shaming is not an end in itself but is a means to correct their behavior. See Schrage, *1 Kor 1,1-6,11*, 354 n. 236.

in this role, Paul could make use of the same full range of kinship responses that actual parents have with their physical children.[37] Thus, it is not a contradiction for Paul to both use the strong rhetoric of 4:1-10 about them and also call them "my beloved children" (τέκνα μου ἀγαπητὰ). Strong verbal correction does not stand in contradiction to, but may, in fact, be proof of love.[38]

Verse 15: Paul sets up a disjunction here between παιδαγωγοὺς[39] and πατέρας and identifies his role/relationship with the Corinthians as that of the latter. There is both semantic overlap as well as disjunction with the terms παιδαγωγοὺς and πατέρας: overlap with respect to caring for children; disjunction because only one has birthed them.[40] And the one who has birthed them, has, according to the cultural norms, the right to be imitated.[41] The legitimacy for Paul seeing himself as parent is linked exclusively to the gospel (διὰ τοῦ εὐαγγελίου). Although some have seen Paul's use of παιδαγωγοὺς as carrying a negative tone, it is not meant to be a pejorative remark against the present Corinthian leaders.[42] The point of comparison is crucial: the παιδαγωγοὶ

---

37 For example: appeal (1:10); admonition (3:1-4), provocative questioning (3:16), irony (4:8-13), warning (4:14), judging (5:3), shaming (6:5), giving directives, teaching (the basic intent of the entire letter), urging imitation (11:1), praising (11:2), not praising (11:17), reminding (15:1), expressing affection (15:58; 16:24).

38 Compare Heb 12:6. Castelli sees this here as anything but a loving parental response. Rather it is a power play to force the Corinthians to act in line with his dictates (Castelli, *Imitating Paul*, 100-01).

39 According to BDAG, this was someone, usually a slave, whose task it was to supervise and guide the conduct of a child when the father was not present.

40 Robertson and Plummer note the "emphatic proximity" of ἐγὼ ὑμᾶς, and see it as implying "whoever may have been the parents of other Churches, it was I who in Christ begat you" (Robertson and Plummer, *First Corinthians*, 354). They correctly link the parenting metaphor of 4:15 with the ἐγὼ ἐφύτευσα ("I planted") of 3:6 and the θεμέλιον ἔθηκα ("I laid a foundation") of 3:10.

41 The inverse of this would also be true: the refusal to imitate would be a rejection of the role, values, and lifestyle of the father.

42 Craig and Short go too far when they write: Paul was not being very complimentary when he referred to the other teachers as guides (παιδαγωγοὶ) . . . . These παιδαγωγοὶ were often worthless slaves. They could be changed as often as one liked, but no one else could take a father's place" (Craig and Short, *1 Corinthians*, 55-56). Collins notes that the perspective on the *paidagogoi* had changed from that of being merely "strict disciplinarians" who used physical punishment to ensure compliance, to those "revered as tutors whose role in the education of the young was truly appreciated" (Raymond F. Collins, *First Corinthians* [SP 7; Collegeville, Minn.: Liturgical Press, 1999], 193). The context of 4:15 bears out Collins' reading. Paul does not deal disparagingly with these παιδαγωγοὶ; the point of comparison is not that they are worthless, but that Paul, by virtue of being their father, has an attachment to them that necessarily goes beyond anything a typical παιδαγωγὸς

have no vested interest in the child but rather are concerned more with their own interests. Conversely, a true father doesn't care for his own interests but for the interests of the child and does whatever needs to be done, using the full range of tools that a parent has at his disposal, to do what he/she thinks will benefit the child the most in his life. Thus, it is not the role of παιδαγωγοὺς on which Paul is focusing, but rather the lack of self-denial they would most likely display.

The additional phrase in 4:15 ἐν Χριστῷ points to the fact that Paul has fathered them so that they might be *in Christ Jesus*. This is the reason he sent Timothy, his son *in the Lord*, with the intention that they learn to follow the way *in Christ* (v. 17). For Paul, ἐν Χριστῷ "is the point of everything . . . , and the other details of the argument must never obscure for us that singular passion of his."[43]

Verse 16: It is within the framework of the spiritual parent-child relationship that Paul urges them (Παρακαλῶ) to imitate him.[44] This admonition would have been completely in line with expected conduct for a natural father as well as a "spiritual father."[45] That he has to urge them to do this is an indication that they were internally distancing themselves from him as their spiritual parent. For this reason Paul needs to reemphasize his spiritual role as father with them. This reestablishes the criterion on which basis they should legitimately imitate him.[46] This may seem strange to modern Western ears, but would have been

---

could have (Fee, *First Corinthians*, 62, also: Fiore, *Personal Example*, 180; Sanders, "Imitating Paul," 355-56).

43 Fee, *First Corinthians*, 186.

44 A few late manuscripts add καθως καγω Χριστου in order to parallel 1 Cor 11:1. Although this is certainly not original, since it is missing in all the early manuscripts, it seems to be in harmony with Paul's thinking (Fee, *First Corinthians*, 183 n. 4; Schrage, *1 Kor 1,1-6,11*, 357).

45 "To admonish (Rom 15:14; Col 1:28; 3:16; 1 Thess 5:12, 14; 2 Thess 3:15) is characteristically the act of a father . . . : positive and creative correction, performed in love. The emphasis is on *as my dear children*, and Paul goes on to emphasize the parental relationship between himself and the Corinthians" (Barrett, *First Corinthians*, 115). See also the expanded discussion of these fatherly characteristics in Fiore, *Personal Example*, 178-80. Fiore notes that teachers of philosophy offer themselves as models "comparatively rarely" (176). That Paul does this seems to be due to the fact that his person, status, and competence has been called into question. When Paul combines the concept of spiritual fatherhood with imitation, he is telling the Corinthians, in effect, "I am your true father and as my true children, you should be imitating me and not others."

46 Thus, Robertson and Plummer are correct when they write that this call to imitation means, "by your conduct prove your parentage" (Robertson and Plummer, *First Corinthians*, 90). Conzelmann sees this call to imitation as not referring to the lifestyle of Paul, but has a missiological intent that is rooted in soteriology. He claims that the call to imitation in 4:16 is "in keeping with the Christological argument for his summons in 11:1: he for his part imitates Christ (cf. 1 Thess 1:6),

seen as natural in light of the role that Paul played with respect to the Corinthians. Joubert, viewing this dynamic sociologically, writes:

> As the person who gave [the Corinthians] access to the benefactions of God, Paul considered himself to be the perfect role-model. He was living proof of the presence of Christ among the Corinthians, since he in turn imitated him as his own Lord and Master . . . He thus not only symbolized the social honour of the new household group as their *paterfamilias*, but also symbolized their ethical honour because he exemplified the contents of his own message.[47]

The term μου focuses the attention on Paul and is not narrowed further than his person.[48] In the previous section 4:6-13, he draws a strong contrast between

---

namely, the preexistent Christ (2 Cor 8:9). The argument is accordingly soteriological. The summons cannot be separated from Paul's missionary work" (Hans Conzelmann, *1 Corinthians: A Commentary on the First Epistle to the Corinthians* [Herm; Philadelphia: Fortress, 1975], 92). This reasoning, however, goes against the grain of the argument of the chapters leading up to 4:16, in which Paul's life is on display as a "Christian personality." The focus is on Paul and how he lived the gospel. When Conzelmann imports the contexts of the other imitation passages into this one, he overrides the way imitation as is configured in this context.

Similarly, Klauck writes: " The appeal to a personal Exemplar, who is worthy of imitation, . . . is solidly anchored in Pauline paraenesis. The objective warrant (*die sachliche Berechtigung*) for this derives from 11:1, where the command to *imitatio Pauli* is based on the addition: As I also am an imitator of Christ" (Klauck, *1. Korintherbrief*, 40). Klauck, following Conzelmann, imports the additional phrase "just as I am [an imitator] of Christ" from 1 Cor 11:1 into this context. Although this may be theoretically true, this idea of the imitation of Christ is simply not found in this passage. The "sachliche Berechtigung" comes from the understanding of imitation common in the culture of that time: people operated on the assumption that teachers, spiritual fathers, and sages would and should be imitated. The concept of Pauline imitation can and does stand on its own without reference to the imitation of Christ.

47 Joubert, "Managing the Household," 219.

48 Wendland, Merklein, and Lindemann all reject this call to imitation as a moral example (Wendland, *Korinther*, 41; Lindemann, *Korintherbrief*, 115; Merklein, *Korinther* [*1-4*], 327). Merklein makes a clear-cut division between Paul's personality and his "apostolic existence that has been marked by the crucified one." This distinction is both textually difficult to sustain, since the two blend together in Paul's person and concrete actions and also practically difficult to sustain, since there is no neat way to determine what is Paul's personality and what is his Christ-orientation.

Surely, Paul's actions are motivated by his role as apostle and stem from his encounter with Christ, but they, nevertheless, inform his attitudes and actions that are to be imitated. This line of reasoning by these scholars is out-of-synch with the way imitation functioned and was understood by people in antiquity. Paul's

his selfless, giving, serving lifestyle and the Corinthians' arrogant, boastful one. Through this description, he provides multiple references to how he lives and thinks. Barrett also notes that Paul in this chapter provides a pattern of a life of humble service that functions as a model for them:

> Paul had lived for months under their eyes, and not merely the details but the whole pattern of his life (as depicted in this chapter) provided an immediate example. If the Corinthians were as ready as he to be humble servants of their church problems would disappear. But they need help.[49]

Verse 17: Through the initial phrase Διὰ τοῦτο[50] ("for this reason"), there is a strong link between v. 16 and v. 17, though some scholars dispute this.[51] Paul links his desire for them to imitate him (v. 16) with the sending of Timothy, a substitute Paul, who will function as an exemplar of Paul and as a living

---

understanding seems to fit in comfortably with the understanding of imitation in antiquity.

49 Barrett, *First Corinthians*, 115-16.

50 The textual variant αυτο inserted after Διὰ τοῦτο is possible, but the external testimony is weightier for its exclusion (Bruce M. Metzger, *A Textual Commentary on the Greek New Testament* [London: United Bible Societies, 1975], 550).

51 This is in contrast to commentators who see a "slight break" between vv. 16 and 17 (Merk, "Nachahmung Christi," 200; Dumm, "Nachahmung," 49). There are two basic problems with Merk's perspective. (1) Merk seeks here to reduce imitation to "the gospel, the word about the cross." Although this is partially true, it is not the whole story, as the context indicates. The whole previous chapters deal with a lifestyle that takes its genesis from "the word about the cross" but proceeds to discuss the implications of how to live in light of the cross in daily life. To reduce it solely to the gospel, when the bulk of the first four chapters have dealt with attitudes of what truly is "wise, strong, and honorable" does not seem to be justified.

(2) The second problem with Merk's perspective is his "slight break" between v. 16 and v. 17. Although it is true that the concept of imitation shifts focus in v. 17—and in so doing may be seen as a break in thought—this should not be used to drive a wedge between vv. 16 and 17 for the following reasons: (a) There is a conceptual unity transported through the kinship language that carries through the verses of this unit 4:14-17 ("my children" v. 14, "your father" v. 15, "my son" v. 17). (b) The reference to τὰς ὁδούς μου τὰς ἐν Χριστῷ (v. 17) is descriptive of Paul's way of living as a follower of Christ, which has been delineated in the previous section (1:10-4:13, specifically 1:23; 2:1-7, 12-13, 15; 3:10, 4:1-4; and especially 4:9-13). (c) It is this *way* of which Paul wants to remind (ἀναμνησει) them by sending Timothy, the one who has been by his spiritual father, and has imitated him the most closely—the one who has imbibed his way of life and corresponding teaching. Thus Fee can write: "[Timothy's] sole task is 'to remind you of my way of life in Christ Jesus,' so that they might imitate him" (Fee, *First Corinthians*, 189). Michaelis and De Boer also see the close connection between these verses: Michaelis, *TWNT* 4:670; de Boer, *Imitation*, 146.

embodiment of Paul's *ways*.[52]

The phrase, "the ways of," corresponds to the Hebrew understanding of *halakah*—a concept which weds teaching and behavior closely together.[53] Fiore picks up the connection between "the ways of" and imitation when he writes, "the fatherly example to be imitated is to be found in *hai hodoi* and in the common teaching of Paul . . . , which Timothy will recall for the Corinthians."[54] Eryl Davies has explored the phrase "walking in someone's ways" and argues that the concept of imitation is implicit in it.[55] His article examines the nature of the *imitatio dei* in the OT and concludes that "walking in the ways of the Lord" goes beyond simple moralistic conformity, but "invites the believer to achieve a pattern of behaviour worthy of God himself, and it does so by providing him or her with a benevolent vision of a goal to which all may aspire."[56] When Paul calls the Corinthians to imitate him and then has Timothy remind them of Paul's, he is mirroring the process and intentions, which Davies describes.

The understanding of imitation in this context is further sharpened through the significant clarification in v. 17 that it is Paul's ways *in Christ* that are in focus.[57] Thus, Paul is not intending to thrust himself into the spotlight; rather, it is his ways *as they are lived* ἐν Χριστῷ, which function as the determinative focus of imitation. He is their example only because and insofar as he lives, thinks, teaches, and acts *in Christ*. This suggests that imitation here does not reduce to a specific trait or aspect of teaching, but to the whole way in which Paul lived as a follower of Christ.[58]

That Paul links the phrase "my ways in Christ" with Timothy ties again into

---

52 Barrett notes correctly: "**For this reason** (that is, because I wish you to imitate me, and wish to provide assistance for you in the task) **I have sent** (or, *am sending*) **you Timothy**" (Barrett, *First Corinthians*, 116; author's emphasis; similarly, Sanders, "Imitating Paul," 357).

53 Jean Hering, *The First Epistle of Saint Paul to the Corinthians* (London: Epworth Press, 1962), 32; Fee, *First Corinthians*, 189; Lang, *Korinther*, 67.

54 Fiore, *Personal Example*, 179.

55 Eryl W. Davies, "Walking in God's Ways: The Concept of *Imitatio Dei* in the Old Testament," in *In Search of True Wisdom: Essays in Old Testament Interpretation in Honour of Ronald E. Clements* (ed. Edward Ball; JSOTSup; Sheffield: Sheffield Academic Press, 1999), 99-115.

56 Davies, "Walking in God's Ways," 115.

57 There are a number of variants here textually: (1) κυριω Ιησ., (2) Χριστω, (3) Χριστω Ιησου. The first and third variants all have later witnesses supporting them. The earlier, more reliable witnesses support the second option as the original.

58 Contra the understanding of Michaelis and Weiss, who see this not referring to the lifestyle of Paul (Michaelis: "expressly not the personal lifestyles [*Lebenswandel*] of the apostle"), but his teaching and his commands (Michaelis, *TWNT* 4:670; Johannes Weiss, *Der erste Korintherbrief* [KEK 9; Göttingen: Vandenhoeck & Ruprecht, 1910], 119-20). Yet Fee claims that to limit imitation to doctrinal instruction "is to miss Paul's own understanding too widely. For him 'doctrine' includes ethics, or it is no doctrine at all" (Fee, *First Corinthians*, 189 n. 37).

the concept imitation. This "reminding" them (ἀναμνήσει) of his ways, is accomplished both as a result of what Timothy relates by way of teaching and by way of his own example. Thus, we observe here four links in an imitation chain: Christ → Paul → Timothy → Corinthians.

Paul extends the kinship terminology with reference to Timothy when he speaks of him as "my beloved and faithful child." Since Timothy is a loved spiritual child of Paul who had observed Paul's ways in Christ, he would function as a legitimate representative of Paul and as a living embodiment of Paul's life and teaching. Timothy, thereby, functions as a surrogate parent to the Corinthians, acting on behalf of Paul, the true parent. He is thus not a παιδαγωγὸς but a πατήρ, since he is coming in the place of Paul.[59]

The additional comment πιστὸν ἐν κυρίῳ ("faithful . . . in the Lord") further clarifies the focus of the imitation: as Timothy is faithful *in the Lord*, so he can faithfully represent the ways of Paul *in the Lord.*[60] The fact that Paul finds it necessary within the span of ten words to write ἐν κυρίῳ, . . . ἐν Χριστῷ indicates Paul is aware of and is stressing the christological dimension of this call to imitation. It is not imitation of Paul, understood as an independent, autonomous individual. It is Paul *ἐν Χριστω*, who is calling others to be, as he himself is, a faithful follower of Christ.

The addition of the phrase "just as I teach everywhere in all the churches" links the concept of lifestyle (τὰς ὁδούς μου) with teaching (διδάσκω). Teaching, as it is configured here, is to be understood as directly integrated with the shape of one's life, not as an abstract set of principles that one cognitively grasps.[61] It was teaching that both informed and formed the actual

59 Thus Fee can write: "The concern over their behavior, and especially that they follow his example, is not posited as the reason for Paul's having sent Timothy to them. This verse implies that Timothy is going in Paul's stead, and therefore that he is to be regarded by them as though Paul himself were present among them" (Fee, *First Corinthians*, 188).

60 There is a question as to what the ἐν κυρίῳ relates: (1) faithful, (2) beloved and faithful, or to (3) child. Contra Mare, ἐν κυρίῳ never modifies an anarthrous adjective in the uncontested letters (W. Harold Mare, "1 Corinthians," in *EBC*, vol. 10 [Grand Rapids: Zondervan], 216). Virtually in every case it modifies either the verb (its subject explicit or implicit) or noun/nominal phrase. In our text, it modifies τέκνον and gives the grounds for him being a child—that is, because of Christ. πιστὸν here is an anarthrous adjective, emphasizing the quality of faithfulness Timothy embodies.

61 As Fiore writes: "precept and instruction [i.e., 'what I teach'] delineate the content and conduct of the Christian life. The example of the founding apostle breathes life into this and provides his community with a stimulus and a hope of emulating Paul" (Fiore, *Personal Example*, 179). Similarly Schrage comments: "It is, in fact the apostle, who preaches the gospel and who in the same way teaches and reminds them of 'the ways' of the Lord—which he at the same time lives out before them" (Schrage, *1 Kor 1,1-6,11*, 359). He correctly observes that the concept of διδαχή "is

lives of the recipients.

A number of commentators, however, do not take it in this way, but see a strong disjuncture between Paul's personal life and his teaching.[62] They see the concept of διδαχή as an authoritative body of laws.[63] However, in our review of imitation in chapter three, we observed that teaching and life for Paul were closely related to and mutually reinforced each other. The lifestyle of the teacher, sage, leader, or parent was understood as pedagogical content—as teaching—to be observed and assimilated.

Fiore notes how these two types of instruction, "my ways" and "my teaching," occur throughout 1 Corinthians:

> It seems *hodos* refers to a person's way of life, and thus 13:1 mentions the *kath' hyperbolen*, which is the way a loving person acts . . . And it is a way which Paul demonstrates (*deiknymi*), recalling like demonstrations of his procedures and convictions in 2:4; 4:9; and 4:19-20. And this demonstration of Paul's way of life becomes explicit in his many precepts (1:10, 31; 3:21; 4:1, 5, 16; 5:9, 12, 13; 6:18, 20; 7 *passim*; 8:9; 10:10, 12; etc.). But the halakic instruction is accompanied by more properly didactic reminders and declarations (1:18ff. the folly of the kerygma of the cross; 2:12, 16 and 3:21 the spiritual gifts; 3:16 and chaps. 5 and 6; 9:13; 24 the recurrent *ouk oudate* formula recalling teachings the community should be aware of).[64]

This ease of shifting to and from references to his own life, to precepts, to instructions indicates how intertwined ethics and teaching are for Paul. Thus de Boer argues correctly that, though words are important, the "*totality of the contact* was included in the process. Paul saw himself teaching Christianity with everything he said, everything he did, and everything he was."[65] Seeing a disjunction between lifestyle and teaching does not seem justified in this context. This way of thinking is

> at odds with the context and with the way one naturally understands Paul's ways . . . . In the context Paul has not been speaking about the formal instruction he had given the Corinthians, but about himself, his conduct, his way of living the Christian life. That Paul could have had these things in mind when he spoke of what he taught everywhere would not be contrary either to Old Testament or to

---

in any case never simply to be understood as doctrine or intellectually in the sense of grasping a theory" (360).

62 Weiss, *Erste Korintherbrief*, 119-20; Michaelis, *TWNT* 4:670; Lietzmann and Kümmel, *Korinther*, 22.

63 Michaelis sees this as referring to laws and other expressions that have legal character (Michaelis, *TWNT* 4:670). Merk also makes a strong bifurcation between Paul's teaching and the concept of imitation (Merk, "Nachahmung Christi," 200).

64 Fiore, *Personal Example*, 179.

65 de Boer, *Imitation*, 151.

classical Greek usage. Furthermore, Paul has just explained that he had written as he had about himself and Apollos that 'in us ye might learn' (4:6).[66]

The concluding καθὼς phrase of v. 17 also points to the fact that the lifestyle and teaching pattern Paul embodies has universal relevance: this is how he is and what he teaches in all the churches (πανταχοῦ) with which he is involved.

5.1.5 Summary of Imitation in 1 Corinthians 4:14-16

We now tie our observations together and summarize how the concept of imitation is developed and understood in 4:16.

(1) 1 Cor 4:1-15 frames the definition of imitation in a decisive way, which brings to a conclusion Paul's argumentation of 1:10-3:23.[67]

(2) Paul defines himself in 4:1 as one whose sole focus and desire is to be at the *service* of Christ and to be a *steward of the divine mysteries*. Both of these images imply working not for selfish goals, but willingly placing oneself at the service of another—God.

(3) The section 4:6-16 continues this theme of servanthood and details Paul's *willful rejection of the world's definition of wisdom, strength, and honor, as well as his willful acceptance of hardship and abuse in humble, selfless service to God on the recipients' behalf.*[68]

(4) Although Paul foregrounds humble service, rejection of pride, and the societal values of wisdom, strength, honor, implicit in the phrase ἐν ἡμῖν μάθητε (4:6) is that these are *only limited examples* of what they should/could learn from and imitate in him.

(5) Paul's reference to being their spiritual father (4:15) carries at least three implications: (a) in contrast to an emotionally-distanced tutor, when Paul frames his relationship with them as a spiritual father, he is highlighting the theme of selfless service on the basis of the strong emotional attachment of paternal love that takes place as a normal result of "spiritually birthing" children; (b) as a spiritual parent, he logically has the right to be imitated; (c) as a spiritual parent, the nature of imitation would be holistic, extending to all aspects of life.

(6) The addition of 4:17 extends the concept of imitation beyond the scope of 4:1-15.[69] Paul's sending of Timothy, his spiritual son, is for the purpose of

66 de Boer, *Imitation*, 152.

67 So, Sanders, "Imitating Paul," 354.

68 The structure of 4:5-16 is in the form of an inclusio with an A-B-A pattern:
(A) "learn from me" (4:6)
(B) Illustrations from Paul's life (4:8-12)
(A′) "Therefore imitate me." (4:16)

69 Fee comes to the same conclusion as we do: "The immediate context for this exhortation is the tribulation list of vv. 11-13, in which Paul describes his own life and ministry in terms consonant with the gospel of a crucified Messiah. It therefore

demonstrating—living out before them—Paul's way of life in Christ. There are at least three implications involved in this that are of importance for the understanding of imitation. (a) Timothy, as Paul's spiritual child, has already learned through observation and imitation Paul's way of life in Christ, and can authentically pass it on. He thus becomes a "spitting image" of Paul and functions as a surrogate parent to the Corinthians. Through his person, Timothy can live out the life of his spiritual father to the Corinthians, and can legitimately say to them: "Imitate me as I imitate Paul." (b) This "way of life in Christ" is holistic in nature, encompassing everything in Paul's life (actions, virtues, emotions, and lifestyle) that flows out of his relationship to and service of Christ. This is not in detail defined by Paul, but assumed that the Corinthians will know what he means. (c) This way of life weds orthodoxy (διδάσκω) with orthopraxy (τὰς ὁδούς μου),[70] both of which interrelate, mutually define, and clarify the other.

These six observations lead us to the following understanding of imitation in this passage: Imitation has a specific as well as a general referent: *specifically* it refers to living a life of humble, sacrificial service to others because of implications of the message of the cross of Christ, which should lead to the rejection of what the world considers to be wisdom, strength, and honor; *generally* it refers holistically to everything in Paul's life (actions, virtues, emotions, and lifestyle) that flows out of his relationship to and service of Christ, which Paul assumes will be understood by the readers, but which we can in part reconstruct through a closer look at his writings and Acts.[71]

5.2 1 Corinthians 11:1

The second reference to imitation in 1 Corinthians comes in the Περὶ δὲ . . .

---

functions as one more item in the long argument of 1:10-4:13 that appeals to the servant nature of discipleship over against their 'boasting' and worldly wisdom. However, by implication, especially from what is said further in v. 17, the concern is now also being raised to the much broader level of their behavior in general, as it is reflected throughout the rest of the letter" (Fee, *First Corinthians*, 186-87). Collins also sees that the reference to imitation includes the entire context beginning in 1:10 (Collins, *First Corinthians*, 195).

70 As Fee also argues: "That Paul was long on behavioral concerns . . . is writ large in his letters. He is never satisfied simply to change people's thinking. That is obviously important because the one (right behavior) flows out of the other (correct theology); but in his letters he never leaves them with an argument that does not have its corresponding paraenesis . . . . It is therefore impossible to imagine that he did not do the same when he was present with the young converts in these newly formed Christian communities" (Fee, *First Corinthians*, 187).

71 Since this is something that he "taught everywhere and in all the churches."

ἐγράψατε portion[72] of the letter, in which Paul responds to a questions posed by the Corinthians via correspondence they had sent him.[73] His response, however, is not in the simple form of "question-answer." He uses these questions to address other topics that have bearing on their attitudes and outlook on the Christian life, as well as their understanding of and relationship with him.

The call to imitation in 11:1 comes at the close of the lengthy section 8:1-10:33, which responds to the question concerning the issue of eating meat sacrificed to idols (8:1). Paul in a most ingenious manner interweaves the crucial issues of freedom, authority, strength, weakness, and discipline together to help them deal in a comprehensive way with the problem of sacrificial meat and other misunderstandings about the Christian life and Paul's actions that have developed since he had seen them last. The masterful approach to these topics directly influences the character and content of Paul's call to imitation in 1 Cor 11:1. In order for us to comprehend this call to imitation, we will need to thread our way through the argument of Paul beginning with 1 Cor 8 and concluding with 11:1.

5.2.1 Development of Argument in 1 Corinthians 8:1-11:1

1 Corinthians 8, as noted above, begins with the transitional marker περὶ δὲ that harks clearly back to the initial περὶ δὲ of 7:1. Although Paul unmistakably defines the topic of this section (τῶν εἰδωλοθύτων—"things sacrificed to idols") in 8:1, we unfortunately do not have the specific question (or issue) the Corinthians had written him and can only reconstruct it based on the response Paul gives in these three chapters. The question, we would assume, could be baldly and simply formulated as follows: "Is it right to eat meat that was sacrificed to idols?"[74]

Paul begins his response (8:1-3) immediately with a warning—particularly appropriate for the Corinthians—about knowledge leading to pride. In contrast, loving God leads to true and appropriate knowledge.[75] Paul continues by explaining to them that idols are not truly gods (8:4-6), but that not everyone knows this: some apparently think that idols are real (vv. 7-8). Paul seems to be dealing with an apparent or potential conflict between those who think eating

---

72 "Now concerning the issues about which you wrote." These sections are: 7:1 (marriage); 7:25 (virgins); 8:1 (meat sacrificed to idols); 12:1 (spiritual gifts); 16:1 (collection for the saints); 16:12 (Apollos).

73 It is unclear when they had written it, but it is probable that Stephanus, Fortunatus and Achaicus (mentioned in 1 Cor 16:17) brought the letter(s) when they visited Paul.

74 Or, alternatively, "How should we think about and handle the issue of meat sacrificed to idols?"

75 8:1-13. This was a basic problem of the Corinthians, that they were so caught up with being "wise" according to the ways of the world that this led to pride (Cf. 1:18-2:16; 3:18-21; 4:10).

meat sacrificed to idols is permissible and others who do not. He proceeds (vv. 9-13) to warn those who have "the free right" (ἡ ἐξουσία)[76] to eat this meat that they should be careful how they exercise their freedom in front of "the weak *in conscience*"—understood as someone who thinks eating idol meat is wrong and who will stumble in the faith as a result of him seeing others eat meat sacrificed to idols. This use of "knowledge" that idols are not real, could destroy those who are weak, who believe they are real.[77]

This leads Paul to express a basic principle that guides his thinking and action with respect to the use of knowledge and rights vis-à-vis the weak as it is applied to the issue of τῶν εἰδωλοθύτων: if eating meat sacrificed to idols would cause someone to stumble in their faith, Paul will refrain from it (8:13).

When we come to 1 Cor 9, there is a shift in topic, with no expressed terminological link to 1 Cor 8.[78] An underlying, non-topicalized theme in chapter eight is that of *freedom*: some people have *freedom* to eat meat and others do not. Paul, however, for strategic reasons, does not mention this word freedom, until 1 Cor 9,[79] where it becomes an underlying theme. The topic of 9:1-27 could be summarized as: "Paul's rights as an apostle are *freely* given up for the sake of the gospel." He introduces the topic (9:1-2) through rhetorical questions (as if he is being accused) by means of addressing the intertwined

---

76 The major translations weaken the terminological link throughout these chapters when they translate ἡ ἐξουσία as "liberty" (ASV, NAU, RSV, NRS, KJV) or "freedom" (NIV, NJB), even though these terms capture part of the intention of Paul.

77 There seems to be an intentional inclusio through the term γινωσκω (8:1 and 11), which indicates that an important issue behind the topic of eating meat sacrificed to idols is a proper use of knowledge.

78 This chapter break is justified, since the topic clearly changes. This topic continues throughout chapter nine and shifts with the beginning of chapter ten. A number of scholars argue against the integrity of this passage. Weiss, Hering, Schmithals hold this text to be an "editorial misplacement" only loosely attached. Lietzman sees it as an excursus, and Conzelmann sees it as a "digression"' or "interruption." See Wendel L. Willis, "An Apostolic Apologia? The Form and Function of 1 Corinthians 9," *JSNT* 24 (1985): 33. Klauck sees chapter nine as the work of an intelligent redactor that has successfully tied together the contradictory texts preceding and following it (Klauck, *1. Korintherbrief*, 77).

However, these and other interpretations do not do justice to the intricacies of the macrostructure of the argument. To posit intricate redactional work seems to be a case of special pleading, which finds no text-critical support. Fee concludes, in our opinion, correctly: "The very fact that there is so little agreement in the theories suggests that the various reconstructions are not as viable as their proponents would lead one to believe" (Fee, *First Corinthians*, 15). For further justification that chapter nine is integrally related to the structure of the book, see David Horrell, "Theological Principle or Christological Praxis? Pauline Ethics in 1 Corinthians 8.1-11.1," *JSNT* 67 (1997): 83-114.

79 ἐλεύθερος appears in 1 Corinthians in: 7:21, 22, 39; 9:1, 19; 12:13.

issues of his own personal "freedom" and "authority" as apostle to the Corinthians.[80]

In the main section of this chapter (vv. 3-18), Paul argues: "Yes, I have the freedom and right to do many things—just as the other apostles do. I am in no way inferior to them."[81] He frames his argument as a defense (ἀπολογία) against his accusers (vv. 3-14),[82] arguing that, yes, he does have the right to eat, take a wife, and receive material support just as the others apostles. However, he does not make use of those rights for a specific reason, which leads him to express another principle, under which Paul operates: "We put up with anything so the gospel will not be hindered" (v. 12)

In the following section (vv. 15-18), Paul provides an explanation of his motivation for writing about these rights. He does not wish them to take him up on these rights, for his desire is to "offer the gospel free of charge." This is a crucial point for Paul. His motivation and actions were completely misread by the Corinthians, and they were drawing false conclusions based on Paul's action (i.e., the rights mentioned in this section that he didn't use). The Corinthians had assumed that since Paul didn't take advantage of these rights, then there must be something inferior about him. Their perception of him was that either Paul didn't feel as if he were an apostle on the same level as the other apostles, or that he didn't feel as if he had a right to these things, possibly because of some weakness in himself.

Paul counters this misperception by providing the rationale for his actions in vv. 15-18: "Everything I do and say is subsumed under my obligation (ἀνάγκη) to the gospel and its proclamation." Since the gospel was for Paul the foundation and radiating center of his life and ministry, he had made the decision to offer it freely to everyone, not taking advantage of a right that would have been his. Only from this vantage point could Paul's actions be properly understood.

After describing his rationale, Paul proceeds in 9:19-23 to explain how he applies this rationale to various groups. In order for the gospel to reach these groups, Paul uses his freedom to take the stance of a slave, that is, to adapt his

---

80 When Paul uses the constructions οὐκ/μή οὐκ/μή, or εἰ + indicative in this passage, he knows all the questions will be answered affirmatively by the Corinthians.

81 The term ἐξουσία occurs ten times in 1 Corinthians, and six of those times are in chapter nine: 7:37; 8:9; 9:4, 5, 6, 12 [2x], 18; 11:10; 15:24.

Two things are happening in these verses and the whole of the chapter: (1) Paul is dealing with the problem that the Corinthian believers have with respect to how they handle *freedom*; (2) at the same time they are calling into question Paul's *authority* as apostle. By the way he shapes the argument, he is able to take on both issues at the same time. The issue of freedom is broached in 9:1 and then taken up in 9:19 again after he has defended his authority in 9:3-18. The references to ἐξουσία at the beginning (3:3) and end (3:18) function as an inclusio. The references to ἐξουσία within the section are used to re-thematizing and underscore the topic.

82 So, Conzelmann, *1 Corinthians*, 153.

mode of interaction with them according to who they are. Paul argues here that he is "weak" not because of some flaw in his character, as the Corinthians surmised. Rather, he is "free" to be "weak" *strategically*, based on his obligation to the gospel.

This view of weakness was diametrically opposed to how some in the Christian community at Corinth saw Paul's weakness. Evidently influenced by the society around them (cf. 4:10), they judged Paul's actions based on the reigning cultural definition of what weakness and strength were. Since Paul looked weak from a worldly perspective, they questioned his apostleship (9:1) and interpreted all that he did as stemming from him being a weak person. Paul here tells the Corinthian believers: "No! My weakness is not a character flaw, but a strategic choice that flows out of my calling to preach the gospel. It has nothing to do with weakness at all. You have misread and misinterpreted me! I have subordinated everything that I have done—acting one way in one situation, and another in other situations—all for the sake of reaching people for Christ.[83] Paul concludes this section with the articulation of a third guiding principle (9:22-23): "My behavior is adapted to the recipient for the sake of the gospel so that we can jointly participate in the gospel."

In the final section of this chapter (9:24-27), Paul interjects the metaphor of competing in a race to bring closure to the topics he has been discussing. By use of the race metaphor, he weaves together the topics of rights, freedom, and the gospel with the topic of self-discipline: Paul freely disciplines himself and gives up his rights for the sake of the eternal prize that awaits him if he runs faithfully (9:25). He then closes by stating a further guiding principle: "I control myself/discipline myself, based on the calling I have and the eternal prize I am seeking" (9:27).

In this section, Paul hints at the concept of imitation: Paul willingly holds himself back and disciplines himself—and he argues the Corinthian believers should also.[84] In other words, "Follow my example in what I have just described for the sake of the prize that awaits us—and so you will not be disqualified." The understanding of discipline is shaped strongly here by the previous discussion of freedom, authority, and the willingness to give up legitimate rights for the sake of the gospel. It is not self-discipline generally in all of life that is in view here,[85] but self-discipline in the practice of relinquishing one's legitimate rights for the sake of the gospel.

After Paul has dealt with his rationale for and use of his authority in 1 Cor 9,

---

83 An inclusio ties his thinking together here, through the reiteration of the principle:

9:19 (a) make myself a slave to everyone,	(b) to win as many as possible.
9:23 (a′) become all things to all men,	(b′) to save some.

84 "Run in such a way as to get the prize" (9:24).

85 Although self-discipline in general is a valid principle, it is not the thrust of Paul's argument here.

he returns to the topic of how to handle the issues of idolatry and meat sacrificed to idols in chapter ten. This topic is divided into three sections, followed by a general conclusion of the argument of the 1 Cor 8-10.

The first section, 10:1-13, is a warning for those who don't discipline themselves based on the example of Israel in the wilderness—a warning that is linked to 9:27, where Paul disciplines himself so that he is not disqualified (ἀδόκιμος). Paul uses the example of the forefathers in the wilderness who "ate and drank" from Christ (10:1-5), but despite this privilege, they were nevertheless disqualified and failed to attain the prize (10:5). The reason they failed is given in the next section, 10:6-10, where the forefathers are described as partaking in idolatrous worship and were subsequently punished because of it.[86] This was evidence that they were ἀδόκιμος (9:27).

In 10:11-13 Paul draws the moral from the story he had retold in 10:1-10 and formulates it as a warning:[87] (a) do not assume you are above this; (b) if you are tempted, God has promised it will not be beyond what you can handle.

In the second section (10:14-22), Paul draws a parallel between Israel and Corinth regarding idolatry and eating sacrificial meat. Just as the Israelites were then in danger of idolatry, so the Corinthian believers are now. He warns them, with regard to the public pagan sacrifices held in Corinth, to flee from it, since it leads to bad ends and invites God's punishment. He draws a direct parallel between the elements of bread and wine ("eat and drink") of Israel and the Lord's table (10:16-17) and reasons: "If the Israelites participated in the spiritual food and drink of Christ—and then fell into idolatry afterwards, beware that the same thing doesn't happen to you." He then describes more specifically what is occurring during a ritual of pagan ceremonial sacrifice (10:18-22). He argues that those who eat the sacrificial meat within the ritual of pagan sacrifice are participating in demons.[88] However, detached from the ritual of sacrifice, the sacrificed meat and the idol are nothing in and of themselves. The danger lies not in the meat or the idol themselves but rather in one's participation in the ritual. The implication Paul is drawing from this (vv. 25-28) is that one should not involve oneself in pagan ritual ceremonies. In other words, Paul is saying, "Do not eat meat as part of the ritual of pagan ceremonial sacrifice. Do not worry about meat sold at the market place, even if some of the meat sold there may, in fact, have come from the pagan ritual sacrifice. Since in itself it is not associated with the ritual offering, it is perfectly fine to eat."

---

86 Exo 32: the Israelites participated in the pagan sacrifice to the golden calf, which was idolatry, which led to sexual sin, and aroused God's jealousy (10:22).

87 Both this section (6-10) and the next (11-13) are introduced with parallel expressions:

6 (a) these occurred as examples,	(b) for us to avoid evil
11 (a′) these happened as examples,	(b′) as warnings

88 This is what happened in 10:6-10, where the Israelites aroused God's jealousy.

In the final section of the body of his argument (10:23-30), Paul gives his closing thoughts on the issue of eating meat. He takes up a potential response that the Corinthians may have had (10:23-24):[89] "It is possible to participate in the ritual since demons are nothing." To this way of thinking Paul responds: "Though this may be possible, it is, however, unwise to do this and may harm others." Paul then gives his concluding verdict on eating meat from the marketplace (10:25-26): "It is permissible, even though the meat may have comes from the pagan ritual sacrifice."[90] Regarding the problem of eating meat in an unbeliever's home (10:27-30), Paul advises that it is permissible to eat the meat, even though it may have come from the ritual sacrifice. They are to partake with thankfulness, and not ask questions. If the unbeliever notes that it is from pagan sacrifice, then they should not eat it—for the other's sake, not theirs—so that the other one does not stumble in his faith.

The conclusion of the discussion on eating meat sacrificed to idols comes in 10:31-11:1.[91] What Paul does here is to distill the principles under which he was operating in 1 Cor 8-10 and weaves them together into summary principles that condense his entire argument in these chapters. Since these verses contain the reference to imitation, we will analyze it more closely in the next section.

5.2.2 Exegetical Notes on 1 Corinthians 10:31-11:1 Bearing on the Concept of Imitation

1 Cor 10:31. This section of Paul's letter begins with the inferential conjunction οὖν, which indicates closure of the preceding discussion and introduction of summary remarks and implications. This unit (10:31-11:1) is clearly marked by the three imperatives, ποιεῖτε ("do"), ἀπρόσκοποι γίνεσθε ("give no offense"), μιμηταί γίνεσθε ("be imitators"), which provide this

89 This may have been part of the letter that had come from the Corinthian believers (7:1).

90 Based on 10:19.

91 The verses 10:31-11:1 can be understood as summarizing the immediately preceding section (10:23-30), since the principles make perfect sense in light of them. However, the addition of καθως καγω in 10:33 cannot be explained simply in light of the previous section, but seems to refer to self-referential statements in 1 Cor 8-10. Those seeing section beginning with 8:1 are Stanley, "Become Imitators," 873; de Boer, *Imitation*, 155; Fee, *First Corinthians*, 357; Mare, "1 Corinthians," 184; Orr and Walther, *1 Corinthians*, 227; Merk, "Nachahmung Christi," 201; Horrell, "Theological Principle," 83. Thus, Schrage correctly concludes that this summary refers not simply to what immediately precedes, but to the entire passage (Wolfgang Schrage, *Der erste Brief an die Korinther, 2 Teilband 1 Kor 6,12-11,16* [EKKNT 7/2; Zurich: Benzinger, 1995], 473).

section with its structure.[92] The crucial question revolves around how these are related to each other and to the preceding context?

The first imperative is preceded by a string of verbs joined together by the conjunction εἴτε ("whether"). The first two elements of the string in v. 31, "eat" and "drink," indicate that Paul is drawing a conclusory implication of his previous discussion *specifically* on eating and drinking sacrificial food—the integrating theme of 1 Cor 8-10. The third part of the string, however, "whatever you do," does not refer to anything in the text, but expands what Paul is talking about to a principle that *generally* applies to any action they perform. As part of this string, it is implied that all their actions will be rooted in and guided by the same reasoning process Paul has developed regarding the first two verbs as reflected in the argument of 1 Cor 8-10.

The first imperative follows on the heels of this εἴτε string and is stated in the form of a global principle. This command to "do everything" (πάντα ποιεῖτε) encompasses all human conduct. The prepositional phrase εἰς δόξαν θεοῦ ("to/for the glory of God") provides the Corinthians with the attitudinal perspective with which they should approach all situations: does it bring glory to God?[93]

What, however, does εἰς δόξαν θεοῦ specifically mean in this context? It appears that the term δόξαν in the context of 10:31 has the meaning: bringing honor to or enhancing the reputation of God.[94] This calling is two-edged: it is, on the one hand, a *positive* call to make sure that all of one's activities enhance the reputation of God. It is on the other hand, a *negative* call to avoid anything

---

92 There are four statements Paul makes in 1 Cor 8-10 that function as guiding principles for himself personally (a-d), which he then takes and derives summary principles by which the Corinthians should live (e-f).
Guiding Principles:
(a) 1 Cor 8:13, "Therefore, if what I eat causes my brother to fall into sin, I will never eat meat again, so that I will not cause him to fall."
(b) 1 Cor 9:12, "Nevertheless, we have not made use of this right, but we endure anything rather than put an obstacle in the way of the gospel of Christ."
(c) 1 Cor 9:23, "I do it all for the sake of the gospel, so that I may share in its blessings."
(d) 1 Cor 9:27, "I beat my body and make it my slave so that after I have preached to others, I myself will not be disqualified for the prize."
Summary principles:
(e) 1 Cor 10:31, "whatever you do, do it all for the glory of God."
(f) 1 Cor 10:32, "Do not cause anyone to stumble, whether Jews, Greeks or the church of God" (the subordinate clause which makes up v. 33 clarifies what Paul means by the principle of v. 32).

93 Fee notes that this πάντα is referring to *adiaphora* (Fee, *First Corinthians*, 488).

94 BDAG, 257. The term δόξα is used twelve times in 1 Corinthians. It occurs only once in 1 Cor 8-10. The rest of the occurrences do not shed much light on its usage in 1 Cor 10:31.

that would detract from his reputation.

Since this reference to glory comes at the end of the string "eat . . . drink . . . everything," it is clear that ensuring God's reputation has *specific relevance* for the issue of food sacrificed to idols,[95] but is broadened to have *general* relevance as well. Specifically, the Corinthians are to avoid damaging God's reputation by how they partake of food sacrificed to idols.[96] That is, they should not participate in pagan ceremony of idol worship, but may eat food that has been sacrificed to idols, if it is not brought into association with the ceremony (10:18-22, 28). Generally, the Corinthians should have God's reputation as their primary concern in all their activities ("whatever you do").

Verses 32-33. The second imperative, "do not cause anyone to stumble,"[97] goes hand-in-hand with the first one, yet shifts the focus away from the intention of the Corinthians' actions with respect to God to: (v. 32) the impact of their actions on those around them (both inside and outside of the church), and (v. 33) the ultimate goal for which they should strive.

The imperative, ἀπρόσκοποι γίνεσθε, is further clarified through the following καθὼς ("just as")[98] phrase, in which Paul brings himself into the picture in order for the Corinthians to have an example of how not to give offense.

The imperatival phrase ἀπρόσκοποι γίνεσθε is placed through the καθὼς in parallelism to κἀγὼ πάντα . . . ἀρέσκω, in which a negative action (avoiding giving offense) is further defined by its being balanced with a positive action (pleasing everyone). In other words, to avoid offense means actively to seek to please others. Rom 15:1-3 provides a strong parallel to 1 Cor 10:32-33, which

95 1 Cor 8:7-13; 10:7-8, 18, 25-28.

96 This mention of protecting God's δόξα seems tied to his discussion in 8:4-6, where Paul stresses that there is but one God in heaven and on earth, who created everything; this God is contrasted with those idols who are merely "so-called gods" (λεγόμενοι θεοὶ). Paul is calling them to protect God's reputation as creator over against these idols.

97 The term ἀπρόσκοποι has been translated "occasion/cause of stumbling" (ASV, NIV) and "offense" (NAU, RSV, NRS, KJV, NJB). It is only used here and Phil. 1:10 in the uncontested Pauline writings. Fee notes correctly that to "'give offense,' . . . does not so much mean to 'hurt someone's feelings' as to behave in such a way as to prevent someone else from hearing the gospel, or to alienate someone who is already a brother or sister" (Fee, *First Corinthians*, 489).

98 A subordinate conjunction, which can indicate comparison, extent, manner, cause, or time. The usage in this context seems to be comparison, by means of illustration. It could be paraphrased: 'be blameless *in the same way as* I seek to please . . . .' Reading it as referring to extent or time does not make sense in the context. To read it as causal (since, insofar as) is possible, but seems forced here. In addition, if the causal element were primary, there are other conjunctions (διά, ὅτι, γάρ) which are better suited for this. What Paul is stressing is the "exemplary" nature of his actions that function as a model for their own actions.

teaches that one should please (ἀρεσκέτω) his neighbor for the good (τὸ ἀγαθὸν=τὸ . . . σύμφορον) for Christ did this also.[99] This is followed by an OT quotation that makes an association with Christ, who did not please himself but others. Christ thus functions in this case as an example to be imitated even though imitation language is not used.

In 1 Cor 10:33 the concept of pleasing others is further clarified, for to have stopped after the term ἀρέσκω would have been unclear. Paul goes on to define more closely what he means by this: he pleases them through seeking the good of many. This, however, is still open to abuse and misunderstanding, so Paul yet further narrows down what he means by clarifying the specific intent of his action: their salvation.[100]

When one looks at the terms Paul uses here—ἀπρόσκοποι, πάντα, ἀρέσκω, σύμφορον, πολλῶν—it seems that he has intentionally chosen them to tie in to the other problems the Corinthians had. As our discussion of 1 Cor 4:16 showed and as a look into other parts of 1 Corinthians reveals, some in the Corinthian church didn't care about others;[101] they sought to please themselves;[102] they weren't concerned about the many, but acted on the basis of their own advantage.[103] Since this way of thinking was a major temptation for the Corinthians, Paul needs to emphasize what he is saying in sweeping terms so that they are forced to reflect on all of life and not just on the issue of eating meat sacrificed to idols.

Since Paul refers to himself and how he seeks not to be a cause of stumbing, it is legitimate to look for references both to Paul's life and to teaching on *not being a stumbling* block in 1 Cor 8-10?[104] When we review these chapters observing the use of the first person singular and plural, we discover a close interweaving of Paul as example and Paul's teaching. There is an explicit warning by Paul to avoid the exercise of a legitimate right if it would be a stumbling block to those who have a weak conscience (8:9), for this might destroy another's faith (8:12). In the issue of meat sacrificed to idols, Paul is ready to go so far as never to eat meat again, if it would cause a weaker one to stumble (8:13). 1 Cor 9 is an extended illustration of how Paul willfully gives

---

99 Karris, following Conzelmann, sees strong verbal parallels in Rom 14:1-15:13, which "repeat, rephrase and echo" 1 Cor 8; 9; 10:23-11:1 (Robert J. Karris, "Romans 14:1-15:13 and the Occasion of Romans," in *The Romans Debate* [ed. Karl P. Donfried; Minneapolis: Augsburg, 1977], 86 n. 51; Conzelmann, *1 Corinthians*, 16).

100 So Schrage, in colorful language, comments: "directly from this final sentence of v. 33 (ἵνα σωθῶσιν) it is necessary to think of an adaptation for the sake of . . . the salvation of others, and not; however, for the sake of currying favor with everyone" (Schrage, *1. Kor 6,12-11,16*, 475).

101 Cf., 1 Cor 1:12; 11:18-22.

102 The thrust of discussion on the immoral brother, 1 Cor 5.

103 Illustrated in the problem of lawsuits, 1 Cor. 6.

104 We will discuss here the more obvious references to this principle.

up legitimate rights in a number of areas in order that "the gospel is not hindered" (9:12).[105] He speaks of deliberately becoming like his various target audiences in order to remove all unnecessary stumbling blocks to the gospel (9:19-23). He is willing to "discipline himself" so that he can avoid being such a stumbling block (9:24-27). In 10:28-29, Paul calls them to avoid the stumbling block of eating meat with an unbeliever, when both know the meat was sacrificed to idols—the implication being that the unbeliever associates it with the ceremonial aspect, and it could be a hindrance to the gospel.

When we seek to isolate Paul's life from his teaching, we are reduced to the personal references in 8:13, (9:1-5),[106] 9:11-12, 15-27; 10:15.[107] An even closer look at these texts reveals surprisingly little about how Paul actually lived, if they were to imitate him. Why this is the case, we will discuss at the end of this section.

Verse 11:1a. When we come to the specific reference to imitation, we observe that it has a simple structure, which in itself gives little clue as to what it means and to what it refers.[108] It is, therefore, radically dependent on the preceding context in order to understand it properly.[109] As we have argued

105 The right to having food and drink (9:3), taking along a believing wife (9:5), and getting support from them (9:12).

106 These verses contain little "content" *per se*, since they are in the form of questions.

107 Schrage also refers to 9:19 and 10:23-24, though the latter is not technically an autobiographical reference. Both texts reveal very little to the modern reader about what specifically the Corinthians were to imitate (Schrage, *1 Kor 6,12-11,16*, 475).

108 While it is true that this reference to imitation should be read with the echo of 4:16 in mind, we need to allow this present context its full right to define imitation here (de Boer, *Imitation*, 154; Michaelis, *TWNT* 4:974 n. 172). Conzelmann rejects the idea that Paul could be referring to himself, and, on the basis of 1 Cor 11:2, argues that imitation is referring to Paul's teaching (Conzelmann, *1 Corinthians*, 180-81). This, however, is a misunderstanding of how imitation in antiquity functioned. This leads Conzelmann, then, to exegetical decisions that run counter to the intention of the text. From the structure of the text, it is hard to maintain that Paul's call to imitation refer to his teachings, since (1) the μου on 11:1 focuses on the person and (2) there is sufficient material in chapter nine that can be imitated. Thus, Clarke rightly argues that Paul reinforces the content of his teaching by using his own conduct as an example (Clarke, "Be Imitators," 342).

109 1 Cor 11:1 is one of the most unfortunate chapter breaks in the English Bible, for it clearly looks back over the last few chapters, especially 10:31-33. It seems there is a clear inclusio that ties 8:1-10:30 together: it begins and ends by talking about the issue of idols. In addition, it begins and ends by similar terminology about not doing anything that would cause anyone to stumble (compare 8:9 and 10:32).

That 1 Cor 11:1 refers to the preceding and not that which follows is held by Robertson and Plummer, *First Corinthians*, 225; Barrett, *First Corinthians*, 246; Fee, *First Corinthians*, 490; Collins, *First Corinthians*, 390; Clarke, "Be Imitators," 346. Schrage is even more forceful when he writes that there is no doubt

above, it should be taken with the immediately preceding imperatives, which function as a summary of the discussion on eating meat sacrificed to idols. There seem to be three options for understanding how this last imperative relates to the preceding ones: (1) it refers to the immediately preceding imperative of 10:32 alone as the lens through which one sees imitation in 1 Cor 8-10. (2) It refers to both of the preceding imperatives as the lens through which one sees imitation in 1 Cor 8-10. (3) The final imperative refers to the life of Paul as expressed in the previous chapters.

5.2.2.1 Option 1: Imitation understood as referring to the Imperative in 1 Corinthians 10:32-33[110]

Speaking for this view are the following observations. (a) There is a clear association between the imperative in 10:32 and Paul's life made explicit through the subordinate conjunction καθὼς, which parallels the structure of 11:1.[111] (b) In 10:33 there is specific content from Paul's life that is imitable, and this same content is also found articulated in the previous chapters. (c) There is no explicit link to Paul's life in the first imperative of 10:31. (d) Paul's reference to the Jews, Greeks, and the church of God (10:32) is parallel to 9:19-23, where he speaks of how he seeks to please them by becoming like them. (e) In both passages, 9:1-23 and 10:33, the goal of his action is their salvation. (f) The way these three imperatives interrelate leads to the conclusion that imitation refers to the second imperative. The first imperative ("do everything") is a broad generalization stemming from Paul's treatment of the issue of eating meat sacrificed to idols. The second imperative, however, focuses on the issue of *how* our actions affect others with respect to the gospel and *what* type of mindset one should have—for which Paul provides a living example that they should imitate (third imperative). (g) All the self-referential statements of Paul in 1 Cor 8-10 are concerned specifically with how Paul's actions affect the faith of others. (h) This concern for the salvation of others and avoidance of causing someone weak to stumble is observable in how Christ ministered to others and interacted with others.

Speaking against this view is the observation that it does not take into

---

whatsoever that 11:1 is the conclusion of the entire argument of chapters 8-10 (Schrage, *1 Kor 6,12-11,16*, 476).

110 So Stanley, "Become Imitators," 874; Belleville, "Imitate Me," 126; Fee, *First Corinthians*, 489. However, Fee sees this section as referring more specifically to the previous section, 10:23-30, with only echoes of these themes in the previous chapters (490). This does not do justice to Paul's call to imitation here, since there is virtually no personal reference in 10:23-30. Fee does not even mention the specific references to Paul in chapter nine, to which, we argue, the call to imitation includes. Craig and Short see this as referring only to 1 Cor 9 (Craig and Short, *1 Corinthians*, 121-22).

111 11:1 μιμηταί μου γίνεσθε . . . καθὼς κἀγὼ . . .=10:32 ἀπρόσκοποι γίνεσθε . . . καθὼς καγὼ.

consideration the close association between v. 31 and vv. 32-33, which together seem to be summarizing these chapters.

5.2.2.2 Option 2: Imitation understood as referring to both Imperatives in 1 Corinthians 10:31-33[112]

Speaking for this option are the following observations. (a) These two principles together seem to function as a summary of the whole previous discussion. (b) Paul's self-referential statements as well as his teaching in 1 Cor 8-10 could be understood to refer to both of these imperatives. (c) These two imperatives are inextricably bound together and function as two sides of one coin: what one says about the one imperative, can also be said about the other. (d) Even if 10:32-33 (more specifically) is the intended referent to imitation here, one could potentially argue that when the Corinthians have fulfilled the command in 10:32-33, they have in actual fact brought glory to God (10:31). Thus, the first imperative is fulfilled automatically through the fulfillment of the second imperative.

Speaking against this is the observation that there are no explicit personal references to Paul noted in association with the first imperative, whereas there are in the second one.

5.2.2.3 Option 3: Imitation refers generally to the picture of Paul as expressed in 1 Corinthians 8-10.[113]

In support of this view are the following observations. (a) The division between teaching and lifestyle is an artificial one; it is in the combination of the two that is important to grasp and imitate. (b) There are relatively few concrete and specific actions of Paul described in 1 Cor 8-10 that one, in fact, can imitate. What one observes is a tightly woven interplay of actions, principles of conduct, and teaching that guide Paul's thinking—the totality of which is to be imitated.[114]

Speaking against this view is the fact that this does not provide an adequate explanation of the strong linkage and parallelism between 10:33 and 11:1.

5.2.2.4 Conclusion

On balance, it seems that from an exegetical standpoint, the first view is the most plausible, the counter-arguments of the other proposals not being weighty

---

112 Fiore, *Personal Example*, 181. Wolff seems unsure if imitation refers to 10:32-33 or 10:31-33 (Wolff, *Korinther*, 242).

113 Fiore does not hold that this refers to the picture of Paul only in 1 Cor 8-10, but of his picture in all the preceding chapters. Nonetheless, he concludes that the "imitation is specified by verses 31-33" (Fiore, *Personal Example*, 181-82).

114 Robertson and Plummer note that the "details of His life are not generally imitable, our calling and circumstances being so different from his" (Robertson and Plummer, *First Corinthians*, 225).

enough to overthrow this reading.

If the first option is correct, then it presents two additional problems to which we have alluded above. (1) If Paul's call to imitation has to do with how Paul embodies the principle in 10:32-33 as revealed throughout 1 Cor 8-10, we note that the self-referential remarks in 1 Cor 8 and 10 reveal virtually nothing about Paul himself.[115] (2) In addition, the few comments in 1 Cor 9 that Paul does make about himself are neither specific nor detailed. We are driven to ask: why is it that there is not more explicit personal information about Paul's life and activity that the Corinthians can imitate? How can they imitate someone, when relatively little is revealed of his life in the text?[116] The answers to these questions have to do with how Paul conceives imitation.

For Paul, imitation involves much more than achieving a simplistic correspondence between external activities, even though it will and should find expression in concrete action. It also encompasses (1) the reasoning process Paul has gone through to arrive at specific activities, (2) the teaching he has presented surrounding these activities, and (3) the ethos he has laid before them in these chapters in which these self-referential statements are made.[117]

Thus, when Paul asks the Corinthians to imitate him, he is asking them to perform a sophisticated act of analogical correspondence. He is asking them (1) to reflectively sift through what he has just written about himself in conjunction with the corresponding teaching, and then (2) to process this in order to arrive at a deep understanding of his explanation in its totality, so that they in turn, (3) can apply this in a contextually appropriate manner to their situation in Corinth.

Verse 11:1b. We have intentionally bracketed a discussion of the content of the phrase καθὼς κἀγὼ Χριστοῦ ("just as I am [an imitator] of Christ") since the concept of Paul's call to imitation is not *necessarily* contingent upon Paul's imitation of Christ. This conclusion is based on two reasons: (1) Most of the references to the imitation of Paul occur without reference to Christ, and are therefore not dependent upon Christ to understand Pauline imitation.[118] (2) The subordinate conjunction καθὼς here parallels its usage as a comparative in the

115 First person singular or plural verbs in 1 Cor 8-10 are found in 8:13; 9:1-3, 4, 11-12, 15-18, 19-23, 26-27; 10:1, 14, 19-20, 29-30.

116 One answer is that they can reflect on his lengthy time with them and draw parallels between what Paul says here and his life as they experienced it. But the thrust of the context indicates that imitation has to do with issues wrapped up with eating meat sacrificed to idols, which would remove imitation from the time he spent with them.

117 This intertwining of teaching and self-reference can be illustrated in 9:6-7 (*self-reference*—"Is it only I and Barnabas that must work?"; *teaching*—"Who serves as a soldier at his expense . . . ?"), and in 9:12-13 (*Self-reference*—"But we don't use this right"; *teaching*: "Don't you know that those who work in the temple . . . ?"). This indicates that in Paul's mind there was no clear division between how he lived and what he taught. The description by Xenophon cited in chapter three of how Socrates' teaching and lifestyle intertwined parallels what is going on here.

118 1 Cor 4:16; Phil 1:29-30; 3:17; 4:9, and compare Gal 4:12.

preceding verse,[119] making it simply *illustrative* of the type of imitation to which Paul is referring and not *foundational* for understanding the imitation of Paul.

In what sense is Paul an imitator of Christ?[120] A number of options have been proposed, not all of them mutually exclusive, but rather a matter of foregrounding and backgrounding the components of imitation that various scholars have detected in this passage.[121] (1) Michaelis also here rejects the possibility that exemplariness (*Vorbildlichkeit*) is intended and argues that it must be interpreted as a command to obey the warning in 10:32.[122] (2) Lietzmann and Kümmel, Schulz, Bruce, Lang, Horrell, Kremer, and Collins see it as referring to Christ who gave up his (divine) rights in order to become a

---

119 I.e., "in the same way that . . ." A number of scholars see this καθὼς as indicating the cause of or grounds for imitation (de Boer, *Imitation*, 164; Wendland, *Korinther*, 84; Wolff, *Korinther*, 242 n. 445; Helmut Merklein, *Der erste Brief an die Korinther (Kapitel 5,1-11,1)* [ÖTK 7/2; Gütersloh: Gütersloher, 2000], 283). Schrage (pointedly against Wolff) argues that the term goes beyond simple causality and functions here as a comparative (Schrage, *1 Kor 6,12-11,16*, 477).

To read this conjunction as causal runs counter to the parallelism with the previous verse, which foregrounds the conception of comparison. Stanley is thus correct when he writes: "Paul does not urge the Corinthians to imitate himself *because* he imitates Christ, but 'just as' he imitates him. [Further,] he does not command them to imitate Christ, but to imitate himself" (Stanley, "Become Imitators," 874).

120 Our discussion in chapter four regarding the illegitimacy of drawing a sharp distinction between the earthly Jesus and the risen Christ also applies here. Paul has in mind the undivided Christ. To discern more closely whether Paul is referring to Christ in his earthly ministry or in his exalted state hinges upon the understanding of Paul's call to the Corinthians to imitate him here.

Dibelius, Lindemann, Kremer and Schrage all conclude that the referent is not the earthly Jesus (Dibelius, "Nachfolge," 395; Schrage, *1 Kor 6,12-11,16*, 477; Kremer, *Korinther*, 222; Lindemann, *Korintherbrief*, 235).

De Boer remarks wisely: "It is questionable whether it is helpful to an understanding of this passage to attempt to distinguish in regard to Christ between the historical man and the pre-existent Son of God" (de Boer, *Imitation*, 159). It is impossible to ascertain to which he is referring from the context, and to argue from silence (i.e., not referring to the earthly life of Christ) is still not proof positive.

121 For a helpful, though limited, summary of various perspectives see Belleville, "Imitate Me," 125.

122 His reasoning is that it is difficult to explain why Paul does not appeal immediately for the Corinthians to imitate Christ and that the imitation of Christ is contentless. His reasoning, however, is based on a number of illegitimate assumptions, the two main ones being (1) the misunderstanding of how imitation functions, and (2) the lack of understanding of orality and traditioning in early Christian communities, which we have discussed in chapter four (Michaelis, *TWNT* 4:671-72).

self-giving servant to humanity.[123] (3) Conzelmann and Fee maintain that the imitation of Christ refers to him willfully giving himself as a sacrifice for salvation.[124] (4) Robertson and Plummer, Barrett, Fowl, Agan, and Fiore see it as referring to the general pattern of the life of Christ in setting others' well-being above his.[125] (5) Thompson, Merk, Wolff, and Lindemann see this as referring specifically to the Passion of Christ, or, in the words of Merk, to "the inimitable salvation event."[126] (6) Orr and Walther see it as referring to Christ's mission to save the lost.[127] (7) De Boer sees it as the self-giving act of Christ for the salvation of the world.[128]

Structurally it would seem that Paul's imitation of Christ should be parallel to the Corinthians' imitation of Paul. In this context it would mean that the Corinthians are to imitate Paul as he makes it his constant aim not to cause anyone, believer or non-believer, to falter in their relationship to God. In other words, he subordinates his own desires and seeks the good of many for the goal of their salvation. By extension, then, Paul would be imitating Christ in the way that Christ made it his goal not to cause anyone to stumble in their relationship to God and subordinated his own desires for the good of many with the goal of their ultimate salvation.[129]

---

123 Lietzmann and Kümmel, *Korinther*, 53; Schulz, *Nachfolgen*, 171; Bruce, *Corinthians*, 102; Lang, *Korinther*, 133; Horrell, "Theological Principle," 109; Kremer, *Korinther*, 222; Collins, *First Corinthians*, 391.

124 Conzelmann, *1 Corinthians*, 181; Fee, *First Corinthians*, 490. However, Conzelmann sees this as referring to the preexistent Christ, whereas Fee does not (490 n. 70).

125 Robertson and Plummer, *First Corinthians*, 225; Fowl, "Imitation," 429; Agan, "Christological Context," 4. Fiore sees imitation referring to "self-effacement for the common good" (Fiore, *Personal Example*, 182). Agan, seeking a middle way between the one extreme of focusing solely on the earthly Jesus (De Boer) and the other extreme of seeing only "the fact of the incarnation, crucifixion, and resurrection of the preexistent Christ" as being in view (Betz), argues sagely for a middle way: "It is Christ who is the object for Paul's imitation, but it is the pattern of self-sacrificial service demonstrated during his earthly existence—and nowhere more than on the cross—that Paul imitated" (5).

126 Merk, "Nachahmung Christi," 202; Thompson, *Clothed With Christ*, 213; Lindemann, *Korintherbrief*, 235. Wolff sums up this perspective aptly: "Paul is imitator of Christ because of the calling he received from the risen one; he experienced in a unique way that the salvation of humanity occurred through the crucified one, through the path of renunciation and suffering. Because of this, Paul is free not to seek his own advantage, but rather to help others grasp eschatological salvation" (Wolff, *Korinther*, 242).

127 Orr and Walther, *1 Corinthians*, 251.

128 de Boer, *Imitation*, 158.

129 A number of scholars argue that this passage teaches that it is actually the Christ who dwells in Paul that is the object of imitation: Craig and Short, *1 Corinthians*, 121-22; Belleville, "Imitate Me," 124; Barrett, *First Corinthians*, 246. Against this

It is relevant to note here a parallel between this reference to Paul imitating Christ and references in antiquity to imitating "heroes" from the past, which we noted in chapter three. Individuals and groups were encouraged to imitate both the general pattern of the life, the virtues, as well as deeds of heroes or ancestors, which had been passed on by oral tradition or in writing. These writers assumed the readers' familiarity with the story of the exemplar's life and key events. Further, they would assume that a simple reference to "imitate the character/action/virtue of X" would be sufficient to recall the relevant tradition surrounding the exemplar, so that the appropriate association would be automatically inferred.

The way that Paul refers to his imitation of Christ fits this pattern. The fact that Paul's reference to his imitation of Christ is so "matter-of-fact"—that is, with no extra effort to justify it and no additional information to point to specific events in the life of Christ—indicates that Paul assumed a simple mention of "imitating Christ" would be sufficient for the readers to recall the relevant portions of the tradition they have received about Christ. He assumes that they would draw the proper parallels and associations from the JT that would correspond to Paul's example, which the Corinthians should imitate in 10:32-33 and generally from 1 Cor 8-10. It is, therefore, aside from the Passion, impossible to know specifically to which events in Christ's life and ministry Paul may have been referring.

In light of our discussion on the historical Jesus and the risen Christ in chapter four, we have argued that Paul would have been well acquainted with the details of the earthly life and ministry of Christ through the Jesus Tradition. Since concrete references to Jesus' earthly ministry are minimal in Paul, we cannot discern what he specifically had in mind when he says that he imitates Christ. Certainly, at least Christ's Passion would come to the fore as an example of subordinating his own desires for the good of many so that they would be saved. Then again this subordination of personal desires could be said to characterize the life of Christ life on earth.[130] A look at the Gospels gives ample evidence that the concepts in 10:32-33 were the general pattern of Jesus' earthly ministry:

(1) *Seeking the good of others and subordinating his own needs.* Jesus was so busy with ministering for the good of the people that he did not take time to eat (Mark 3:20). He would not be deterred even by family matters for the sake

---

is that in this entire section, there is no description of Christ's actions or attitudes. The focus in these chapters has been consistently on the actions and attitudes of Paul and his companion.

130 "No doubt, Paul has [Christ's self-giving in his incarnation and death] chiefly in view. However, there are indications that he has more features of the historical Jesus in view than just the two moments of his life, incarnation and death" (Kim, "Imitatio Christi," 6). Kim goes on to list in detail texts in 1 Corinthians that are allusions Christ's earthly life as transmitted in the Gospels.

of ministry (Mark 3:31-32). Even though tired from ministry, he was moved to compassion when he saw the needs of others and would continue to minister to them (Mark 6:34). Everywhere he went he was thronged by people who wanted to be healed, and he did not refuse them (Mark 6:56). He spoke for three days on end for the sake of the hearers (Mark 8:2-3), and at the end of this time thought of their needs, without mentioning his own.[131] The foot washing ceremony (John 13:1-17) is a symbolic summary of how Jesus conducted himself with respect to his disciples: serving them, so that they would have an example for themselves to follow. He endured the hate of the world (John 15:20-24) throughout his ministry. He wept over the plight of Jerusalem for he had "often longed to gather [her] children" (Luke 13:34).

(2) *Becoming like all people to save some.* Jesus was willing to associate with people (tax collectors and "sinners") to bring them to salvation (Mark 2:15-17), which parallels 1 Cor 9:19-23, where Paul has become all things for all people to save some.

(3) *Seeking to save the lost as a core goal.* The whole pattern of his life could be summarized as ministering for the good of others. He understood his mission to be to "seek and to save the lost" (Luke 19:10, compare Luke 4:18-20) and everything he did contributed to that end. He was constantly healing[132] and speaking to people[133] for their good and their ultimate salvation and subordinating his own desires toward this end.

(4) *The ultimate example of subordinating his own desires, seeking the good of others, for their salvation: Christ's Passion.* Jesus is described in the Gospels as knowingly and willingly laying down his life for his friends and the world (John 3:16; 15:13; Mark 10:32-34; 14:24). Jesus' knowledge of his impending death is used as an example for others to take up their crosses (Luke 9:22-27). Paul seems to have picked up this theme. There are a number of strong parallels in Mark 10:42-45[134] that seem to be echoed in 1 Cor 10:32-11:1, where the shared concepts of (1) "subordinating one's desires" (2) "for the others good" (3) "in order that they might be saved" are brought together from the perspective of Christ's impending Passion.[135] In Rom 15:1-3, as we have seen above, the same parallels arise also pointing to association with the Passion of Christ.

We would conclude that when one asks the question, "Does Paul have in mind *exclusively* the Passion when he says καθὼς κἀγὼ Χριστοῦ, or is he referring to Christ's earthly ministry?" one is setting up an unnecessary dichotomy that would have been foreign to the way Paul and the early

131 "[They] have nothing to eat. If I send them home hungry, they will collapse on the way."

132 Cf. Mark 1:40-45; 2:1-12; 3:5, 10, etc.

133 Cf. Mark 8:2; Matt 5-7; 13; 18.

134 Par. Matt 20:25-28; Luke 22:24-27.

135 Thompson, *Clothed With Christ*, 213.

Christians would have thought. Certainly, the Passion functions in Paul's writings as the ultimate example of the way Christ conducted his entire life on earth, yet the supreme example of Christ's Passion emerges out of, is continuous with, and cannot be separated from the context of his entire life and ministry.

5.2.3 Summary of Imitation in 1 Corinthians 11:1

Imitation in I Cor 11:1 refers most immediately to the content of the directly preceding verses (10:32-33), which in turn functions as a lens through which Paul wishes the Corinthians to look at the preceding discussion for the personal references to Paul's action. Paul is calling the Corinthian believers to imitate him in the way that he makes it his constant aim *negatively* not to cause anyone—believer or unbeliever—to falter in their relationship to God, and *positively* to intentionally seek the good of the many so that they may be ultimately saved. This is seen reflected in the personal examples of himself in 8:1-10:30: (1) how he would refuse to eat meat if it would cause a brother to stumble (8:13);[136] (2) how he freely gives up his legitimate rights as an apostle (9:1-6, 15) so that the gospel would not be hindered (9:12); (3) how he is compelled to preach the gospel and that his reward is to offer it "with no strings attached" (9:15-19); (4) how he "makes himself a slave" to everyone (9:19) by becoming like them (or adapting to them) in order that they may experience salvation (9:19-23); and finally (5) how he disciplines himself (9:27) in that he relinquishes his legitimate rights to certain things (such as points 2-4) in light of the eschatological reward awaiting him (9:23-25).

---

136 This first point is somewhat debatable and may not be what Paul intended because (1) it *per se* is not what Paul has done, but what he would do; (2) it has to do with the issue of eating meat, which relates more to 10:31 than 10:32-33; and (3) it is not part of the section (chapter nine) in which the concrete personal examples occur. However, on the basis of the following observations, we see strong reason for including it as something Paul intended: (a) 8:13 does function as an example to be imitated in the way Paul phrases it, since he describes what he theoretically would do in a concrete situation; (b) it does have relevance to the issue of being ἀπρόσκοποι and seeking the good of others.

CHAPTER 6

Imitation of Paul, Part III: Philippian Correspondence

Introductory Comments

There are two passages that directly bear on the concept of imitation in Philippians: "join in imitating me" (Συμμιμηταί μου γίνεσθε) in 3:17 and "Keep on doing the things that you have learned and received and heard and seen in me" (ἃ καὶ ἐμάθετε καὶ παρελάβετε καὶ ἠκούσατε καὶ εἴδετε ἐν ἐμοί, ταῦτα πράσσετε) in 4:9. However, as we will see, the concept of imitation runs throughout this letter, which is replete with personal examples. It will hopefully become clear throughout our discussion that Paul's letter deliberately sets out distinct theses for imitatory purposes.

The introductory matters of times and place bear little on the concept of imitation in this letter.[1] The explicit occasion of the book is Paul's wish to

1 Thurston and Ryan provide a relatively up-to-date summary of the issues surrounding the literary integrity of Philippians. They summarize various proposals for the fragmentary composition of the letter, along with their proponents (Murphy-O'Connor, Goodspeed, Bornkamm, Gnilka, Keck, Barth, Beare, Collange, Fitzmyer, Fuller, Koester, Lohse, Marxsen) and also present the arguments for the unity of the letter and their proponents (Bloomquist, Dalton, Fee, Garland, Jewett, Kümmel, Pollard, Watson) (Bonnie Bowman Thurston and Judith Ryan, *Philippians and Philemon* [SP; Collegeville, Minn.: Liturgical Press, 2005], 34-38).

Though there is a debated reference in Polycarp (*Phil* 3:2) to the "letters" of Paul to the Philippians, there is no manuscript evidence that the letter ever existed in any but its present form. For a discussion of this reference in Polycarp, see Carson and Moo, *Introduction*, 510; Thurston and Ryan, *Philippians* 32; Morna D. Hooker, "The Letter to the Philippians," in *The New Interpreter's Bible. New Testament Survey* (Nashville: Abingdon, 2006), 233-34. Arguments for the fragmentary composition of Philippians reduce down to what individual scholars imagine to be "Pauline" writing style. Divergence from this assumed style, then, indicates the work of a redactor. Reed, in his massive discussion on the arguments for and against unity, concludes that multiple letter theories are beset with a fundamental problem of circularity: "Paul would not have done this, but a redactor would have" (Jeffrey T. Reed, *A Discourse Analysis of Philippians: Method and Rhetoric in the Debate over Literary Integrity* [JSNTSup 136; Sheffield: Sheffield

thank the Philippians for the gift that they sent to him through Epaphroditus.[2] He takes this opportunity to write to them about specific issues of which, no doubt, Epaphroditus informed him, having been sent by the Philippians to meet the needs of Paul.

There is considerable divergence among scholars regarding the purpose of this letter.[3] For example, Luter and Lee, following Dalton, narrow it down to "partnership in the gospel."[4] Black proposes "ecclesial unity in the cause of the Gospel" as the main theme.[5] Melick argues for the twin purposes of thanks for the Philippians' gift for him and a plea for unity in the church.[6] Although these do have data to justify these conclusions, it seems that narrowing down the purpose of Philippians to one or two items does not do justice to the variety of themes present in Philippians. Reed argues that the epistolary classification of

---

University Press, 1997], 412). There is simply no final arbiter to determine what Paul would have done and what a redactor would have done.

Perhaps the most rigorous and convincing defense of the unity of the letter is by L. Gregory Bloomquist, *The Function of Suffering in Philippians* (JSNTSup 78; Sheffield: JSOT Press, 1993). He meticulously lists the lexical and thematic parallels throughout Philippians. These parallels, he argues, "must be considered significant indexes of the integrity of the letter if they are such as are not to be found in Paul's other letters. And, in fact, this is the case: the most striking parallels *within* Philippians are *unparalleled* in Paul's other letters" (103). He then concludes, "When one adds to this the recurrence of specific, unique phrasing, one is left with the probability of intentional cross-referencing of vocabulary and themes within the same letter. . . . So I believe we may proceed—if not with absolute certainty, at least with probability—to treat Philippians as one integral letter" (103). For other substantial arguments for the unity of the letter, see David E. Garland, "The Composition and Unity of Philippians: Some Neglected Literary Factors," *NovT* 27, no. 2 (1985): 141-73; David Alan Black, "The Discourse Structure of Philippians: A Study in Textlinguistics," *NovT* 37 (1995): 16-49; Gerald F. Hawthorne, "Letter to the Philippians," *DPL* 709; Jeffrey T. Reed, "Philippians 3:1 and the Epistolary Hesitation Formulas: The Literary Integrity of Philippians, Again," *JBL* 115 (1996): 63-90; John T. Fitzgerald, "Epistle to the Philippians," n.p., *ABD on CD-ROM.* Version 3.0a. 2006; Casey Wayne Davis, *Oral Biblical Criticism: The Influence of the Principles on the Literary Structure of Paul's Epistle to the Philippians* (JSNTSup 172; Sheffield: Sheffield University Press, 1999); Luke Timothy Johnson and Todd C. Penner, *The Writings of the New Testament: An Interpretation* (Rev. ed.; Minneapolis: Fortress, 1999), 369-70.

2 4:10-19.

3 For a helpful up-to-date survey of major proposals regarding the purposes for this letter, see Thurston and Ryan, *Philippians* 34-38.

4 A. Boyd Luter and Michelle V. Lee, "Philippians as Chiasmus: Key to the Structure, Unity and Theme Questions," *NTS* 41 (1995): 99; William J. Dalton, "The Integrity of Philippians," *Bib* 60 (1979): 97-98.

5 Black, "Discourse Structure," 43.

6 Richard R. Melick, *Philippians, Colossians, Philemon* (NAC 32; Nashville, Tenn.: Broadman, 1991), 29.

Philippians "allows for (almost demands) multiple purposes in the letter."[7] For this reason, Hawthorne lists eight distinct purposes for this letter and Kümmel concludes that "the reasons for writing this very personal letter are . . . numerous."[8]

Decisions regarding the purpose of the letter, however, are bound up with decisions regarding its structure.[9] Unfortunately, attempts at discerning the unifying theme and the structure of the book have been beset by subjectivism combined with "a notable deficiency of rigorous text-centered analysis that makes explicit how the various text-sequences function interactively in achieving the overall communicative function of the text."[10] Some commentators claim that there is no discernible structure, with Paul writing in "stream of consciousness" mode.[11] Even the employment of rhetorical epistolary convention with the desire to provide objective controls has not been successful in achieving consensus, as is evident when comparing Watson's and Bloomquist's epistolary analyses.[12] Both claim to be developing their understanding of the letter based on epistolary categories, but they arrive at divergent outcomes.

Attempts at rhetorical analysis also have produced divergent results. Alexander sees the letter to the Philippians as a "family letter."[13] White, Stowers, Witherington, and Fee see the letter as having characteristic of being a "friendship letter" as well as a letter of "moral exhortation," although Fee admits that 3:1-4:9 and 4:10-20 "do not easily fit the scheme."[14] Black

---

7 Reed, *Discourse Analysis*, 178, 415 n. 27; Stanley E. Porter and Jeffrey T. Reed, "Philippians as a Micro-Chiasm and Its Exegetical Significance," *NTS* 44 (1998): 226.

8 Gerald F. Hawthorne, *Philippians* (WBC 43; Waco: Word, 1983), 324; Kümmel, *Introduction*. Similarly Frank Thielman, *Philippians* (NIVAC; Grand Rapids: Zondervan, 1995), 22.

9 For attempts to come to grips with the purpose and structure of the book, see the works of Garland, Black, Reed, Luter and Lee, Porter and Reed, and Davis (see previous footnotes) as well as A. Boyd Luter, "Ears to Hear: Pauline Orality and the Structure of Philippians" (paper presented at the annual meeting of the ETS, Nashville, Tenn., 16 November 2000), 1-15.

10 Black, "Discourse Structure," 19.

11 T. Evan Pollard, "The Integrity of Philippians," *NTS* 13 (1966): 59. Cited in Duane F. Watson, "A Rhetorical Analysis of Philippians and its Implications for the Unity Question," *NovT* 30 (1988): 57.

12 Watson, "Rhetorical Analysis," 61-88; Bloomquist, *Suffering*, 137.

13 Loveday Alexander, "Hellenistic Letter-Forms and the Structure of Philippians," in *New Testament Essays in Honour of David Hill* (ed. Christopher Tuckett; Sheffield: JSOT Press, 1989), 95.

14 L. Michael White, "Morality Between Two Worlds: A Paradigm of Friendship in Philippians," in *Greeks, Romans, and Christians: Essays in Honor of Abraham J. Malherbe* (ed. David L. Balch, et al.; Minneapolis: Fortress, 1990), 206; S. K. Stowers, "Friends and Enemies in the Politics of Heaven," in *Pauline Theology:*

considers this to be a "deliberative" letter intended to solve the problem in 4:2-3.[15] Reed also loosely classifies this letter as a subgenre of friendship or family letters, but cautions against pressing the issue because of elements that do not completely fit.[16] Holloway argues that it is a letter of consolation written to encourage the downcast Philippians because of Paul's imprisonment and suffering.[17]

It is this observation that the letters of Paul can be made to fit various rhetorical schemes which leads Black to conclude that

> Paul's letters not only accord with the pattern of ancient rhetorical convention; they radically differ from that pattern as well. This means that textual features other than purely rhetorical conventions need to be considered in order to arrive at an adequate literary background against which the letter can be interpreted.[18]

Black's approach is to use the tools of discourse analysis to trace the thought-flow of the text, guided by topical, logical, and textual connectors between the sections. It is the *macrostructure* of the text that influences the *microstructure* of the text.[19]

Although the insights of text-linguistics are important, another aspect needs to be factored into the understanding of Paul's letters and their structure: the oral dimension. Davis argues that "while [discourse analysis] approaches the NT as a literary product, [oral biblical criticism] recognizes from the beginning that the material is, fundamentally, an oral product which has been written down." He goes on to say that the writers of the NT "expected their compositions to be read aloud to a gathered community, who would, in turn, use that material to establish a dialogue among themselves and, especially in the case of a letter, with the reader, who was often the writer's official representative.[20] Davis, in this work, has worked out in impressive detail various oral patterns that are part of and interplay with the structure of the text.

Thessalonians, Philippians, Galatians, Philemon (ed. Jouette M. Bassler, et al.; Minneapolis: Fortress, 1991), 107; Ben Witherington, *Friendship and Finances in Philippi: The Letter of Paul to the Philippians* (Valley Forge, Pa.: Trinity Press, 1994), 15-6; Fee, *Philippians*, 2-5, 14. Silva, however, questions this noting that "nowhere in Philippians does Paul make explicit reference . . . to the Greco-Roman concept of friendship . . ." (Moises Silva, *Philippians* [BECNT; Grand Rapids: Baker, 1992], 19).

15 Black, "Discourse Structure," 16.

16 Reed, *Discourse Analysis*, 289.

17 Paul Holloway, *Consolation in Philippians: Philosophical: Sources and Rhetorical Strategy* (SNTSMS 112; New York: Cambridge University Press, 2001), 55.

18 Black, "Discourse Structure," 21. For a similar perspective see Reed, *Discourse Analysis*, 295.

19 It is "the thought that determines and controls the choice of words and the construction of sentences" (Black, "Discourse Structure," 43).

20 Davis, *Oral Biblical Criticism*, 60, 62.

In light of all these factors it seems best to view this letter having following multiple purposes. Based on his and the Philippians' joint partnership in the gospel[21] and their mutual affection for one another,[22] Paul desires to inform them of the spread of the gospel[23] despite the suffering he is experiencing[24] and to give them perspective on their own suffering for the gospel.[25] He wishes to encourage them to continue to grow in their faith, love, and knowledge.[26]

His major concern in this letter, however, seems to be that they walk worthily (ἀξίως . . . πολιτεύεσθε) of the gospel,[27] which is specifically understood in this letter as the need for unity in the body[28] manifesting itself by

---

21 Cf. κοινωνία 1:5; 2:1; 3:10; 4:15; συγκοινωνός 1:7, 4:14.

22 This can be seen, for example, in the following texts: "your partnership in the gospel"(1:5); "through your prayers [for me]" (1:19); the sending of Epaphroditus to take care of Paul's needs (2:25-30); the sending of Epaphroditus to Paul as representative of the Philippians since they all could not come to help as they would have liked (2:30); "you have revived your concern for me" (4:10) and "sent me help for my needs" by means of monetary support of Paul (4:14-17) just as the Philippians had done previously (4:15), which Epaphroditus delivered to him (4:18).

23 1:12-18.

24 1:12-18, 30; 2:17; 4:10-12. As we will argue below, the one external problem of the "Judaizers" (3:2), i.e., those who promote circumcision in conjunction with the gospel, is only mentioned here and does not significantly influence the other topics of this letter outside this one passage. "That Paul does not mention them again would seem to indicate that they are not present—although they surely will have tried their wares in Philippi in times past—and that a present threat of 'Judaizing' does not seriously exist" (Fee, *Philippians*, 294). The same can be said for those mentioned in 1:15; 3:18.

25 1:30.

26 1:6, 9-11; 2:12-13; 4:1.

27 "The focal point of the letter may be seen in the rhetorical proposition [of 1:27]. Paul's desire for the Philippians is that they conduct themselves in a manner worthy of the gospel. The specific manifestation of this command is that they stand firm in one spirit, struggling together with one mind for the faith" (Davis, *Oral Biblical Criticism*, 156). Reed, however, sees this as one of several focal points. We discuss his proposal below.

The suggestion that "joy" is the major topic of Philippians based on high frequency of usage is not necessarily an indication of topics: "It is rarely legitimate simply to make a word count and draw conclusions from it, since concepts involve far more elaborate structures than individual words" (Black, "Discourse Structure," 17). Contra Reed, *Discourse Analysis*, 217. See discussion on 1:27-30 below under "Thought-flow."

28 Seen through the following terms: φρονέω (1:7; 2:2 [2x], 5; 3:15, 19; 4:2, 10 [2x]); τὸ αὐτὸ (1:30, 2:2[2x], 18; 4:2); ἐν (1:27 [2x]; 2:2); συν- compounds: -συναθλοῦντες (1:27; 4:3); σύμψυχοι (2:2); συγχαίρω (2:17, 18); συνεργὸν (2:25; 4:3); συστρατιώτην (2:25); συμμορφιζόμενος (3:10, 21?); συμμιμηταί (3:17); συλλαμβάνου (4:3); ἰσο- compound: ἰσόψυχον (2:19); the problem with Euodia and Syntyche

means of selfless service for others in the cause of the witness to the gospel.[29] Paul uses teaching interwoven with positive personal examples (Paul himself, Christ, Timothy, and Epaphroditus) to describe how selfless service looks in practice.[30] The issues of unity and selfless service for the sake of the gospel is so important to him because of the surpassing value of knowing Christ, to which any human reason for boasting in comparison is "dung" or "refuse."[31] Paul's desire is that their lives be motivated by and conformed to this gospel[32] so that they ultimately—individually and corporately—can stand blameless before God and bring praise to him.[33]

If pressed to reduce the themes of Philippians to a single sentence, we would argue that Paul desires the Philippians to walk worthily of the gospel, which in their case involves primarily the need for unity in the cause of together living out and advancing the gospel.[34]

6.1 Philippians 3:17

6.1.1 Understandings of Imitation in This Context

The call to imitation in 3:17 is unusual in the NT since it is the only instance of a prefix attached to the term μιμητής. A search of the term συμμιμηταί in the TLG revealed only five instances of the term—only one instance of which occurs before Paul's usage here. These instances reveal relatively little about

---

(4:2). Black (along with Vos and Bruce) sees the "theme of unity as an essential aspect of Christian living and witness" as the main one of the letter (Black, "Discourse Structure," 17). Garland also notes that unity is the theme, but sees it as "unity in order to withstand the external enemy" (Garland, "Composition and Unity," 172). This seems implausible since "the enemy" is only marginally thematized. O'Brien, in our opinion, correctly, does not tie the theme of the book down to the concept of unity exclusively, but weds it to other themes: "[Paul] had a number of purposes in mind as he wrote . . . especially [he wrote] to urge his Christian friends to stand firm for the gospel and to be united in Christian love" (Peter T. O'Brien, *Commentary on Philippians* [NIGNTC; Grand Rapids: Eerdmans, 1991], 38).

Hooker, however, disagrees, since Paul only offers a "mild rebuke" to two leaders in 4:2 (Morna D. Hooker, "The Letter to the Philippians," in *NIB*, vol. 11 [Nashville: Abingdon], 475).

29 1:12-14; 2:14-16.

30 1:12-2:30; 3:4-14. This is contrasted with the negative examples of the Judaizers (3:2) and of Euodia and Syntyche (4:2).

31 3:4-14. See Fee for background on the term σκύβαλα. (Fee, *Philippians*, 319).

32 1:9-11, 27-30.

33 1:11; 4:20.

34 This is a similar conclusion to those of Black and Davis (Black, "Discourse Structure," 16; Davis, *Oral Biblical Criticism*, 156).

the term.[35]

There are two basic issues that need to be clarified with respect to imitation in 3:17: how the term συμμιμηταί is to be understood, and to what imitation in this text refers.

Regarding the first issue, the term συμμιμηταί could be understood in at least four basic ways:[36] (1) the Philippians are to be fellow imitators with Paul of Christ;[37] (2) they are to be fellow imitators of others already imitating Paul;[38] (3) the Philippians together are to be imitators of Paul;[39] (4) the prefix συν- has no specific significance and is equivalent to the simple term μιμηταί.[40]

Regarding the second issue, there have been six proposals for what imitation might refer in this passage. (1) Imitation refers to a general call to imitate Paul's way of life and thought in Christ.[41] (2) Imitation refers to 1:12-26 or

---

35 Plato, *Pol.* 274D. Three instances are direct quotations of this passage with limited commentary on this passage: Basil Theol., *reg. Mor.* 31.848; Joannes Damascenus, *Comm. Paul* 95.876; Theodoretus, *Int. epist. Paul.* 82.584. The last text is a non-religious text: Mauricius, *Strategicon* 8.2.70. The sense in the texts by Plato and Mauricius is that of a group of people jointly imitating something or someone.

36 Both Fee and O'Brien provide helpful overviews of the options commentators have chosen (Fee, *Philippians*, 364 n. 10; O'Brien, *Philippians*, 445).

37 "But Paul expresses the exhortation to 'imitate with' (*Mit-Nachahmen*) in such a way that he does not present himself as the glowing model; rather, he appears with others together as imitators of the Lord Christ and his way of humiliation (*Niedrigkeitsweges*)" (Nikolaus Walter, "Der Brief an die Philipper," in *Das Neue Testament Deutsch*, vol. 8/2 [Göttingen: Vandenhoeck & Ruprecht], 84).

38 Homer A. Kent, Jr., "Philippians," in *EBC*, vol. 11 (Grand Rapids: Zondervan), 146; Werner de Boor, *Der Brief des Paulus an die Philipper* (WSB; Wuppertal: Brockhaus, 1989), 128; Dumm, "Nachahmung," 55. De Boor lists the following as also holding this position: Estius, Erasmus, Vatablus, Lapide, Wiesinger, B. Weiss, Ellicott, Schmidt and Franke (177 n. 259). Fee also adds Meyer, Vincent, Silva, Melick, and Earle as holding this (Fee, *Philippians*, 365 n. 10).

39 The major commentators hold this view. Among them Fee cites Lightfoot, Meyer, Kennedy, Jones, Plummer, Collange, Martin, Kent, Bruce, Hawthorne, O'Brien, and Betz (Fee, *Philippians*, 364). Also holding this position are Marvin R. Vincent, *A Critical and Exegetical Commentary on Epistles to the Philippians and to Philemon* (ICC; New York: Scribners, 1897), 115; J. Hugh Michael, *The Epistle of Paul to the Philippians* (MNTC; London: Hodder & Stoughton, 1927), 168; Ernest F. Scott and Robert R. Wicks, *The Epistle to the Philippians* (IB 11; New York: Abingdon-Cokesbury, 1955), 95-96; Francis Wright Beare, *A Commentary on the Epistle to the Philippians* (BNTC; London: Black, 1959), 132; de Boer, *Imitation*, 179.

40 Michaelis, *TWNT* 4:667, 669.

41 "Bring to expression in your lives the Christianity and the Christian way you see portrayed in me"(de Boer, *Imitation*, 186). Similarly, Hawthorne, *Philippians*, 159-60. De Boer takes great pains to stress that it is not the personality of Paul that is the object of imitation: "Paul can not point to an inherent worth in his conduct and recommend this to others. The whole matter of imitation here has nothing to do

more specifically to "suffering with joy."[42] (3) Imitation is a call to obedience based on his apostolic authority.[43] (4) Imitation has to do with the model he left them when he was with them.[44] (5) Imitation is a call to adopt Paul's attitude in 3:4-14 of "his refusal to boast on the grounds of flesh categories, and his refusal to consider himself as already made perfect."[45] (6) Imitation refers specifically to the content of 3:4-14.[46]

6.1.2 Development of the Argument: Thought-flow of Philippians

To understand and appreciate the breadth and content of these two calls to imitation in 3:17 and 4:9, they need to be placed within the flow of Paul's thought. The thought-flow in Philippians has heightened relevance for the concept of imitation because of the prominent role that exemplars play in the central section of the book.

Davis notes eight factors that impinge upon discerning the structure of the

---

with a personal exemplariness as this is commonly understood" (de Boer, *Imitation*, 184). Although this is on one level true, the term "personality" is quite slippery. We would argue that it is Paul's Christ-oriented conduct, which is intended in contrast to modern understandings of personality.

42 So Jean-Francois Collange, *The Epistle of Saint Paul to the Philippians* (London: Epworth, 1979), 136; Heinrich Schlier, *Der Philipperbrief* (Einsiedeln: Johannesverlag, 1980), 67; Fee, *Philippians*, 364. Fee leans strongly on 1 Thess 1:6 for his understanding of imitation in Phil 3:17. He sees a parallel context in which suffering and joy are the key components. However, he also holds that it refers to 3:4-14: "They [i.e., the ones mentioned in 3:17b] are to walk, and to watch for others who so walk, in keeping with the example of Paul just given in vv. 4-14" (366). Gnilka also sees imitation as having the character of suffering, but also notes this call to imitation as being strongly tied to the previous section of 3:4-14 (Joachim Gnilka, *Der Philipperbrief* [HTKNT 10; Vienna: Herder, 1968], 201-02). He effectively combines options 2 and 6 in a similar way as does Fee. (See footnote under option 6 for further discussion.)

43 Michaelis, *TWNT* 4:670; Ralph P. Martin, *The Epistle of Paul to the Philippians* (TNTC 11; Grand Rapids: Eerdmans, 1987), 142.

44 A suggestion made by O'Brien, but not adopted by him (O'Brien, *Philippians*, 446).

45 Garland, "Composition and Unity," 171.

46 Karl Barth, *The Epistle to the Philippians* (London: SCM, 1962), 112; William Hendriksen, *Philippians* (NTC; London: Banner of Truth Trust, 1962), 179; Wilhelm Egger, *Galater, Philipperbrief, Philemonbrief* (NEchtB 9; Würzburg: Echter, 1985), 68; O'Brien, *Philippians*, 447; Bernhard Mayer, *Philipperbrief, Philemonbrief* (2 ed.; SKKNT 11; Stuttgart: Verlag Katholisches Bibelwerk, 1992), 58; Black, "Discourse Structure," 41; Fee, *Philippians*, 366. Gnilka holds that imitation has primarily to do with 3:4-14, but (similar to Fee) that the broader background of imitation is dealing with tribulation (Gnilka, *Philipperbrief*, 201-02).

text and textual units:[47] (1) chiasm,[48] (2) introductory and concluding formulae, (3) changes in genre, (4) logical relationships often signaled by conjunctions and prepositions, (5) units of grammatical consistency, (6) sound, word, and topic grouping, (7) temporal and spatial frames, and (8) the use of climax.

When these factors are attended to, we would suggest the following structure of the letter in the box below.[49] We will then comment on the thought-flow leading up to the imitation texts.

---

47 Davis, *Oral Biblical Criticism*, 98-140. A similar discussion, though not taking into account the issue of orality, is found in Black, "Discourse Structure," 16-26. Our own findings dovetail closely with Davis' conclusions.

48 Know also as inclusio, parallelism, or concentric patterns. For a detailed understanding of this see Davis, *Oral Biblical Criticism*, 112-18. He follows the conclusions of N. W. Lund, *Chiasmus in the New Testament: A Study in the Form and Function of Chiastic Structures* (Chapel Hill: University of North Carolina, 1942), especially 41-42. Davis (90) quotes Havelock: "The basic method for assisting the memory to retain a series of distinct meanings is to frame the first of them in a way which will suggest or forecast a later meaning which will recall the first without being identical with it" (E. A. Havelock, "Oral Composition in the Oedipus Tyrannus of Sophocles," *NLitHist* 16 [1984]: 183). Davis goes on to list the types of repetition that function chiastically: repetition of sounds, grammatical constructions, words, and topics (80).

In their jointly-written article, Reed and Porter fundamentally question the whole study of chiasm, since in the ancient rhetorical handbooks the topic is virtually non-existent. "If chiasm is identified in ancient documents, apart possibly from instances of reverse parallelism in four-clause sentences, a modern category is being utilized, one probably unknown and unrecognized by the ancients. At the most, the ancients would have had a vague idea of inverted parallelism, although certainly no clear formulation of how it was constructed and what defined its elements, and certainly not that it was a category that could be applied to entire literary works" (Porter and Reed, "Philippians as a Micro-Chiasm," 217).

Although this may be the case, the thrust of their argument leads one to conclude that any type of parallelism or mirroring of thought throughout a longer work is illegitimate. Although "grand chiasm" may not have been a rhetorical category, the concept of parallelism and "concentric patterns" can be observed. The question is: were these intentional or unintentional parallels of the author? Porter and Reed are skeptical, since they are concerned primarily with "quantifiable" or "firm" criteria for the detection (218-19). We would argue, along with Davis, that in the letter to the Philippians there is intentional paralleling and concentric patterning both on a micro-structural level as well as on a macro-structural level (Davis, *Oral Biblical Criticism*, 168-77). Since, as Porter and Reed and others have pointed out, the term chiasm is an anachronism, to use the term may well be inappropriate. Whichever nomenclature one prefers, it seems clear that concentric oral and textual patterns in Philippians were an intentional strategy of the author.

49 This outline has been, in part, informed by Davis, *Oral Biblical Criticism*, 98-140.

Parallel Structures in Philippians

(1:1-2) Opening Greeting

- A. (1:3-11) Partnership in the Gospel
  - B. (1:12-26) **Example** (Paul): joy in difficult circumstances because of advance of gospel
    - C. (1:27-2:4) **Instruction**: walk worthily by standing united (general situation)
      - D. (2:5-11) **Example** (Jesus): selfless service
        - E. (2:12-18) **Instruction**: selflessness/unity impacts gospel witness
          - F. (2:19-24) **Example** (Timothy) selfless service for the gospel
          - F′. (2:25-30) **Example** (Epaphroditus) selfless service for the gospel
        - E′. (3:1-3) **Instruction**: warning against selfish individuals who distort the gospel
      - D(i)′. (3:4-16) **Positive Example** (Paul): selfless service because of the value of Christ
      - D(ii)′. (3:17-21) **Negative Example** (enemies of the cross): selfish interests because the mind is set on earthly things
      - D(iii)′. (4:1-3) **Negative Example** (Euodia and Syntyche): plea for selflessness and unity
    - C′. (4:4-9) **Instruction**: how to walk worthily by standing united (specific situation)
  - B′. (4:10-13) **Example** (Paul): joy in the midst of any circumstances
- A′. (4:14-20) Partnership in the Gospel

(4:21-23) Closing Greeting

Paul begins with a brief introduction in which subsequent themes of selfless servanthood and unity are hinted at.[50] The structure of the letter follows epistolary convention, with a clear introduction (1:1-2), body (1:3-4:20), and

50 For example, in 1:1-2 the special mention of πᾶσιν τοῖς ἁγίοις . . . σὺν ἐπισκόποις καὶ διακόνοις are important for the thrust of the letter in which disunity (hence the use of πᾶσιν), common mission (hence σὺν) and serving others (hence δοῦλοι) are pivotal. The closing of the letter (4:21-23) echoes the introduction using identical terminology: ἁγίοις/ἅγιον, ἐν Χριστῷ Ἰησοῦ, σὺν, χάρις ὑμῖν . . . κυρίου Ἰησοῦ Χριστοῦ/Ἡ χάρις τοῦ κυρίου Ἰησοῦ Χριστοῦ). This section and the following prayer and thanksgiving section (1:3-11) are clear textual units, according with epistolary convention.

conclusion (4:21-23).[51]

The thanksgiving and prayer section (1:3-11) introduces themes that will be developed in the body of the letter: joy, fellowship, the work begun in you, complete, day of Christ, think this way, desire, compassion of Christ.[52]

The body of the work (1:12-4:9) begins with a description of Paul's imprisonment and the effect that it had on the advancement (προκοπὴν)[53] of the gospel (1:12-26). Everyone knows that Paul is in prison for the sake of the gospel and believers have therefore been emboldened in their witness (1:12-14). Paul makes a special point of expressing his joy that despite the questionable motives of other proclaimers of the gospel, at least the gospel is advancing (1:15-18a). Paul is so gripped by Christ that he would rather leave this life and be with him, but he knows that he will stay in order to serve them and help them advance (προκοπὴν) in their faith (1:18b-26).

Paul then addresses the Philippians directly, calling them to walk worthily of

---

51 There is debate as to whether the prayer and thanksgiving belongs to the letter introduction or to the body. Black sees the prayer and thanksgiving section as being the "body opening" (Black, "Discourse Structure," 26). For further discussion and bibliography of formal epistolary style, see Davis, *Oral Biblical Criticism*, 95.

52 The introductory thanksgiving sections in Paul's letters contain "some of the major themes and motifs which bind the whole letter together" (O'Brien, *Introductory Thanksgivings*, 37-38). Some of the themes and important terms that are mentioned here, which are referenced again in the letter are (1:6) ἐναρξάμενος ἐν ὑμῖν ἔργον . . . ἐπιτελέσει (compare 3:12, 15, 19), ἡμέρας Χριστοῦ (compare 1:10; 2:16); (v. 7) τούτο φρονεῖν (compare 2:5; 3:15); (v. 8) ἐπιποθῶ (compare 2:26), σπλάγχνοις Χριστοῦ (compare 2:1).

In addition to these terms, there is strong verbal correlation between the body opening and the body closing, which indicate the themes Paul wishes to emphasize in the body. The chart below lists these verbal parallels and indicates where these terms also occur in the body.

Body Opening (1:3-11)	**Body Closing (4:10-20)**	**Body (1:12-4:9)**
χαρᾶς (4)	ἐχάραν (10)	1:25; 2:2, 29; 4:1
κοινωνίᾳ . . . εἰς (5)	ἐκοινώνησεν εἰς (15)	2:1; 3:10
ἐυαγγέλιον (5, 7)	εὐαγγελίου (15)	1:12, 16, 27 (2x); 2:22; 4:3
τὸ ἐυαγγέλιον ἀπὸ τῆς πρώτης ἡμέρας (5)	ἐν ἀρχῇ τοῦ εὐαγγελίου (15)	---
φρονεῖν (7)	φρονεῖν, ἐφρονεῖτε (10)	2:2 (2x), 5; 3:15 (2x), 19; 4:2
φρονεῖν ὑπὲρ (7)	ὑπὲρ . . . φρονεῖν (10)	---
συγκοινωνούς (7)	συγκοινωνήσαντές (14)	---
περρισεύῃ (9)	περισσεύειν (12 [2x]), περισσεύω (18)	1:26
πεπληρωμένοι (11)	πεπλήρωμαι (18) πληρώσει (19)	2:2
καρπὸν (11)	καρπὸν (17)	1:22
εἰς δόξαν (11)	ἐν δόξῃ (19), ἡ δόξα (20)	2:11; 3:19, 21

53 The term προκοπὴν occurs twice at the beginning (v. 12) and end (v. 25) of this section functioning as an inclusio and division marker.

this gospel by standing united together in the advancement of the gospel (1:27-30) with respect to those outside the church.[54] Paul uses the disclosure of himself in 1:12-26 as a basis for this paraenesis.[55] This topic of unity becomes the major focus of Paul's that continues through 4:3, with further echoes of the topic in 4:4-23.[56]

In 2:1-18, he shifts to dealing with the need for unity within the church.[57] Based on their experience of the gospel (2:1-4), he calls them to walk in unity, reject pride (v. 3), and put the needs of others before one's own (v. 4). He then (2:5-11) gives the supreme example of Christ, who did exactly this: put aside his rights in order to serve.[58] Paul then, in the next section (2:12-18) pleads with

---

54 Davis, Watson, and Witherington observe that 1:27-30 is positioned as the main proposition of the letter (Davis, *Oral Biblical Criticism*, 154; Watson, "Rhetorical Analysis," 66; Witherington, *Friendship and Finances*, 61). Reed argues, however, that this is just one of many propositions, and attaches no elevated status to it in the letter (Reed, *Discourse Analysis*, 218). However, the fact that this is the first imperative in the whole book may indicate that it is a positioning proposition that sets the frame-work for the subsequent discussion. In addition, it seems that one can logically and easily tie all the parts of the main section of the letter (2:1-4:9) back to this proposition, thus corroborating Davis' view.

Black sees the theme of 1:12-26 and the following paraenesis in 1:27-30 as "unity in the face of external opposition" (Black, "Discourse Structure," 35). This, however, does not do full justice to 1:12-26, since the topic of unity is absent in these verses, only being thematized in v. 27.

The phrase ἀξίως . . . πολιτευέσθε has both a corporate and individual dimension. On the one hand, it is to be understood based on the exemplary "citizenship" of Paul described in the previous verses. On the other hand, it speaks to the need for the Philippians' corporate credibility, which should evidence itself through their unity (στήκετε ἐν ἑνὶ πνεύματι, μιᾷ ψυχῇ συναθλοῦντες). (Similarly, Reed, *Discourse Analysis*, 217). This call to unity, which is hinted at up to this point (1:1, 4-9), now becomes the major focus in the next chapters.

There are two sets of inclusios, which function as boundary-markers. (1) The paraenetic section of 1:27-30 is marked off in an inclusio: ἰδὼν . . . ἀκούω (v. 27)—εἴδετε . . . ἀκουέτε (v. 30). (2) In addition, a further set of terms mark off a larger segment: πολιτεύεσθε, στήκετε, συναθλοῦντες (v. 27)—πολίτευμα, στήκετε, συνήθλησάν (3:20; 4:1, 3), and as a result, the discussion between these sets of terms is framed and informed by them.

55 Wick writes that "Paul used his self-portrayal in order to give the Philippians an example for the paraenesis" (Peter Wick, *Der Philipperbrief: Der formale Aufbau des Briefs als Schlüssel zum Verständnis seines Inhalts* [BWNT 135; Stuttgart: Kohlhammer, 1994], 158).

56 Cf. 4:8 (ἀδελφοί), 14 (συγκοινωνήσαντές), 15 (ἐκοινώνησεν).

57 This section is tied together as an inclusio through the term χαρὰν (2:2) . . . χαίρω, συγχαίρω, χαίρετε, συγχαίρετέ (2:17-18).

58 Contra Käsemann and Martin, Betz and others, who see this reference to Christ as non-exemplary with a redemptive thrust, we take this to be a call to the Philippians to orient their lives based on the pattern of Christ's life as a reference point for their

them to work out their salvation, which in this context means: let Christ bring

---

own attitudes and actions. (See Käsemann, "Phil 2:5-11," 19-22, 87-89; Hurtado, "Lordly Example," 113-26; Ralph P. Martin, *Carmen Christi: Philippians ii. 5-11 in Recent Interpretation and in the Setting of Early Christian Worship* [New York: Cambridge University Press, 2005]; Betz, *Nachfolge*, 167-68). The foundational analysis of Fowl, who builds on the works of Larsson, Stanley, and Hurtado, shows that while Käsemann and Martin sought to identify the origins of this hymn, they have not done sufficient justice to the function of this Christ hymn in the context of the complete letter. Morna Hooker dryly states: "Whatever the origin of Phil 2:5-11, the passage belongs in its present context" (Morna Hooker, "Philippians 2:6-11," in *Jesus und Paulus: Festschrift for W. G. Kümmel* [ed. Earl E. Ellis and E. Grässer; Tübingen: Mohr Siebeck, 1975], 152). Similarly, Kraftchick notes: "It should be stated . . . that Käsemann's denial of the ethical interpretation is directed to the hymn itself and not necessarily to the hymn in its epistolary context. In fact, Käsemann allows that Paul uses the hymn in his exhortation to the Philippians to practice humility and obedience, but he insists that the context for this is 'in the sphere of Christ'" (Steven J. Kraftchick, "A Necessary Detour: Paul's Metaphorical Understanding of the Philippian Hymn," *HBT* 15 [1993]: 4).

Fowl argues that "the issue in Philippians is not whether to be obedient or not, whether to live in Christ or in sin. Rather, Paul is anxious to impart to the Philippians an understanding of what would constitute an obedient life in their situation (cf. 1:27). To assert, as Käsemann claims Paul does in 2:5-11, that the Philippians are under Christ's lordship, therefore they must obey, answers the question of whether or not to obey. This, however, is not the issue addressed in the epistle. Käsemann has made a naïve ethical example reading of 2:5-11 untenable, but his own formulation is also an inadequate explanation of the way in which this hymnic passage functions to support Paul's paraenesis because it does not deal with the concerns of the epistle" (Fowl, *Story of Christ*, 81-82). Fowl notes, further, that "one might well question whether anyone actually ever held the view that Käsemann ridicules" (79 n. 4). Similarly, Davis argues that the "debate over whether v. 5 should be interpreted as an ethical exhortation to follow Christ's example . . . or as a kerygmatic imperative to treat others properly within the church, does not change the fact that Christ is an example. Whether or not the Philippians are specifically called to imitate him, he is presented to them as an example in the same way that Paul himself, Timothy and Epaphroditus are given as examples without a specific call for imitation until 3:17" (Davis, *Oral Biblical Criticism*, 115). For further argumentation for Christ functioning in this text as "exemplar", see Larsson, *Vorbild*; Hooker, "Philippians 2:6-11."; Hurtado, "Lordly Example."; William S. Kurz, "Kenotic Imitation of Paul and of Christ in Philippians 2 and 3," in *Discipleship in the New Testament* (ed. Fernando F. Segovia; Philadelphia: Fortress, 1985), 103-26; Gerald F. Hawthorne, "The Imitation of Christ: Discipleship in Philippians," in *Patterns of Discipleship in the New Testament* (ed. Richard N. Longenecker; Grand Rapids: Eerdmans, 1996), 163-79; Stephen E. Fowl, "Christology and Ethics in Philippians 2:5-11," in *Where Christology Began: Essays on Philippians 2* (ed. Ralph P. Martin and Brian J. Dodd; Louisville, Ky.: Westminster John Knox, 1998), 140-53.

healing to your community based on (1) adopting the attitude of Christ (as one who humbled himself, did not live for his own interests, but the interest of others) (2:12-13), as well as (2) avoiding complaints and arguing.[59] The rationale for this is that unity is crucial for the gospel witness before the watching world (2:14-16).[60] Paul concludes this paraenesis with an appeal to reciprocity: his desire to boast about them on the day of Christ (cf. 1:6) and the reiteration of the theme of gladly giving himself to serve them. Paul then introduces two others individuals who serve as examples of selfless service for the sake of the gospel: Timothy and Epaphroditus (2:19-30).[61]

In the second half of this letter (3:1-4:9), indicated by the transitional adverb, τὸ λοιπόν, the themes introduced in the first half are further developed and no new ones are introduced.[62] This section has a chiastic pattern, beginning

---

59 Harking back to or echoing 2:3-4.

60 Taking up the theme of 1:27-30.

61 These two examples are also marked off by inclusio: Timothy (2:19-24): ἐν κυρίῳ, ταχέως (v. 19) . . . ἐν κυρίῳ, ταχέως (v. 24); Epaphroditus (2:25-30): λειτουργὸν (v. 25) . . . λειτουργίας (v. 30).

There are a high number of thematic parallels between this passage and the preceding and following sections: 2:19, 20 τὰ περὶ ὑμῶν (cf.2:4 τὰ ἑτέρων); 2:20 ἰσόψυχον (cf. 1:27 μιᾷ ψυχῇ, 2:2 σύμψυχοι); 2:20 γνησίως (cf. 4:3 γνήσιε); 2:21 τὰ ἑαυτῶν ζητοῦσιν (cf. 2:4 τὰ ἑαυτῶν . . . σκποποῦντες); 2:22 σὺν, 2:25 συνεργὸν, συστρατιώτην (cf. 1:1; 4:21, and συν- compounds 1:23, 27; 2:2; 3:10; 4:3 etc.); 2:22 ἐδούλευσεν (cf. 1:1; 2:7); 2:25 χρείας (4:16); 2:26 ἐπιποθῶν (1:8; 4:1); 2:29 μετὰ . . . χαρᾶς (1:4, 25; 2:2); 2:30 ἔργον (1:6, 22); 2:30 μέχρι θανάτου (2:8). This leads us to see this section not as a simple, informational "travelogue" but as content deliberately intended to contribute to the overarching themes of this letter. Davis writes: "As is typical of oral composition, Paul does not leave the discussion of working for the benefit of the gospel in the theoretical world. He immediately follows up his commands with two very practical examples. Furthermore, these examples are not icons to be imagined but men with whom the Philippians are quite familiar" (Davis, *Oral Biblical Criticism*, 117).

Although Watson argues that this is a digression (Watson, "Rhetorical Analysis," 71-72), we concur with Black (following Culpepper) who sees Paul intentionally inserting two *exempla* to illustrate his preceding paraenetic comments (Black, "Discourse Structure," 29; R. Alan Culpepper, "Co-workers in Suffering: Philippians 2:19-30," *RevExp* 77 [1980]: 357).

62 Davis, *Oral Biblical Criticism*, 151. The "seam" in 3:1 between these sections of 1:12-2:30 and 3:1-4:9 has caused problems for exegetes, since τὸ λοιπόν has been understood to mean "finally," indicating closure of the letter. The term μόνον ("only") both furthers the argument of the preceding section and provides the transition to the topic of unity. Silva, following Schenk and Gnilka, translate this as an emphatic ("above all") akin to how it is used in Gal 2:10 and 5:13 (Moisés Silva, *Philippians* [2nd ed.; BECNT; Grand Rapids: Baker Academic, 2005], 79). Davis argues that it is an adverbial inferential conjunction that "break[s] away from, while at the same time, drawing a conclusion from, what has been said in the previous unit" (Davis, *Oral Biblical Criticism*, 122).

with instructions (3:2-3), followed by a presentation of three examples (3:4-4:3), concluding with instructions (4:4-9). Paul's use of a warning at the outset of this section (3:2-3) is used as a reminder of the value of the gospel, which nothing can surpass. That which is truly valuable is not what the Judaizers think, i.e., earthly accomplishments and external ritual.[63] They therefore need to beware of them. Paul himself could potentially boast about such things (3:4-6). But that which is of ultimate value is knowing Christ (3:7-11). Everything is refuse in comparison to surpassing greatness of knowing Christ, and it is this, which is Paul's greatest desire.

Paul is clear that he has not "arrived" (3:12-16) but that he makes it his top priority to pursue this goal of knowing Christ (recalling 1:6, where the work in them has begun and needs to be completed). He appeals to them (3:15-16) to adopt this perspective as well.

On the heels of this discussion of Paul's ultimate passion, he again addresses the Philippians directly (3:17-21), calling them to imitate him (3:17) as well as to seek out other exemplars (τύπον) to imitate. He then presents two sets of negative examples. The first set (3:18-21) is provided as a direct contrast to the example of Paul. He wants the Philippians not to imitate those who characterized as enemies of the cross, selfish (i.e., they do not seek unity), and earthly minded (3:18-19).

Another factor that has been at times overlooked is the function of the two instances of τὸ λοιπόν in this section (3:1; 4:8). They seem to function as an inclusio, tying this second half of the body together.

Black argues further: "the passage itself reveals a typical Pauline strategy. We have seen how Paul cites Christ, Timothy, and Epaphroditus as examples bolstering his exhortations in 1:27-2:4. The only example conspicuously absent is Paul himself. His own example of proper thinking in chap. 3 would act as a logical extension to his argument in 1:12-2:30. Adducing himself or certain aspects of his behavior to buttress his hortatory appeals is a typical Pauline move" (Black, "Discourse Structure," 40 n. 39).

63 The fact that so little time is spent dealing with those mentioned in 3:2 leads us to understand this as somewhat of a foil. Paul, in leading up to the delicate situation of 4:2-3, wishes to underscore the importance of the gospel. He thus does this on the backdrop of those who radically distort this gospel. We concur with Davis who writes: "It is my contention that their [i.e., the adversaries] identity is of little concern to Paul in this letter. Rather than using certain grounds to argue against a specific threat to the church, as is the case in letters such as those to the Galatians and Corinthians, he is dealing with the topic of unity in the church (the problem with Euodia and Syntyche in 4:2-3) and, in reference to that topic, drawing antithetical examples as the need arises. Whether the opponents are within or outside of the church in 1:28, Jews or Judaizers in 3:2, or Judaizers or libertarians in 3:18-19, is neither discernable from the letter nor important to his discussion. In the same way, whether Paul is referring to threats which are past, present or future is also unknowable" (Davis, *Oral Biblical Criticism*, 125-26 n. 93; Garland, "Composition and Unity," 166).

The description of these enemies functions as a transition for final negative example found in 4:1-3. Davis observes that Paul's strategy is to narrow "the circle of opponents to a tight group which displays characteristics seen in Euodia and Syntyche." By doing this he is "preparing for the direct application of his instruction to an immediate problem in the church."[64]

The re-use of two key terms στήκετε, συνήθλησαν clearly echoes 1:27, functioning as an inclusio, to draw his discussion of this section to a close.[65] The verbal parallels are striking:

> 1:27 οὗ εὐαγγελίου τοῦ Χριστοῦ πολιτεύεσθε, ἵνα εἴτε ἐλθὼν καὶ ἰδὼν ὑμᾶς εἴτε ἀπὼν ἀκούω τὰ περὶ ὑμῶν, ὅτι στήκετε ἐν ἑνὶ πνεύματι, μιᾷ ψυχῇ συναθλοῦντες τῇ πίστει τοῦ εὐαγγελίου

> 3:20-4:3 ἡμῶν γὰρ τὸ πολίτευμα ἐν οὐρανοῖς ὑπάρχει . . . οὕτως στήκετε ἐν κυρίῳ . . . τὸ αὐτὸ φρονεῖν ἐν κυρίῳ . . . ἐν τῷ εὐαγγελίῳ συνήθλησάν μοι

Paul brings up here for the first time in the letter an extremely sensitive issue: a dispute between two women in the church who have been co-strugglers and co-workers (συνήθλησάν . . . καὶ συνεργῶν) of Paul (4:2-3). This is a dispute that has mushroomed into a community-wide problem, and we would argue is probably the covert reason for the writing of this letter.[66] With the explicit terminological linkage back to 1:27, the *general* call to stand firm and strive together (στήκετε, συνήθλησαν) finds its *specific* expression in the call of 4:1-3 for the church to stand firm (στήκετε, 4:1) and aid Euodia and Syntyche, who strove (συνήθλησάν, 4:3) as Paul's coworkers in the gospel, to overcome their disagreement.

Here is where the concept of Pauline letters as "oral performance" is key to understanding the logic of the letter's development:[67] The previous chapter

---

64 Davis, *Oral Biblical Criticism*, 131.

65 Black argues that στήκετε in 4:1 is linked back to 1:27 and refers here to 4:2-9, which provides "a concrete description of how the Philippians are to 'stand firm'" (Black, "Discourse Structure," 42. n.45). This is contra Silva, who argues that it refers to the previous section (Silva, *Philippians*[1992], 217). Davis, also noting the link with 1:27 argues that it is bringing the entire discussion between 1:27 and 4:1 to its climax (Davis, *Oral Biblical Criticism*, 86).

66 "It is my contention that Paul carefully and covertly wove his argument to lead up to the impassioned summons in 4:2. He wrote primarily to defuse the dispute between these two women that was having disastrous repercussion for the unity of the church" (Garland, "Composition and Unity," 173). Davis picks this up and concludes that "if [Garland] is correct, this sub-unit is the climax, not only of the unit 3.1-4.3, but of the entire letter" (Davis, *Oral Biblical Criticism*, 133).

67 For the importance of orality on the development of the structure of the letter, see the following discussions: Fee, *Philippians*, 14-15; John D. Harvey, *Listening to the Text: Oral Patterning in Paul's Letters* (ETSS 1; Grand Rapids: Baker, 1998); Gordon D. Fee, "To What End Exegesis? Reflections on Exegesis and Spirituality

(3:1-21), which recalls the importance of knowing Christ as the ultimate goal in life, will have played a crucial role in emotionally preparing the community to deal adequately and sensitively with this problem. This church would have all been together listening to the reading by the messenger (Epaphroditus?). They will have still ringing in their ears Paul's vivid, emotional description of the value of knowing Christ as the ultimate goal in life, to which nothing can compare, and for which everything else is worth giving up to attain. The listeners will have present in their mind's eye, the examples of Christ, Timothy, Epaphroditus, and Paul in how they lived selfless lives for the advancement of the gospel. With all this still resounding in their minds and hearts, they will have been mentally and emotionally prepared to receive Paul's instruction on how to deal with their problem.[68]

As we come to the final paraenetic section of the body of the letter (4:4-9), Paul gives instructions that grow out of his previous discussion. The first set of instructions (4:4-7) deals with the topics of rejoicing, prayer, and experiencing the resulting peace of God. The themes and examples mentioned previously in the letter (unity, humility, service, advancing the gospel, persecution) would still be ringing in their ears and would speak powerfully to their present situation and the need for joy, prayer, trust, peace.

The final (τὸ λοίπον) set of instructions (4:8-9) are phrased in global language (ὅσα, ἃ) and brings to a conclusion the instructional section of the letter.[69] A dual call is presented here: (1) they should train their minds to focus on positive, virtuous things (in contrast to focusing on things that cause grumbling and disputes) (4:8, cf. 2:14), and (2) they are called to holistic imitation by putting into practice all (ἃ) that they have received from him, either in written form or in person (4:9).

The letter closes with extended thanks for the physical proof of their gift (συγκοινωνήσαντές) the gift they sent to him through Epaphroditus (4:10-20), followed by the official letter closing (4:21-23).

6.1.3 Exegetical Notes Bearing on the Concept of Imitation

The call to imitation in 3:17 comes at the end of a series of examples (Jesus 2:5-11), Timothy (2:19-24), Epaphroditus (2:25-30), and Paul (3:4-16). The paragraph of 3:17-21 draws out the paraenetic implications of the previous discussion and functions as a conclusion to the discussion up to this point. This

---

in Philippians 4:10-20," *BBR* 8 (1998): 75-88; Davis, *Oral Biblical Criticism*, 11-63.

68 Paul's moving, emotional description of the unsurpassing value of knowing Christ would have probably caused them, by the sheer nature of the contrast with their own petty problems, to see that there was truly no reason to cling to their disagreements.

69 Davis, *Oral Biblical Criticism*, 136.

paragraph has three discernable sections: (1) a call to imitation of proper models (v. 17); (2) a warning and description of those who do not walk as Paul does (3:18-19), who are marked by selfish desires;[70] and (3) the earthly mindset between these individuals in v. 18-19 as contrasted with the heavenly mindset exemplified by Paul (3:20-21).

Grammatically, the call to imitation in 3:17 has a strong parallel structure, which needs to be unpacked in order to determine the nature, content, and focus of this imitation.[71]

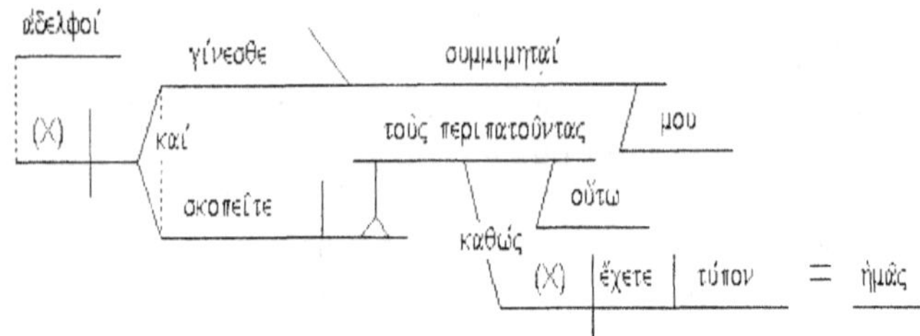

(V. 17a.) How is the term συμμιμηταί as well as the complete phrase συμμιμηταί μου γίνεσθε to be understood? This phrase has been translated in the following ways: "be imitators/followers together of me" (ASV, KJV); "join in imitating me/following my example" (ESV, NAU, RSV, NRS); "take me as your example" (BBE); the NJB, in line with the theme of unity in the letter, translates it as "be united in imitating me;" the NIV's "join with others in following my example" leaves it unclear as to who these "others" are and hints that these "others" may be outside the Philippian fellowship.

The term συμμιμηταί is a hapax legomenon, but as Fee points out, there are a considerable number of compound words beginning with συν, and a number of them are also unique in the NT.[72] The high number of hapaxes with the prefix

70 The terminology indicates that these are individual who claimed to be believers who either have rejected the Christian message or have a strongly distorted understanding of it. O'Brien argues that these enemies of the cross most likely refer to those professing to be Christians, "since the wording suggests some kind of claim to being related to Christ's saving death, and is unlikely to have been used of unbelieving Jews or Gentiles" (O'Brien, *Philippians*, 452). The theme of living for selfish purposes resurfaces here.

71 BibleWorks on CD-ROM. Ver. 7.0, 2006.

72 Hapax legomena in the NT: συναθλεω (1:27; 4:3), σύμψυχοι (2:2), συμμορφιζὸμενος (3:10), σύζυγε (4:3). Pauline hapax legomena: συγκοινωνήσαντές (4:14, compare Eph 5:13; Rev 18:4), συλλαμβάνου (4:3) (Fee, *Philippians*, 19 n. 53-54). In addition, Fee correctly points out that the hapaxes that are derived from compound terms of

συν gives indication that, as we have seen above, Paul is intending to stress the theme of unity among the Philippians. It seems natural, then, to read συμμιμηταί as another instance of Paul wishing to reinforce this theme of unity within the Philippian community—that is, they are to be jointly imitators together.[73] This way of reading it would indicate that the joint imitation refers to the Philippians specifically and not to being fellow imitators with Paul.[74] Further, this reading argues against a generalized understanding of imitation, since the issue of unity in the Philippian church is the object of concern in this letter. "Those already imitating Paul" are not mentioned and are of no relevance to imitation here. Paul does not seem to be appealing to these others to encourage their imitation.

To summarize: the phrase συμμιμηταί μου γίνεσθε refers specifically to the joint imitation of the Philippians of Paul.

What, however, are they specifically to imitate in the context of this passage? We will argue against the first five proposals mentioned above and opt for the sixth one.

(1) The proposal, that it is a general call to imitate Paul's way of life in Christ, does not do sufficient justice to the contextual shape of imitation as Paul understands it, as well as the emphases he is stressing here. This does not imply that Paul does not see himself as a general example (the call to imitation in 4:9 indicates this), but simply to say that this proposal is an assertion that does not deal with the specific argument Paul has developed up to 3:17.[75]

(2) The view that imitation refers to 1:12-26—more specifically to Paul's experience of "suffering with joy" (parallel to 1 Thess 1:6)—simply bypasses the immediately preceding context as insignificant. In fact, the reverse is the case. The primary understanding would be the immediate context of 3:4-14, with 1:12-26 as being secondary and supportive material to his discussion in 3:4-14. It is not that these passages stand in opposition to one another. Rather, it is simply that Paul would have had 3:4-14 primarily in mind, since that

---

preposition + known noun/verb should be seen with respect to the term from which they derive (19 n. 55).

73 Louw and Nida translate it thus as "joint imitator" (L&N 1989, 508.). BDAG, however, leaves it open: "join (w. the other) in following my example" (958). Stanley sees it also as referring to unity, but translates it as "remain united in becoming imitators of me" (Stanley, "Become Imitators," 871). This could be justified from the intention of the letter, but such a translation is somewhat strained in this context.

74 This argues against option one mentioned above under "Understandings of Imitation." This way of reading—that it is joint imitation with Paul—suffers also from not being able to explain the μου, which in all the other cases of μιμητής + γίνομαι + μου always refers to the object of imitation.

75 Hawthorne, for example, imports the various understandings of imitation from other sections of the Pauline corpus into this context and does not specifically anchor his understanding of imitation to the immediate context (Hawthorne, *Philippians*, 159).

immediately preceded it. The counter-argument, that in 3:4-14 there is nothing "concrete" to imitate, and that all one could imitate is a mental change in ones thinking, is relativized by the overview of imitation in antiquity we presented in chapter two, in which we saw that there was no strict division between internal values and external actions with respect to the concept of imitation. Imitation could and did refer to both.

(3) Michaelis sees the call to imitation here, as he does in every imitation text, as a call to obedience based on Paul's apostolic authority.[76] However, a number of points work against this view: (a) The emphasis on apostolic authority is lacking in this context.[77] (b) Indeed, Paul avoids the use of authority and takes pains to stress here that he is, in some sense, on their level as a "brother" (ἀδελφός).[78] (c) The whole thrust of the prior argumentation is

---

76 Michaelis, *TWNT* 4:670; Wilhelm Michaelis, *Der Brief des Paulus an die Philipper* (THKNT 11; Leipzig: Deichertsche Verlagsbuchhandlung, 1935), 61.

77 Fiore vigorously opposes Michaelis' view since "the notion of apostolic command is quite alien to this passage" (Fiore, *Personal Example*, 185). However, Fortna is convinced that the letter of Philippians displays the height of Pauline egotism: "Yes, Philippians is surely Paul's most self-centered letter, the most subtly arrogant of all . . . . The honesty of Paul's display of shamelessness is almost admirable" (Robert T. Fortna, "Philippians: Paul's Most Egocentric Letter," in *The Conversation Continues: Studies in Paul and John in Honor of J. Louis Martyn* [ed. Robert T. Fortna and Beverly Roberts Gaventa; Nashville: Abingdon, 1990], 230). Fortna approaches the letter to Philippians with a modernist understanding of what constitutes humility and self-centeredness, gravely misunderstand the role Paul plays with respect to the Philippians, the pedagogical dynamics involved in his interaction with them, the mindset of the Greco and Judaic world of that time, and ancient understandings of what constitute humility and egotism.

Indeed, the tone of the whole letter controverts Fortna's case. Paul is described as one who lives a self-sacrificial life for the sake of Christ and for the sake of his spiritual children. His rhetoric would be easily parallel to physical parents in their appeals to their physical children. Arrogance should not be confused with the explanation of the nature and dynamics of Paul's relationship to the church he founded. Thus, we concur with Scott and Wicks: "[Paul's] apparent egotism in this and similar appeals has often been misunderstood. We need to remember that his readers were Gentiles to whom the Christian ethic was altogether new. They could make nothing of it unless they saw it in action, and Paul considered it one of his chief duties to exemplify in his own person the things he taught" (Scott and Wicks, *Philippians*, 95-96).

78 Andrew Clarke has recently deflated the notion that the term ἀδελφοι by definition implies equality: "It may be that Paul's use of egalitarian language is disingenuous. This may be analogous to the widespread social custom of a Graeco-Roman patron publicly addressing his client as 'friend' (*amicus*), when the relationship is self-evidently one of hierarchy, and fuelled by debt, not affection" (Andrew D. Clarke, "Equality or Mutuality? Paul's Use of 'Brother' Language," in *The New Testament in Its First Century Setting: Essays on Context and Background in Honour of Bruce W. Winter on His 65th Birthday* [ed. P. J. Williams, et al.; Grand Rapids: Eerdmans,

appealing to his example (3:4-14). (d) Paul is seen as reasoning with them (3:15-16), something unnecessary, if he could simply assert his authority. The expression τοῦτο φρονῶμεν (3:15) invites reflection, is written as a subjunctive not imperative, in which Paul himself (first person plural) is included. (e) In 3:17b he includes others as equally legitimate examples to follow.

(4) The suggestion that Paul was intending them to reflect on the model he left with them when he was with them also does not carry full weight since there is no hint of that in the context. Surely, the Philippians would have thought back on Paul's time with them and would have brought that into alignment with what he had just mentioned, but that is not mentioned in this context as the primary focus.

(5) Garland's suggestion that imitation here refers back to 3:4-14, specifically to adopting Paul's attitude of refusing to pride oneself on the basis of "flesh categories" as well as acknowledging that he is not yet perfect[79]—is correct insofar as it goes. However, it does not grasp the breadth of the content of 3:4-14 sufficiently. There is more to imitation in 3:4-14 than these two aspects he suggests.

(6) We hold the sixth option—that the content of 3:4-14 is what Paul intended them to imitate—to be the correct one for the following reasons.[80] (a) The call to imitation comes immediately after Paul has given an extended explanation about himself and his thinking. (b) This way of thinking (τούτο φρονῶμεν . . . φρονεῖτε) can be imitated, and has been used with reference to the Philippians imitating Christ in 2:5 (τοῦτο φρονεῖτε). (c) When one considers the thought-flow of Paul as he was writing/dictating the letter, it is most natural to assume that what Paul most recently had mentioned about himself is the referent to imitation. (d) When one considers the oral dimension of the letter

---

2004], 157). After a look at the documentary papyri, Clarke concludes that "brotherly love" is concerned more with mutuality than with equality and (quoting Arzt-Grabner) expresses "closeness, solidarity and some kind of bond or engagement" (164).

Although I would not deny this, nonetheless it does seem that Paul in some sense uses the term to indicate that they are spiritually on the same level. At the same time, it is clear that, from the standpoint of their faith, he is their spiritual father and that there is a natural status differential because of that. Thus, he is at the same time an equal as well as a model.

Looking at this text from the vantage point of Paul exerting power and authority over the Philippians, there seems to be no hint of pride in this context. On the contrary, Paul describes himself as not having arrived (3:12-14) and as seeking to be a servant to them for the sake of the gospel. Yet, he is nevertheless confident that his embodiment of the gospel and its values are a reliable guide for the Philippians. For a similar perspective, see Hawthorne, *Philippians*, 161.

79 Garland, "Composition and Unity," 171.

80 These reasons overlap to varying degrees, but contain different nuances that can be understood as further arguments.

and the thought-flow, we suggest that when the Philippians heard this call to imitation, there would have been an immediate association in their minds with what Paul had most recently related about himself. (e) The other options do not answer adequately the question as to why Paul does *not* intend 3:4-14 as the content of imitation. (f) Further, there are no textual indicators around 3:17 that Paul intended these other options mentioned above. We conclude that the phrase συμμιμηταί μου γίνεσθε looks back at the illustration of Paul's example that is reflected primarily in 3:4-14, and only secondarily to other references to Paul's example in Philippians.

The specific content of imitation in 3:4-14 can be more narrowly delineated to include the following: (1) Paul's decision to put confidence in Christ and not in the flesh ([οὐκ] ἔχων πεποίθησιν καὶ ἐν σαρκί, i.e., accomplishments and external factors, which society considers important) (3:3-6). (2) Paul's utter rejection of all these factors (mentioned in the previous point) because of the surpassing value of knowing Christ (3:7-9). (3) Paul's pursuit of the ultimate goals of knowing Christ, his resurrection power, and the fellowship of his sufferings in order to attain to the resurrection from the dead (3:10-11). (4) Paul's acknowledgement of not having yet achieved and his intense pursuit of these things (3:12). (5) The way that Paul intensely pursued these things: as one pursues an ultimate prize (σκοπὸν)—i.e., forgetting the past and straining toward the future (3:14).

Another dimension of the imitation of Paul in this section has to do with the strong parallelism between 3:4-14 and 2:5-11. As has been mentioned above in the sections "Thought-flow," there are close terminological, structural, and thematic parallels between Paul's self-description in 3:4-14 and the description of Christ in 2:5-11. This direct paralleling indicates that Paul intentionally conformed his thinking and lifestyle to that of Christ. Indeed, the intense focus on pursuing Christ to the radical exclusion of everything else in life, graphically described in 3:4-14, strongly reinforces this parallelism between these two sections. Thus to imitate Paul was virtually to be imitating Christ.[81]

The understanding of imitation is given more nuance also by the additional comments following the call to imitation in 3:17b and 3:18-21.

(V. 17b) The structural parallelism with the preceding command (γίνεσθε = σκοπεῖτε, both second person plural imperatives) indicates that the careful observation is for the purposes of imitating these individuals. The term σκοπεῖτε[82] indicates carefully observing or paying careful attention to

81 Further, if this is in fact the case that Paul is intentionally patterning his life on Christ's, then one could legitimately take the paraenetic section of 2:1-4, which frames Paul's use of the example of Christ, and see that as applying to Paul as well, defining how Paul also thought and lived.

82 There are six instances of this term in the NT, once in the Gospels (Luk 11:35) and five times in the uncontested Pauline letters: Rom 16:17; 2 Cor 4:18; Gal 6:1 and twice in Philippians (2:4; 3:17).

something.[83] The object of σκοπεῖτε is the phrase "those who live" (τοὺς . . . περιπατοῦντας) and reveals another dimension to the understanding of imitation in this context. The term περιπατοῦντες indicates it is not merely the thought-processes and values that are in view; rather, the totality of the lifestyle is what is intended to be imitated.[84] One's basic values shape the thoughts, which then are translated into concrete action, the long-term outcome of which is the development of a lifestyle.

Davis observes that oral cultures are characterized by appeal to proper and improper examples:

> It must be remembered that in an oral community, people tend to act a certain way not because they consider it philosophically right but because they are following the example of a hero or avoiding the example of a villain.[85]

This is certainly an aspect of the argumentation here. We note especially the contrasts here developed between (a) "the dogs" (3:2) and Paul (3:4-14) as well as (b) the positive examples of 3:17 and their negative counterparts (3:18-19 and 4:1-3).

To whom is Paul referring, when he speaks of τοὺς . . . περιπατοῦντας? There seem to be a number of possibilities, among which are: (1) Christians or churches in other places;[86] (2) Paul's colleagues in the work of ministry, including Timothy and Epaphroditus; (3) various itinerant teachers who traveled through the area;[87] (4) The church leaders in Philippi.[88]

---

83 BDAG, 931. The translation of the ASV, KJV, and RSV "mark" does not accord with modern usage, with its negative connotation ("he's a marked man") and is easily misunderstood. The translation "observe" (NAU, NRS, NAB) or "pay attention to" (CJB) does not bring across the concept of *careful* observation sufficiently. The NIV's "take note of" is better, but would have been strengthened by "take *careful* note of." The ESV's "keep your eyes on" is close, but the NJB's translation "keep your eyes fixed on" and the NET's "watch carefully" bring out the meaning of the term in this context admirably.

84 Again, this must not be understood to be wooden copying. Danker sums up the metaphorical usages of περιπατεω as: 'to conduct ones life,' 'live as a habit of conduct' (BDAG, 803).

85 Davis, *Oral Biblical Criticism*, 66.

86 Michaelis, *Philipper*, 61.

87 This is Fee's suggestion, who notes this with reference to those described in 3:18-21: "Fully aware that not all who would come through were of the same mind as Paul regarding walking in the ways of Christ, he has frequently warned them of such itinerants (as vv. 1 and 18 indicate)" (Fee, *Philippians*, 366). It is further of note that the emphasis here is not on false teaching, but rather a false lifestyle, which is implied by the use of περιπατέω.

88 So Alfred Plummer, *Commentary on St. Paul's Epistle to the Philippians* (London: Robert Scott, 1919), 81; O'Brien, *Philippians*, 449; de Boer, *Imitation*, 181-82. Lohmeyer, falsely, sees "Philippian martyrs" as behind much of the discussion in

There are a number of indicators in the text that help to clarify to whom he is referring. The insertion of the adverb οὕτω as well as the subordinate clause καθὼς ἔχετε τύπον ἡμᾶς clarifies and delimits what type of imitation is being referred to: it is parallel to how Paul himself conducts his life as outlined in 3:4-14. The articular participle τοὺς περιπατοῦντας seems to indicate a class of people broader than just the Philippians,[89] who share the characteristic of living/thinking as Paul did. The subordinate conjunction καθὼς is used in a comparative/correlative sense, paralleling the lifestyle with the example[90] Paul gave them.

The word τύπον, however, indicates that these people are more mature in the faith and would be looked upon in some sense as leaders. Nevertheless, Paul does not wish to limit the exemplars it to an identifiable group and speaks broadly of τοὺς . . . περιπατοῦντας. He leaving it up to the Philippians themselves to determine—based on drawing analogies between Paul and these exemplars—whom they should imitate. It seems then, that τοὺς . . . περιπατοῦντας in this context refers to all people who live in line with the lifestyle of Paul portrayed as portrayed in 3:1-14, including Fee's suggestion of itinerants, as proper objects of imitation.[91]

When we consider the development of the argument in this letter in light of the oral performance of the reading of this letter, it would seem that the hearers would immediately associate this with the examples that Paul provided immediately before his own example, that is, the examples of Timothy (who is soon to visit) and Epaphroditus (one of their own and the carrier of this letter) as they are portrayed in 2:19-30. Paul has described these two individuals in language that thematically parallels Paul's own perspective in 3:4-14 and the example of Christ in 2:5-11.[92]

Another strong indication that Timothy and Epaphroditus are intended is the

---

this letter and argues that they are in mind here (Ernst Lohmeyer, *Die Briefe an die Philipper, an die Kolosser und an Philemon* (KEK; Göttingen: Vandenhoeck & Ruprecht, 1929), 151-52).

89 Fee, *Philippians*, 366; Markus Bockmuehl, *A Commentary on the Epistle to the Philippians* (BNTC; London: Black, 1997), 229.

90 τύπον is translated "pattern" (NIV, NAU), "example/ensample" (RSV, NJB, NRS, KJV, ASV), "model" (DRA, DBY, NAB).

91 Similarly, Fee: "Although this may well include some among the Philippians 'who walk thus' (Epaphroditus, for example), the grammar and language of this clause imply a more comprehensive group of people, reaching beyond the Philippians themselves" (Fee, *Philippians*, 365-66).

92 Timothy: taking a genuine interest in other's welfare (2:20); looking out for the interests of Christ (2:21); serving in the work of the gospel (2:22). Epaphroditus: fellow worker and soldier (2:25); longing for the Philippians and being distressed for them (2:26); almost dying for the work of Christ (2:30); risking his life in place of the Philippians (2:30).

accusative pronoun "us" in the phrase ἔχετε τύπον ἡμᾶς.[93] Some commentators see this as a "rare editorial we" in which only Paul is intended.[94] Others see it as referring to Timothy as co-author.[95] However, a simpler explanation is that it was Paul along with his colleagues, Timothy and Epaphroditus he had just mentioned that Paul had in mind. This reading nicely deals with the problem of the unusual editorial "we" and also makes sense of the language Paul chose to describe Timothy and Epaphroditus in 2:19-30.[96] It also dovetails with Davis' observation that "the imperative call to imitation in v. 17 . . . draws not only from vv. 4-16 but from the rest of the examples in the earlier part of the letter."[97]

(V. 18-19) We are further helped in understanding the meaning of imitation in 3:17 through the strong contrast Paul provides in vv. 18-19: the Philippians are to be imitators of Paul *in contrast to* the individuals described in 3:18-21.[98]

The term περιπατέω is picked up from v. 17 and re-used in v. 18 to contrast the lifestyle of those individuals who live in a manner diametrically opposed to the positive examples mentioned in the letter to this point (Jesus, Paul, Timothy, Epaphroditus). This passage is linked closely both terminologically and thematically with Phil 3:17 and the preceding section (3:4-14). This

---

93 There are two basic usages of the double accusative: (1) identifying personal and impersonal objects and (2) identifying primary and secondary objects, in which the secondary object is in apposition with the primary object (James A. Brooks and Carlton L. Winbery, *Syntax of New Testament Greek* [Washington D.C.: University Press of America, 1983], 47). The second makes best sense of this text, making τύπον an apposition to ἡμᾶς: i.e., "just as you have us as your example."

94 For a clear argumentation of this position, see Hawthorne, *Philippians*, 160-61.

95 So Fee, *Philippians*, 61.

96 This is also the argumentation of O'Brien, who "that regards ἡμᾶς as referring to both Paul, the dominant member of the team, and his associates such as Timothy and Epaphroditus. The change from singular . . . to plural . . . in the middle of the sentence tells against the idea that the plural speaks of Paul alone" (*Philippians*, 450). O'Brien also notes that an "adequate explanation for this change has not been given by those who suggest that ἡμᾶς refers to Paul alone" (450 n. 26). So also Llewelyn: "Philippians, though the opening greetings are by Paul and Timothy, must be considered the most individual of Paul's letters. All plural with the exception of one (Phil.3:17) must be classed as literary plurals" (S. R. Llewelyn, "Ammonius to Appolonios [*P.Oxy.* XLII 3057]: The Earliest Christian Letter on Papyrus?" *NewDocs* 6:171-72).

97 Davis, *Oral Biblical Criticism*, 130.

98 Even though Paul does not explicitly verbalize this, the sheer juxtaposition of Paul's self-description (3:4-14) with these enemies of the cross (3:18-19)—in the midst of which is sandwiched the call to imitation (3:17)—implies that there are other potential exemplars, which the Philippians should not imitate. Thus Jewett correctly observes, these people "present a tempting model for Christian existence" (quoted in O'Brien, *Philippians*, 453).

negative model[99] provides further information to the Philippians as to what characteristics they are and what they are not to imitate. Through this rhetorical strategy, we can add precision and depth to the content of their imitation.[100]

Paul frames his discussion of these negative exemplars (see below) by beginning with a categorization of who they are ("enemies of the cross")[101] and ending with a categorization of the fundamental mindset that leads one to become an enemy of the cross ("earthly thinking"). The second descriptive element indicates their ultimate destiny ("their end is destruction"). The third and fourth elements ("whose god is their belly" and "whose glory is their shame"), grammatically linked together and are the concrete expression of the general description of the closing element—earthly thinking.[102]

1) They live as—or declare themselves to be—enemies of the cross.
2) Their ultimate destiny is destruction.
3) Their "god" is their own selfish desires.
4) Their glory is their shame.
5) Their mindset is oriented toward earthly things.

By implication, if the Philippians were imitators of Paul and τοὺς οὕτω περιπατοῦντας (v. 17b), they would be characterized by the flip-side of these characteristics; that is,

1) they would commit themselves to the cross and all it encompasses;
2) their ultimate destiny is eternal life;
3) they would not serve their selfish, earthly desire, but the God of heaven;

---

99 Fee already sees them in 3:17b (as does Davis), but the shift to these others only occurs grammatically in 3:18 (Fee, *Philippians*, 366; Davis, *Oral Biblical Criticism*, 130).

100 VV. 18-19 is one intricate sentence. For a solid discussion of the grammatical structure and exegetical issues, see Fee, *Philippians*, 368-75.

101 The narrower identification of who these were does not concern our focus on imitation, nor does it seem possible to discover who they were (Silva, *Philippians*[2005], 180). Fee does, however, make a strong case (as mentioned above) that these πολλοὶ . . . περιπατοῦσιν refer to other religious itinerants who were traveling about (Fee, *Philippians*, 366). That the concept of religious itineracy is established seems clear from the reference to those preaching Christ for less than positive motivations in 1:15-17, who in that context, function as negative exemplars. What may be observed, however, is Paul's emotion in v. 18 νῦν δὲ καὶ κλαίων, which seems to indicate former believers who either have rejected the gospel, or have, as the "dogs" in 3:2, so severely distorted the gospel that they are now preaching a doctrine that is the polar opposite of Paul's gospel.

102 Commentators are all over the map, what these two phrases might mean. Beyond the understanding of the individual words themselves, "in terms of specifics, we are largely in the dark" (Fee, *Philippians*, 373).

4) their glory is that which is honorable;
5) their mindset is oriented toward heavenly things.

The only item in this list that is not inimitable is the second one. All other items clearly echo fundamental themes of selfless service for others for the sake of the gospel that run throughout the entire letter and are evident in the description of Paul in 3:4-14.

6.1.4 Summary of Imitation in Philippians 3:17

To summarize: συμμιμηταί μου γίνεσθε refers specifically to the joint imitation by the Philippians of Paul. The content of Paul's call to imitation in 3:17a is specifically found in 3:4-14. The main elements of this imitation are the following. (1) One should put exclusive confidence in Christ as the source of what is of value and not on those things society considers as important (3:3-6). (2) One should reject all that society considers of value in light of that which is most valuable of all: knowing Christ (3:7-9). (3) One should intensely pursue that which is of ultimate value, which is described as knowing: (a) Christ's resurrection power, (b) the fellowship of his sufferings in order to (c) attain to the resurrection from the dead (3:10-11). (4) One should humbly acknowledge one's own imperfection and at the same time pursue relentlessly those things mentioned in the previous point—being fully cognizant that it is for these reasons that Christ has pursued us (3:12). (5) One should develop the mindset that has a singular focus as an athlete in pursuit of the ultimate prize, which is further characterized by letting go of things in the past and looking intentionally toward the future.

This content of Pauline imitation is further amplified in 3:18-19, where Paul contrasts what one should not emulate. Inverting the description of these negative examples gives us three additional characteristics, which are implicit in 3:4-14: (1) they do not focus on satisfying selfish desires ("Their God is [not] their stomach"). (2) Their glory is that which is honorable and leads to honor in the sight of God. (3) Their mindset is characterized by a fundamental orientation toward the values and goals of heaven.

A final comment: Even though these things are the specific focus of Pauline imitation here, this does not imply that Pauline imitation generally is reduced to these elements. It means simply that the focus of imitation in this context is on these items. This call to imitation is, however, expanded in 17b to include others who walk in the same manner as Paul.

6.2 Philippians 4:9

Phil. 4:9 does not contain technical imitation terminology of the sort we encountered in the previous passages, but the thrust of this verse indicates clearly that Paul is intended to function as a model for the Philippians to imitate.

6.2.1 Understandings of Imitation and Other Issues in this Context

There appears to be little debate in the literature about the understanding of imitation in this context. Virtually all the commentators see this call to imitation in global terms that encompass the totality of Paul's Christ-centered message and his manner of life and thought that has emerged out of Paul's experience and understanding of Christ. Three major questions stand out as important with respect to understanding imitation in this passage. (1) How should one understand the verbal string "you have learned and received and heard and seen" and what is the interrelationship of these verbs one to another? Do they all refer to the same thing? To different things? Is there a natural grouping intended by Paul? (2) How does the prepositional phrase ἐν ἐμοί relate to the four preceding verbs? Does it refer to all the verbs? To a subset of these verbs? (3) How does this verse relate to the previous verse and to the preceding context? We will seek to answer the first two questions below under "Exegetical Comments." The third question is related to the development of the argument, to which we now will turn.

6.2.2 Development of the Argument[103]

After Paul in 4:2-3 finally discloses the concrete problem of disunity he has been covertly addressing throughout the letter, he moves into paraenesis from 4:4-9, which is divided into two sections, the first of which (4:4-7) seems to build directly on 4:2-3, indicating the way one should deal with such problems as in the case of Euodia and Syntyche. Paul emphasizes the need for intentionally rejoicing in the Lord (4:4), dealing gently (ἐπιεικὲς) with one another (4:5), and underscoring the role of replacing worry with faith-filled prayer, which results in a supernatural experience of peace (4:6-7).

The last set of instructions (4:8-9)[104] is marked off from the others through the phrase τὸ λοιπόν, indicating a strong transition.[105] These verses contain the final two commands/calls of the letter, which are framed in global terms (ὅσα v. 8, ἃ v. 9). These seem to bring to a close both the paraenetic section 4:4-9 as

---

103 The fuller discussion of this has been undertaking in the discussion of Phil. 3:17. We limit our comments to a brief discussion of the logic and flow of 4:4-9.

104 Gnilka sees these two verses as the work of the redactor (Gnilka, *Philipperbrief*, 200-02).

105 Hawthorne emphasizes that τὸ λοιπόν "does not signal the end of the letter . . . or even its near end, but rather the last of the imperatives in a parenetic section that states in detail how one is to 'stand firm as a Christian'" (Hawthorne, *Philippians*, 185). For other options of how to understand this, see O'Brien, *Philippians*, 503 n. 19.

well as the major teaching section of the letter beginning with 1:27. We turn now to look more closely at these two calls, the last of which is a call to imitation.

6.2.3 Exegetical Notes Bearing on the Concept of Imitation

(V. 8) The first of these two calls presented in v. 8 has to do with developing virtuous thought-patterns ("think about these things," ταῦτα λογίζεσθε). The call is to focus intentionally one's thoughts on anything that in general is virtuous and praiseworthy (τις ἀρετὴ καὶ εἴ τις ἔπαινος).[106] The use of the term virtue (ἀρετὴ) would most likely call to mind cardinal virtues of Hellenism.[107] These six adjectives, common in the moral literature of the Greco-Roman world, would most likely have found approval by all in Roman Empire at that time. Yet Paul's specific list of virtues finds no direct parallel in Hellenistic literature.[108]

Since this is a list of Paul's own making, what purpose would Paul have in inserting such a catalogue with its unique form and content? We would suggest that this list of six virtues was intended to be a direct contrast to the unvirtuous ways of the Philippians hinted at in this letter. This would include the way of thinking embodied by Euodia and Syntyche in 4:2-3, the grumbling and disputes mentioned in 2:3-4, 14 (cf. 1:27) and the negative examples throughout the letter (cf. 1:15-18; 3:2, 18-19). Paul uses this opportunity, as founder of this community, to highlight and position key virtues, which the community should characterize their thinking (λογίζεσθε), and which should define their life together.

Yet these virtues are not to be understood within the framework of Greco-Roman morality, but within the framework of the example of Jesus as highlighted in this letter. As Fee correctly notes, "in Paul [these virtues] must be understood in light of the cross, since that is surely the point of the final proviso in v. 9 that whatever else they do, they are to follow Paul's teaching and thus imitate his cruciform lifestyle."[109]

(V. 9a) This *generalized* list of virtues in v. 8 is then supplemented by the

---

106 For a helpful discussion on how to understand these virtues and their background, since they are unusual terms for Paul and are rare in the NT, see O'Brien, *Philippians*, 499-503; Fee, *Philippians*, 414-19.

107 Plato in *The Republic* was to first to list self-control (σωφροσύνη), prudence (φρόνησις), justice (δικαιοσύνη), and courage (ἀνδρεία) as cardinal virtues (4.427-33).

108 So Fee, *Philippians*, 416. He notes that the closest parallel to the language of Paul here can actually be found in James 3:13-18 and in the wisdom tradition as mediated by Wisdom of Solomon.

109 Fee, *Philippians*, 417.

content of the second call—the call to imitation—in v. 9a,[110] in which the *specific* Christian content would shape their personal and community life. This content would be derived from the model of Paul himself, as the founder of the community, who has patterned his life on the model of Jesus. This content was transmitted to them in varied ways: learning, receiving, hearing, seeing (μάθετε καὶ παρελάβετε καὶ ἠκούσατε καὶ εἴδετε). This four-fold string of verbs highlights all the possible means available to receive instruction from another. This shift from general (v. 8) to specific (v. 9) is significant in that "general matters (ὅσα) are not now in view, but rather those particular things (ἅ) that Paul himself had taught and which the Philippians had learned from him."[111] Thus, these two calls inform one another, and help the Philippian believers to integrate the general good they know (v. 8) with their new Christian existence (v. 9), and to see the good in light of their new life in Christ.[112]

How should one understand the terms μάθετε καὶ παρελάβετε καὶ ἠκούσατε καὶ εἴδετε and how do they interrelate? We will begin with the second question, since there are clues in the context and in other parts of the letter that help us answer the first one.

Regarding the interrelationship between these four verbs, there seem to be four possibilities.[113] (1) They are a simple string of verbs that are

---

110 The structure of v. 8 and v. 9 are symmetrically developed and parallel one another closely:

v. 8 ὅσα . . . ταῦτα λογίζεσθε
v. 9 ἅ. . . ταῦτα πράσσετε

Sevenster seeks to drive a wedge between v. 8 and v. 9, seeing v. 9 as a "corrective" to v. 8, and also seeing a disjunction between λογίζεσθε and πράσσετε (J. N. Sevenster, *Paul and Seneca* [Leiden: Brill, 1961], 156). This is, however, not a correction. V. 9 is Paul's way of providing proper perspective on the commonly held values mentioned in v. 8. In addition, if Paul meant a disjunctive contrast, he could have used a disjunctive conjunction (ἀλλὰ, δὲ). For further justification of this view, see O'Brien, *Philippians*, 508. Bockmuehl summarizes this well: "The 'common sense' and general virtues of verse 8 are given definition by an appeal to this letter's specifically Christian framework of imitation" (Bockmuehl, *Philippians*, 254). He also notes that "sentences beginning with *ha kai* often introduce a further and specific elaboration of the preceding subject at hand" (254) and cites as examples 1 Cor 2:14; Gal 2:10; 1 Pet 3:2; Acts 11:30; 26:10; 2 Macc 4:33; 3 Macc 3:1.

111 Hawthorne, *Philippians*, 189.

112 Fee also notes this connection between vv. 8-9: "Read [the list of virtues in v. 8], he now tells them, in light of 'what you have learned and received and heard and seen in me,' and above all else 'put these things (you have learned, etc.) into practice'" (Fee, *Philippians*, 420).

113 For a helpful overview of the options, see O'Brien, *Philippians*, 508.

unconnected.[114] (2) The first three refer to Paul's teaching and the last to his example.[115] (3) The first two and last two are grouped together, the first pair referring to his teaching, the last pair referring to his example.[116] (4) These are seen as two pairs, the last set being seen as the content of the first set.[117]

The strongest case can be made for option three. When we examine the usage of both of these pairs both in the book and in other contexts, the first two items and the last two are clearly linked together. The clearest linkage is with the term in the second pair, ἀκούω and ὁράω. There are four indications that these two terms are to be understood together in the context of the letter. (1) These verbs have been used together three times earlier in the letter (1:27, 30; 2:26, 28). (2) The references in 1:27 and 30 refer specifically the hearing and seeing with respect to Paul and the Philippians. In 1:27 Paul is hearing and seeing them, and in 1:30 the Philippians are hearing and seeing Paul. (3) The sentence structure of the third and fourth elements in 1:30 (εἴδετε . . . καὶ νῦν ἀκούετε) points to a close relationship between seeing and hearing. This connection is further strengthened by the addition of the νῦν ("and now"). (4) The logical association between the two sensory activities of sight and hearing.

The first two items in 4:9, ἐμάθετε and παρελάβετε, are also closely linked together.[118] It is clear that one usage of each of these terms conveys the notion of teaching/learning.[119] In addition, Paul's earliest role with the church at Philippi, and the other churches he founded, was that of a teacher, from whom they are *learning* how to live as followers of Christ and from whom they have *received* the Christian Tradition.[120]

The conclusion that these first two terms are to be understood together is strengthened by examining them more closely and by identifying to what specifically they refer in this context.

---

114 Most of the translations as well as Schlier, *Philipperbrief*, 76; Hawthorne, *Philippians*, 189-90; Martin, *Philippians*, 175.

115 BBE, O'Brien also cites Goodspeed as holding this view (O'Brien, *Philippians*, 508).

116 GWN, NJB, NLT and also J. B. Lightfoot, *St Paul's Epistle to the Philippians* (London: Macmillan, 1868; repr., Lynn, Mass.: Hendrickson, 1981), 162; Vincent, *Philippians*, 140; Lohmeyer, *Briefe*, 176; Hendriksen, *Philippians*, 200; Gnilka, *Philipperbrief*, 222; Kent, "Philippians," 152; Egger, *Galater*, 71; O'Brien, *Philippians*, 509; Bockmuehl, *Philippians*, 254. Fee holds a somewhat modified view of this (Fee, *Philippians*, 420).

117 So GNB and Phillips.

118 Further argumentation is found in the discussion below of these terms.

119 Cf. μανθάνω: Deut 4:10; 1 Chr 25:8; Matt 24:32; John 7:15; παραλαμβάνω: 1 Thess 4:1; 2 Thess 3:6. Each of these terms can also refers to informal teaching/learning: (μανθάνω:) cf. Phil 4:11; Tit 3:14; (παραλαμβάνω:) Col 2:6(?); 4:17; Acts 23:18. Gal 1:12 is especially instructive, since it indicates that reception of the gospel (παρέλαβον) and teaching (ἐδιδάχθην) go hand-in-hand. See the discussion below.

120 Cf. Acts 16:13-21; Gal 1:9; 1 Cor 11:23: 15:1, 3; 1 Thess 2:13.

The first term, ἐμάθετε, has four basic usages in the NT.[121] In this context, it seems to indicate the acquisition of knowledge or skill by the act of being taught. Calling this usage into question is the use of μανθάνω two verses later (Phil 4:11), which indicates learning not from a teacher but through the experiences of life. Although this may be the usage in 4:9, the sequence of the four verbs Paul has chosen indicates that he is beginning with the reception of tradition (first two elements) and shifting to observing his life (last two elements). If ἐμάθετε refers to formal instruction in 4:9, then the accent here is on the active role of the learner.[122] What was it they learned from Paul? Although this is not defined, we are aided in our understanding of μανθάνω by the following verb, παρελάβετε, which, as we will argue below, refers to the passing on of the core elements of the Christian Tradition. This may indicate that ἐμάθετε is a broader term that "focuses on the Philippians' appropriating the teaching and instruction Paul had initially given to them."[123] This would encompass the core elements of the Christian Traditions that they *received* (παρελάβετε) but go beyond that to include all that Paul had taught them.

The second term, παρελάβετε, is used eight times in the uncontested Pauline writings, and (leaving aside Phil 4:9 for the sake of argument) refers each time to the reception of the Christian message/tradition.[124] This provides strong indication that the Christian Tradition is what Paul had in mind in 4:9.[125] This tradition (παράδοσις) can refer to the core of the gospel (1 Cor 15:1-5), core ritual acts (1 Cor 11:23-26), and ethical practice (1 Cor 11:2).[126] Although O'Brien concludes that the third usage is in view in Phil 4:9, this would lead to a virtual overlap in understanding between ἐμάθετε and παρελάβετε in this context. Given the summarizing quality of 4:9, it seems inappropriate to drive a wedge between these different understandings of παρελάβετε, but to view the term as encompassing all three dimensions.

As was argued above, the third and fourth verbs (ἠκούσατε καὶ εἴδετε) are to be understood together. The understanding of these terms in the context of 4:9 is aided by comparing it to how they are used in other parts of this letter:

---

121 "To gain knowledge or skill by instruction;" "to make the acquaintance of something;" "to come to realize, with implication of taking place less through instruction than through experience or practice;" "to hear" (BDAG, 615).

122 This is in distinction to the term διδάσκειν, which places the emphasis on the teacher.

123 O'Brien, *Philippians*, 509.

124 1 Cor 11:2, 23; 15:1, 3; Gal 1:9, 12; 1 Thess 2:13; 4:1 (cf. 2 Thess 3:6).

125 Most of the commentators hold this to be the case. However, against this see K. Wegenast, *Das Verständnis der Tradition bei Paulus in und in den Deuteropaulinen* (Neukirchen-Vluyn: Neukirchener, 1962), 113-14. Kent also makes little distinction between the two terms and sees them as "virtually synonymous" (Kent, "Philippians," 153).

126 Suggested by O'Brien, *Philippians*, 510.

1:27 ἵνα εἴτε ἐλθὼν καὶ <u>ἰδὼν</u> ὑμᾶς εἴτε ἀπὼν <u>ἀκούω</u> τὰ περὶ ὑμῶν
1:30 οἷον <u>εἴδετε</u> ἐν ἐμοὶ καὶ νῦν <u>ἀκούετε</u> ἐν ἐμοί
2:26 διότι <u>ἠκούσατε</u> ὅτι ἠσθένησεν.
2:28 ἵνα <u>ἰδόντες</u> αὐτὸν πάλιν χαρῆτε κἀγὼ ἀλυπότερος ὦ.
4:9 καὶ <u>ἠκούσατε</u> καὶ <u>εἴδετε</u> ἐν ἐμοί

The usage of these terms in 4:9, even down to their grammatical structure, clearly echoes 1:30. In addition, the use of these terms in 1:27 and 30 functions as an inclusio, setting off 1:27-30 as the central proposition of the letter,[127] which follows hard on the heels of 1:11-26, where the example of Paul suffering for the sake of the gospel is the focus. The other two instances of these two terms in the letter revolve around the example of Epaphroditus.

Since 4:9 clearly recalls 1:30, it seems that the content of the hearing and seeing in both contexts would be referring to the same things. The verb "to see" in both 1:30 and 4:9 is in identical grammatical form (εἴδετε, second person plural aorist). What they had seen was Paul's struggle for the gospel while he was with them (Acts 16:19-40). Thus, they were eyewitnesses of Paul's gospel oriented lifestyle when he was among them.[128]

There is a distinction between the form of the verb "to hear" in 1:30 and 4:9. In 1:30 it is in the present tense and is combined with a particle (νῦν ἀκούετε) that indicates current information received by a third party. This information was most likely brought and transmitted to them by Epaphroditus, the bearer of the letter. In 4:9 the verb is changed to aorist, indicating in this context something that had already taken place. The content of this hearing is captured well by O'Brien when he notes that "the Philippians had heard about Paul's character and demeanour, how he faced his trials, and so on. This occurred particularly when he was with them, but they no doubt heard positive accounts during his absences as well."[129] This would indicate that even third party information about Paul—how he lived, how he thought, what he taught—would be useful to the Philippians to shape their own thinking and lifestyle. Thus, this would indicate a mediated Pauline imitation, but imitation of Paul nonetheless.

This way of reading fits well the context of 4:9. It would indicate that Paul's Christ-oriented manner of life (in contrast to his teaching, the focus of the first two verbs) was in view by the use of the last set of verbs. This would highlight the twin aspects of how the Philippians directly experienced Paul: by experiencing him directly (εἴδετε) and by what they heard about him (ἠκούσατε)

---

127 Davis, *Oral Biblical Criticism*, 112, 147.

128 This would be similar to Paul's recalling to the Thessalonians mind "how we [i.e., Paul and his companions] lived among you" in 1 Thess 1:5 and also "you are witnesses . . . of how holy, righteous and blameless we were among you" in 1 Thess 2:10.

129 O'Brien, *Philippians*, 511.

through others.[130]

The scope of these four verbs is clarified by the prepositional phrase, ἐν ἐμοί, placed after the final verb. Regarding the meaning of this phrase, two questions arise. (1) How is it used in this context? (2) How does it relate to the verbs that proceed it? A complicating factor in the answering of these questions is the fact that these questions cannot be answered in isolation from each other.

Most of the translations opt to render ἐν as "in," leaving it open whether it is to be understood as a locative ("in my person") or dative of respect ("with respect to").[131] Other translations simply opt to translate this prepositional phrase with the pronoun "me," indicating "with respect to."[132] O'Brien translates this "from me," indicating source.[133]

It is at this point that the second question pushes itself to the fore. If one sees this phrase as relating to the last item or the last two items, the meaning seems to be either locative or dative of respect. If it is to be understood as relating to all four, then it would seem that the phrase would need to be understood more loosely along the lines of "in connection to or with."[134] We will need to answer to the second question before we can determine which of these meanings the ἐν has.

How does ἐν ἐμοί relate to the four preceding verbs? The three options that have been seriously considered are that the phrase refers (1) to the last verb, (2) the last two verbs, or (3) to all four verbs.

O'Brien argues that "strictly, the ἐν ἐμοί is connected with εἴδετε alone."[135] Simply from the grammatical flow, a good case can be made for this. However, this would leave the other verbs indeterminate and highly ambiguous (i.e., what and from whom did they learn, receive, and hear?). Some sort of prepositional phrase or qualifying term would have to be understood. None of the commentators seriously entertain this option.

A stronger case can be made that the prepositional phrase ἐν ἐμοί refers to the last two verbs, since both εἴδετε and ἀκούετε echo the way they are used in

---

130 Against a number of commentators who understand this as directly hearing from Paul: J. B. Lightfoot, *St Paul's Epistle to the Philippians* (Lynn, Mass.: Hendrickson, 1981), 162; Vincent, *Philippians*, 140; Plummer, *Philippians*, 98; Martin, *Philippians*, 175; Kent, "Philippians," 152. Arguing for seeing this as referring to "hearing from others" are Hendriksen, *Philippians*, 200; Hawthorne, *Philippians*, 190; O'Brien, *Philippians*, 510; Bockmuehl, *Philippians*, 255. Arguing that both are intended is Heinrich Schlier, *Der Brief an die Galater* (KEK 7; Göttingen: Vandenhoeck & Ruprecht, 1949), 76.

131 ASV, BBE, ESV, KJV, NAB, NRS, NIB, NET, etc.

132 For example, CJB: "what you have heard and seen me doing." So also GWN, NJB, NLT.

133 O'Brien, *Philippians*, 511.

134 A "marker denoting the object to which someth. happens or in which someth. shows itself, or by which someth. is recognized" (BDAG, 329).

135 O'Brien, *Philippians*, 511. Similarly Hawthorne, *Philippians*, 190.

1:30, where they are both modified by ἐν ἐμοί.[136] What speaks against this, however, is that there are no grammatical or contextual indicators in 4:9 that set these verbs off from the other two. It may be counter-argued, however, on the strength of the pattern established in 1:30, that it would have been natural for Paul's readers to associate seeing and hearing with ἐν ἐμοί when they came upon these verbs in 4:9, and that they simply understand that it refers to the last two items. This is theoretically possible, though it does not resolve the issue that the first two terms require some sort of qualifier.

The strongest case can be made for ἐν ἐμοι referring to all four verbs for the following reasons. (1) All these verbs demand some sort of prepositional phrase to narrow down their scope. (2) The grammatical structure of verb + conjunction repeated four times with no intervening modifiers which then closes with ἐν ἐμοὶ, would naturally cause the reader to infer it was referring to the entire string. (3) Even though other prepositions would have been more precise or appropriate, Paul allows it to refer to all four verbs for the sake of rhetorical symmetry.[137] (3) The phrase ἐν ἐμοί can easily modify all four verbs without special pleading.

It seems then, on balance, that ἐν ἐμοί does refer to all four verbs and that it

---

136 It is for this reason that Michaelis only ties this prepositional phrase to the last two items (Michaelis, *Philipper*, 69). The NIV also ties ἐν ἐμοί to the last two elements, but then must shift the way ἐν ἐμοί modifies the verbs: "whatever you have . . . heard *from me* [source?], or seen *in me* [location? respect?]."

137 The term μανθάνω occurs 13 times in the NT (outside our passage) with prepositions: seven times with ἀπό, four times with ἐν, and twice with παρά. There is one usage that has a parallel structure with our passage (1 Cor 4:6, ἵνα ἐν ἡμῖν μάθητ. The rest do not refer to a person, but to the sphere or the manner in which one learns (Phil 4:11; 1 Tim 2:11; 2 Tim 3:14).

The use of παραλαμβάνω in the uncontested Pauline epistles is used in every instance in association with the reception of the Christian Tradition (1 Cor 11:23; 15:1, 3; Gal 1:9, 12; 1 Thess 2:13; 4:1). Where agency is explicit, either the prepositions ἀπό or παρά are used. Ἀπό is used only once (1 Cor 11:23) and seems to indicate direct reception of something, probably via direct revelation being indicated. Παρά is used five times (1 Cor 15:3; Gal 1:9, 12; 1 Thess 2:13; 4:1) and indicates "the mediating instrument of the tradition," "by the hands of," or "by the one who passes on the tradition."

In the contested Pauline epistles, παραλαμβάνω refers once to the reception of the Christian Tradition (2 Thess 3:6), once from the reception of Christ (Col 2:6). It is used only one time clearly with the preposition ἐν, referring to "receiving a ministry" (Col 4:17), which does not seem to be related to the passing on of a tradition (contra O'Brien, *Philippians*, 259). Instead, it has to do with receiving a specific ministry, which is described as being ἐν κυρίῳ. This usage is quite different than the one in Phil 4:9, since there a physical person is in view, whereas in Col 4:17 it is the ministry which is the object. The category that best describes the usage of ἐν in Col 4:17 seems to be "a close personal relation in which the referent of the ἐν-term is viewed as the controlling influence" (BDAG, 327).

is to be understood loosely to mean "in connection to or with something." This usage would fit well if it were simply referring only to the last two verbs or to all four of them, with no shift in meaning, and it also resolves the issue of all four verbs needing some qualifier to narrow the scope down. Thus O'Brien is correct, even if he is somewhat tentative, when he suggests that "ἐν ἐμοί has been placed at the end for rhetorical effect, that is, to indicate in an emphatic way that everything they had learnt, received, heard, and seen had been embodied in Paul himself."[138]

The specific call to imitate Paul comes at the end of this verbal string in the form of the present, imperative command, "keep on doing" (ταῦτα πράσσετε). Paul's ultimate goal of all that they learned from him, captured in these four verbs, is the integration of what they received from Paul into the fabric of their life and thought. When we compare the verb Paul chose (πράσσω) with other possible verbs he could have chosen (such as ποιέω or ἐργάζομαι, etc.), it seems Paul wishes to emphasize the element of continual (present tense) involvement in and practice of that which they received from Paul over against the mere act of doing, which these other verbs often convey.[139]

Paul is not merely concerned with the mental cognition of truth. It is the embodiment of those truths intentionally practiced in everyday life that is the goal of his instruction. Orthodoxy and orthopraxy go hand-in-hand and cannot, according to Paul, be divorced from one another.[140] All that Paul taught and lived out before them is for the purpose of their ultimate transformation into the image of Christ, which is also the highest goal for his own life (3:4-14).

6.2.4 Summary of Imitation in Philippians 4:9

Imitation in 4:9 is presented as "global imitation" of all that Paul did and acted, especially as he is pictured in this letter. In the context of all that precedes this call to imitation, it is clear that the direction of Paul's entire life was defined and motivated by the ultimate passion of what can be summed up as "knowing Christ" (3:10). Paul's call to imitation in 4:9 is surely to be understood in light of this.

---

138 O'Brien, *Philippians*, 511.

139 BDAG cites this usage of πράσσω as virtually equivalent to ποιέω with the meaning of "do" or "accomplish" (860), but since Paul uses ποιέω three other times in Philippians (1:4; 2:14; 4:14) and uses πράσσω only in 4:9, the choice of πράσσω over other terms seems intentional and nuanced. In fact, BDAG's second usage, "to engage in activity or behave in a certain way" comes closer to the intent of Paul here than the meaning they have adopted.

140 So also Gnilka: "significant is the connection between word and person. The apostle stands by his word and offers himself to be imitated . . . This connection cannot be severed, and the witness of the apostolic word must be assimilated by faith in the same way as the witness of the apostolic example was" (Gnilka, *Philipperbrief*, 222).

In vv. 8-9 Paul gives his final commands to the Philippians, which he phrases in broad generalizations (ὅσα, ἅ). He describes the ethos, mindset, and lifestyle that should characterize their lives as a Christian community. He begins in v. 8 by listing general attributes that should characterize their way of thinking, attributes which they would share with their Greek compatriots, but which they would, based on the content of v. 9, understand in terms of the Christian message as embodied and taught by Paul.

Paul mentions four verbs in v. 9 that they should put into practice. These four verbs together indicate that Paul intended them to see this call to imitation as encompassing all of Paul's Christ-oriented life, with no artificial distinction between Paul's "public" and "private" life, or between what he taught and how he lived. Paul used these four terms to represent all the dimensions and aspects of how they could learn from him, both in his formal teaching (the first two verbs) and in the example of his life (the last two verbs). Each of these verbs carries a different accent and together they present a picture of Paul in his total existence as a model for the Philippians. This can be summarized in the following way:

Emphasis on Paul's Teaching

ἐμάθετε	His general teaching
παρελάβετε	His teaching of the Christian Tradition

Emphasis on Paul's Christ-Oriented Life

ἠκούσατε	What they heard from others about Paul
εἴδετε	What they personally experienced of Paul when he was with them.

These verbs are qualified by the prepositional phrase ἐν ἐμοί, which is best understood as indicating relationship to Paul ("in connection to or with Paul"), while leaving the nature of that relationship general.

The intention of all these verbs comes at the end (for heightened rhetorical effect) by means of the command, ταῦτα πράσσετε, which indicates not a mindless doing (ποιέω), but an intentional integration of all they learned from him.

In essence, Paul is telling them in 4:9a: "Look at everything about me: how I lived, what I said, what I wrote, and what you heard from others about me. Everything about me is there to teach you, to be a model for your life as a follower of Christ. Learn from all of it. Intentionally reflect on all this and seek to put it into practice in your own context."[141] The same intention can be

141 As Bockmuehl writes: "While the invitation to imitate ones teacher or rabbi was of course standard Graeco-Roman as well as Jewish didactic procedure, in Paul's case that invitation derives both its authority and its limitations from his own faithfulness to the prior example of Christ, who is himself the prototype and measure of all Christian discipleship (2:5ff and *passim*). Paul's own ministry is merely the

discerned in Acts 20:20-21 in which the author of Acts quotes Paul as saying: "I never shrank from letting you know anything that was for your good, or from teaching you alike in public and from house to house, bearing my testimony, both to Jews and Greeks."[142]

Fee aptly summarizes the role of this verse in the context of this letter when he writes:

> With this sentence Paul brings the exhortations to conclusion. It is not surprising that they end on the note of "imitation." . . . Paul's concern throughout has been the gospel, not its content ("doctrinal error" is not at issue), but its lived out expression in the world. To get there he has informed them of his response to his own present suffering (1:12-26), reminded them of the "way of Christ" (2:6-11), and told his own story (3:4-14), all of which were intended to appeal, warn, and encourage them to steadfastness and unity in the face of opposition. . . . Paul is once again calling them to the kind of cruciform existence he has been commending and urging on them throughout.[143]

---

apostolic illustration and exemplification of that mind of Christ" (Bockmuehl, *Philippians*, 254).

142 This parallel also noted by Hawthorne, "Letter to the Philippians," 189.

143 Fee, *Philippians*, 419-20.

CHAPTER 7

Imitation as a Pauline Power Play? A Response to Elizabeth Castelli's *Imitating Paul*

Introduction

Elizabeth Castelli in her book *Imitating Paul: A Discourse of Power*, which is a reworking of her dissertation, has developed an intriguing and provocative reading of Pauline imitation that makes a clear break from the traditional approaches that handle this theme. Although there have been a number of book reviews,[1] a few articles (or portions thereof)[2] and one section of a dissertation[3]

---

1 Ronald J. Allen, "review of Elizabeth A. Castelli, *Imitating Paul: A Discourse on Power*," *Enc* 53 (1992): 292-94; William R. Baird, "review of Elizabeth A. Castelli, *Imitating Paul: A Discourse on Power*," *Mid-Stream* 31 (1992): 272-74; Paul T. Coke, "review of Elizabeth A. Castelli, *Imitating Paul: A Discourse of Power*," *AThR* 74 (1992): 520; Christoph Heil, "review of Elizabeth A. Castelli, *Imitating Paul: A Discourse of Power*," *BZ* n.s., 36 (1992): 279-81; Margaret M. Mitchell, "review of Elizabeth A. Castelli, *Imitating Paul: A Discourse of Power*," *JR* 72 (1992): 581-82; B. Keith Putt, "review of Elizabeth A. Castelli, *Imitating Paul: A Discourse on Power*," *SwJT* 35 (1992): 61; George Aichele, "review of Elizabeth A. Castelli, *Imitating Paul: A Discourse on Power*," *CrCur* 43 (1993): 130-33; George Aichele, "review of Elizabeth A. Castelli, *Imitating Paul: A Discourse of Power*," *ThTo* 50 (1993): 130; John M. Court, "review of Elizabeth A. Castelli, *Imitating Paul: A Discourse of Power*," *ExpTim* 104 (1993): 281; David B. Howell, "review of Elizabeth A. Castelli, *Imitating Paul: A Discourse on Power*," *PRSt* 20 (1993): 317-20; Calvin J. Roetzel, "review of Elizabeth A. Castelli, *Imitating Paul: A Discourse on Power*," *CRBR* 6 (1993): 213-15; F. Scott Spencer, "review of Elizabeth A. Castelli, *Imitating Paul: A Discourse of Power*," *CBQ* 55 (1993): 573-74; Dorothy Jean Weaver, "review of Elizabeth A. Castelli, *Imitating Paul: A Discourse of Power*," *Int* 47 (1993): 313-14; Willis Peter de Boer, "review of Elizabeth A. Castelli, *Imitating Paul: A Discourse of Power*," *CTJ* 29 (1994): 236-40.

2 Agan, "Pauline Epistles;" Anthony C. Thiselton, *Interpreting God and the Postmodern Self: On Meaning, Manipulation, and Promise* (Edinburgh: T&T Clark, 1995), 140-42; Clarke, "Be Imitators," 329-60; Fowl, "Christology and Ethics," 148-49; P. J. Watson, "Girard and Integration: Desire, Violence, and the Mimesis of Christ as Foundation for Postmodernity," *JPT* 26 (1998): 318-19;

written on her book, there has to our knowledge been no extended response to her position challenging her hermeneutic and proposing an alternative.[4] In this chapter, we will seek to provide such a response.

Elizabeth Castelli develops her argumentation based on the work of Michel Foucault as he understands the nature of power relations[5] and applies this to Paul's understanding of imitation. Her work is comprised of five chapters,[6] the contents of which we will summarize below. We will follow this by a critique of the core issues that arise from the development of her argumentation.

7.1 Summary of Castelli's Argument

In chapter one Castelli discusses the philosophical problems she sees implicit in the concept of imitation—primarily the dimension of power implicit in the term. She views imitation as a "critical relationship of power" in which the "model sets the terms of the relationship, which is both hierarchical and asymmetrical" (22). The inferior element strives progressively to become similar to the superior (21). The ideological force at work here is that sameness is good and difference is problematic, dangerous, and threatening (22). Since the copy must focus on the model, it reinforces the distinction between them, which the copy can never fully attain (22).

Castelli observes that in the NT the concepts of power and identity are referred to only sporadically. It is these *power relations* that are "underwritten or enabled" by these NT texts, which she seeks first to expose and then examine (23).

Castelli notes that there have been two moves in Pauline scholarship regarding mimesis which she wishes to question: (1) "a spiritualizing gesture

---

Trevor J. Burke, "Pauline Paternity in 1 Thessalonians," *TynBul* 51 (2000): 59-80; A. K. M. Adam, "Walk This Way: Repetition, Difference, and the Imitation of Christ," *Int* 55 (2001): 19-33.

3 Simon Gathercole, "The Influence on New Testament Studies of Post-Structuralism with Special Reference to John Dominic Crossan and Elizabeth Castelli (Part II Dissertation submitted for Tripos)" (Ph.D., King's College, Cambridge University, 1996), 40. Although we concur in general with Gathercole's solid critique, it does not go into in-depth analysis of Castelli's argumentation and does not provide a sustained counter-proposal. Our discussion attempts to do just this.

4 The reason for this may be, as Gathercole notes: "Castelli's work is still new (and marginal) enough to have elicited little response" (Gathercole, "Influence on New Testament Studies," 22 n. 82).

5 Castelli, *Imitating Paul*, 39.

6 Chapter one: "Imitation and Problems of Power, Ideology, and Interpretation;" chapter two: "Theoretical Frameworks: Foucault and Power;" chapter three: "Mimesis in Antiquity;" chapter four: "'Be Imitators of Me': Discourses of Mimesis in Paul;" chapter five: "Reading Effects: Imitation, Power and Claims to Truth."

towards the text" (23), which does not take seriously the "interestedness of the text;" and (2) an investment in the notion that "tradition itself as authoritative, monolithic, and univocal" (23) She discerns in the Pauline texts a subtle power play, in which one power holder is muted while the other is "authorized" (23) It is this muting by Paul of other legitimate voices she wishes to unmask. In addition to noting how Paul uses the mimetic relationship as a strategy to grasp and maintain power, Castelli seeks to analyze "the mimetic gesture, which reinscribes the textual effects of power and thereby authorizes the texts claims to truth as truth" (24).

After these positioning remarks she surveys various scholars who have dealt with this concept (Tinsley, Michaelis, de Boer, Betz, Schulz, Schütz, Fiore, and Furnish) with respect to how they treat the issue of power. Castelli's major critique of all these approaches is twofold: (1) they simply assume the authority of Paul and do not call into question the legitimacy of that authority; a corollary to this is that (2) they do not deal with the dimension of power implicit in the concept of imitation. This failure to create "ironic distance between the readings of the text and the text itself" (29) limits scholarly discourse and leads to sheer repetition of the positions to date.[7]

At the conclusion of chapter one, she turns to two quotations of Furnish, which serve as a springboard for the main theses of her book. The first quotation deals with the Paul's radical christocentrism. "[I]t is clear that Paul regards himself not only as a bearer of *traditions* but also as a bearer of Christ. . . . To imitate Paul and Christ means to conform to Christ's suffering and death in the giving of ones self over to the service of others."[8] Her observation is that, although Furnish sees Paul's ethic as strongly christocentric, "it says nothing about the privileged position that Paul has implicitly claimed for himself" (32-33).

Castelli uses a second quotation from Furnish to press the case that Paul is reinforcing his power illegitimately:

> It is noteworthy that none of these imitation passages singles out any particular qualities of the earthly Jesus with the insistence that they be emulated. Rather, it seems always to be the humble, giving, obedient *love* of the crucified and resurrected Lord to which the final appeal is made.[9]

Castelli deduces from this fact that "the call to imitation has no particular content" (32), which she interprets as indication that Paul uses imitation as a

7 She does note that Schütz and Fiore mention the topic of power, but do not deal with it. Castelli, on the one hand, finds Fiore's study convincing, but on the other hand calls it into question because "it seems to cast certain distinctions in terms which are too harsh and its point is overdrawn" (Castelli, *Imitating Paul*, 30). She however, provides neither examples nor justification whatsoever for her criticism.

8 Furnish, *Theology and Ethics*, 222-23.

9 Furnish, *Theology and Ethics*, 223.

foil to maintain power and control over others. She proceeds, based on this, to formulate the basic argument of her work:

> I will argue . . . that the lack of content of the object of imitation is itself a rhetorical gesture which both reinforces the power of Paul's example and implicates the imitators in the economy of sameness by forcing them always to be 'policing' themselves, because their model is conspicuously imprecise. (32)

Her stance with respect to Pauline authority can be summarized as follows: Paul does not have a legitimate claim to a privileged position with respect to Christ in his role as founder of these churches. Since he does not have this legitimacy, then he must rhetorically manipulate/coerce the recipients of the letter into accepting his authority. He does this through illegitimately claiming a unique position with Christ, which he buttresses by a unique reading of the Old Testament, which reinforces his unique status. With these two authoritative heavyweights on his side, he is able to *force* others into conformity ("sameness") with his desires, thereby effectively undermining any rival's claims to authority and quelling any attempts to diversity, which would undermine his sole position as authoritative.

In *chapter two* Castelli describes the theoretical framework of power that Foucault has developed, which she then will use in the subsequent chapters to critique the conception of imitation in antiquity (*chapter three*) and in Paul (*chapter four*). At the outset of chapter two she states a basic intention of hers in this work: "to challenge the 'specialness' usually attributed to early Christianity—an attribution which masks a theological claim to a privileged truth for Christianity and a concern to uncover, at the 'origins' of Christianity, a particularly pristine version of that truth."[10] This challenge she bases squarely on the premises of Michel Foucault's philosophy. She approvingly quotes Foucault:

> It is one of my targets to show people that a lot of things that are a part of their landscape—that people think are universal—are the result of some very precise historical changes. All my analyses are against the idea of universal necessities in human existence. They show the arbitrariness of institutions and show which space of freedom we can still enjoy and how many changes can still be made.[11]

Taking this Foucauldian assumption as her point of departure, Castelli comments: "With Foucault, I reject the notion that there is anything universally human about cultural and social formations and institutions. Societies are organized and power relations emerge in response to very particular historical circumstances" (37). Based on this foundational axiom of Foucault, Castelli takes on the task of critiquing Christianity as an arbitrary, historic institution

10 Castelli, *Imitating Paul*, 35.

11 Quoted in Castelli, *Imitating Paul*, 36.

with no legitimate claim to universality. She adopts this Foucauldian framework and interprets the Pauline claim to special revelation as an attempt at coercive, manipulative, self-seeking power over others. It is this she seeks to unmask for what it is. Castelli maintains that the operative dynamic in the writings of Paul is that of a struggle for power. Every action, every word, every phrase from Paul is critiqued in answer to the question, "what does this tell us about Paul's attempt at forcing his authority/power onto those under him?" *Power* functions as the lens through which Pauline texts are to be read—including, and especially, the imitation texts.

Following Foucault, Castelli assumes that the concept of power is the basic dynamic around which not just Paul's writings but all human institutions revolve. As a result, Castelli attempts in this work a "rethinking" of early Christianity based on the "analytics of power" (51). Power is understood by Castelli as "a fluid and relational force that permeates and cirulates [sic] within a social body. Power is coterminous with social relations in general" (52).

After her general introduction to the concept of power, she turns to the nature of "discourse" and "rhetoric" and states that they are "non-innocent terms." *Discourse* is not innocent since it is "an active constructor of ideology; it is through discourse that ideology makes its claims to truth. In this sense, discourse serves the social construction of power relations" (53). *Rhetoric* is also not innocent since it fashions the "perspectival nature" of a text, i.e., its political tone (54). The text thus becomes an ideological force. "The claim to truth which undergirds so much of Paul's discourse must be seen through this lens of the rhetorical nature of the text: it is a *claim* to truth, but not truth itself" (54; author's emphasis).

It is through the vehicle of discourse that Paul shaped "the contours of the social experience of early Christian communities" (56). This is the framework in which Pauline imitation functions. It functions as "a discourse of power."

> What is the sense of the ambiguous genitive? Should it be read as a genitive of possession? Is "imitation," then, "power's discourse," the very articulation of power? Or perhaps it could be read as a genitive of respect: "imitation" as a way of articulating power relations and claiming for them a grounding in truth. I see it as both of these. (56)

These two understandings of "discourse of power," Castelli concludes, comprise together the implicit nature of imitation, be it specifically Christian or pagan. The exemplar sets himself up as *truth*. This Castelli views as illegitimate and notes that she herself "attempts to resist the arrogant singularity of the drive toward truth, recognizing its elusive and contingent status" (57).

Armed with this understanding of power, she proceeds in *chapter three* to analyze the nature of imitation in antiquity. After a review of illustrative references to imitation in Greco-Roman and Judaic texts, she makes a key observation: "The point cannot be made strongly enough: there exists in the notion of imitation this tension between the drive to sameness and the inability to achieve it, an inability which creates hierarchy."[12] Implicit in the concept of imitation is the impossibility of equality. This basic thesis is a thorn in Castelli's flesh.

Castelli draws three conclusions based on her survey of mimesis in Greco-Roman antiquity: (1) "[M]imesis is constituted through a hierarchy in which the model is imbued with perfection and wholeness, and the copy represents an attempt to reclaim that perfection." (2) The model is seen as of "superior value" and based on this "the model has authority to which the copy submits." (3) Mimesis implies that "sameness" is to be preferred over difference. "Sameness and unity and harmony have positive value while, by implication, difference is associated with disunity and discord" (86). Castelli maintains that the Pauline conception of imitation functions upon the same lines as those of Greco-Roman antiquity, to which she then turns in the next chapter.

In *chapter four* she turns to the reading of the Pauline imitation texts and "reads" (i.e., critiques) them from the standpoint of what they imply about the use of power. She notes in 1 Thess 1:6 that the equivalence set up between Paul and Christ "can be read as a rhetorical attempt to undergird the authority of Paul's message by equating it with God and Christ" (92). In 1 Thess 2:14 Castelli observes the "notably passive quality" of the imitators, which Paul praises, since "they have . . . performed their receptive function well" (94). She draws the implication from this that it was Paul's intention all along to bring them to a point of passive receptivity.

In Phil 3:17 she notes three crucial elements of power going on. (1) The term συμμιμητής reinforces the necessity for unity, since diversity is a danger. This is reinforced by the contrasted fate of others who are the enemies of the cross of Christ. (2) The passage reinforced a clear hierarchy: Christ—Paul—Christians. This places Paul in a strategic mediating position of power and "reinscribes Paul's privileged position within the hierarchy" (96). (3) The call to unity is underlined through the humility of Christ as displayed in Phil 2:5-11. The connection of unity with humility for Paul is a felicitous one. This strategic move provides him with authority over the readers.

> The impact of this rhetoric is powerful. Christian identity is linked, on the one hand, with the humility displayed by Christ on the cross and, on the other hand, with the imitation of Paul. There exists only one alternative to this identity, and that is to "live as enemies of the cross." (96)

Turning to 1 Corinthians, Castelli notes at the outset that this book "offers the richest context for producing a reading of the discourse of mimesis in Paul's letters" (97). It is significant for Castelli that in the midst of the dissension and factions, Paul calls the Corinthians twice (1 Cor 4:16, 11:1) to imitate him.

---

12 Castelli, *Imitating Paul*, 75 (see also pp. 22 and 80).

> The idea of mimesis . . . is felicitously linked in Paul's discourse to notions of social order and power, and each reinscribes and reinforces the other's "truth." That Paul would exhort the Corinthians twice in this one document to become his imitators, when he is dealing with problems of social diffusion and dispersed authority, is both striking and telling. (98)

Paul positions himself at the beginning of the book by means of a master stroke of rhetorical strategy when he writes in 1 Cor 1:17, "For Christ did not send me to baptize but to preach the gospel, and not with eloquent wisdom, lest the cross of Christ be emptied of its power." This

> clever rhetorical gesture . . . paradoxically ascribes to Paul both a privileged status vis-à-vis the gospel, bestowing upon Paul a special authority to speak, and also a contentless-ness, an emptiness which removes him from the fray. He is the one who is supposed to speak while it is not he who speaks at all, but Christ through him. (99)

In the context immediately preceding the first imitation reference in 1 Cor 4:17, Paul uses a patriarchal image to describe himself and to set the framework for imitation. Castelli notes that virtually all the commentators view this paternal metaphor "to evoke a sense of kindness and love."[13] However, she maintains that ever since the modern ("especially feminist") critiques of this symbol by Ochshorn, Trible, Daly, and Schüssler Fiorenza such "naïve and utopian readings of Paul's use of this image are no longer justifiable" (101). Far from seeing these references to imitation as benign, Castelli sees this paternal imagery as analogous to military imagery. Her justification for this comes from a text in Epictetus: "Otherwise, go call the general a meddler when he oversees and reviews and watches over his troops, and punishes those who are guilty of a breach of discipline."[14] Reading this text by Epictetus alongside to Paul's call to imitation, she comments: "Whatever else one might want to claim about the relationship between a general and his troops, it is difficult to imagine that the general acts out of love and kind feeling" (101). Paul is thus cast by Castelli as a military general, whose primary motivation is the desire to maintain power.

Castelli then goes into considerable detail into the argumentation of 1 Cor 1-4 leading up to the imitation reference in 4:17, noting the dimensions of power implicit in the rhetoric Paul employs. When Paul arrives at this verse, he identifies no specific content to the imitation. She draws from this that

> the lack of specific content in his exhortation to imitate him reflects an aspect of the political nature of the relationship between him and the community. The call to imitation constructs power relations in the community precisely because of the slipperiness of the object of imitation. Foucault has ably demonstrated in his work

13 She cites Conzelmann, Sanders, de Boer. (100)

14 Epictetus, *Diss.* 3.22.95.

> on technologies of power how the more generalized and unpredictable the technology's application, the more effective its result. (110)

Further, when Paul refers to "my ways in Christ," the rhetorical effect is to reinforce authority for himself and secure that claim through linking it to Christ himself.

In 1 Cor 11:1 Paul links imitation of himself with imitation of Christ. This linkage places Paul in a mediating position. This is a "presumptuous" move because it places Paul structurally on the level of Christ, which is interpreted by Castelli as Pauline "identity confusion" (112). In addition, a strong hierarchical arrangement is seen here (God→Christ→Paul→Community) which is based on non-reciprocity. The implicit assumption of "sameness is good" and "difference is bad" is also present and underlined in the text. This sameness (imitating Paul), however, is dressed in urgency since it is linked with the access to salvation. "Paul's call to imitation . . . possesses a more profound level of meaning because the imitation of Paul's example is itself a privileged mode of access to salvation" (115).

The final passage Castelli looks at is Gal 4:12, which she briefly handles. She notes that (1) Paul is in the position of being the "privileged model" for the Galatian community, and that (2) the metaphor of fatherhood (i.e., read: "military commander") is invoked, and finally (3) the hierarchical dimension is accentuated by Paul.

As she concludes this chapter, she summarizes her observations of Pauline imitation:

> Paul's discourse of mimesis uses rhetoric to rationalize and shore up a particular set of social relations or power relations within the early Christian movement. His use of the notion of mimesis, with all of its nuances, reinforces both Paul's own privileged position and the power relations of the early Christian communities as somehow "natural." That is to say, the hierarchy of power is in tune with a much larger and more self-evident structure which incorporates both the earthly community and the divine order. Participating positively in the mimetic relationship with Paul, the early communities are to be rewarded with salvation. Resisting the mimetic relationship, by contrast, has dire consequences. (116)

Her conclusion notes two further implications. (1) The invocation of imitation implies sameness is privileged and difference has exclusively negative connotations. (2) The implications of a hierarchy place Paul in a secure and privileged position of power.

In the *final chapter*, she discusses issues that should have been raised earlier: her stance on authorial intention and how she perceives her own reading. She intentionally has left this for the end of her work:

> I have bracketed the whole matter of conscious authorial intent. I assume here that the author's intent—the motive residing in the mind of the writer—is unattainable

> because it involves inaccessible aspects of the author's psychology. In any case, to assume that verbal expression is continuous with authorial intent is to assume that language is transparent and self-evident. (120)

Since, according to Castelli, it is not possible to discern authorial intent, this implies that there is no *singular, right* way to read the text. There can be no controls for determining authorial intentionality. All interpretations are, therefore, equally valid. She thus acknowledges: "my reading is not the only possible or plausible one" (121). Another result of the irretrievability of authorial intent is that one can legitimately, without losing intellectual respectability, read the text based on personal preference. That is the reason Castelli can openly write: "I have framed my discussion according to my interests" (121). She makes explicit her presuppositions when she writes:

> By focusing on the effects of reading rather than on the author's intentions, I have joined those biblical critics who have been shifting the terms of the discussion, asking readers to pose questions of meaning from a different point of view from the one often taken in biblical studies. (121)

She is thus bound to say that although her reading of Paul "does not claim to stand as the singularly true reading of Paul's discourse . . . . I hope [it is] persuasive."[15]

The chapter continues in the same vein, but pulls back to look more generally at truth-claims, using the work of Jacques Derrida as her starting point. This section takes us beyond the issues of Pauline imitation and will therefore not be pursued here.

7.2 Isolating the Key Issues

The sweeping Foucauldian agenda Castelli presents in this book goes much deeper than a challenge to the understanding of the traditional approaches to imitation in Paul. It calls into question at the same time (1) what the primary task of exegesis should be, as well as (2) the "specialness" of Christianity. The use of Paul appears to be a foil for this more foundational agenda. "My focus on Paul" writes Castelli, "is a matter of necessity, because his texts are the earliest coherent expression of what one might call an early Christian position" (35). If her argument is persuasive, then the "specialness" of Christianity is nullified.

A point-by-point exegetical response to Castelli's approach is inadequate

15 Castelli, *Imitating Paul*, 121. Elsewhere she writes: "In pursuing a 'Foucauldian reading' of Paul, my purpose was not to demonstrate a privileged truthfulness of Foucault's perspective, nor to produce a totalized new reading of Paul. Rather, I have attempted to imagine what a reading-otherwise might look like, and Foucault is a congenial if sometimes erratic partner in such a project" (57).

and unhelpful.[16] A proper response to Castelli is needed on a foundational level, since it is on the hermeneutical level that she mounts her attack. There are a number of issues Castelli raises, but we will look at five fundamental ones. The first issue could be said to be *the* crux issue, since it is the foundational premise for Castelli's book: the question of authorial intention. If Castelli (read: Foucault) is wrong here about authorial intent, then the remainder of her argumentation founders as well. To this first issue we will devote considerable attention. The second issue relates to Castelli's use of Foucault as a starting point. The loss of authorial intent opens up new ways of reading and Castelli opts to use Foucault's theory of power as her starting point. Issues three (Paul and Christianity: issues of specialness, power, and authority), four (three implications of imitation), and five (Paul, benevolent or malevolent leader) can also be grouped together, since they flow out of the conclusions that Castelli has drawn from the first two issues, and, being derivative issues, will therefore not require such detailed argumentation.[17]

7.2.1 Authorial Intent – Revisiting Hermeneutical Starting Points

To frame our discussion of authorial intent, we will restate a crucial remark by Castelli in the closing chapter of her study on imitation:

> I have bracketed the whole matter of conscious authorial intent [until now]. I assume here that the author's intent—the motive residing in the mind of the writer—is unattainable because it involves inaccessible aspects of the author's psychology. In any case, to assume that verbal expression is continuous with authorial intent is to assume that language is transparent and self-evident. (120)

Since the mind of the author cannot be discerned, Castelli, continues, "to assert that 'Paul did not mean that,' in relation to [my] reading, is therefore irrelevant" (121). With this strategic move, she has allegedly checkmated any attempt to controvert her conclusions. Every critic that begs to differ is thereby shut up.

This conclusion frees Castelli from the constraints of author-centered readings and opens up the many possibilities of reader-centered approaches to texts, allowing her to approach Paul's writings "according to my interests"

---

16 As de Boer writes: "With Castelli's moving authorial intent to the realm of the irrelevant, there is little incentive to enter into exegetical debate with her on some of her conclusions about the imitation texts" (de Boer, "review of Castelli," 238).

17 Another issue Castelli notes—of imitation being contentless in Paul—will not be touched on here, since we have dealt with the content of Pauline imitation it in the previous chapter, which we have found to be anything but without content. We argued also in our discussion "Jesus of history, Christ of Faith" in chapter three that Paul's appeals to Christ are far from contentless when one takes a closer look at the use of the Jesus Tradition in the Pauline writings.

(121). Her intention is not to produce "the singularly true reading of Paul's discourse" (121). Her intention is to present a "possible, plausible, and I hope also persuasive" reading of Paul's discourse (121).

What, however, does she mean by the term "persuasive"? One can only conjecture, but the thrust of her book and its rhetoric implies that it is *her* Foucauldian reading of power, which is *the* properly basic reading, and if another reader comes to an opposing conclusion, then the reader has simply not grasped what was truly going on in the text.[18] She thus attempts to mask her authoritarian intentions through a thinly veiled disclaimer of subjectivity.

If it can be maintained that Paul did intend something with his text and that this can be discerned, then Castelli's interpretive framework of power is radically called into question. If we grant her Foucauldian premises, then her case may be *a* legitimate reading.

Castelli's negation of authorial intention, combined with her "focus on the effects of reading" (121), has obvious and dramatic implications for the use of any text, especially religious ones. To paraphrase what she is doing by way of analogy: In contrast to viewing the text as a tool in the hands of an author who *intends* to communicate a specific message with the text she has written, Castelli views the text as putty in the hands of school children— each free to do what he wishes with the text, endlessly fashioning and refashioning the clay as he desires.[19]

This effectively allows her, on the one hand, to develop willy-nilly any reading she fancies without ever putting herself in a position, where she herself can be critiqued. On the other hand, she is able willy-nilly to critique Paul and paint him as a manipulative power-monger without allowing him to defend himself.

It is at this point, we need to ask: Can we so easily set aside the intention of an author? Is it true that the intention of the author cannot be discovered? What would happen if we turned the tables and asked Castelli why she herself has written her piece? Can she also deny intentionality in writing her book? Can she deny the discovery of that intentionality? Does she, in fact, wish to say this? Or has she written for a purpose and has she written in a way that we can discover that purpose?

It seems the consistent use of her approach would necessarily lead one to

---

18 Gathercole also has observed this: "So, although Castelli denies production of a 'totalizing discourse' in her work, she effectively excludes most other readings of the text" (Gathercole, "Influence on New Testament Studies," 18).

19 De Boer also notes this shift and responds: "For all their debatability and difficulty of detection, the author's intended meanings are crucial to the communication process. Failure to detect the author's intention is a breakdown in the communication process. Cutting oneself loose from authorial intentions means sailing rudderless on an unending sea of all possible and any conceivable meanings. We're set adrift in rankest subjectivism. I hope human communication has not come to that" (de Boer, "review of Castelli," 238).

epistemological and verbal solipsism, which would universally undermine any reason to communicate with others at all. Yet, the whole human communication enterprise in any form, written, oral, or otherwise, is founded on the implicit assumption that one can satisfactorily and truly, though not completely, impart one's intentions and meanings to others. If this is not actually possible, then one must legitimately ask: why, then, has the mass of humanity throughout the millenia acted upon on the assumption that this *is* possible? In the normal activity of reading virtually any text, humanity seeks to understand what the writer is intending. Does that mean that for all of these millenia, humanity was simply misguided? And that it was only through the insights of Foucault, Castelli, and others, that we have finally discovered that, what humanity has always assumed, is simply not possible? Or is it, rather, that Foucault and Castelli are simply operating on inadequate assumptions and tools of description, which do not do justice to the whole human communicative enterprise? Castelli, following Foucault, seems to be foisting a philosophical system onto reality and then on the basis of that philosophy, claiming certain things about reality—in our case, that authorial intention is a factual impossibility. This however, as we have said, is not, in fact, how humanity operates on a day-to-day level. Humans *do* operate on the assumption that one can adequately, if not fully, know the intentions of the author as inscribed in texts. It seems that Castelli has developed a straw-man argument, which she eloquently shoots down. In the process, however, she has not addressed the more fundamental nature of how humans actually communicate in written form. Thus, an adequate model for determining textual intentionality needs to be presented.

It is significant, that Castelli herself is not true to the hermeneutical axioms she espouses.[20] Let us look at a few examples in her work that illustrate this. In chapter one she analyzes the works of Tinsley, Michaelis, de Boer, and others and comes to conclusions based on her reading of what they *intended*. Then she proceeds to explicate her own *intentions* over-against these authors by writing: "I am arguing for . . ." (28). True, she does not use the word *intention*, but is it possible to understand the phrase "I am arguing for . . ." in this context in another way than "this is what I am intending to accomplish"?

Another example of this is in her comments regarding a text of Furnish. After critiquing this text and coming to conclusions as to what he *intended* (again, not using the term), she writes: "I will argue, in contrast, that . . ." (32).

20 Gathercole also notes this. Although Castelli proclaims herself a follower of the post-modern Foucault, "she shifts to seemingly modernist categories very quickly [when she writes]: 'What does it mean to imitate? In what fields of meaning is *imitation* inscribed?'" (Gathercole, "Influence on New Testament Studies," 17 [quoting Castelli, p. 21]). It is just this modernist way of argumentation that Foucault wished to critique! Gathercole takes Castelli to task for an inaccurate und uneven application of Foucault's approach (17).

She then proceeds to describe her intentions.

Turning to her understanding of Foucault, she writes: "I have certainly not done justice to his [Foucault's] . . . thought" (57). In other words, she is attempting to discern the intentions of Foucault. Yet, if, as she theoretically claims, the author's intent is unattainable, then why does she herself exert so much effort into doing something that is per definition impossible? What she in theory denies, in practice she cannot avoid.

Castelli is certainly correct in stating that intentionality cannot be bound up with the psychology of the author, for the psychology of an author is textually intangible and non-verifiable. But does that imply that intentionality cannot be discerned? Is there a model of authorial intentionality that is not grounded in the psychology of the author? How does one legitimately and verifiably determine authorial intentionality? To develop a full-blown hermeneutic of authorial intentionality is far beyond the strictures of this work. What follows, however, is a summary of the model that Kevin Vanhoozer presents in *Is There a Meaning in This Text?*[21] We will summarize his main arguments and at the same time interact with and critique the hermeneutic of Castelli.

7.2.1.1 Resurrecting the Author: Meaning as Communicative Action

Vanhoozer begins his reconstruction[22] of authorial intent with an observation from criminal law: "You cannot take the top of a man's head off and look into his mind and actually see what his intent was at any given moment. You have to decide it by reference to what he did, what he said and all the circumstances of the case."[23] Vanhoozer concurs with Castelli when he refuses to tie intentionality to the psychology of the author. This truly is an impossibility. Just as in criminal law, the author's intent is based on what he did—i.e., the act of intentionally producing a text.[24] Intentionality is fundamentally related to the concept of "directedness" with respect to communicative action.[25]

Intentionality is expressed through various media: thinking, saying, and doing—all of which are intentional: "Intending—to think or to say or to do something—always has an object: a thought, in the case of thinking; a proposition, in the case of saying; a project, in the case of doing" (246) With

---

21 Kevin J. Vanhoozer, *Is There a Meaning in This Text? The Bible, the Reader, and the Morality of Literary Knowledge* (Grand Rapids: Zondervan, 1998).

22 It is a "reconstruction," since the first half of his book deals with the "deconstruction" of the author.

23 Vanhoozer, *Meaning*, 246 (Quoting from Antony Duff, *Intention, Agency, and Criminal Liability: Philosophy of Action and the Criminal Law* [Cambridge, Mass.: Blackwell, 1990], 29).

24 "What an author planned to write is not necessarily the same as what an author succeeds in doing. What is needed is an account that explains the author's intent in terms of action rather than psychology" (Vanhoozer, *Meaning*, 246).

25 "To intend . . . is a matter of directing one's mind towards a certain object or idea" (246).

respect to an author, this intention has two basic components: an object ("the propositional content to which the author's activity is directed") and a disposition related to that object ("the stance an author takes with regard to the object," 247). The textual meaning is not found in the experience of the writer, but rather the discovery of the directedness of the text.

> It is the author's intention that determines the direction (and manner) of fit between words and world. Understanding takes place when both author and reader *attend* to the same matter in the same manner. Interpretation . . . is largely a matter of following directions: the direction of the author's attention (e.g., to a proposition), the direction of fit between words and world (e.g., the kind of illocution). (247)

7.2.1.2 The "Wink" and Intentionality

Using the illustration of a wink, Vanhoozer persuasively develops his case for intentionality. There are involuntary winks (a physical reflex) and voluntary ones (for example, to get someone's attention). The same bodily action is involved in both cases. The rapid closing and opening of the eye can be an act or a non-act. The difference between them is solely located in the intentionality of the voluntary act. This voluntary wink, however, is an "institutional fact" that cannot be described as a "brute fact" without losing explanatory power (248). It is true that one could explain intentional acts as involuntary events, as for example, an intentional wink may be described in terms of its physiology. "Yet even a thoroughgoing physiological explanation of an eye movement may be incomplete; it may only get us as far as the blink, not the wink. Ultimately, it is the agent's intention that makes an action what it is" (248).

A further aspect of understanding the intentionality of the wink is the unity of the act of winking. One cannot simply analyze the various components of a wink and arrive at understanding. If one analyzes the neural patterns that together form a wink, one ultimately loses that component that turns the *blink* into a *wink*. A consequence of this is the loss of the entire communicative act.

> When I intend a wink, I originate and unify all the infrastructural systems that I need to put in motion in order to enact my wink. Each of these stages could be examined in itself, but not one stage is the locus of the intention or of the wink. Yet if the wink is indeed a communicative act, then its explanation is incomplete and inauthentic unless reference is made to the intention that initiated and enacted it. Intention is not the first in a series of events that initiates an action, but rather the principle that unifies the whole act. (248)

The same type of reasoning can be applied to the textual process of communication. It is here that Castelli makes a fundamental flaw in her approach to texts. Vanhoozer writes:

> The author's intention is the originating and unifying power that puts a linguistic system (the infrastructure) into motion in order to do something with words that the system alone cannot do. The author's intention is the real causality that alone accounts for why a text is the way it is. It is important to locate the cause of the text at the right level: not at the level of the infrastructure (the sign system) or at the level of the superstructure (e.g., the ideology), but at the level of the completed act—the level of that to which the author was attending. The author's intention is a necessary condition of the text taken as a unified and completed act. (249)

Castelli's work can be said to be a study in the analysis of the "superstructure," the "ideology" in the text. Or, to put it more accurately, her analysis of the ideology is *based on her own ideological standpoint.* She completely dismisses that to which the author was attending and intending as an invalid object of study, and uses her perception of the superstructure to analyze what she sees as going on in the text.[26] For Castelli, the superstructure (ideology) is all-important.

A further important, though complex, step Vanhoozer takes is to bring in recent thought on consciousness as it relates to the body-mind relationship. He claims that meaning, similar to the mind, is an "emergent property."

> An emergent property is one that characterizes a higher order phenomenon (e.g., the brain) that has attained such a level of organizational complexity that it displays new properties (e.g., mental rather than physical) and requires new categories (e.g., the mind) to describe them. (249)

The phenomena on the higher level cannot be described in terms of the lower level phenomena upon which the higher-level phenomena are based. They become, in fact, a completely new phenomenon that follows a new set of rules, which cannot be extrapolated from the rules that apply on the lower levels.[27]

These recent insights have ramifications for reader-centered approaches to texts, which Castelli exemplifies. Such readings reduce "higher level phenomena (e.g., meaning) to lower, materialistic levels (e.g., signifying systems)" (249). Castelli imputes meaning to the material level of the signifying systems and ignores the dimension of the author's meaning—which imparts to the whole text its unifying principle. Since this higher level is bypassed, the replacement unifying principle is found in *her* reading of various

---

26 "My account of intention resists what I call 'eliminative semiotics'—the tendency to reduce meaning to morphemes in motion or to explain meaning in terms of the immanence of the language system" (Vanhoozer, *Meaning*, 249).

27 Vanhoozer follows Nancey Murphy at this point: "The new concepts needed to describe the emergent properties are neither applicable at the lower level nor reducible to (translatable into) concepts at the lower level" (Nancey C. Murphy, *Anglo-American Postmodernity: Philosophical Perspectives on Science, Religion, and Ethics* [Boulder, Colo.: Westview, 1997], 20).

lower-level systems, which may or may not, in fact, be present.[28]

7.2.1.3 The Role of Context with respect to Intention

A significant component in discerning textual (authorial) intentionality is the all-important role that context plays. "Context" is defined by Vanhoozer as

> the various factors one has to take into consideration together with the text in order to understand the author's intention. Any number of circumstances or contexts might be relevant to this task: historical, linguistic, literary, canonical, sociological, and so forth. (250)

The understanding of the appropriate context of the author makes it possible for the reader to understand the author's words as he/she understood them. The breadth or narrowness of the context is based on what is necessary for making sense of the text of an author as a "communicative act" (252).

7.2.1.4 Illocution, Perlocution, and Accidents

Another factor in determining meaning is the necessity of distinguishing the intended results (illocution) of the author from both the *desired* consequences (perlocutions) and *unintended* consequences (accidents). As far as authorial intention goes, the author is responsible for illocution but not for the rest. One cannot impugn the writer for the misconstrued readings and results of those readings, which were never intended by the writer at the time of writing. Thus the patriarchal narratives cannot be found guilty of promoting partriarchalism, since it was an "unforeseen and unintended consequence of the text" which was not the original intention of the author (255).

Here also Castelli's argumentation falters, since she imputes the effects of her reading of Paul's texts on subsequent generations. She writes that

> it is crucial that we think beyond the first century and look at the reading *effects* of Paul's discourse in our own context . . . . The Bible, into which Paul's occasional letters were woven, is obviously a major source for the master narratives that have constructed Western culture. Even now, twenty centuries and a number of epistemic shifts later, the *effects* of these biblical texts continue to modulate and reverberate culturally.[29]

---

28 Vanhoozer writes: "I believe that the theory of communicative action yields a fuller explanation of how things at the lower linguistic levels get taken up into more complex literary forms and provides a better account of what we must postulate in order to account for the emergence of textual meaning. The author's intention, reconceived in terms of agency, explains how we get from the physics to the semantics. *I believe in the reality of the author's intention, for without it I cannot explain the emergence of meaning, that is to say, how meaning supervenes on written marks*" (Vanhoozer, *Meaning*, 249; author's emphasis).

29 Castelli, *Imitating Paul*, 119-20 (emphasis mine).

According to Vanhoozer, this move on Castelli's part is illegitimate, for Paul could not have foreseen and did not intend the negative outworkings of his writings to be construed in various ways. In addition, Paul never intended his writings to be construed in the way that Castelli reads them.[30]

7.2.1.5 On Ambiguity and Multiple Meanings

In order to discern the author's intention, one is often confronted on the one hand with *ambiguity* (i.e., uncertainty of meaning giving rise to various understandings) and *multiple meanings* (i.e., intending more than one thing at one and the same time). This concept of ambiguity is a reason for Castelli's rejection of the possibility of recovering authorial intention. She observes that since the intention cannot be adequately and fully reconstructed, it must not be attempted: "[T]o assume that verbal expression is continuous with authorial intent is to assume that language is transparent and self-evident, a conduit of communication which leaves no remainder."[31] According to Castelli, since a full reconstrual of the intention of the author is in essence impossible, one must infer that the intention of the author cannot be adequately recovered. This leap in logic is unwarranted. In seeking to discern the intention of the author, lack of *full* understanding of the author's intentions does not negate *sufficient* understanding of them. To argue in this way is to set up an unjustifiable either-or dichotomy.

Turning to the concept of *multiple meanings*, Vanhoozer asks whether an author is capable of intending multiple things at one time (256). Vanhoozer denies this possibility, since intention implies authorial awareness. "All claims that a text alludes to some previous text, that it is ironic, or that it is fiction rather than history depend, logically and ontologically, on what the author was actually doing."[32] This is a crucial point. Our interest is not with any structures that Castelli may have discovered in the text. Our interest is in the intentionality of Paul in what he said. Did he *intend* these power structures, that Castelli reads into his discourse, to have a message? Were they an intentional part of that, which he was trying to convey to his readers? Based on our exegesis of the imitation passages, Paul did not have these intentions.

---

30 The support for this statement is found in the cumulative effort of seeking to understand Paul's intention when he refers to imitation, which we have discussed throughout this work.

31 Castelli, *Imitating Paul*, 120.

32 Vanhoozer, *Meaning*, 256. This needs to be qualified somewhat. We would argue that one cannot intend two things at a given time that knowingly are self-contradictory. When one performs an action, one can have multiple intentions that mutually support one another. There is, I would maintain, one foundational intention that may drag other intentions along with it.

7.2.1.6 The Importance of Distinguishing "Meaning" from "Significance"[33]

The two questions, "What did the author mean?" (*meaning*) and "What does it mean to me?" (*significance*) need to be held apart in the task of interpretation, since the symbiosis of the two leads to interpretive confusion. *Meaning* we have discussed above, but *significance* can be understood as the ways a text has come to be understood in contexts not envisioned by the author.[34] *Significance* is the proper object of the study of *criticism* understood as "all of the indefinitely extendible interpretations that any work might be given by individuals or societies pursuing their own interests unchecked by intentions."[35]

The first question (what the author meant) is properly basic to the second (what it means to individuals in other contexts), and the second can only be answered successfully, presupposing a desire to honor the intentionality of the author, if the first is satisfactorily understood. This distinction obviously presupposes a fixed and stable meaning in the text throughout time. Applying this to the teachings of Jesus, Vanhoozer writes,

> For the realist, one cannot change the past simply by interpreting it differently . . . The *meaning* of Jesus is independent of our attempts to express his *significance*. That is not to say that we cannot have new interpretive insights, but to insist that these insights, insofar as they enable a more adequate reading of the text, reveal something already there that had previously escaped notice.[36]

When we look at the work of Castelli, she appears to have no interest in *meaning* as we understand it here. Rather, she jumps right to significance without first considering meaning. She then takes significance to be *a* meaning of the text:

> My line of inquiry is meant to be both provocative and illuminating, looking at the text not simply as a historical artifact from a period quite removed from our own (and the questions that concern our own period of history), but as a continuously-producing source of *meanings* as timely and urgent now as at first writing.[37]

This conflation of *meaning* with *significance* leads to constant confusion in her book. When she refers to *meanings* in this quotation, she is speaking of "what the text means *to her*" that is, the implications that these texts have for

---

33 Building on the works of E. D. Hirsch: *Validity in Interpretation* (New Haven, Conn.: Yale University Press, 1967), and *The Aims of Interpretation* (Chicago: University of Chicago Press, 1976).

34 Vanhoozer, *Meaning*, 260.

35 Wayne C. Booth, *A Rhetoric of Irony* (Chicago: University of Chicago Press, 1974), 19. Cited in Vanhoozer, *Meaning*, 260.

36 Vanhoozer, *Meaning*, 263 (author's emphasis).

37 Castelli, *Imitating Paul*, 121 (emphasis mine).

her in her contemporary situation. However, since she has ignored the task of the first question ("What did Paul mean by the texts he wrote?") and since she has detached it from its relationship to the second question ("What it means to me?"), it is questionable that *what it means to her* corresponds with Paul's actual intentions in the text.

It is abundantly clear throughout the work that Castelli has come to the text with her own agenda, with the intention of squeezing out of the texts anything that hints at an ideology of individual and institutional power. Although she claims to be "reading the text," she in effect is "reading *into* the text" her own meaning.

In light of this, it is illuminating to analyze how she has strategically developed the argument of her study of Pauline imitation. She begins with an overview of the major interpreters of Paul and how they understand Pauline imitation and notes the universal, glaring ignorance of the dimension of power.[38] She then shifts in the next chapter to discuss the Foucauldian understanding of power, which then becomes the *Castellian* understanding—that is, leadership implies a drive to grasp and maintain power and control over others in an authoritarian and malevolent manner. After she has established this framework as *a* valid framework for understanding power, she puts on these Foucauldian glasses and looks at the references to imitation in the Greco, Roman, and Judaic contexts, which she then follows by an analysis of the Pauline imitation texts.[39] Paul is thus "framed" by Foucault from the very outset, and is pre-judged to be a power-hungry, authoritarian, malevolent leader.[40] Her reading of Paul simply confirms her starting point. No alternative seems possible, based on how she has stacked the argumentation.

Vanhoozer argues vigorously against such biased readings and speaks, as if targeting Castelli's work directly:

> Without this basic distinction between meaning and significance, subsequent distinctions—between exegesis and eisegesis, understanding and overstanding, commentary and criticism—will be difficult, if not impossible, to maintain. Without some such criterion for discriminating "what is meant" to the author from "what it means" to the reader, interpreters risk confusing the aim of the text with their own aims and interests. It is one thing to fuse horizons, quite another to

38 This in itself is revealing. Since these interpreters were interested in the intentionality of Paul and sought to understand what he meant when he referred to imitation, there was general unanimity in understanding it not in terms of power, as Castelli wishes to see it, but in benevolent, self-sacrificial terms.

39 Although she uses the term "a possible reading," the distinct impression one has in reading her work is that it is in actual fact *the* correct reading. This conclusion is derived from the fact that all other readings that she discusses are dismissed as inadequate and naïve (23-34). Thus her explicit mentioning of her reading being "a possible" reading masks her intention of it being *the true* reading.

40 Castelli, *Imitating Paul*, 89.

> *confuse* them. Contemporary readers who reject the meaning/significance distinction, refuse hermeneutic realism, and ignore the author's intended meaning as a goal and guide, condemn themselves to such confusion, and to interpretive narcissism besides. Bereft of intrinsic meaning, a text becomes a screen on which readers project their own images or a surface that reflects the interpreter's own face.[41]

7.2.1.7 Concluding Comments on Authorial Intention

If the hermeneutical theory of the communicative act of written texts that Vanhoozer has presented is an accurate description of how texts really work, which we believe it does, then the starting point of Castelli, upon which she bases her work, is radically called into question. This illegitimate starting point undermines both the foundation of her work and her argumentation based on that foundation.

The remaining points of critique of Castelli's work can be responded to based on the perspective of what Paul, the author, intended to do with the words and texts that he wrote. We have seen how Castelli has read Paul from the framework of power. We now respond to Castelli's use of Foucault as a starting point.

7.2.2 The Foucauldian Starting Point – Ideology, Truth, and the Danger of Reading with Tinted Glasses

Castelli frames her discussion in chapter two of Foucault's theory of power with a quotation from Foucault himself, which functions as the interpretive framework within which she herself operates:

> It is one of my targets to show people that a lot of things that are a part of their landscape—that people think are universal—are the result of some very precise historical changes. All my analyses are against the idea of universal necessities in human existence. They show the arbitrariness of institutions [42]

Castelli then applies this statement to what she is intending in her work:

> With Foucault, I reject the notion that there is anything universally human about cultural and social formations and institutions. Societies are organized and power relations emerge in response to very particular historical circumstances. (37)

Thus, any institution that sets itself up as a "totalizing, fully explanatory system of meaning (tradition)" must be understood as an illegitimate ideology. The rationale for this is that any such claim is not self-evident (33). Since this is

41 Vanhoozer, *Meaning*, 263 (author's emphasis).

42 Quoted in Castelli, *Imitating Paul*, 36.

descriptive of *all* institutions, it is clear that Christianity must also be understood as an arbitrary, historical phenomenon with no legitimate, self-evident claim to universality: "My study attempts . . . to challenge the 'specialness' usually attributed to early Christianity—an attribution which masks a theological claim to a privileged truth for Christianity" (35). Clearly, the task of dismantling Christianity's claim is the thrust of her work.

Since there is no "specialness" attached to Christianity, from her Foucauldian starting point, Paul's claim to privilege and special revelation must be interpreted as an attempt at coercive, manipulative, self-seeking power over others. We will deal with the reasoning implicit in this claim when we address the issue of "specialness" in the next section. Our point here is simply to note this as her starting point for the choice of "power" as her hermeneutical stance.

As noted above, Castelli's rejection of the concept of authorial intent as well as her discarding any claims of Christianity's specialness enables her to select any standpoint from which she can launch a critique. And as noted, she has chosen Foucault's notion of power as her framework for such a critique. It is at this point that Castelli is vulnerable.

This adoption of Foucault's notion of power is telling. What she has effectively done is traded one "totalizing, fully explanatory system" for another. Despite her claim that she "attempts to resist the arrogant singularity of the drive toward truth, recognizing its elusive and contingent status" (57), nevertheless her adoption of Foucault's notion of power functions *de facto* as just such a totalizing explanatory system, which she then uses to silence other readings.

This seems to us the inherent philosophical dilemma out of which radical relativism cannot extricate itself: the rejection of any truth-claim as arrogant is claimed on the basis of an alternate truth-claim. The sheer attempt at making an utterance is to utter a truth-claim, whether one is saying "I *believe* this is so" or "This *is* so."

It is important to reflect more carefully on Foucault's notion of "power" as his operating paradigm: In Castelli's understanding of Foucault, her basic paradigm is that of a "power struggle." Every action, every word, every phrase from Paul is critiqued on the basis of "what does this tell us about Paul's attempt at exerting his authority/power onto those under him?" She reads the Pauline texts in general with this lens but specifically focuses on Paul's references to imitation. She, following Foucault, assumes that this is the basic paradigm, upon which all human institutions are based. However, power, is not the only model by which one can view institutions and relationships. It is not *the* universal starting point. It is highly instructive that she mentions no other alternative to analyzing institutions except for the tool of power.

However, just as one can critique anything from the vantage point of power, so one can legitimately critique institutions and relationships from a number of vantage points: i.e., from the paradigm of love, service, kindness, usefulness, profitability, etc. It is an illegitimate oversimplification to isolate power from the other realities of life and lift it up—in its isolation—as *the* basic paradigm by which everything should be critiqued. Isolating one factor to the exclusion of the others is an illegitimate distortion of reality that does not do justice to the totality of persons in relationship with one another. To view social structures as providing "the possibility for desires to meet and conflict, and for the agents within power relations to engage one another"[43] is reductionistic and does not reflect the multifaceted totality of how human beings live, feel, and interact.

Castelli (and Foucault) are surely correct in seeing that the component of power is present in every social relationship. But every social relationship is a blending of complex, multiple motivations—of which one may be predominant. The question, which Castelli never asks, is: "Is the desire for power *the main motivating factor* in Paul's relationships with the congregations he founded?" A correlated question is: "Is the quest for power *the main motivating factor* for the letters that he wrote?" Castelli simply assumes *power* to be the main motivator based on her Foucauldian starting point, without substantiating her claim, and proceeds with interpreting Paul based on this.

If the assumption of Castelli's—that Paul was using the texts as a literary power play—was not the driving force Paul's letters, then her results end up to be a fundamental misreading of these texts. This provokes the further question of how one seeks to determine true motivation or intention from a piece of writing. The approach that we have attempted to follow is that which has been outlined in the previous section—analyzing the intentions of the author as they are scripted into the shape of the text.

7.2.3 Paul and Christianity – The Issues of Specialness, Power, and Authority

As has been evident in the survey of Castelli's position and in the previous point, one of Castelli's major criticisms of traditional approaches to Pauline imitation is that they simply assume the "specialness" of Paul and do not call into question the legitimacy of that uniqueness. She, however, never asks the question: "Does Paul, in fact, have a legitimately privileged position?" She simply assumes, based on her Foucauldian starting point, the impossibility of this.

Castelli's basic assumption is that there can be no specialness, no unique revelation that has a legitimate claim to be ultimate truth. The logic of this argumentation is questionable since it begs the question. If one's starting point is that there cannot be unique revelation, then that starting point has predetermined the outcome one will receive and will exclude any evidence as invalid that runs counter to that starting point.

There is a further implicit assumption of Castelli's that is closely tied to the previous one. The assumption is that, since one cannot *prove* special revelation or unique privilege, then there *cannot be* special revelation or unique privilege.

---

43 Castelli, *Imitating Paul*, 50.

Yet, it is important to distinguish between *claims* to specialness and *evidences* of those claims. Castelli's intention is surely laudable to restrict illegitimate claims to specialness and privilege. But one does not accomplish this with her line of argumentation. Other criteria are needed to discern between legitimate and illegitimate claims to specialness.

Is there a "specialness" to Christianity? Did Paul have a privileged status? If so, how can one know? In other words, what are the proofs of such claims to uniqueness. Peter Berger's brilliant essay, "Amid Different Follies," begins with a reflection on the sociological dimensions of knowledge, where he claims that "every human society has its own corpus of officially accredited wisdom, the beliefs and values that most people take for granted as self-evidently true."[44] This corpus is for that society their "plausibility structure." Any group in society that deviates from this plausibility structure by setting up a competing corpus of wisdom, beliefs, and values, will be viewed as a threat to the dominant society and will be treated by them with contempt and disdain.

It was just this state of affairs in which the Corinthian believers, holding to "the foolishness of the cross" in the face of the "wisdom of the world" (1 Cor 1:18, 20), found themselves. The Christian message contained an understanding of truth, which stood in radical contradiction to the reigning plausibility structures. To feel the emotional impact of the predicament of the Corinthians, Berger asks the reader to imagine the following:

> [T]o appreciate the outlandishness of Paul's message, we should perhaps "translate" these discrepancies [between the Christian message and the prevalent assumptions in Corinth] into contemporary terms. Take anything which in your immediate milieu is taken for granted as scientifically established knowledge or as self-evident common sense—and then imagine your reaction to someone who confidently and aggressively proclaims the opposite.[45]

The point Berger is making is that the Christian message stood at that time, as it does now, with paradigms of what some cultures hold to be true or false. What is self-evident in Tokyo is not necessarily self-evident in New York, Vienna, or Madras. Castelli, Foucault, and others are correct in observing that there is no Archimedean standpoint, no universal standard, to which all can appeal to be the final arbiter of what constitutes conclusive proof of truth or falsehood. This Enlightenment quest for objective truth that can adjudicate between rival truth-claims cannot—in light of the social dimension of knowledge—be realized. There is no ultimate court of appeals, which can adjudicate between competing truth-claims represented by the religions and philosophies in the public square.[46]

---

44 Berger, *Far Glory*, 9.

45 Berger, *Far Glory*, 8.

46 "There is no external criterion above [competing truth-claims] to which I and my opposite number can appeal for a decision . . . . [T]he ultimate outcome is at the end

Yet this stance does not necessarily imply relativism. It simply points to the inadequacy of logical proofs to span the various philosophical or religious systems, since any "proof" is contingent upon the system within which the proof is considered valid. Each system of truth has warrants and arguments that "make sense" within that system, the validity of which would be denied in another system of truth.[47] Verification of "truth" or "proof" turns, then, on both the coherence of the system as well as the ability it has to integrate the greatest amount of data into a coherent whole. As N. T. Wright states,

> There is no such thing as "neutral" or "objective" proof; only the claim that the story [i.e., system] we are now telling about the world as a whole makes more sense, in its outline and detail, than other potential or actual stories that may be on offer. Simplicity of outline, elegance in handling the details within it, the inclusion of all the parts of the story, and the ability of the story to make sense beyond its immediate subject-matter: these are what count.[48]

To develop a full-blown argument for the uniqueness of Christianity and the special role that Paul had based on the criteria that N. T. Wright describes would go beyond the purview of this work. Impressive arguments for the uniqueness of Christ and for the unique position of Paul as interpreter of the life and message of Christ have been marshaled.[49] Yet these arguments may fail to convince those with a differing plausibility structure that follows its own

---

when the one who alone is judge sums up and gives the verdict"(Lesslie Newbigin, *Foolishness to the Greeks: The Gospel and Western Culture* [Grand Rapids: Eerdmans, 1986], 65).

47 For example, a grammatical proof has no relevance to the study of biology, since the criteria and the systems of each are of a radically different nature.

48 N. T. Wright, *The New Testament and the People of God* (Minneapolis: Fortress, 1992), 42. A full-bodied discussion of epistemology is not possible. See the compelling argument for a critical-realist epistemology by N. T. Wright on pages 31-45.

49 For a limited sampling on the uniqueness of Jesus, see N. T. Wright, *The Resurrection of the Son of God* (London: SPCK, 2003); Dunn, *Jesus Remembered*; Larry W. Hurtado, *Lord Jesus Christ: Devotion to Jesus in Earliest Christianity* (Grand Rapids: Eerdmans, 2003); Larry W. Hurtado, *How on Earth Did Jesus Become a God? Historical Questions About Earliest Devotion to Jesus* (Grand Rapids: Eerdmans, 2005). For discussions on the significance of what occurred on the road to Damascus as well as Paul's understanding of his unique commission as apostle see the following sources and the literature noted there: K. H. Rengstorf, "ἀπόστολος," *TWNT* 1:402-48; Seyoon Kim, *The Origin of Paul's Gospel* (WUNT 4; Tübingen: J. C. B. Mohr, 1981); Hans Dieter Betz, "Apostle," n.p., *ABD on CD-ROM*. Version 3.0a. 2006; Richard N. Longenecker, *The Road from Damascus: the Impact of Paul's conversion on His Life, Thought, and Ministry* (Grand Rapids: Eerdmans, 1997); Witherington, *Paul Quest*, 73-78, 156-62; Paul W. Barnett, "Apostle," *DPL* 45-50; Schnelle, *Apostle Paul*, 87-102.

internal system of what it holds as valid warrants and arguments.

Yet, as we have seen and will continue to see, Castelli's rejection of the uniqueness of Christianity and the specialness of Paul raises more questions than it answers. None of the fundamental arguments for the uniqueness of Christ or of Paul's special place in the early church has been addressed in Castelli's work. In addition, her reconstruction does not meet the criteria of N. T. Wright that we noted above with respect to verification of truth-claims. While she may have produced a simple outline—reducing Paul and his message to that of strategy for power—this outline turns out to be reductionistic in that it collapses the entirety of Paul's life and thought to one concept that does not have sufficient explanatory and integrating power for the breadth of what Paul did and said. She does not attempt to include all the data in the texts, but deals selectively with it, choosing those aspects, which support her thesis, reinterpreting others to align them with her thesis, and ignoring other data that runs counter to her thesis. Finally, she is not able to explain the breadth of human relationships beyond the Pauline material based on her reconstruction.

7.2.4 Castelli's Threefold Conclusion of the Nature of Imitation

Castelli, in her analysis of imitation in antiquity and in Paul, perceives three problems that she concludes are inherent in the concept of imitation: (1) the problem of implicit hierarchy; (2) the model is superior in value; (3) "sameness" is a virtue and "difference" is therefore undesirable. We will briefly respond to these charges.

7.2.4.1 On the Problem of Implicit Hierarchy

The first critique Castelli brings is that imitation implies hierarchy and thus inequality. This rubs against her egalitarian assumptions that all are created equal. Castelli, however, confuses *ontology* with *ability* and *status*. *Ontologically* there are no differences between individuals. All are equal. The programmatic passage in Gal 3:28 bears witness to this: "There is neither Jew nor Greek, slave nor free, male nor female, for you are all one in Christ." Before Christ, we are all children of God[50] and brothers and sisters of one another.[51]

Regarding *ability* or *status/role* in life, it is a fact of life—irrespective of the dimension of power—that humans do not have the same abilities and do not

50 "The Spirit himself testifies with our spirit that we are children of God" (Rom 8:16; cf. Gal 4:3). With the first person plural, Paul is placing himself on the same level, demonstrating his equality with them before God.

51 See the abundant references to ἀδελφοί in Paul's writings, in which he places himself, in some sense, on the same level—as a brother—with the recipients. In a remarkable text, Christ is presented as our brother, thus displaying identification with us. (Rom 8:29)

play the same roles. Here, it is true: there is inequality. This, however, need not be implicitly negative, as Castelli paints it. It is a fact, that certain individuals have competencies in certain areas and others do not. It is a fact that there are master carpenters and there are apprentices. There are parents, and there are children. There are students, and there are teachers.[52] It is a fact that there are people who display virtues in their lives that are desirable—and then there are others that could use more virtue.

The same distinction between ontology and ability/role relate to Paul. In Paul's texts he stresses two relational realities: With respect to ontology, Paul saw himself as a child of God and a sibling to the recipients. With respect to role, Paul was a spiritual father to them.[53] With respect to ability and experience, Paul, since he had a deeper experience of Christ, could call the recipients to imitate him.

7.2.4.2 On the Model as Superior in Value

Castelli writes: "The distance between the model and the copy is never completely erased . . . the copy is a derivation from the perfection of the model."[54] This criticism of Castelli, that the model is considered of superior value, is integrally related to the previous point. The distinction between ontology and ability/role, which we have argued above, apply here as well. The argumentation of Castelli on this point does not follow logically: the distance between model and copy is one that will never be erased and thus leads to permanent frustration and subordination. This does not necessarily follow since it is possible for a student as she gains skill and experience to surpass her teacher. An apprentice can learn her trade and surpass the skills of the master carpenter. That Paul does not mention this has less to do with his superior value, and more to do with the relative immaturity of the congregations, which he is addressing. Castelli's criticism does not hold.

7.2.4.3 On "Sameness" as Virtue and "Difference" as Undesirable

Castelli's understanding of imitation as demanding "sameness" and squelching diversity is problematic. She understands "sameness" to be the equivalent of the superficial "cookie cutter" variety: everyone thinking and acting the same. She claims this both with respect to mimesis in antiquity as well as in Paul: "The mimetic relationship replicates the harmonious quality of the cosmos; sameness and the desire to achieve it are tied to the cosmic order. By inference, difference is relegated to the realm of discord and chaos" (81). However, a closer reading of the texts of antiquity as well as of Paul does not bear this out.

52 We grant that these roles are culturally determined, but every culture makes similar or corresponding role distinctions.

53 Gal 4:19: "My dear children, for whom I am again in the pains of childbirth until Christ is formed in you." Also 1 Cor 4:14.

54 Castelli, *Imitating Paul*, 80.

Imitation does not imply the obliteration of all distinction and uniformity in all aspects. The calls to imitation we looked at in chapter three[55] indicate an individual, creative process, an imaginative act that metaphorically translates virtues observed in the model (living or dead) in a given situation (or situations) into a completely new context, where other dynamics are operative. There is similarity, but the application of that virtue is not an exact replica.

Paul's conception of unity and diversity is much broader and differentiated than Castelli would lead us to believe. His understanding of gifting (corresponding to the category *ability/role* discussed above) is crucial here. Paul celebrated diversity in his letters but is also realistic about the need for unity in certain areas. A group could not exist without this interplay between unity and diversity, and Paul acknowledges this. The passage in 1 Corinthians 12 speaks to this eloquently. Everyone has a different gifts but there is "one Spirit" (1 Cor 12:9). There is not "sameness" in the sense Castelli uses it but rather harmony in the midst of diversity. The unity is based on "the same Spirit . . . the same Lord . . . the same God" (1 Cor 12:4-6, cf. Rom 12:3-8). This diversity does not stand in contradiction to Phil 2:2, which stresses the need to "have the same mind, the same love, being one in spirit and purpose." This multiple unity is integrally related to the Christ-Hymn of vv. 6-11 and speaks to the "glue" that is necessary for the functioning of relationships. Again, this sameness is not mindless uniformity, but presupposes and implies diversity—or else the call to unity would be unnecessary.

Thiselton notes several important studies that analyze Pauline rhetoric and which come to the opposite conclusion of Castelli with regard to the issue of sameness.[56] Pogoloff's research shows that it was Paul's desire in Corinth to protect those who might easily have been despised, disadvantaged, and socially inferior. This was the motivating factor for his call to unity and imitation. Marshall argues that the call to humility is a confrontation with those Corinthian believers who discriminated based on social status, and not motivated by a drive to conformity. Paul championed the case for the weak and those who were not highly esteemed.[57]

55 See specifically: "Descriptive Imitation Texts."

56 S. M. Pogoloff, *Logos and Sophia: The Rhetorical Situation of 1 Corinthians* (Atlanta: Scholars Press, 1992); P. Marshall, *Enmity at Corinth: Social Conventions in Paul's Relations with the Corinthians* (Tübingen: J. C. B. Mohr, 1987); Wendel L. Willis, *Idol Meat at Corinth. The Pauline Argument in 1 Corinthians 8 and 9* (Chico, Calif.: Scholars Press, 1985).

57 Marshall, *Enmity*, 295. (Directed to this and sources in previous footnote by Thiselton, *Interpreting God*, 132).

7.2.5 Paul–Benevolent or Malevolent Authoritarian? On Patriarchal Symbolism and Discerning Authorial Emotions

Castelli from the outset denies that any Pauline reference to paternity contains a positive connotation. She writes: "My point is that the image of the father must be read in cultural context, that is, in relationship to the nature of the paternal role in Greco-Roman society—which is a role of possessing total authority over children"(101). She links these paternal images with the military general's assertion of his power. She further reinterprets any positive intention or emotion into a Pauline strategy for asserting his power.

A response to these criticisms must begin again at the issues discussed under authorial intent above. Castelli assigns meaning to her perception of the superstructures in the text and mutes meaning that the author may have intended. This superstructure is then imposed on and supersedes any intentionality that the author may have had. Since Castelli's discovered structure is Foucauldian power, then everything the text speaks of must speak of this power. Thus, any positive imagery, any benevolence that one observes in the text, and any positive emotions in the text are transmuted in Castelli's reading into strategies to exert and assert power and maintain the ascendancy of Paul over-against the subordinated readers. If, however, the locus of intention and meaning are taken away from her reading of the superstructure (i.e., the Foucauldian starting point as well as *her construct of* Greco-Roman society) and returned to the authorial intention located in the text, her reading becomes effectively a *mis*reading. The analogy of the wink discussed above applies here. Castelli has analyzed the neural patterns of the wink (structures, superstructures), and has ignored completely the reason (authorial intention) for the wink itself.

When intentionality is taken away from the structure that Castelli imposes on the text, a completely different picture emerges of Paul, and his use of power/authority is cast into a different light altogether. A number of points must be taken into consideration in order to understand Paul's relationship with the recipients *in its totality*[58] and, further, in order to understand Paul's use of power/authority.[59]

7.2.5.1 Paul's Motivation for Life and Ministry

The genesis of Paul's motivation came with his supernatural encounter with the

---

58 Burke comes to the same conclusion: "[My contention] is that any correct understanding of Paul's role as 'father' towards the Thessalonians needs to account adequately for his hierarchical position and authority *and* his affection for his converts, and that these two aspects are not mutually exclusive" (Burke, "Paternity," 61).

59 We note only a few texts, which provide the general tenor of these various aspects of Paul's life and thought.

living Christ, which caused a radical reorientation in every sphere of his life.[60] Paul's desire then becomes to live for Christ.[61] He considered every earthly gain in status to be of no value. Instead, he desired to know Christ and be fully united with him.[62] He expresses his motivation for ministry as being compelled by the love of Christ,[63] which has ignited a desire in Paul for all to be reconciled with God. In 1 Cor 9 he twice repeats the motivation for his action: "we put up with anything rather than hinder the gospel of Christ" (v. 12) and "I do all this for the sake of the gospel" (v. 23). These texts give strong indication that his life and ministry revolved exclusively around this principle and can only adequately be understood if these are seen as the core principle out of which flowed everything that Paul said and did.

7.2.5.2 Paul's Roles with Respect to the Recipients

Growing out of his motivations for life and ministry were *the roles that he played with respect to the recipients*. Since Paul's roles of parent, teacher, and leader have already been explicated at the end of chapter two, we only note them here. Since the specific problematic imagery for Castelli seems to be the paternity of Paul, we will focus on this. It is clear that Paul saw himself as the spiritual parent of the recipients.[64] Most times, he uses paternal language to describe this relationship,[65] but he also uses maternal imagery as well.[66] It is important, as we will observe below, to note that the paternity of Paul was full-orbed; that is, it encompassed the full range of emotions and responses that an actual parent would have. This includes both authority and love, and sees these emotions not as mutually exclusive, but as interrelated.[67]

---

60 See the foundational work of Seyoon Kim, who argues that the source of Paul's call and the subsequent development of his theological understanding of salvation are directly related to his encounter with Christ (Kim, *Origin of Paul's Gospel*).

61 "For to me to live is Christ, and to die is gain." (Phil 1:21)

62 Phil 3:8-11.

63 2 Cor 5:14. He also writes that he is inwardly compelled to preach the gospel: "Woe is me if I do not preach the gospel" (1 Cor 9:16).

64 For references, see chapter two.

65 1 Cor 4:14-16; 1 Thess 2:11-12.

66 Gal 4:19; 1 Thess 2:7-8.

67 Similar to our observations in chapter three, Burke sees both dynamics as part of the concept of paternity in antiquity. Castelli, on the other hand, suppresses these positive qualities and favors the negative ones. In Burke's analysis of Castelli's use of the primary sources, he concludes: "Castelli's legalistically driven analysis completely neglects the affective aspect of paternal responsibility. This is partly due to her overly selective choice of primary sources. For example, she is critical of scholars who try, in her view unsuccessfully, to use some of Epictetus' writings (e.g. *Diss*. 3.22.95ff.) to argue a case for paternal love. However, Castelli fails to consider other passages in the same discourse where affection is clearly manifested (e.g. *Diss*. 1.11.4, 5-6; 1.23.5; 2.22.4)" (Burke, "Paternity," 65).

7.2.5.3 Paul's Explicit Desires for his Recipients

Another factor that affects how we envision Paul is with respect to how he understood his desires for his recipients. He expresses his desire for his recipients in a number of complementary ways. He describes himself as longing for "Christ to be formed in them."[68] He writes of desiring to share the gospel with them.[69] Further, his desire for them is that they "live lives worthy of God,"[70] which broadly refers to all of life conforming to and being informed by the gospel. The implications of accepting the gospel was not only a cognitive experience, but embraced the totality of a person's life. It did not happen at once. For this reason, it is a constant thread in Paul's epistles that they "grow in grace," that they mature.[71]

7.2.5.4 Paul's Self-less Service for Others

Out of Paul's personal motivations and his explicit desires for his recipients emanated *his selfless service for others,* which was often coupled with *suffering* on other's behalf. Compelled by this encounter with Christ and love for Christ, he was willing to go to great lengths to invite others to be reconciled with God. He endured hardship of every kind—being brought to the point of death several times—for the sake of the gospel.[72] He battled deep discouragement,[73] being misunderstood, mocked and misrepresented;[74] he put himself in positions of emotional weakness for other's sake.[75] All these things he endured, on the one hand, because of his own experience of the love of Christ, and on the other hand, because he desired to help others experience this same love of Christ.

7.2.5.5 Paul's Display of Positive Emotions and Expressions of Benevolence for the Recipients

His selfless service was coupled with *positive emotions and benevolent expressions on his part for the recipients.* Reflected in the letters we see his care for individuals. In Rom 16, Paul mentions twenty-seven people by name,

---

68 Gal 4:19.

69 1 Thess 2:8. This parallels somewhat the desire of Paul for his ministry, understanding himself as an "ambassador of reconciliation" (2 Cor. 5:20). Ralph Martin argues that this is the unifying theme of Paul's theology (Ralph P. Martin, *Reconciliation: A Study of Paul's Theology* (Grand Rapids: Zondervan, 1990); Ralph P. Martin, "Center of Paul's Theology," *DPL* 93-95).

70 1 Thess 2:12.

71 Cf. 1 Cor 14:20; Phil 2:12-14; 3:15 (possibly with a touch of irony); Rom 12:2. Paul's personal goal, expressed in Phil 3:12-14 functions, in the structure of the letter, as a model for them also to follow.

72 2 Cor 1:8-9; 6:3-10; 11:23-30; Phil 4:14.

73 2 Cor 4:7-12.

74 1 Cor 4:8-13, cf. Acts 17:5-7, 32.

75 "I came to you in weakness and fear, and with much trembling." 1 Cor 2:3. Also 2 Cor 12:9-10; 13:2-4.

often using terms of endearment. He speaks of his love for Timothy[76] and Onesimus.[77] He thanks God that Titus has developed "the same concern" Paul has for the Corinthians.[78] In a poignant passage Paul writes: "For I wrote out of great distress and anguish of heart and with many tears, not to grieve you but to let you know the depth of my love for you."[79] He writes to the Corinthians, further, that he works for them for their joy.[80] He expresses the lengths he will go because of his love for them: "I have said before that you have such a place in our hearts that we would live or die with you."[81] Especially to the Philippians, Paul expresses his loving concern for his "brothers and sisters, whom I love and long for, my joy and crown."[82] Of the Philippians he says: "I yearn for you all with the affection of Christ Jesus."[83] He displays his care for other churches, which are in need and helps to raise funding for relief.[84]

The most striking metaphors of loving concern, however, revolve around the parental language of Paul. Particularly striking is his use of maternal metaphors to describe his relationship to the recipients. Especially striking is the metaphor in Gal 4:19, where Paul writes, "My dear children, for whom I am again in the pains of childbirth until Christ is formed in you." It is significant that this metaphor occurs within the context of a disputed imitation passage, Gal 4:12, which Castelli treats.[85] In her discussion of this text, she does not refer to Paul's use of the maternal metaphor in 4:19 (or for that matter, to any other maternal metaphor in her entire work). She does, however, mention Paul's use of fatherhood imagery in Gal 4:1-3, emphasizing the hierarchical nature of father-child relationship. By not dealing with all the material of Paul and leaving out material that controverts her assumptions and conclusions, she has unfairly stacked the deck of her argumentation.

Yet it is instructive to look more carefully at this maternal imagery Gal 4:19: This highly emotive, maternal language indicates a strong sense of identification with women and the pains involved in the birthing process. Gaventa asks the perceptive question:

> Is maternal imagery a language that can readily be used by a man who has no underlying sympathy with or identification with the lives of women? Pressing a little further, I want to suggest the physical struggle involved in giving birth and the vulnerability involved in caring for a child are images not readily used by a

76 1 Cor 4:17.

77 Phm 10-12.

78 2 Cor 8:16.

79 2 Cor 2:4.

80 2 Cor 1:24.

81 2 Cor 7:3.

82 Phil 4:1.

83 Phil 1:8.

84 Gal 2:10 (for a church that is not one that he founded); 2 Cor 8-9.

85 Castelli, *Imitating Paul*, 115-16.

> man so alienated from women and so hierarchical as Paul is sometimes assumed to be.[86]

Another maternity text in Paul's writing that Castelli does not mention is found in 1 Thess 2. She does discuss imitation language in 1:6-7 and 2:14, noting its passive nature (95). Although Castelli acknowledges this,[87] she claims that "the passive nature of the imitation described in 1 Thessalonians 2 points to the power relations involved in such imitation" (95).

In 1 Thess 2:7-11, Paul blends both maternal as well as paternal metaphors together into a moving picture of how Paul lived among the Thessalonians. After mentioning his suffering for the gospel in v. 1, he encourages the Thessalonians to reflect on how he lived with them. Although it is not addressed in the form of question-response, the structure indicates that Paul is inviting them to scrutinize his motivation and lifestyle in order to verify if what Paul says about himself and his companions corresponds to their experience of them.

He begins this chapter (1 Thess 2:2-6) reemphasizing that his motives revolved around the Gospel and wanting to please God. He claims that he was not motivated by impure motives (v. 3); on the contrary, he was motivated by the gospel (v. 4a); there was no desire on his part to please men, only God with how they acted among them (v. 4b); there was no hint of flattery or greed that motivated Paul's coming to them (v. 5). Can this invitation to scrutinize his life, his actions, and his motives be construed as Paul making a power play?

It is at this point, in vv. 7-12, that he introduces the maternal imagery:[88]

> As apostles of Christ we could have been a burden to you, but we were *gentle* among you like a mother *caring for her little children*. We *loved you so much* that we were delighted to share with you not only the gospel of God but *our lives as well*, because *you became so dear to us*. Surely you remember, brothers (and sisters), our toil and hardship; we worked night and day in order not to be a burden to anyone while we preached the gospel of God to you. (emphasis mine)

The emotive language here is striking and contains no nuance of authoritarianism. The image of a concerned, selfless mother absorbed in the well-being of a beloved child is evoked in the language that Paul chooses here.

---

86 Beverly Roberts Gaventa, "The Maternity of Paul: An Exegetical Study of Galatians 4:19," in *The Conversation Continues: Studies in Paul and John in Honor of J. Louis Martyn* (ed. Robert T. Fortna and Beverly Roberts Gaventa; Nashville: Abingdon, 1990), 199.

87 "The mimetic relationship articulated here does not reveal the clearly defined relations of power evident in the other texts involving mimesis" (95).

88 See Malherbe's illuminating study of this maternal imagery on the backdrop of Cynic philosophy, Abraham J. Malherbe, "'Gentle as a Nu[illegible] The Cynic Background to 1 Thess 2," *NovT* 12 (1970): 203-17.

One is certainly hard-pressed to interpret this as a power strategy on Paul's part.

In the next section (v. 10-12), the maternal metaphor is replaced with a paternal one, yet the emphasis Paul highlights with this metaphor is not one of domineering and commanding, but of fatherly encouragement toward right living:

> You are witnesses, and so is God, of how holy, righteous and blameless we were among you who believed. For you know that we dealt with each of you as a father deals with his own children, *encouraging, comforting and urging you* to live lives worthy of God. (emphasis mine)

Paul uses a rhetoric of persuasion to encourage the Thessalonians to orient their lives toward God. He deliberately avoids a rhetoric of command.[89] The text indicates no hint of Paul wishing to bind them to himself. The phrases "you are witnesses" and "for you know" in. vv. 10-12 parallel similar invitations in vv. 1, 2, 5, and 9 for the Thessalonians to scrutinize Paul's life and motives to see whether what he was saying about his paternal concern for the Thessalonians was in alignment with his actual way of being with them.

Outside of contexts that refer to Pauline imitation, there are a few other passages where Paul uses paternal language to indicate loving concern and empathy. Paul tells the Corinthians, "We have opened our hearts wide to you . . . . As a fair exchange—I speak as to my children—open wide your hearts also."[90] In 1 Cor 4:14, Paul expresses how dear the Corinthian community is to him, even as he admonishes them—which brings us to Paul's use of negative emotional language and instances in which he asserts his authority.

7.2.5.6 Paul's Display of Negative Emotions and Use of Authoritarian Language

Even a cursory reading especially of the Corinthian correspondence and the letter to the Galatians, as well as in his other letters, reveals Paul's use of rhetoric that could be classified as authoritarian, negative, derogatory, and/or bitingly sarcastic with respect to the churches that he founded. We see taunting sarcasm,[91] outbursts of frustration, as from an angry parent.[92] We observe clear directives he commands the church to carry out[93] and the top-down issuing of instructions for the churches,[94] and we read of threats of punishment if these

89 It is also highly instructive, as Burke notes, that "Paul never issues instructions based upon his apostolic status" (Burke, "Paternity," 72).

90 2 Cor 6:11-13.

91 1 Cor 4:8-13.

92 Gal 1:6; 1 Cor 5:1-6.

93 1 Cor 5:9-13; Phil 2:12; Phm 2.

94 Cf., 1 Cor 11:17; 1 Thess 4:2.

directives are not followed.[95] How, then, does one explain the negative emotions and the authoritarian language on the one side, and the positive, non-authoritarian rhetoric on the other?

We would suggest that the broad spectrum of Paul's rhetoric is to be understood from the standpoint of Paul's unique call to apostleship, his understanding of the mission given to him by divine revelation, and from the goals that that mission entailed as outlined above.[96] Indeed, the contexts in which Paul's negative language occurs bear this out. In Galatians, Paul appeals to his divine commissioning as an apostle (Gal 1:1, 11).[97] He vents his anger at them not for personal reasons, but in order to preserve the gospel from becoming distorted (Gal 1:6-7). The reason Paul opposed Peter (Gal 2:11-12) was also not for personal reasons, but because the gospel was being compromised (Gal 2:14). The underlying cause of Paul's anger at what is occurring in the Galatian church is described in Gal 4:19-20, a passage we have discussed above, in which Paul reveals his "maternal instincts" for them. Just as mother, who has gone through the entire birthing process, addresses her children with the phrase of endearment, "my little children," so Paul, who was the spiritual parent of the Galatian Christians also experiences maternal emotions of love for them. In fact, the birthing process Paul describes here is for the purpose of Christ being formed in them (v. 19). The following verse indicates that his use of negative language is as a means of last resort: "I wish I . . . could change my tone." Based on this, Paul's default emotion was one of loving concern for the spiritual welfare of the churches he founded, and the negative and authoritarian language was only used when the situation compelled him to "change his tone."

In 1 Corinthians Paul rejects the notion of "personal fan clubs" (1 Cor 1:10-16), which would be bound to him exclusively, and reminds the church that his calling was to proclaim a gospel that transcends all human parties (1 Cor 1:17). This indicates that what he wrote to them and the manner in which he wrote was based on his responsibility to be true to that gospel. As a result of this calling, he became the spiritual parent of the Corinthians (1 Cor 4:15). The phrase "*in Christ Jesus* I became your father" indicates Paul's focus was on calling them to conformity to the character of Christ.

Paul's motivation for writing the Corinthians was because they were his "beloved children" in Christ (1 Cor 4:14). Paul indicates that shame that they

---

95 "We will be ready to punish every act of disobedience" (2 Cor 10:6). See also 1 Cor 4:19-20.

96 See section 7.2.5.1-3.

97 "Gal 1.1 taken in isolation can easily give the impression that Paul's primary concern was to defend his apostleship. But the first main section of the letter (chs. 1-2) shows that it was his gospel which Paul was most concerned about. . . . Apostolic authority was conditioned upon the gospel and subject to the norm of the gospel" (Dunn, *Theology of Paul*, 572).

may have felt as a result of the sarcastic rhetoric he aimed at them in 1 Cor 4:8-13 was not done to "shame" them as an end in itself, but that, out of his care for them, he desired to awaken them to the reality of Paul's selfless service on their behalf and their corresponding selfishness.

In 2 Corinthians, Paul indicates his motivation for all that he did, which must include the rhetoric he chose, was done "not to proclaim [himself, but] . . . to proclaim Jesus Christ as Lord and ourselves as your slaves for Jesus' sake" (2 Cor 4:5). He explains further that "if we are beside ourselves, it is for God; if we are in our right mind, it is for you" (2 Cor 5:13). Paul goes on to describe that he is compelled by the love of Christ (2 Cor 5:15) to be an "ambassador for Christ" (2 Cor 5:20). When he writes, "We are putting no obstacle in anyone's way, so that no fault may be found with our ministry" (2 Cor 6:3), this is, in fact, an invitation to the Corinthians to examine both Paul's motives and the way he ministered in their midst. Someone bent on maintaining power over others would not extend such an invitation.

Paul administers strong words to the Corinthians as a means of correcting self-damaging behavior based on his role as their spiritual parent.[98] In a moving passage in 2 Corinthians, he writes:

> Even if I caused you sorrow by my letter, I don't regret it. Though I did regret it—I see that my letter hurt you, but only for a little while—yet now I am happy, not because you were made sorry, but because your sorrow led you to repentance. For you became sorrowful as God intended and so were not harmed in any way by us. Godly sorrow brings repentance that leads to salvation and leaves no regret, but worldly sorrow brings death. See what this godly sorrow has produced in you: what earnestness, what eagerness to clear yourselves . . . . (2 Cor 7:8-11)

Four observations on this text are relevant for our concerns: (1) This text reveals that Paul's default emotion toward the Corinthians was one of loving concern for his spiritual children (see 2 Cor 6:13). (2) Only when circumstances warranted would he be driven to find a suitable rhetoric to aid them in bringing their lives into conformity with the gospel. (3) The sorrow Paul caused was motivated not by selfish desires for power and control, but by concern for the health of the individuals and the health of the Corinthian church as a whole. (4) Finally, this sorrow is framed in the context of leading them to salvation as their lives were brought into conformity with the gospel.

When we place the texts in which Paul evidences negative emotions and authoritarian language, these can best be understood in light of his divine call to apostleship, his unique calling and mission in service of the gospel, and the spiritual parenting role he played in founding these communities of faith. It is this perspective that has the explanatory power to integrate both the positive and negative rhetoric of Paul. Burke's observation is an apt one:

---

98 He refers to them as such in the previous chapter (2 Cor 6:13).

> Paul's role as father is a richly complex one. The apostle's hierarchical relations . . . need not, and in our view does not, exclude the natural affection he also felt and manifested towards his converts. Any proper understanding of Paul's paternal role must account for the dialectic between the power, influence and authority implied in such a role *and* the benign, affective associations it also implies.[99]

If Paul's words are not considered from this vantage point, then he indeed may look like a power-hungry authoritarian. But when these negative texts are taken together with the many texts emphasizing caring concern, one discerns simply the intensity of Paul's desire for the welfare of his spiritual children.

Naturally, it is possible, as does Castelli, to adopt a hermeneutic of suspicion toward Paul. One can call into question Paul's appeal to his apostleship, the references to his selfless service and suffering on behalf of others, and his consistent grounding of his ministry in Christ and the gospel as stemming from a manipulative strategy to "impose power and to eliminate deviancy."[100]

But does this way of reading do justice to the entirety of Paul as inscribed in his letters? Is it legitimate to isolate one element, such as power, and to read Paul and understand his theology exclusively through this solitary lens? Does this way of reading do justice to the full spectrum of human communication at the time of Paul and in our own?

It would seem that a reading of Paul that seeks to account for this entire spectrum of interaction between him and his churches, as opposed to collapsing this spectrum into the will to power—would lead one to answer "no" to all these questions.

7.3 Summary and Concluding Remarks

Elisabeth Castelli's claim that Paul uses imitation language as a "discourse of power," by which he reinscribes his position as apostle and thus reemphasizes the "hierarchical power relationship" between him and the congregation, to ensure conformity, cannot be sustained. This is due to the twin factors of her illegitimate *a priori* denial of authorial intention and her use of Foucault's understanding of relational power, which she applies to, and, we would argue, forces on the text.

The linchpin in Castelli's work is her rejection of authorial intent. We noted that she herself does not follow the principles she asserts in her work with respect to authorial intent. On the contrary, we have observed that she implicitly operates on the basis of authorial intention. We countered her proposal by means of Kevin Vanhoozer's argument for authorial intent, and we critiqued Castelli's argumentation as we progressed through the approach that Vanhoozer offers. After "resurrecting the author," we critiqued Castelli's

---

99 Burke, "Paternity," 80 (author's emphasis).

100 Thiselton, *Interpreting God*, 141.

Foucauldian starting point and countered, based on authorial intention, that *meaning* is not found in the superstructures one brings to the text (in this case Foucault's understanding of relational power); on the contrary, meaning is controlled by the intention of the author, as the author he has inscribed them in the communication act of the text.

After dealing with these two core issues, we then critiqued three further issues that formed the bulk of Castelli's agenda. (1) Castelli's assumption that Christianity was not "special" and Paul was not "privileged" was seen as logically question-begging, since it assumes that there can be no privileged position. In addition, her assumption was predicated on the implicit supposition that since one cannot prove "specialness" based on criteria, to which everyone would agree, there can therefore not be "specialness." Since truth-claims are system-immanent, having their force within the system from which they derive, there can be no Archimedean standpoint to adjudicate between the competing truth-claims. We concluded that, in line with N. T. Wright, the reconstruction that has the best claim to validity is the one which demonstrates "simplicity of outline, elegance in handling the details within it, the inclusion of all the parts of the story, and the ability of the story to make sense beyond its immediate subject-matter."[101]

We then (2) challenged Castelli's threefold conclusions of the nature of imitation. We observed that her understanding of hierarchy did not distinguish between ontology and ability. We noted, further, her idea of the model being of superior value was weak, and her understanding of "sameness" and "difference" was a caricature of Pauline thought, which, to the contrary, displays a highly nuanced interplay of unity and diversity in the body of Christ.

The final issue we critiqued is Castelli's understanding of Paul as malevolent patriarch. We noted that she did not handle the paternity texts from antiquity evenly, ignoring Paul's expressions of benevolent paternity. We also noted that there indeed were texts that used strong, authoritative language. But to understand that language we needed to locate these expressions of authority in the context of Paul's life as he himself defined it. We proceeded to look at Paul's understanding of his own motivation for life and ministry, the role he played with respect to the recipients of his letters, the explicit desires he had for his recipients, and—growing out of his selfless service for them—the expressions of positive emotions and benevolence toward the recipients. These factors then function as the backdrop into which Paul's negative outbursts of emotion and authoritarian language need to be placed. These negative outbursts have little to do with Paul wanting to exert his authority for self-aggrandizement, since this runs directly counter to the ethos and values he repeatedly expresses. He even challenges his recipients to scrutinize his life to see if this is the case or not. The instances of negative emotions have to do with (1) the gospel being distorted, (2) his spiritual children being made to stumble,

101 Wright, *NTPOG*, 42.

or (3) his children's behavior being damaging to themselves and not in line with the gospel.

We maintain that this reading of Paul is more in harmony with his explicit intentions and in harmony with the full breadth of what Paul wrote. In contrast, Castelli's reading is explicitly an exercise in mono-dimensional reading that ended up excluding evidence to the contrary.

> In the final analysis, Castelli's critique reads more as a critique of modern society . . . than of Paul's theology, and she assumes rather than justifies her hermeneutic of suspicion. One must grant her presupposition that power-hungry authority figures often employ rhetoric to advance their own ends; it is not as clear that one must grant her presupposition that Paul was (consciously or not) a wolf in shepherd's clothing.[102]

102 An unpublished manuscript by James Agan quoted in Clarke, "Be Imitators," 332 n. 12.

CHAPTER 8

Summary of Pauline Imitation

8.1 Summary of Imitation in Antiquity as it bears on Pauline Imitation

Of the numerous references to imitation in antiquity using the term μιμητής and its cognates, there are five general categories of subjects that were imitated, of which one large category is the imitation of living persons.[1] There are, broadly speaking, three main objects associated with all human imitation: the classical virtues, concrete actions of the model (commonly associated with the virtues), and "global" imitation, referring to the totality of the model's life (i.e., the model's character and manner of life). The concept of imitation is found often in three relational spheres: parent-child relations, teacher-student relations, and leader/sage-people relations. In all three of these constellations, kinship language is common: the parent/teacher/leader is often referred to as "father," and the child/student/people-group is referred to as "child" or "children." It would be assumed in the Greek and Jewish cultures of antiquity that imitation would be occurring within these constellations.

The concept of "shame" and "honor" played a vital role both in society in general as well as with respect to the concept of imitation. Since people were identified primarily not as isolated individuals, but with respect to the societally recognized groups to which they belonged,[2] the use of shame and honor functioned as "glue" to keep the members properly aligned with those groups. Thus, the individual "children" brought either honor or shame to their "parents" through aligning themselves with—or rejecting—the values, teaching, and actions of the parents.

The basic *purpose* of human imitation was the improvement of the character or the specific skills of an individual (the imitator) through orienting herself on a "virtuous" model. Based on this exemplar, one could observe with all the senses how a virtuous person lived, thereby having a pattern for one's own life.

---

1 (a) Imitation of living persons, (b) imitation of persons of antiquity, (c) imitation of people groups, (d) imitation of God or the gods, angels, and the devil, (e) imitation of animals (i.e. their characteristic traits).

2 For example: families, voluntary associations, cities, countries, etc.

The *process* of imitation in antiquity could be described as follows:[3] (a) initial contact with the model; (2) attraction to the model; (3) desire to be like the model; (4) intentional scrutiny of and reflection on the model (using the thoughts and imagination [φαντασία]); (5) "performing the model"—that is, attempting to assimilate those qualities of the exemplar into one's own life. This process was not performed in thoughtless mimicry, but required a "metaphorical leap" from the life-situation of the model's to one's own life situation. This demanded a thorough knowledge by the imitator of the model's lifestyle, intentions, and goals.

8.2 Summary of Pauline Imitation

When Paul called people to imitate him, he was acting in line with the common understanding of imitation that had developed in antiquity, in both the Greek as well as the Jewish contexts. In his person, Paul united all the roles in which imitation was normally found: (fictive) parent, teacher, and leader. Paul was therefore not saying anything unusual when he encouraged the members of the communities he helped establish to imitate him. This simply "went with the territory" of Paul's position/role.

Imitation was something that Paul both called his churches to do[4] as well commended them for doing.[5] His calls to imitation were always rooted in concrete situations of the churches' life together, and each call must be understood within the framework of those individual situations. Each reference to the imitation of Paul is thus unique and specific. When we seek to summarize Paul's thought on imitation, it is important to remind ourselves that Paul never intended to develop a full-orbed treatment of "Pauline imitation." What we have is a jigsaw puzzle in which only a few pieces are in place surrounded by gaping holes. This needs to be kept in mind when we attempt to draw these disparate contexts together into a composite reconstruction of Pauline imitation.

In addition, there are at least three dangers inherent in such attempts at systematization. (1) By virtue of the act of systematization, the contexts in which these references to imitation occur automatically recede into the background tend to be treated as of secondary importance. (2) This backgrounding of the context could potentially skew our understanding of how

---

3 These individual stages do not necessarily represent clean-cut divisions. Some may well overlap with one another. Also, we do not imply that the imitator would even be conscious of the individual stages of the process. These stages simply indicate how we perceive the process to have occurred. These divisions simply highlight from our perspective the individual stages of the imitation process based on our analysis of the texts.

4 1 Cor 4:16; 11:1; Phil 3:17; 4:9.

5 1 Thess 1:6.

Paul intended imitation to occur. (3) The imposition of the systematician's own grid onto the data could distort the conceptualization of the original author. We wish to avoid these dangers, if possible. It is therefore vital to read the summary below contextually. In other words, the connection with individual contexts, in which these references to imitation are embedded, must be kept in mind as we seek to tie these elements together.

We have divided the summary below in three major sections. In the first section, we look at the ways Paul presents and describes himself in the various contexts. In the second section, we look at the orientation and content of these references to imitation. In the final section, we look at the means of imitation.

8.2.1 Paul as Model: Self-Designation and Description

With respect to his being a model, Paul presents himself in four ways.

(1) *Without a self-designation and the designation "brother."* In 1 Thessalonians, Paul opens the book with no self-designation at all (1:1). This hints at Paul intentionally emphasizing commonality with them and reinforcing the bond of friendship they share. This focus on commonality is also seen through Paul's use of the term ἀδελφοὶ. In the context immediately preceding the reference to imitation in 1 Thess 1:4, he addresses the recipients as "brothers," as he also does in other imitation contexts (Phil 3:17; 4:8 and 1 Cor 4:6). The term "brother" highlights reinforces to the readers that there is, before God, no ultimate distinction between Paul and his recipients.[6]

(2) *Spiritual father.* Another self-designation Paul uses in connection with imitation is that of being a "spiritual father" to his "spiritual children" (1 Cor 4:15-17). He indicates the emotive bond between himself and the recipients when he sets the terms παιδαγωγός and πατήρ up against one another. Thus, even though the term πατήρ has an authoritative dimension, Paul chooses—in the context of a call to imitation—to emphasize the caring concern of a loving father and to distance himself from the uncaring, disciplinarian dimension, which could be associated with a παιδαγωγός.

(3+4) *Servant and steward.* The last two self-designations Paul uses in association with imitation are found in the 1 Cor 4:1, in which Paul chooses to see himself "as servants of Christ and stewards of God's mysteries." The terms ὑπηρέτας and οἰκονόμους are intimately related to one another and in this context mutually define how Paul wishes to be seen by the Corinthians.[7] These terms are intended as a deliberate, rhetorically potent contrast to the mind-set of the pride-oriented Corinthians (4:6), who sought to be associated with *leaders* deemed to have higher societal standing, so that they could "boast in men" (1

6 This is not to argue that there is no role distinction implied in the term, but simply to highlight the bond of friendship between them.

7 The address in Phil 1:1 also should be placed in this category, in which Paul describes himself and his companions as "servants of Christ" (δοῦλοι Χριστοῦ).

Cor 3:20). Paul deliberately chooses to present himself in the polar-opposite role, as one who is exclusively under the command of another—that is, as one whose sole focus and desire is to be at the *service* of Christ and to be a *steward* of heavenly mysteries. Both of these images imply working not for selfish goals, but willingly placing oneself at the service of another—God.

Thus, Paul seeks—with respect to imitation of himself—to accentuate both equality as well as maternal/paternal concern for the recipients based on understanding himself as exclusively in the service of God in Christ.

It is, in closing, noteworthy that Paul nowhere explicitly calls for imitation of himself in connection with his role as apostle. Even though he uses the phrase "as apostles of Christ" of himself and his team in 1 Thess 2:7, he intentionally downplays the aspect of apostolic authority and foregrounds the "maternal dimension" with which he lives out his role as an apostle. This downplaying of authority parallels 1 Cor 4:15-17, in which the authoritative dimension of the father role is also downplayed and the nurturing, caring aspects are accentuated.

8.2.2 Orientation and Content of Pauline Imitation

Paul does not neatly distinguish between "orientation" and "content" with respect to imitation. Rather, this orientation is understood to be part-and-parcel of the content of imitation. We are struck by the pervasiveness of references to Christ and the gospel in every reference to imitation, and it these that function as the orienting framework of Pauline imitation, within which the content of imitation is to be understood.

8.2.2.1 Orientation of Imitation: Christ and the Gospel

All of Paul's references to imitation of himself are directly linked to and tied to Christ and his gospel. This consistent orientation toward Christ and his gospel functions for Paul as the radiating center out of which all of Paul's life, thought, and ministry orbited. It is for this reason that Michael Gorman identifies *cruciformity* as the ultimate goal of Paul for himself and for his readers:

> One of the chief hallmarks . . . of Paul's spirituality is this life of "mutual indwelling" between Christ and believers that results in conformity to Christ . . . . We may refer to this conformity to Christ crucified as *cruciformity* . . . . [T]his is not a onetime experience but an ongoing reality. It begins at the first moment of faith, expressed in baptism, and continues throughout life. Believers both die and rise with Christ in baptism (Rom 6:1-11); the paradox is that the new or "resurrection" life to which they rise is a life of ongoing "death"—ongoing conformity to the death of Jesus.[8]

---

8 Michael J. Gorman, *Apostle of the Crucified Lord: a Theological Introduction to Paul and his Letters* (Grand Rapids: Eerdmans, 2004), 120-21 (author's emphasis).

If this theme is neglected or marginalized, it will distort not only Paul's conception of imitation but will also skew how one understands his theology as well.

Philippians 3:4-14 provides probably the most graphic, emotively descriptive understanding of Paul's core motivation for his life and ministry. As we have argued in our discussion on Phil 3:17, the preceding passage (3:4-14) provides the content of imitation for 3:17. The exclusive focus around which Paul orients his life and ministry is "knowing Christ" (3:7-9; cf. Phil 1:21), the meaning of which he unfolds in these verses. Paul holds experiential, holistic knowledge of and union with Christ to be the ultimate value and goal in life that leads Paul to reject those elements which society considers of value that are not in alignment with Christ and his gospel (3:3-6). Everything Paul does and thinks is controlled and informed by this way of knowing Christ, and it is for this reason that personal glory, prestige, and honor are considered valueless.

Similarly, in the context of 1 Cor 11:1, the gospel is seen as the ultimate value, under which all other values and actions should be subsumed and against which all human interaction should be measured. The proper understanding of the gospel is the decisive and exclusive point of orientation for the Corinthians' life together. This gospel has concrete implications for the individual lives of the Christian community as well their life together as a community.

These two terms "Christ" and "gospel"[9] are used at times interchangeably and accent different aspects of one and the same reality. Generally, the term "gospel" stresses more the content, whereas the term "Christ" expresses the relational dimension. Together, these provide the focal point for Pauline imitation.

8.2.2.2 Content of Imitation

When we look at the further content of Pauline imitation, we observe two general categories that correspond to the categories of imitation in chapter three: "global/holistic imitation" and "imitation of the virtues."

8.2.2.2.1 Global/holistic Imitation

There are a number of references to Pauline imitation in 1 Thess 1:6, 1 Cor 4:16-17, and Phil 4:9, which can be described in terms of "global" or "holistic" imitation—that is, they refer to the imitation of the totality of Paul's life. In 1 Thess. 1:5 the phrase "just as you know what kind of persons we proved to be among you" informs the understanding of imitation in 1:6 as functioning within the context of the life of Paul and his companions as the Thessalonian believers experienced them. The gospel message of 1:5a is tied to *how they were* when Paul and his team were with them in 1:5b. Thus Paul and his companions are seen to holistically integrate both the verbal communication of truth as well as

9 As also in phrases like "knowing *Christ*" (Phil 3:7-14) and "doing all things for the sake of the *gospel*" (1 Cor 9:23).

the embodiment of truth lived out before them.

This concept of Paul and his team being models to be globally imitated is repeated in parallel expressions in 1 Thessalonians 2. This is most clear in 1 Thess 2:8 ("we were determined to share with you not only the gospel of God but also our own selves") and 2:10 ("blameless our conduct [ἐγενήθημεν] was toward you believers"). The focus of 2:1-12 is, in large part, an invitation to the Thessalonians to scrutinize every aspect of Paul and his companions' exemplary lives.

It is apparent in the literature that commentators read the plural "you became imitators *of us*" as an actual singular that refers to Paul alone. The work of E. Randolph Richards on the role of co-authorship, however, argues that the co-authors mentioned in the prescript played an active role in the actual writing of the book.[10] Correspondingly, this would imply an actual and active role throughout the letter for the individuals indicated in second plural references. This would mean that, for example, in 1 Thess 1:4-6 as well as 2:1-12 these verses indicate that it is not simply Paul's life being the focus of imitation; rather, it points to Paul *in-community-with-his-companions*—in all of its dimensions—as the object and content of imitation.

In 1 Corinthians 4 there are two expressions that indicate that imitation in this context is to be understood globally as referring to the life of Paul beyond its specific referent in 4:16. The first is in 4:6 ("so that you may learn [μάθητε] through us") and the second in 4:17 ("to remind you of my ways" [ἀναμνήσει τὰς ὁδούς μου]). Both of these expressions indicate that, whatever the specific referent of imitation, the Corinthians could, in a general way, learn from the total shape of Paul's life in Christ. The expression τὰς ὁδούς μου in 4:17 is an expression referring to the overall lifestyle of a person. Thus all aspects of that lifestyle are potential objects for scrutiny and imitation. However, Paul's ways here are explicitly tied to Paul's life "in Christ" (ἐν Χριστῷ). Thus, Pauline imitation encompasses everything in Paul's life (actions, virtues, emotions, lifestyle) that flows out of his relationship to and service of Christ.

In Phil 4:9 imitation is presented as encompassing all that Paul did and said.[11] The global pronoun in v. 9 ("the things" [ἅ]), along with the four elements the Philippians obtained from Paul ("learned . . . received . . . heard and saw") indicates that the totality of Paul's teaching and person was the objects of imitation. Every aspect of his life was an open book to be read and scrutinized and which they could and should imitate. No artificial distinction was made between Paul's "public" and "private" life or between what he taught and how he lived. These four terms in 4:9 represent all the possible ways they could learn from him, both in his formal teaching (first two verbs) and in the

10 E. Randolph Richards, *Paul and First-Century Letter Writing: Secretaries, Composition, and Collection* (Downers Grove: InterVarsity, 2004).

11 Again, this would be understood through the orientation-point Paul mentioned earlier of "knowing Christ" (3:10).

example of his life (last two verbs). Orthodoxy and orthopraxy are seen to go hand-in-hand for Paul and imitation here encompasses both.

8.2.2.2.2 Imitation of Pauline Virtues

Beyond the call to global imitation, we also observe specific virtues that Paul lifts up for imitation. These "Pauline virtues" are all embedded in the contextual realities in which the recipients found themselves. These virtues are not to be understood as abstract principles or values, but rather as "lived-out principles" or "incarnated values." As we observed in our discussion of the imitation of the virtues in antiquity in chapter three, the specific Pauline virtues here also have three dimensions to them: (1) the principle itself as an ideal, (2) the effective integration of this principle into the lifestyle of the individual, which is then (3) evidenced in specific actions of the individual that can be seen as the outworking of that principle. These three dimensions would not be clearly differentiated in the understanding of the Greco-Judaic society of Paul's time.

What is significant about these specific "Pauline virtues," is that they are all exclusively oriented to Christ and the gospel and reflect a cruciform life. Paul does not, for example, simply call them to imitate his virtue of "humility" or "discipline." Paul calls them to imitate the virtues of humility and discipline "because of Christ" or "for the sake of the gospel." Paul spends no time on theoretical discussions of virtues or ideals as universal abstractions. On the contrary, the Pauline virtues are to be understood with respect to their Christocentric orientation.

In the Pauline imitation texts discussed in earlier chapters, we identified various Pauline virtues, or groupings of virtues, that Paul called his recipients to imitate. All of these virtues could be listed and discussed in isolation. However, since these items were never intended to be understood in isolation from the contexts in which they occurred, we have considered it best to summarize these virtues within the groupings in which Paul has placed them. This will then reflect his thinking more accurately.

A further note is in order at this point. We are also not wishing to imply that the items in this list are the only Pauline virtues that one could imitate. It is only to say that these are the ones Paul has mentioned in connection with imitation. Other Pauline virtues can legitimately be extrapolated from his writings on the basis of his call to global/holistic imitation discussed above.

(1) *Willfully (a) rejecting the world's definition of wisdom, strength, and honor, (b) accepting hardship and (c) choosing humble, selfless service to God on behalf of others because of the message of the cross of Christ* (1 Cor 4:16). Paul intentionally uses the images of a servant and a steward to emphasize not working for selfish goals, but volitionally placing oneself in the service of God. He discards the Corinthian society's perspective of that which is considered wise, strong, and honorable in light of the "message of the cross" (1 Cor 1:18-31). His life is focused on preaching the message of the cross of Christ and

living in line with the implications of that cross.

(2) *(a) Disciplining oneself for the sake of the gospel, (b) avoidance of causing others to stumble in their relationship with God, (b) seeking the good of others, (c) giving up individual rights so the gospel is unhindered, (d) making oneself a "slave to everyone" in order to win them to Christ* (1 Cor 11:1). This passage contains a perspective similar to 1 Cor 4:16: selfless service for the sake of the advance of the gospel. Pauline imitation is focused (negatively) on not wishing to cause anyone to falter in their relationship to God and (positively) on intentionally seeking the good of the many so that they may be ultimately saved. This entails willful surrender of legitimate rights and freedoms for the higher good of the advance of the gospel. Further, this entails becoming like/adapting to those to whom he ministers in order to "win them for the gospel." All these elements are included in actively "disciplining oneself" for the sake of an eternal prize (9:27), which parallels an athlete who goes into rigorous conditioning in order to win a race.

(3) *(a) Singularly focusing, as would an athlete, on the surpassing value of knowing Christ to the exclusion of all other competing values, (b) humbly acknowledging imperfection, and (c) relentlessly pursuing the future prize (Phil 3:16).* This passage contains similar themes to the passages in 1 Corinthians: the gospel orientation and its surpassing value, the element of disciplining oneself for the sake of a higher goal and subordinating one's own desires and values for the sake of others and the gospel. Pauline imitation is here oriented to the "surpassing value of knowing Christ," which rejects all competing claims to that which is valuable. This orientation is described in terms of an intense pursuit of experientially knowing (a) Christ, (b) his resurrection power, and (c) the fellowship of his sufferings for the purpose of attaining the resurrection from the dead. This pursuit is undertaken, on the one hand, in humble acknowledgment of not yet having attained, and on the other hand, with the dogged determination of an athlete focusing all his powers on the ultimate prize (σκοπός). Thus, by very nature of this "athletic contest" in which Paul is competing, there is an intentional orientation to the future and a letting-go of the past insofar as it hinders him in this "competition."

This content of Pauline imitation is further supplemented by 3:18-19, in which three additional characteristics of Pauline imitation emerge, which are implicit in 3:4-14:[12] avoidance of satisfying selfish desires, seeking God's glory, and intentionally focusing on "heavenly" values and goals—i.e., values that are in line with spiritual realities.[13]

12 These are derived by the process of inverting the description of the negative examples presented 3:18-19.

13 In light of the discussion in 1 Thess 1:6, there may be a fourth virtue that Paul highlights for imitation: *with joy despite difficulty*. Our discussion of this text concluded that the content of imitation here was most likely referring to "holistic" imitation, but that there were also strong exegetical indications that imitation here

8.2.3 Means/Media of Imitation

In this final section, we summarize the various means and media (and aspects thereof) that Paul used with respect to imitation of himself. The first three highlight the medium used for Pauline imitation. The last two highlight the specific objects of Pauline imitation.

(1) *Mediated through a letter.* It is patently obvious, and thus perhaps often overlooked, that Paul's calls to imitation were always mediated through the form of written correspondence.[14] This in itself is significant, because Paul was not present with them for them to "see him." This was apparently not a problem for the recipients, since there is not the slightest hint of this being a barrier to imitation.

Imitation of Paul in these passages was thus always at least one remove from the reality of his physical presence. By its very nature, then, Pauline imitation was "metaphorical"—that is, it required an act of the imagination to draw parallels between Paul's text and their lives. In other words, they were to draw out the understanding of imitation described in these written texts—sifting appropriately through the paraenesis and personal examples that Paul presented there—and then apply this appropriately to their own lives.

(2) *Mediated through memory recall*: A further aspect that comes to the fore in 1 Thessalonians 1 and 2 is the role and function of memory. This is seen through the use of the terms "knowledge" (οἶδα, 1:5b; 2:1, 2, 5, 11) and "remember" (μνημονεύω, 1:3; 2:9) as well as the phrase "you are witnesses" (ὑμεῖς μάρτυρες, 2:10). These terms and expressions would trigger the recall of the Thessalonians' experience of Paul and his companions. It would be as if Paul were asking the Thessalonians to take an internal video recording out of storage, place it in a player, and watch it in order to inspect the motives, lives, and ministry of the apostolic band. This process would both confirm and reinforce the imitatory process and further solidify those values and way of life they had seen on display before them. Thus, the memory of Paul and his companions is reinforced through these calls to remember throughout the letter.

(3) *Mediated through a representative of Paul.* Paul's call to imitation in 1 Cor 4:16 is reinforced in the following verse, which also extends the concept of imitation beyond the scope of 4:1-15. Paul refers to the sending of Timothy, his

---

may refer to how the Thessalonians had received the message—with joy despite difficulties. These two options do not stand in opposition to one another, but are a matter of emphasis based on the goals Paul was following in this letter. If that is the case, then Paul is highlighting the Spirit-produced response of joy (χαρά) that enabled them not only to endure difficulty but also to live above the difficulty because of the Spirit's indwelling presence.

14 One could also include here the concept of letter reading as "oral performance," by a representative of Paul who read the letter to the congregation. This reader could then interpret, expand, and illustrate the points of the letter with additional information reinforcing their memory recall.

spiritual son, *for the purpose of* the Corinthians imitating Paul through the medium of his representative, Timothy. Timothy is sent to them in order to demonstrate—that is, live out before them—Paul's way of life in Christ. Since Timothy is Paul's child in the faith, he has learned through observation and imitation Paul's way of life in Christ, and can authentically pass it on. He has so imbibed the image of Paul that he can function in the place of Paul as model to the Corinthians. Timothy is sent, in effect, to the Corinthians with the message: "Imitate me as I imitate Paul," or: "by imitating me you will be imitating Paul."

(4) *Paul alone as the object of imitation.* We have noted throughout references to imitating Paul alone as well as to imitating Paul as part of a group. Since this entire study has had this as its focus, we simply mention it here for the sake of completeness with no further comment.

(5) *Paul in connection with his team as the object of imitation.* The imitation of Paul in concert with his team is most clearly displayed in 1 Thessalonians 1:6, the only text which refers to imitation in the plural form (μιμηταὶ ἡμῶν ἐγενήθητε). From the information provided in the prescript (1:1), this must refer to Paul and his co-authors, Silas and Timothy. The use of the plural in 1 Thess 1-2 bears out that the interaction of this apostolic team with one another was to be an object of imitation. This observation indicates the social dimension of Pauline imitation and counters seeing Pauline imitation in exclusively individualistic terms.

CHAPTER 9

Issues and Implications of Pauline Imitation to the Practice of Spiritual Direction

Before we look at the implications of our study for the practice of spiritual direction, it is necessary to look at three additional issues that have ramifications for the use of imitation in spiritual direction today.

9.1 Pauline Imitation: Special Issues with Respect to Pauline Imitation

9.1.1 Paul's Personality and Imitation

What role does Paul's personality play in the concept of imitation? Is the imitation of Paul bound up with Paul's personality? Was Paul calling his recipients to imitate his personality? These and related questions are valid to pursue, but are, at the same time, fraught with methodological and definitional difficulty, since "human personality almost defies description."[1] To date, there is no consensus in the psychology and counseling profession as to what ultimately constitutes personality.[2]

When we look at the Pauline letters, and more specifically the imitation passages, we do not detect any hint of the concept of personality, irrespective of how one defines it, playing a role in what Paul intended them to imitate. Indeed, the category "personality" would have been foreign to the apostle Paul.

The closest Paul comes to discussing differing characteristics in persons is the concept of spiritual gifts.[3] There is also an acknowledgement that some individuals are, for example, "idlers," "faint-hearted," and "weak" (1 Thess 5:14), possibly indicating deep-seated tendencies in certain people.[4] One can extrapolate from this, that Paul could have characterized persons in other ways as well. However, in the imitation passages, no categorization of individuals based on such characteristics are mentioned, thereby implying that Paul had

---

1 James R. Beck, *Jesus and Personality Theory: Exploring the Five-Factor Model* (Downers Grove: InterVarsity, 1999), 17-18.

2 "No one is able to draw a line around the personality and define it with great precision" (Beck, *Personality Theory*, 18). See also pp. 20-36 for Beck's helpful overview of the various attempts at defining and characterizing personality.

3 Cf. Rom 12:3-8; 1 Cor 12:1-30.

4 The precise understanding of these terms in this context is debated. For an overview of the options, see: Holmes, *Thessalonians*, 181.

everyone in these congregations in view irrespective of individual traits.

When we turn to look at Paul's references to his own character traits in the imitation passages, we note that Paul nowhere links imitation of himself to his person *qua* personality in the modern senses of the term. Even when he focuses exclusively on himself as the object of imitation, the imitation of Paul is implicitly understood to be with reference to the defining orientation of Paul's life—his Christocentric focus. Thus, from these texts, it is impossible to abstract "Paul as personality" from "Paul in his orientation to Christ and his gospel." His personality, however one chooses to define it, plays no observable role in either his own imitation of Christ or in his congregations' imitation of him.

Further, the specific content of Pauline imitation is not focused on qualities of personality but on fundamental virtues that flow out of Paul's understanding of Christ and the gospel. These virtues are in operation on a more basic level than personality, which would apply to every "personality type."

One final observation: as we have argued in chapter two and confirmed in chapter three, a "cookie-cutter" understanding of Pauline imitation runs counter to the thrust and intent of human imitation in antiquity and in Paul. These virtues would have a common core of meaning that all those practicing them would hold in common. Yet the embodiment of those virtues would necessarily be lived out in unique and individual ways. The differences would be based on the countless factors that characterize their divergent contexts (both in the external situation as well as in the personal histories of the individuals). Yet both, in their divergent ways, could be faithfully living out the same values.[5]

9.1.2 Paul's Unique Apostolic Role and Imitation

The contemporary practice of the concept of imitation based on the Pauline model requires us to ask a further set of questions revolving around Paul's unique apostolic role. The basic question is: Is it hermeneutically legitimate to apply Paul's call to imitation to ourselves (i.e. to suggest that others should imitate us), since Paul played a unique role as an apostle in the development of Christianity—a role which we cannot play?[6]

In order to answer this question, the more fundamental question needs to be answered: Does Paul tie his call to imitation to his apostolic role? As we have argued above, Paul avoids explicit connection between imitation and apostleship. In fact, it seems he intentionally avoided connecting imitation with

---

5 We will explain the hermeneutical dynamics of this more fully below in the section "Imitation and Metaphor-making."

6 Cf. Acts 9:15, "This man [Paul] is my chosen instrument to carry my name before the Gentiles and their kings and before the people of Israel."

apostolic authority.[7] If Paul does not appeal to his apostolic authority to legitimate his call to imitation, then how did he legitimate it? Again, from our observations of the texts, it seems that the ground of Paul's call to imitation had to do with Paul understanding himself as an authentic and reliable follower of Christ, who embodied in his thought and action the life of Christ in such a way as to become a model for others. His position as apostle and founder of the Christian communities was of secondary importance to the primary significance of his authentic embodiment of Christ and his message as their spiritual parent.

This reading is supported by at least five observations, which we mention here briefly. (1) The reference to Timothy who is sent to remind the Corinthians of "my way of life *in Christ*" (1 Cor 4:17) indicates the legitimation centered on his authentic embodiment of his life as he lived *in Christ* life. (2) Paul connects imitation of himself with imitation of Christ (1 Cor 11:1; 1 Thess 1:6). (3) Paul points to other models as exemplars, who are not apostles (Phil 3:17). (4) The content of the call to imitation in Phil 3:17 is linked exclusively to Paul's radical orientation to Christ displayed in the previous verses (4-14). (5) The explicit role he associates with imitation and appeals to for legitimation is that of spiritual father (1 Cor 4:15-17).[8] These five observations, coupled with the lack of explicit connection between apostleship and imitation in these texts, leads to the conclusion that apostleship does not play a direct role in the legitimation for Paul's call to imitate him.

This returns us to a final aspect of the initial question posed: "What is the legitimation for the application of Paul's call to imitation for us today?" The way this question is framed, however, implies that there needs to be one-to-one correspondence between Paul and us with respect to our roles. We would argue that to seek a one-to-one correspondence between the situation in the biblical text and our lives today is not in harmony with how one should read and apply biblical teaching to our modern context. We would suggest that a "metaphorical reading" of these texts, as we discuss below under "Imitation and Metaphor-making," is the appropriate hermeneutical tool, which allows us to apply the teaching of Paul on imitation in a legitimate manner.

9.1.3 Misunderstandings and Dangers of Pauline Imitation

In this section, we will note various misunderstandings and misconceptions that have emerged with reference to Paul's call to imitate him. When we have discussed these misunderstandings elsewhere, we simply note this here without further discussion. We will focus our comments on those misunderstandings

---

7 That it was functioning on an implicit level goes without saying. The question, however, remains: is imitation linked to the apostolic role?

8 Fiore comes to the same conclusion: "Paul calls for imitation, then, as a consequence . . . of his fatherhood of the community in Christ" (Fiore, *Personal Example*, 179).

not discussed in the preceding chapters.

(1) Imitation as superficial copying or "aping." See the discussions in chapter three, sections 3.3.4 and 3.6 and chapter five, section 5.2.2.[9]

(2) Calls to imitation imply over-developed egotism or a desire for power. In our extended interaction with Castelli's thesis, we have argued the contrary. In addition, the overview of imitation in antiquity and in Paul does not make this causal connection. Calls to imitation were pedagogical devices that did not intrinsically imply egotism any more than a parent or artisan, calling her children or apprentice to do what she does, would be seen as egotistical,.

(3) Imitation as a strategy to enforce uniformity and squelch individuality. This charge goes hand-in-hand with the misunderstanding of imitation as superficial copying. The difference is the social element: all are copying in the same way. This also has been discussed in connection with Castelli in chapter seven. We have argued that this is a fundamental misunderstanding of the nature of imitation as "analogical parallelism," which we will discuss below ("Imitation and Metaphor-making"). In contrast, the call to imitation is understood through the process of "metaphoric transfer," as Gaventa describes:[10]

> [Paul] does not praise the Thessalonians for wearing what Jesus wore or eating what Paul ate. He praises them for embodying in their own setting a response to the gospel that is consistent with Jesus' own faithfulness and with the faith of their teachers.[11]

(4) Imitation as a psychologically problematic technique to effect foundational transformation of a person. The methodology of much psychotherapy and counseling technique begins with the assumption that cognitive insight is the beginning of the transformation of the person.[12] With

---

9 Schrage and Fiore also argue strongly against this way of understanding imitation: "It is not a specific, particular behavior and certainly not a meticulous (*minutiöse*) or 'cookie-cutter' (*schablonenhafte*) copying . . . that is called for; rather [what is called for] is a relationship based on *conformitas* to Christ" (Wolfgang Schrage, "Das apostolische Amt des Paulus nach 1 Kor 4,14-17," in *L'Apôtre Paul, Personnalité, Style et Conception du Ministère* [ed. A. Vanhoye; BETL; Leuven: Leuven University Press, 1986], 114). "Not that Paul seeks a servile and minute imitation. Rather he wants the community to acquire the deepest and most central attitudes of the Christian life and apply them properly in particular cases" (Fiore, *Personal Example*, 179-80).

10 Gaventa does not use the term "metaphorical," but her description parallels our understanding of metaphorical transfer discussed below.

11 Gaventa, *Thessalonians*, 17.

12 This is true of classical psychoanalysis (Freud), the interpersonal school of Adler, transactional analysis, rational-emotive therapy (Ellis), client-centered therapy (Rogers), analytical psychotherapy (Jung) and gestalt therapy (Perls). Less true is

the exception of reality therapy and behavior modification, if the person discovers the crucial roots to her problem and/or achieves insight into who she truly is/what her true desires are, then this insight can lead to a legitimate change in thought which then affects the emotions and behavior. If the cognitive insight is lacking, then simply changing one's external behavior will not produce lasting effects. This basic approach does have some validity but also its limitations. Because it is not possible to deal in depth with this topic, we limit our comments to key elements that impinge on imitation as a psychological method to effect transformation in persons.

"Pauline psychology" seems to operate on the opposite premise: the extended and continual practice of proper behavior and thinking—rooted in the understanding of one's relationship to Christ and empowered by the Holy Spirit—leads to long-term transformation of the person.[13] The crystallization of Paul's perspective can be discerned in the sequential development of thought in Rom 12:1-2, whereby the individual realizes that life is: (1) rooted in the mercies of God, (2) which provides the rationale for *presenting* one's body as a living sacrifice,[14] (3) which intentionally *does not conform* itself to the pattern of this world, but (4) *is transformed* by the renewing of one's mind, in order that (5) the will of God can be *approved by testing*.

(1) Paul's psychology is rooted in "the mercies of God," which is a shorthand summary of chapters 1-11.[15] This provides the proper frame of reference for what follows in the next verses. Based on these mercies, Paul calls for the *performance* of the truth, through specific behavioral actions:[16] (2)

---

this of reality therapy (Glasser) and behavior modification (Pavlov, Skinner, Wolpe).

13 For interesting parallel understandings to ours, which go into more detail about Paul as psychologist, see Willard, *Spirit of the Disciplines*, 95-129; Robert C. Roberts, "Outline of Pauline Psychotherapy," in *Care for the Soul: Exploring the Intersection of Psychology & Theology* (ed. Mark R. McMinn and Timothy R. Phillips; Downers Grove: InterVarsity, 2001), 134-63. Willard comments astutely: "We customarily think of Paul as a great theologian, not as a master psychologist. But he clearly perceived and explained the fundamental structures and processes of the human self related to its well-being, its corruption, and its redemption. His Letter to the Romans can never be fully appreciated unless it is read as, among other things, a treatise on social and individual psychology. The fact that he viewed his doctrine of redemption as a doctrine of the transformation of the self required him to be a psychologist" (112).

14 Note the metaphorical nature of Paul's statement.

15 This phrase "underscores the connection between what Paul now asks his readers to do and what he has told them earlier in the letter that God has done for them" (Douglas J. Moo, *The Epistle to the Romans* [NICNT; Grand Rapids: Eerdmans, 1996], 749). This pattern is in accord with all the letters of Paul, in which parenesis is predicated on and rooted in the gospel of grace.

16 This seems to be the consistent pattern in all of Paul's letters.

"present your bodies" (παραστῆσαι) and (3) "do not conform yourself" (μὴ συσχηματίζεσθε).[17] (4) The result of this performance leads to a transformation (μεταμορφοῦσθε) by the Spirit.[18] In other words, when one performs these two actions of presenting and not confirming, the person places himself in a position, in which the Spirit can transform him. (5) The outcome of this whole process, after a person has performed the truth and been transformed by the Spirit, is that he will then be in a position to discern the will of God. Knowledge and insight come at the end of the process. This type of knowledge is not insight into the inner-workings of the psyche, nor does this provide comprehension into why a person is driven to think or act in certain ways, though such an insight may occur. This type of knowledge results in discerning what is truly good, pleasing, and perfect. It is for this reason that Richard Hays writes:

> The New Testament itself repeatedly insists on the necessity of embodiment of the Word. The sequence of the verbs in Romans 12:1-2 is significant: "*Present* your bodies as a living sacrifice . . . . Be *transformed* . . . that you may *discern* what is the will of God, what is good and acceptable and perfect." Knowledge of the will of God *follows* the community's submission and transformation. Why? Because until we see the text lived, we cannot begin to conceive what it means. Until we see God's power at work among us, we do not know what we are reading. Thus, the most crucial hermeneutical task is the formation of communities seeking to live under the Word.[19]

To summarize our discussion thus far: one searches in vain in the letters of Paul for explorations of the human psyche. Instead, we find explorations in theology and corresponding performance. We understand Paul to be saying, in its simplest form: when a person "does the truth" with the full engagement and integration of "heart, soul, mind, and strength" (Mark 12:30), this will lead to her being transformed.

Is it psychologically legitimate to bypass reference to the human psyche and focus on performance? Would this not lead to deeper psychological problems, if an individual is compelled by an external authority to perform actions that are not in accord with the inner world of their self-understanding? Since this is not the focus of this work, we cannot here pursue this broad and complex issue.

The "Pauline approach to psychology" has, however, been strengthened by

---

17 There is debate with regard to συσχηματίζεσθε as to whether it is to be understood as active "do not conform" (NIV, NJB), middle "do not conform yourselves" (TEV) or passive "do not be conformed" (KJV, NAS, NRS). Moo, following Turner, notes the penchant in Hellenistic Greek for using middle or passive verbs with an active sense (Moo, *Romans*, 755; Nigel Turner, *Syntax* [Grammar of New Testament Greek, vol. 3; Edinburgh: T&T Clark, 1963], 57).

18 Understood as a passive (Moo, *Romans*, 755).

19 Hays, *Moral Vision*, 306 (author's emphasis).

research into the "biology of habit"—that is, the biological and neural aspects of habit formation.[20] The essence of this research highlights the psychological impact of performance upon the brain structure of the performer: one becomes what one does. The act of loving, for example, leads to one becoming a loving person.

Jeffrey Satinover, medical doctor, past president of the C. J. Jung Society and professor at Harvard Medical School, has outlined the bio-neural processes of habit-formation, and we summarize his thoughts here.[21] Research into habit-formation in the medical field reveals how deeply our thoughts, emotions, and external actions are "programmed" into the structure of the brain. Every thought we think, and every activity we perform causes neurological and chemical reactions to take place within our brain-structure, which then, in turn, has an effect upon the structure of the whole physical body—our muscles, skin, blood vessels, nerves, etc. The more we think something or the more we do something, the more these ways of thinking and doing become embedded and anchored within the brain and the body. Over time, these neurological and chemical reactions transform the structure of the brain. This process has both a positive and a negative side.

> The neocortex is the part of the brain that we might consider as the seat of the will. . . . It is also the part of the brain whose connections between the neurons will be slowly modified over time, strengthening some connections, weakening others, and eliminating some entirely—all based on how experience shapes us. This ongoing process embeds the emerging pattern of our choices ever more firmly in actual tissue changes. *These changes make it that much more likely for us to make the same choice with less direct effort the next time—and that much more difficult to make a different choice.*[22]

The more we decide to do something, the more this decision shapes our brain-structure. We become, in fact, what we do and think. Performing that which is good and true will then, over time, transform the individual into someone who is good and true.[23] The therapeutic approaches of "cognitive therapy" or "cognitive behavior modification" have taken up these insights, albeit from other vantage points, with positive results and provide intriguing parallels to the psychology of Paul.[24]

---

20 Jeffrey Satinover, *Homosexuality and the Politics of Truth* (Grand Rapids: Baker, 1996), 133.

21 Satinover, *Politics of Truth*, 130-45.

22 Satinover, *Politics of Truth*, 135-36 (author's emphasis).

23 We do not wish to imply that Paul understood this. We simply use this to show that Paul's approach can be psychologically validated.

24 See, for example, the works of Michael J. Mahoney, *Cognition and Behavior Modification* (Cambridge: Ballinger, 1974); David D. Burns, *Feeling Good: The*

In highlighting these approaches, we do not intend to nullify other psychological approaches. Many approaches have validity and can be fruitfully integrated with "the Pauline approach," which could enhance the transformation process. As Willard writes:

> The processes of spiritual formation . . . require precise, testable, thorough knowledge of the human self. Psychological and theological understanding of the spiritual life must go hand in hand. Neither of them is complete without the other.[25]

This emphasis on performance must not be understood as a return to the legalism of the past with its emphasis on (mindless) external conformity to the neglect of the interior shape of the soul.[26] This legalistic practice "led waves of believers [to seek] healing and grace in the office of the . . . psychologist."[27] Genuine and lasting transformation is a result of opening all of ourselves to the work of the Spirit within us—with our heart, soul, mind, and strength.

The means of this transformation have traditionally been called "spiritual disciplines."[28] Although we discuss these below in more detail, we note here that

> these disciplines are not, in themselves, meritorious or even required. . . . They do, however, allow the spirit or will . . . to direct the body into contexts of experience in which the whole self is inwardly restructured to follow the eager Spirit into ever fuller obedience.[29]

New Mood Therapy (New York: New American Library, 1981). These sources are noted in Willard, *Spirit of the Disciplines*, 129 n. 11.

25 Dallas Willard, "Spiritual Formation in Christ: A Perspective on What it is and How it Might be Done," *JPT* 28 (2000): 256. For similar perspectives, see J. P. Moreland and David M. Ciocchi, *Christian Perspectives on Being Human: A Multidisciplinary Approach to Integration* (Grand Rapids: Baker, 1993); J. P. Moreland and Dallas Willard, *Love your God with All Your Mind: The Role of Reason in the Life of the Soul* (Colorado Springs, Colo.: NavPress, 1997); J. P. Moreland, "Restoring the Substance to the Soul of Psychology," *JPT* 26 (1998): 29-43.

26 For an exploration of the process and means of spiritual formation, see Willard, *Spirit of the Disciplines*; Dallas Willard, *Renovation of the Heart: Putting on the Character of Christ* (Colorado Springs, Colo.: NavPress, 2002); Michael W. Mangis, "Spiritual Formation and Christian Psychology: A Response and Application of Willard's Perspective," *JPT* 28, no. 4 (2000): 259-62.

27 Mangis, "Spiritual Formation," 262.

28 Willard lists a few of them: solitude and silence, prayer and fasting, worship and study, fellowship and confession, etc. Willard, *Spirit of the Disciplines*, 156-93; Willard, "Spiritual Formation in Christ," 256.

29 Willard, "Spiritual Formation in Christ," 256.

Unfortunately, this brief discussion leaves many questions unanswered, and many topics must be explored elsewhere. Our main intent has been to show that Paul's call to imitation, when properly understood, is a psychologically legitimate pedagogical tool for the genuine spiritual transformation of an individual.

(5) Revisiting the question: What is the relationship between spiritual direction and psychology/(psycho)therapy?[30] As discussed in chapter two, the relationship between the fields of spiritual direction and therapy is unclear in large part due the ambiguity of the question posed. There is not (1) one type of spiritual direction, (2) one school of (psycho)therapy, and (3) one unified theological position, which can adjudicate between them. The question as posed is ultimately unanswerable. As a result, positing a general relationship between these two fields is also not possible.

If we, however, take our findings of Pauline imitation as our starting point, the following observations can be made of the relationship between spiritual direction, psychology, and theology.

If one can pardon anachronistic categories, we observe that Paul was theologian, anthropologist, psychologist, and spiritual director all in one. For Paul, anthropology emerged out of theology—both of which guided his psychology and practice of spiritual direction. For Paul, none of these fields can be understood in isolation from the others, since they necessarily impinge upon and inform each other. Paul's theological reflections always had a practical psychological and sociological dimension, and he would not have considered divorcing these fields of study from one another nor pitting one against the other.

As we have argued, the decisive factor for Paul's understanding of all branches of knowledge was his conversion to Christ and the resulting understanding of the gospel of Jesus Christ. This reframed his theology, anthropology, psychology, and practice of spiritual direction. Everything else in life—including psychology—was understood in light of this.

Thus, one can legitimately argue that if Paul were living today, psychology is subordinate to theology. His theology would be the determining factor for acceptable and legitimate therapeutic concepts and practices. All those insights and practices of modern therapy, which could be harmonized with his theology and anthropology, would—and should—be welcome. Conversely, it would be difficult to imagine a positive valuation of some of the foundational themes in modern therapy, such as self-actualization and individuation, since these concepts imply an orientation toward the self and not toward God. Indeed, Paul's radical orientation toward Christ and his call to a lifestyle of rigorous cruciformity would put Paul on a collision course with many schools of therapy

30 As in our discussion in chapter two, we are using the terms (psycho)therapy, psychology, and counseling interchangeably in this section, as they all have to do with the inner and outer transformation of the individual.

today.

A Pauline understanding of Christianity speaks to the modern understandings of spiritual direction movement as well and in similar ways as it speaks to the therapeutic schools. Pauline Christianity speaks to modern spiritual direction's need to keep the orientation on Christ central. Thus, the techniques that spiritual directors use—be they "spiritual" or "psychological" in nature—that encourage and advance this orientation to Christ and the cruciform life would be appropriate. The other foci and emphases of the various schools of spiritual direction, which run counter to this vision of God and the nature of humanity, would thereby be called into question.

9.2 Implications of Pauline Imitation for Spiritual Direction Today

9.2.1 Caveats, Notes, and Cautions

In our overview of leading practitioners of spiritual direction in the second chapter, we noted that the concept of imitation does not play a key role in their published writings. There are no calls by directors paralleling Paul's invitation to his recipients to "imitate me" and surprisingly few self-referential remarks that even hint at something akin to a call to imitation. We noted further in chapter three that one of the key roles that Paul understood himself to play with respect to the congregations he founded was that of "father in the gospel"—that is, a spiritual father, who was responsible for the growth of his spiritual children. This, we argue, is roughly similar to the role of spiritual directors today,[31] even if there are dimensions to Paul's apostolic role that would go beyond the general practice of spiritual direction in its present forms.[32] With these discussions as a framework, we are now in a position to revisit the questions posed at the beginning of our work: What relevance does Paul's concept of imitation have for the practice of spiritual direction today? What implications for spiritual direction can we derive from our analysis of the nature of Pauline imitation as Paul, the spiritual director, practiced it? In the remainder of this final chapter, we would like to explore the answers to these questions. We begin, however, with a few caveats and introductory remarks.

In our discussion below, we do not in any way intend to denigrate the emphases of contemporary practitioners of spiritual direction. Our intention is to develop the implications we have discerned as a result of our reflection upon the imitation texts analyzed in chapters four through six. In other words, our intention here is to highlight the Pauline shape of spiritual direction.

A further cautionary note is in order. As indicated above, we do not possess

---

31 In chapter two, we suggested the working definition of spiritual direction as "the variegated means by which one person intentionally influences another person or persons in the development of his/her life as a Christian with the goal of developing his/her relationship to God in the world."

32 For example: the already mentioned apostolic/missionary role, the founding of churches, and the leadership development of the churches.

a full picture of Pauline imitation. What we have are a few pieces of a larger, unfinished puzzle. Therefore our implications are, by the very nature of the information available, sketchy, and incomplete.

Despite their incompleteness, however, we would argue, however, that these Pauline pieces of the puzzle should play a decisive role. To be more specific, we suggest that the conclusions regarding Pauline imitation presented in chapter eight should build the heart of the contemporary practice of Christian spiritual direction, around which other themes and practices in contemporary spiritual direction should orbit. In this way, the shape of Pauline spiritual direction can function as an orientation and guide for contemporary approaches. Thus, if contemporary emphases are in harmony with the heart of Pauline spiritual direction, they can appropriately be deemed *Christian* spiritual direction. If, however, contemporary emphases run counter to or subvert the central emphases of Pauline spiritual direction, then their specifically "Christian" dimension may be called into question.

A final introductory caveat: the term "spiritual direction" has developed into a technical term with a certain mystique associated with it and standard methodologies that have strong analogies to and association with the therapeutic profession. Although these other fields are undeniably helpful at times, we would maintain that spiritual direction can happily exist independently of them. The implications of Pauline imitation for spiritual direction have relevance for all Christians and not just for those who have professional training in psychology. The title of Gordon Jeff's work on spiritual direction captures this intention: *Spiritual Direction [is] for Every Christian.*[33] It is for this reason that our discussion below is intended to relate both to those who formally practice spiritual direction as well as those who informally practice it.

9.2.2 Shifting from Pauline Imitation to the Contemporary Context: Pauline Imitation as Metaphor-Making

When we turn our discussion away from the historical and textual analysis of imitation to the application and implications of Pauline imitation for today, we enter the field of applied hermeneutics. We would propose that the act of human imitation is at its core an exercise in "metaphor-making." Indeed, we see the same metaphorical dynamic occurring between Paul's call to imitation in the canonical texts, and our contemporary appropriation of these texts today.

A full development of the wide-ranging, cross-disciplinary understanding of metaphor is not possible here.[34] We seek here to sketch out the relevant points

33 Jeff, *Spiritual Direction.*

34 For a helpful overview of the issues and options with respect to the topic of metaphor as well as key bibliographic sources, which we cite below, see Kraftchick, "Detour," 1-37.

that impinge directly on the topic of imitation and its appropriation for today, based on the writings of Hays, Kraftchick, and McFague TeSelle.[35]

Metaphor, as we are using it here, refers not primarily to the classification "figure of speech," but operates more broadly on the level of discourse and refers to a mode of cognition.[36] By its very definition, metaphor juxtaposes incongruent elements with one another, yet through this act of juxtaposition they are forcibly brought into relationship with one another. Kittay has argued that the fundamental nature of language is metaphorical, since language is "a bringing together of diversities into a unity of meaning which is contextually supported."[37] The difference between the two is that literal language compares items within given categories, and metaphor associates categories that are usually seen as distinct from one another.

Further, metaphor functions as a structuring device, by which the structure of one field is transferred to another, thereby shifting the way one thinks about the metaphorized object.[38] This allows a reconceptualization of the item, which foregrounds some aspects and backgrounds others. This juxtaposition both reorients as well as distorts the object in order to force one to see it in a new light.

Gerhart and Allan argue that the metaphoric process is a radical one, which has the power to reorient significantly one's worldview.[39] Thus, it is not so much a vehicle of explanation but rather of invention. Through the juxtaposition of two dissimilar objects, a cognitive act occurs in which learning takes place. This factor transcends mere linguistic categories and transports it into the epistemological realm, in which a new way of knowing occurs.

The distinction between "analogy" and "metaphor" is significant.[40] Analogy deals primarily with items of a similar nature:

> Standard analogy proceeds . . . by generalization and compatibility of . . . two regions. The comparison of the first region and its information to the other results in an orientation of the second region's information but no actual distortion of its structure or the area itself.[41]

---

35 Richard B. Hays, *Echoes of Scripture in the Letters of Paul* (New Haven, Conn.: Yale University Press, 1989), 91-102; Hays, *Moral Vision*, 291-312; Kraftchick, "Detour," 9-22; Sally McFague TeSelle, *Speaking in Parables: A Study in Metaphor and Theology* (Philadelphia: Fortress, 1975), 38-65.

36 Kraftchick, "Detour," 9-10.

37 Eva Feder Kittay, *Metaphor: Its Cognitive Force and Linguistic Structure* (Oxford: Clarendon, 1989), 17.

38 Kraftchick, "Detour," 14.

39 Mary Gerhart and Allan Russell, *Metaphoric Process: The Creation of Scientific and Religious Understanding* (Fort Worth, Tex.: Texas Christian University Press, 1984), 108-09.

40 Its importance with respect to imitation will be discussed below.

41 Gerhart and Russell, *Metaphoric Process*, 108-11.

On the other hand, metaphor can be understood as "forced analogy:"

> [I]n standard analogy, relations in one region are mapped onto another, but in this mapping the proffered analogy strains our abilities because we are mapping not from one formed or structured region to another unformed region but to another already *formed/structured* region. The result is a fissure in the relationship internal to each of the formed regions. The resulting tension and potential distortion of relationships completely reorients our conceptions of meaning within the regions and so they are reformed.[42]

Metaphor, thus, implies intentional warping and distortion of normal ways of understanding meanings—not only on the level of figure of speech, but also on the level of discourse—which then ultimately forces a re-perception of reality.

Gadamer pushes the understanding of metaphor to the more fundamental level of epistemology, arguing that the nature of language and thereby our way of knowing is bound up with the "metaphorical transference."

> Transference from one sphere to another not only has a logical function; it corresponds to the fundamental metaphoricity of language. The well known stylistic figure of metaphor is only the rhetorical form of this universal—both linguistic and logical—generative principle.[43]

When we turn to the New Testament and, in particular, Paul's writings, we note that "metaphoricity" is operating on all three levels of figure of speech, discourse, and epistemology. For example, Kraftchick argues that in the Christ-hymn of Phil 2:6-11 Paul intends the Philippian readers to pattern their lives on the story of Christ through metaphorical application and not, as some have argued, through one to one correspondence:

> Because metaphor is not an isomorphic mapping of all relationships within one field to another, but a highlighting of some and suppression of others, it is not necessary to make a one to one mapping of the Christ onto the believer. Neither is it necessary to argue that what the Christ did must be replicated by the believer, nor that the validation of the Christ by God be seen as a reward, as the ethical interpretation would require. Instead, on a metaphorical reading the hymn provides a structural relationship that reorders one content domain [i.e., the conduct of the Philippians] in light of a semantic field [i.e. the Christ depicted in this hymn].[44]

The relevance of metaphorical understanding answers the strong objections

---

42 Kraftchick, "Detour," 16-17.

43 Hans-Georg Gadamer, *Truth and Method* (2nd ed.; New York: Crossroad, 1992), xxxi.

44 Kraftchick, "Detour," 23 (brackets are ours).

Käsemann and followers have regarding the ethical reading of this hymn, and further is relevant to the understanding and appropriation of Paul's call to imitation today. We would argue that when Paul calls his recipients to imitate (or applauds them for imitating) him, he intended this to be understood in metaphorical, not analogical, terms. The analogical understanding of imitation, in which two parallel items are compared, leads to the search for one to one correspondences between Paul and the Philippians. This understanding results in strained, awkward, and impossible attempts at copying or paralleling external activities of Paul.

In contrast, the metaphorical understanding of imitation, in which two dissimilar items are compared, leads to comprehension on a deeper level, whereby the different contexts are acknowledged, forcing the reader to make a metaphoric leap in the transference from one unique situation to the reader's unique situation. We would argue, therefore, that a one to one correspondence between the metaphor (Paul's situation) and the item metaphorized (the Philippians' situation) is neither intended and nor called for. An attempt to do such would miss the intention of Paul completely.

This way of reading the biblical texts is also adopted by Hays with respect to New Testament ethical judgments:

> The use of the New Testament in normative ethics requires *an integrative act of the imagination,* a discernment about how our lives, despite their historical dissimilarity to the lives narrated in the New Testament, might fitly answer to that narration and participate in the truth that it tells . . . . *[W]henever we appeal to the authority of the New Testament, we are necessarily engaged in metaphor-making, placing our community's life imaginatively within the world articulated by the texts.*[45]

Hays argues that the bridge between the writings of the New Testament and our world today is accomplished by a "spark of imagination" in which "the Word leaps the gap."[46] The example of 1 Corinthians 10 illustrates how this occurs. Paul takes the story of Israel in the wilderness and reads it metaphorically—using Christian terminology to describe what was going on in the original event and drawing an application from it.

> The metaphorical conjunction between Israel and the Corinthian situation provides the warrant for the moral judgment that Paul calls the Corinthians to make: "Therefore, my dear friends, flee from the worship of idols".[47]

---

45 Hays, *Moral Vision*, 298-99 (author's emphasis). Although Hays is writing broadly about ethics, the concept has relevance for imitation.

46 "The temporal gap between the first-century Christians and Christians at the end of the twentieth century can be bridged only by a spark of the imagination" (Hays, *Moral Vision*, 302).

47 Hays, *Moral Vision*, 303.

By the metaphorical juxtaposition of this incident in Israel's life with the Corinthians' own situation, Paul thereby disorients their pattern of thinking and behavior and forces. This juxtaposition forces the Corinthians to reorient and recalibrate how they think and act.

In the same way that the Word "leapt the gap" from Old Testament Israel to the Corinthian community of Paul, so Paul's word to the Corinthians can "leap the gap" to us today. Hays' comments further on this passage are instructive:

> A moment's reflection will suggest that Paul's advice to the Corinthians can in turn become a metaphor for our own struggle to resist the temptations of idolatry . . . . If and when that metaphorical transfer occurs, the Word leaps the gap from Corinth to America, just as it leaped from Exodus to Corinth.[48]

We would suggest, correspondingly, that the same dynamic is operative in the Pauline imitation texts. Paul's call to his recipients to imitate him can and should be metaphorically read to apply to us today.[49] By the very nature of metaphorical reading, the outcome of the reading cannot be predetermined. Attempts to determine a "once and for all" application are thus misguided. With every fresh reading of Scripture we "seek, under the inspiration and guidance of the Holy Spirit, to reread our own lives within the narrative framework of the New Testament, discerning analogies—perhaps startling ones—between the canonical stories and our community's situation."[50]

The challenge one faces with metaphorical reading is how to discern which readings are legitimate and which are not. Since the scriptural writings are occasional in nature, establishing a universally agreed upon reading is not possible. We are left in a position similar to the apostle Paul at the beginning of the Christian era, who had the Old Testament writings and metaphorically brought these into conversation with his experience of Christ and the concrete situations, which confronted him and the congregations he founded. Today, we have the collected record of the experiences of Israel and the church as resources from which we draw—in connection with the indwelling Christ—and

48 Hays, *Moral Vision*, 303.

49 We re-emphasize: this is intended to be seen not in terms of attempting external correspondence, but as occurring on a more fundamental level. The comments of Hays on the account of the church in Acts 2 and 4 are instructive here: "Such metaphorical mappings of the biblical stories onto our lives do not require us to imitate the narrated practices point for point or to repristinate ancient conventions in detail. (Indeed, one of the salient characteristics of metaphor is its power to sustain the tension of simultaneous likeness and unlikeness between the semantic fields that are joined metaphorically.) Rather, the metaphorical conjunction between the narrated church of Acts 2 and 4 and the church that we experience unsettles our 'commonsense' view of economic reality and calls us to rethink our practices in radical ways" (Hays, *Moral Vision*, 302-03).

50 Hays, *Moral Vision*, 303.

bring them into metaphorical relationship with our context today. Hays writes:

> There are no foolproof procedures [for the metaphorical appropriations of the New Testament]. Our metaphorical reading must be tested prayerfully within the community of faith by others who seek God's will along with us through close reading of the text. The community that seeks to be shaped by Scripture must in the end, claim responsibility for adjudicating between good and bad readings. . . . [W]e must ask whether any given interpretation is consonant with the fundamental plot of the biblical story.[51]

We would suggest, therefore, that the application of the Pauline imitation texts by means of metaphor-making to be hermeneutically the most appropriate. This way of reading is in harmony with the way that imitation functioned in antiquity (chapter three) and is in harmony with Paul's own appropriation of the Old Testament. Our metaphorical reading of Scripture today is simply an extension of and in continuity with Paul's hermeneutic.[52]

After this exploration of metaphor-making as a means of appropriating and applying New Testament teaching, we turn again to the imitation texts of Paul. We seek to explore how these texts can 'leap the gap' and speak to us in our modern context. The discussion below of the implications of Pauline imitation is our attempt at applying the metaphor of Pauline imitation to spiritual direction today. In the following discussion, we have intentionally sought a close harmony with the central features of the Pauline letters as we have discovered from our analyses in the previous chapters.

9.2.3 Implications Regarding the Self-understanding of the Spiritual Director

There are a number of important implications of Paul's self-understanding with respect to asking others to imitate him that are relevant for the practice of spiritual direction today.

9.2.3.1 Unadorned Equality

The unadorned way Paul introduces himself in 1 Thessalonians indicates simplicity and directness without the pretence of title or position. Paul does not introduce himself as "apostle" or "leader" or with other terms emphasizing authority. He is simply "Paul" (1:1). This stress on unadorned equality is important to preserve in the practice of spiritual direction. This may be similar to the practice of 12-Step groups, in which the participants introduce themselves at the beginning of each session in the form of: "Hi! I'm Jim. I'm

---

51 Hays, *Moral Vision*, 304.

52 This harmonizes with N.T. Wright's discussions of Scriptural authority in N. T. Wright, "How Can the Bible be Authoritative?" *VE* 21 (1991): 7-32; N. T. Wright, *The Last Word: Beyond the Bible Wars to a New Understanding of the Authority of Scripture* (San Francisco: HarperSanFrancisco, 2005).

an alcoholic." No titles are used to impress or mask the true condition of the person, be they facilitator or member. In similar fashion, the spiritual director is simply "Jim" or "Jane" on the same level as the directee.

Similarly, Paul's use of the term "brother (ἀδελφοὶ) emphasizes the mutuality Paul shares with his recipients.[53] In 1 Thess 1:4 Paul presents himself as a brother because they have a common father (v. 3). He addresses them as "beloved brothers and sisters" (ἀδελφοὶ ἀγαπήμενοι). When we take this term into consideration along with the other terms of endearment Paul uses to describe them as well as the language Paul uses to emphasize emotional caring (especially evident in Philippians and 1 Thessalonians), we are struck by *the fundamental relationality* of the practice of spiritual direction.[54]

We would maintain that this way of thinking is crucial for the practice of spiritual direction. Clinical distance does not seem to be a value that Paul would condone with respect to spiritual direction. The "sharing of life" needs to be factored into the understanding of spiritual direction.[55]

Another implication that arises out of Paul's self-understanding as a co-equal of his recipients before God is that he in no way exempts himself from that which he calls his recipients to do. When Paul writes, "as I imitate Christ" (1 Cor 11:1), he is telling them in effect: "I am not asking you to do anything that I myself am not actively engaged in. I am doing the same thing that I am calling you to do."

An apt modern analogy to this is the concept of the "player-coach." Paul is, on the one hand, a full-fledged *player*, who is required to undergo all the training and exercises that all the other players must do. Yet, on the other hand, he is also their *coach,* who has more experience in the game, knows the plays, the dangers, and the strategy. He does not give instructions from the sidelines, but remains on the same field of play as his fellow teammates. He does not see himself as privileged with "exceptional status," thereby avoiding menial tasks required of regular players. His call to imitation has legitimacy and authority on the basis that he continues to "discipline himself" (1 Cor 9:14-17). His call to imitation has authenticity and persuasiveness because of his "playing experience" (cf. 1 Cor 4:11-13, compare 2 Cor 4:7-12; 6:3-10; 11:1-12:10).

Similarly, the spiritual director today should be marked by being a player-coach, who has "played the game" long and well—and is still actively involved

---

53 Recall the discussion of this term in chapter six (6.1.3).

54 Perhaps most poignantly expressed in the words, "We loved you so much that we were delighted to share with you . . . our lives . . . because you had become so dear to us" (1 Thess 2:8).

55 "We take this [pastoral] office and bring to it our personal being, our unique experience, our existential life and language, and we then infuse the office with our personality. The office of preaching needs the imprint of personality, without being reduced to it. You must risk telling your own story, not as an end in itself, but rather as a sharply focused lens through which the whole Christian story is refracted." (Thomas Oden, *Pastoral Theology* [San Francisco: Harper & Row, 1983], 131).

in Christocentric life and ministry. The director should be perceived as authentic and legitimate based on how she has lived.

9.2.3.2 Servant of God

Another metaphor that Paul uses frequently that speaks to the modern practice of spiritual direction is his self-understanding as a servant of God. The abundance of references to the word *servant* in the Pauline writings together with the (over)use of the term both within the church-setting as well as in society (cf. "public *servant*") dulls the modern reader to the radical nature of Paul's understanding of servanthood. The terms servant (ὑπηρέτας) and "steward" (οἰκονόμους) in 1 Cor 4:1 indicate that Paul understood himself as exclusively under the authority of Christ, that governed his every thought and action. These terms implicitly indicate that he was not motivated by self-serving concerns (pride, aggrandizement, power, etc.) that would lead him to abuse his relationship with them.

This self-understanding is also crucial for the practitioner of spiritual direction today. The spiritual director needs to see herself as exclusively and ultimately responsible to God in the ministry of direction. This requires a constant checking of her fundamental motivations for this ministry in order to avoid manipulating others for selfish purposes and in order to remind herself that she is involved in this ministry exclusively because she is serving God even as she is serving the directees.

9.2.3.3 Spiritual Father/Mother

A further key metaphor that Paul uses in conjunction with his calls to imitation, which has far-reaching implications for the practice of spiritual direction today, is the metaphor of being a "father in the gospel" (cf. 1 Cor 4:15). This metaphor is perhaps the most easily misunderstood and abused of all the metaphors associated with imitation and therefore needs more clarification than the others.

The term "father" (πατήρ) carries with it a further relational aspect to spiritual direction that we touched on above with respect to the term "brother" and appears to stand in contradiction to it. This would, however, be a misunderstanding of Paul's use of these terms. The "brother" metaphor emphasizes the horizontal standing that Paul and his recipients experience jointly before God. The "father" metaphor emphasizes the vertical role he has played in their conversion. Both are present realities emphasizing different aspects of the relationship between Paul and the recipients.

In general, the language of parenting that Paul uses in the imitation contexts portrays Paul as emphasizing the nurturing dimension of the parent metaphor.[56]

---

56 This comes out most clearly in the letters of 1 Thessalonians and Philippians. However, that is not to say that the dimension of authority is not present. Rather, we simply observe the grammar and rhetoric that Paul uses highlights the nurturing dimension of Paul as parent. The discussion of Paul as *paterfamilias* in chapter five bears out these other dimensions of Paul's fatherhood.

His concern for the development of his children, his love for them, his sense of responsibility and duty to them are evident throughout his writings.

These intertwining aspects of parental concern, love, responsibility, and duty speak to the practice of spiritual direction today. A Pauline-informed spiritual direction would be marked by these qualities. This would shift the understanding of spiritual direction away from direction models patterned after therapy sessions—with the tendency toward clinical distance between a director (who is objective and reserved) and the directee.[57] In contrast, the director would be marked by evident caring relationality and involved concern, which are also evident in concerned, engaged, and loving parenting.

On parenting and "creating space." Another implication of Paul as spiritual parent can be explored by means of the metaphor of "creating space" for the members of his community. The founding of these new communities of believers functioned as a means of creating space for the gospel as well as space for people to grow into the gospel. Paul, as *paterfamilias*, ensured that this space—in all its physical, emotional, temporal dimensions—was ensured, preserved, and protected. Paul was watchful for anything encroached on this space—influences detrimental to the understanding and embodiment of the gospel.[58]

An example of Paul's metaphorical use of space and its relationship to learning occurs in 2 Corinthians 6 and 7, where Paul is emphasizing emotional space. In 2 Cor 6:13, this emotional space is compared either to the door of one's heart or a cramped room: "open wide your hearts also." This openness of the Corinthian believers' hearts had become severely constricted. As a result, the space in this room for Paul, the gospel, and learning to live the gospel had virtually been squeezed out. Paul appeals to his children as one who had "opened his heart wide to them" (2 Cor 6:11)—as one who had emotionally held nothing back from them and had created space in his life for them. He calls his directees to respond in kind: "as a fair exchange—speaking to you as my children—open wide your hearts also" (2 Cor 6:11, NIV; cf. 2 Cor 7:2).

---

57 This functions often on the level of implicit assumptions. That a clear connection exists can be demonstrated simply by noting the titles of various articles on spiritual direction: Ganje-Fling and McCarthy, "Comparative Analysis."; Jim Lantz and Jan Lantz, "Franklian Psychotherapy and Spiritual Direction," *JRH* 31 (1992); Rachel Julian, "The Practice of Psychotherapy and Spiritual Direction," *JRH* 31 (1992); Joseph Driskill, "Pastoral Counseling and Spiritual Direction: Where the Twain Meet," *PastPsych* 41 (1993); Adrian L. Van Kaam, *Transcendence Therapy* (FormSpirit 7; New York: Crossroad, 1995); Nicholas C. Howard, Mark R. McMinn, and Leslie D. Bissell, "Spiritual Directors and Clinical Psychologists: A Comparison of Mental Health and Spiritual Values," *JPT* 28 (2000): 308-20. Yungblut has a description of "The Dynamics of the Counseling Session," which are virtually a one-to-one parallel with a Jungian therapy session (Yungblut, *Gentle Art*, 113.

58 Cf. Phil 3:1-3; Gal 1:6-9; 2 Cor 11:1-15.

In the same way, the spiritual director today should provide physical, emotional, and temporal space for directees, in which the gospel can take root in their lives and in which they can learn how to embody the gospel in their own life through observation of the pattern of the director's life. Through the person of the director, this space is offered to the directees as a spiritual *room* in which they can enter and dwell. This emotional space is crucial for learning to take place.

The Christian educator Parker J. Palmer develops this metaphor of space with respect to teaching. He defines the nature of teaching in spatial terms: "to teach is to create a space in which obedience to truth is practiced."[59] Taking his cue from the Desert Fathers, Parker writes that the Desert Fathers and their followers

> left the crowded cities to meet truth in the desert; one of the most open and spare spaces on earth. They went there not only to enter an outer space free of the cities' clutter, but also to open up an inner space of heart and mind, free of inward noise. In desert emptiness the soul is able to settle on truth, to concentrate on that which is essential to salvation.[60]

Palmer sees this learning space as being characterized by openness, boundaries, and hospitality. The characteristic of *openness* removes the impediments to learning and discovering the truth. The characteristic of *boundaries* makes possible the hard and painful work of encountering truth. Fleeing from these boundaries leads to evasion of the truth that can be found only within them.[61] The characteristic of *hospitality* makes it possible for the learner to endure the pain of openness and of boundaries. Everyone in this learning environment (including the teacher) is welcomed and fully accepted "as is"—with his struggles, in an atmosphere that is characterized by openness and caring.[62]

These characteristics Palmer outlines dovetail well with our understanding of developing physical, temporal, and emotional space in the spiritual direction relationship—characteristics, which are observable in Paul's interaction with his recipients.[63] The ministry of spiritual direction today is facilitated when the spiritual director envisions themselves as ones who create physical, emotional, temporal space in which the embodied gospel can be holistically observed in the life of the director and incarnated into the thought and lifestyle of the directees.

---

59 Parker J. Palmer, *To Know as We are Known: Education as a Spiritual Journey* (San Francisco: HarperSanFrancisco, 1993), 69.

60 Palmer, *To Know as We are Known*, 69.

61 Palmer uses the symbol of the cells of the Desert Fathers, in which these fathers counsel their disciples to "sit in your cell and it will teach you everything" Palmer, *To Know as We are Known*, 73).

62 Palmer, *To Know as We are Known*, 71-75.

63 As evidenced, for example, in 2 Cor 6 and 7; 1 Thess 2:1-12.

9.2.3.3.1 Concerns with the Metaphor "Spiritual Parent"

When we speak of "spiritual parentage," however, a number of legitimate concerns surface, which require clarification and explanation, since a simplistic adoption of this metaphor has led to abuse in the past, which needs to be avoided today.

(1) The Illegitimate use of the Spiritual Parent Metaphor. The birthing aspect of Paul's relationship with his recipients is a critical difference between Paul's practice of spiritual direction and the general practice of spiritual direction today, for today's spiritual director has not been involved in the immediate conversion process. This strongly influences the nature of the relationship, since the normal and healthy spiritual bonding that develops between one person leading another to faith is absent in the dynamic between director and directee. The spiritual bonding in the conversion experience by its very nature infuses more openness and readiness to assimilate the advice and direction of the spiritual parent. When this spiritual bonding is absent, the openness and readiness to accept the guidance from the director is dependent on a number of other factors.[64] This difference needs to be acknowledged in the practice of spiritual direction today.

In addition, we observed in chapters four through six that Paul used the full range of emotions and rhetoric that a natural parent would use in the nurturing of a child: encouraging, displaying anger, showing deep affection, warning, praising, etc. The legitimate question needs to be asked: Is it appropriate for the spiritual director, who is *not* a spiritual parent of the directee, to act in the same way? This is an extremely sensitive issue, which does not allow for a simple answer. Perhaps a closer look at 1 Cor 4:8-16 would clarify the issues.

As we saw from our discussion of 1 Cor 4:16 (especially the verses 8-13 preceding it) in chapter five, Paul's display of emotion and use of rhetoric in communicating to his recipients was driven by the fundamental motivation of the long-term well-being of the church and its members—as understood and defined by the gospel. In the case of the Corinthians, drastic circumstances called for drastic rhetoric in order to shake the Corinthians awake and to show them the danger of their thinking and resulting lifestyle. A rhetorically subdued, calmly reasoned pastoral letter would simply not have affected the thinking of the Corinthians in the way they needed to be affected. Paul sensed that they would only respond to him if they were verbally jarred to their senses. Paul was thus free to adapt his rhetoric based on the nature of the situation and the stance of the readers. However, the motivation remained constant: the recipient's well-being as understood through the lens of the gospel.

One possible implication for spiritual direction today is the need, when appropriate, to confront directly wrong thinking and wrong action of the

64 The discussion of these factors would lead us away from our discussion of implications for spiritual direction.

directee.[65] It needs to be clear to all involved at the outset of the spiritual direction relationship that the motivating factor for confrontation is not personal opinion or taste; rather, it is the long-term well-being of the individual or group from the standpoint of the gospel and its implications for life-style choices.

This, however, brings us into direct conflict with some implicit values of western culture, in which (1) individualism and tolerance are highly prized societal virtues, (2) lifestyle choices are seen as a private issue, and, therefore, (3) direct confrontation regarding issues related to lifestyle choices is perceived as breaking a societal taboo. The hesitancy to delve into another's "personal life" is strengthened by the fact that spiritual directors have adopted the values, ethos and practice of contemporary psychotherapy. In this setting, explicit "judgment" of the client's thinking and lifestyle is restrained, and the client is seen as having the inherent inner strength and insight to solve her own problems, with only guiding questions from the therapist.[66] The spiritual director, who operates outside of these societally defined parameters and adopts a different paradigm and corresponding methodology could be perceived as ignorant and insensitive.

While we most strongly agree that sensitivity is essential and that individuals have the capacities for proper action and decision-making, we also note that the gospel Paul proclaimed does not easily square with contemporary cultural values. The gospel does not originate from ourselves or our culture. It comes to us from without. It is alien to us and to our culture, standing in contradiction to many societal values and axioms. This includes many assumptions we hold of the nature of the individual. As Jeffrey Boyd writes:

> While secular American psychology encourages you to believe that you are the captain of your own ship, biblical psychology says, "You are not your own; you were bought at a price" (1 Cor 6:19-20). Human nature is not human-centered but God-centered. We belong to him, we are his property (Isa 44:5; Acts 27:23). We may reject that idea and seek some other framework for living, but we wobble, stumble, and fall if we do, because there is only one author of life (Acts 3:15), and it is not we ourselves.[67]

The Christocentric nature of Paul's gospel was "foolishness to the Gentiles"[68]

---

65 How this confrontation is done will vary. Our contention is that it *should be* done.

66 This is most clearly seen in classical psychoanalysis (Freud), analytic (Jung), interpersonal (Adler), client-centered (Rogers), and client-centered therapy.

67 Jeffrey H. Boyd, "Biblical Psychology: A Creative Way to Apply the Whole Bible to Understanding Human Psychology," *TJ* n.s., 21 (2000): 8.

68 1 Cor 1:23. See the works of Newbigin and Berger, who work out this fundamental opposition between the gospel and society: Newbigin, *Foolishness*; Lesslie Newbigin, *The Gospel in a Pluralist Society* (London: SPCK, 1989); Berger, *Far Glory*.

and remains so to modern western—or any other—society.

The spiritual director today, therefore, is faced with the same challenge as Paul: to call people to embody a Christ-oriented mindset and corresponding way of life that challenges the western values of individualism, freedom, and "tolerance."

On the other hand, the desire to remain true to the gospel must in no way be construed as an invitation to insensitivity, to abuse one's position, or to engage in self-righteous judgmentalism. We would suggest four fundamental safeguards against such abuse, based on the example of Paul: (1) the development of a strong Christocentric orientation to life and ministry (cf. Phil 3:7-14); (2) a sustained reflection of the servant nature of the ministry of spiritual direction, in which the metaphors "servant of Christ" (cf. 1 Cor 4:1) and "slave" to others (cf. 1 Cor 10:33)—for the purpose of their well-being, as defined by the gospel—are prominent; (3) the development and maintenance of a deep love and respect for the directees (cf. Phil 1:7-8); and (4) the knowledge that God is at work in the directees' lives (cf. Phil 1:6; 2:12-13). The proper embodiment of these safeguards will guard against authoritative domination and self-righteous legalism.

(2) The Influence of Negative Parenting Models. Another difficulty, which is encountered when one speaks of spiritual direction in terms of parenting, is the number of detrimental parenting models individuals have either personally experienced or of which they are aware. There is, in this regard, the very real danger of projecting onto Paul—or reading into him—one's own negative parenting experience when one encounters Pauline parenting metaphors. The problems of spiritual direction based on a parenting model are legion. For example: (1) "over-mothering" ; (2) encouraging unhealthy dependence upon the director; (3) the desire for ego-gratification by the director; (4) the desire by the director to feel important and needed; (5) maintaining a state of dependency on the director as opposed to encouragement toward development in maturity, etc. These problems have been flagged—correctly—by Castelli as potential dangers.

Although we do not see evidence of these problems in Paul as described in his letters, spiritual directors may, intentionally or subconsciously, be guilty of these problems. Alternately, others, who read Pauline parental metaphors through the lens of these problems, may too easily dismiss the metaphor of parenting as irrelevant or dangerous to spiritual direction today.

(3) Parenting as Paternalistic Subjugation. A third difficulty, which is encountered when one speaks of spiritual direction in terms of parenting, is the issue of paternalistic subjugation. This is, in essence, the critique of Elizabeth Castelli regarding Paul, who understands Paul as having the goal of keeping his spiritual children in perpetual subordination in order to maintain his position of power and authority. There is this danger any time one person comes to another for advice or guidance. The spiritual director needs to be constantly aware of this.

(4) Perpetually Children, Frozen in Immaturity? A fourth issue, which Castelli also raises in her work, is the issue of the directees perpetually being seen as children frozen in a state of permanent inferiority. Although this may be a danger in spiritual direction, it is not inherently so. However, the potential problem does raise the issue of dealing properly with the development of the directee. It is important to realize that Paul's letters are addressed to communities, who were relatively young in the faith. The content and rhetoric of his letters reflect this.

We would argue that Paul adjusted how he interacted with his recipients as their level of maturity increased. A few indications of how Paul adapted his style of interaction with others will need to suffice. On the one hand, Paul can address some recipients as babies, when he writes in 1 Cor 3:1: "Brothers, I could not address you as spiritual but as worldly—mere infants (νηπίοις) in Christ."[69] On the other hand, Paul can send a co-worker who evidences such a high level of spiritual maturity that he can be sent as a "substitute parent" in Paul's place (1 Cor 4:17).[70] Paul also considers Epaphroditus a brother, a co-worker (συνεργὸν), and co-soldier (συστρατιώτην) (Phil 2:25), who shares the same characteristics, which Paul himself exhibits—thus indicating that he is "on the same level" as Paul with respect to these characteristics.

That Paul can address some believers as νήπιοι and others as συνεργοί indicates Paul's implicit approval of the maturational process. It is also clear from Phil 2:19-30 that Paul's relational interaction shifts with the maturity of the individual. Paul's use of the prefix συν- in Phil 2:25 indicates that Paul treats them as full colleagues and makes this treatment public.

It is true, however, that in one sense, those who have come to faith through Paul will always be his "children in the faith." This, however, is a statement about their shared history and not about their inability to develop in maturity or Paul's hindering them from development. It is equally true that individuals can rise to the same maturational level of being συνεργοί and συστρατιῶται—co-equals with respect to the gospel.[71]

---

69 Cf. also 1 Cor 14:20 "Brothers, stop thinking like children."

70 In addition, the term συνεργός (Rom 16:3, 9, 21; 2 Cor 8:23; Phil 2:25; 1 Thess 3:2?) indicates that Paul sees these individuals at least in some sense as equals, albeit, with acknowledgement that Paul is an "older brother," or "senior colleague."

71 One of Castelli's objections to Pauline imitation has to do with the issue of "comparison as competition" between Paul and the recipients. The issue of comparison (who is more mature and who is not) is, however, a non-issue for Paul with respect to the gospel. The goal is for everyone "to know Christ" and "to press on toward the goal" (Phil 3:10, 14). The phrase "Let those of us then who are mature be of the same mind" (Phil 3:15) indicates that everyone should be jointly striving for the same goal and not be caught up in jealously comparing. In addition, the reference, for example, to "encourage one another and build one another up" (1 Thess 5:11), and the other uses of "one another" (εἰς ἀλλήλους, cf. Rom 12:10; 13:8; Gal 5:13) indicates that Paul sought to foster a spirit of mutuality among the

Correspondingly, the spiritual director today needs to take into account the growth of his directees and adjust the nature of the interaction based on the ever-changing levels of maturity. At the beginning of the relationship, this will be by-and-large mono-directional. As the directee grows, mutuality will emerge. The goal in the whole process is to become co-equals in the common pursuit of Christ and to encourage one another in this pursuit. Thus, Paul can speak of Timothy as a co-equal, who is capable of doing what Paul himself can do: "We sent Timothy, who is *our* brother, . . . to strengthen and encourage you in your faith" (1 Thess 3:2).

9.2.3.4 The Non-Exclusive Paul

A fourth aspect of Paul's self-understanding has implications for spiritual direction today: Paul did not think in exclusivist terms: "follow me and no one else." At least four converging observations support this: (1) the reference in 1 Thess 1:6 to "you imitated *us*" and the subsequent references to the apostolic team in 1 Thessalonians (especially 2:1-12), of which Paul says that *all of them* were on display; (2) Paul's approval of other models, who are hallmarked by a similar orientation to Paul's own (Phil 3:17); (3) Paul's praise of the Thessalonians for being "imitators of God's churches" (1 Thess 2:14);[72] (4) Paul's sending of Timothy so that they could imitate Paul through him (1 Cor 4:17).

The implications of this for direction are significant. We note three of them. (1) The spiritual director should not bind the directees to himself exclusively, but should realize that there are other models, which are important for the well-rounded growth of the directees. (2) Well-rounded spiritual direction often includes a communitarian aspect. That is to say, directees benefit from seeing the spiritual director "in action" with others. In this way, they can learn how to live out the relational implications of the gospel.[73] (3) Any model, which authentically embodies the message of Christ and his gospel should be actively praised by the director and held up as an example for emulation.

The advantages of this non-exclusive way of thinking are at least threefold: (1) it works against individualism and emphasizes group life; (2) it counteracts pride, since the significance of exclusiveness is relativized; (3) it avoids the false notion that one person has all the gifts and knowledge necessary to help other individuals to grow.

---

recipients with respect to a common goal or task—in which he himself was also involved. The goal was not to compete against one another so much as to encourage one another to pursue the goal together.

72 Whether this is "active" or "reflective" imitation (see chapter three above, "Unintentional Imitation: Paralleling Reality" on this distinction), the point is that Paul saw them imitating other people's actions and commended them for it.

73 "*We* loved you so much that *we* were delighted to share with you not only the gospel, but *our lives* as well" (1 Thess 2:8).

9.2.3.5 Rejection of Positional Power to Influence the Directees

The final implication with regard to the self-understanding of Paul has to do with Paul's rejection of the use of positional authority in his attempt to influence his directees. As noted earlier, all the references to imitation are void of appeals to positional authority along the lines of, "since I am an apostle, you must imitate me." This avoidance is evident in 1 Thess 2:7: "As apostles of Christ we could have been a burden to you, but we were gentle among you, like a mother caring for her little children."[74] Paul's positional rights as an apostle are set aside as inadequate and inappropriate for his pedagogical intentions.

Instead of using positional authority in imitation contexts, Paul pleads with them (παρακαλῶ, 1 Cor 4:16), stresses what he shares in common with them (ἀδελφοί, Phil 3:17; 4:8-9), stresses his love for them (1 Thess 2:7-9), and appeals to his own example of how to live and think.

In the same way, we would argue, it is important for the ministry of spiritual directing to be based not on the externals of titles or degrees, but rather on appeals to the directees, which are based on the faithful, exemplary embodying of the model of Christ and the gospel in the life of the director. Just as Paul does not exempt himself from the actions and attitudes to which he calls the recipients but rather calls direct attention to his own striving to live the cruciform life, so the spiritual director today needs to do the same. Spiritual direction that is rooted in the reality and shape of the director's life provides significant orientation for the life of the directee.

9.2.4 Implications Regarding the Orientation and Content of Spiritual Direction

In the following discussion of the implications regarding the orientation and content of spiritual direction based on our understanding of Paul's call to imitate him, we limit our remarks to two general areas: (1) implications with reference to the life and thinking of the spiritual director, and (2) implications with respect to the accents and emphases that should be present in the practice of spiritual direction.

9.2.4.1 Orientation of Spiritual Direction

9.2.4.1.1 Conversion to Christ: Unapologetic Christocentrism

As we have mentioned above, Pauline imitation is exclusively and unapologetically oriented to Christ. Everything in Paul's life revolved around and was subordinated to Christ. Paul cannot be properly understood unless one grasps the all-pervasive influence of his relationship with Christ. We observe three fundamental features of this christocentrism in the letters of Paul. (1)

---

74 To argue that Paul's reference to his apostleship is a thinly veiled exertion of his authority misses the point Paul is seeking to make. Paul is emphasizing the nurturing nature of his interaction while he was among them.

Anything that advanced and was in harmony with the gospel (cf. Phil 4:8) was encouraged. (2) Anything that compromised the understanding and the outworking of the gospel was challenged by Paul, no matter what the fallout might be. (3) There was no kowtowing to anyone, no matter how great, if either the understanding of the gospel or the lifestyle that flowed out of this understanding was distorted.

The genesis of this unapologetic christocentrism was Paul's encounter with the risen Christ on the Damascus road, which had so radically altered him that he dedicated his life to drawing others into relationship with Christ and to conforming his and other's lives to be in harmony with that relationship with Christ.[75] Conversion to Christ causes the core of life to become God-in-Christ oriented and is accompanied by a corresponding turning away from former "idols," irrespective of what these may be (cf. 1 Thess 1:9). Although there are other texts that discuss conversion (cf. 2 Cor 5:20), it is here sufficient to note that a full turning to God and a forsaking of those things, which compete with one's ultimate allegiance to God, that comprise the foundational hallmarks of conversion in Paul. It is this "turning from . . . to . . ." movement that builds the basis not only for Paul's understanding of the Christian life but also his spiritual direction as well.

Consequently, Pauline spiritual direction today should be fundamentally informed by the director's conversion to Christ, understood holistically as a Christocentric orientation that encompasses every aspect of the human person—mental, emotional, physical, and spiritual. This would encompass both the private and public spheres of life, since, as argued earlier, the distinction is ultimately artificial. Everything that emerges in the spiritual direction process, from the banal to the sublime, should be reflected upon with respect to its Christocentric orientation.

9.2.4.1.2 Aligning Life to the Implications of the Gospel

Flowing out of this Christocentric orientation is the alignment of every area of life to the implications and values of this Christocentric orientation. One summarizing statement, which encapsulates Paul's foundational desire for his recipients, is to live their lives in a manner "worthy of the gospel" (Phil 1:27). This statement implies that spiritual direction for Paul had primarily to do with conforming all of one's life to Christ and the implications of his gospel. Every action, every thought, every virtue was to be understood in light of the implicit question: "Is this worthy of, is it in line with, and does it flow from the gospel?" Much in the epistles of Paul could well be understood as his reflections and comments on the recipients' lifestyle from this vantage point of it being "worthy of the gospel."

---

75 There is ongoing debate as to whether Paul's Damascus road experience is to be understood in terms of conversion or call to ministry. For our purposes, it is unnecessary to formally decide between the two. What one can say is that it truly was a conversion *to Christ*.

In the same way, the spiritual director today has as her basic task to look at all of life (both the directors as well as directees) from the perspective of gospel worthiness. This is a call to personal and community examination to see if the shape of one's individual life and one's life-in-community corresponds to the ramifications of Christ's gospel. Pauline-informed spiritual direction thus seeks to bring thought and action into alignment with the nature of the gospel.

Utter care must be taken in how this is done, and legalistic application must be avoided at all costs. The twin motivating factors of love for Christ (cf. Phil 1:21-24) and love for the directee (1 Thess 2:7-9) need to be emphasized as the controlling values. These two factors coalesce poignantly in Gal 4:19 and indicate the basic stance necessary in spiritual direction: "My dear children, for whom I am again in the pains of childbirth until Christ is formed in you."[76]

9.2.4.2 Content of Spiritual Direction

We turn now to implications for the specific content of spiritual direction today. We will comment only briefly on these, since the content is integrally related to and has in general been covered by the two preceding points and can easily be extrapolated from the summary of Pauline imitation at the beginning of this chapter.

9.2.4.2.1 Encompassing All of Life

Just as Paul intended the recipients of his letters in a number of passages to imitate the general shape of his Christocentric life, so the spiritual director today needs to see that spiritual direction encompasses the whole of life, and not merely the explicitly religious segment of it. Since we have dealt with this above, we simply note it here and add that, by its very nature, the examination of life will be a deeply personal and reflective undertaking.

9.2.4.2.2 Servanthood and the Other Pauline Virtues

A key thread running through all the Pauline imitation texts is the theme of servanthood for the sake of the gospel. Paul's understanding of servanthood has two foci: God and people. Paul understands himself as a *servant of God*, a metaphor used to describe his primary allegiance. Flowing from this servanthood to God is his service to people on God's behalf. Paul's own model for servanthood is patterned after Christ's life (Phil 2:6-11), which continues, through Paul's own example, to function as a pattern for Paul's recipients.

This metaphor of servanthood in Paul's writings integrates many of the virtues we have observed in association with Pauline imitation: giving up one's rights, humility, subordinating all standards (Paul mentions specifically wisdom, strength, honor) to the "message of the cross," seeking the good of others, and enduring hardship joyfully. The elucidation of the implication of these individual themes here would not be helpful, since the nature of

---

76 Although this Galatians text does not contain a reference to explicit imitation, the language of parenting implies the presence of imitation.

servanthood is person- and context-specific. A fruitful exploration could be undertaken through a metaphorical, meditative reading of Paul's letters under this theme of servanthood while reflecting on the question: "How could Paul's understanding of servanthood as reflected in his letters be worked out in the shape of my life today?"

The two remaining Pauline virtues, mentioned in connection with the imitation of Paul are: having a singular focus (as defined by the content in Phil 3:7-14) and acknowledging imperfection (Phil 3:15-16). These could be explored in a similar way as suggested in the previous paragraph.

As is at times implied by an analogical hermeneutic, none of these virtues has a single, specific, one-to-one application to our lives today. Rather, the metaphorical reading, we suggest, implies many legitimate applications. The application process should be undertaken in a deeply reflective manner, which takes seriously, on the one hand, the shape of these virtues in Paul's life and context, and, on the other hand, how these virtues can "leap the gap" and find expression in the context of our lives today.

It must be noted, in this context, that a Pauline informed spiritual direction is not exclusively limited to the virtues mentioned in this section. We would argue that any virtue in alignment with the life and teachings of Christ should be included as legitimate in spiritual direction today.

9.2.4.3 The Role of the Display of Emotions in Spiritual Direction

From our discussion in chapter five on the text of 1 Corinthians 4:16, we noted that the rhetoric Paul used with his recipients reveals a great breadth of emotions. This is evident in Paul's interactions with the communities he founded: from extreme frustration and anger (cf. Gal 4:20; 1:6-9) to maternal love (cf. 1 Thess 2:8; Phil 4:1; Gal 4:19), from friendly and familial (Phil 1:3-8) to caustic and critical (1 Cor 4:8-13). From the standpoint of Paul's goal of cruciformity for himself and his congregations, the specific emotions he displayed seem to have been strategically and deliberately chosen, as each case demanded, to encourage, influence, motivate, reprimand, or shock his recipients toward this goal.

Gal 4:19-20 highlights the closeness of these seemingly self-contradictory emotions of love and anger, and, at the same time, this text indicates provides insight into the primary motivation that could generate such diverse emotions and rhetoric. In these verses, Paul is seen as vacillating between anger, frustration, and love. The metaphor of childbirth blends these disparate emotions into one, as different facets of a diamond. The primary motivation generating these emotions emerges in the phrase "until Christ is formed in you." This evocative metaphor indicates that Paul experienced pain analogous to those of a woman in childbirth. Further, it indicates the maternal instincts of nurturing and protecting he felt for the Christ, who was yet to be fully birthed in his children. The full range of emotions and rhetoric are thus not contradictory, but find their explanation in the "maternal heart" of Paul.

It is for a similar reason that Paul, motivated by love for the Corinthians and a desire for their welfare, uses harsh language in his first letter to them (cf. 1 Cor 4:6-14, 21). Harsh language was commensurate with the occasion.

The implications of the use of the complete range of emotions for the spiritual direction relationship are broad and not uncontroversial. The director needs always to have as his primary goal the well-being and the needs of the directees. The director today should be solely concerned with and committed to Christ being formed in the directees. This would need to be the explicit goal of the direction relationship and be agreed upon and affirmed at the outset by both director and directees.

This would imply, at times, that direct confrontation (with authentic emotions not being suppressed) of thought and action that is not in harmony with Christ and the gospel may be appropriate. In order for this to be effective in the life of the directees, however, the directee must sense that the director is not motivated by anything else save the sole concern of Christ being formed in them.

Double-sided sensitivity is required in this process—both to the directee and to the gospel. This is by no means an excuse for a heavy-handed, authoritarian approach. It is, however, a call to be true to the gospel and its lifestyle implications. Steering a clear, sensitive course between the Scylla of relativistic permissiveness and the Charybdis of heavy-handed authoritarianism can be avoided through continuous reflection upon the way of Jesus as seen in the four Gospels and the letters of Paul, which are read and reflected upon within a community of faith dedicated to the close reading and practice of these texts.[77]

9.2.5 Implications Regarding the Spiritual Director: Living a Life Worthy of Being Imitated

The final area in which we will explore implications for imitation and spiritual direction is reserved for the very heart of the concept of imitation: the shape of the life of the director herself. We will focus our discussion on three areas: (1) the life of the spiritual director as the foundation for the direction relationship; (2) cultivating the life of the spiritual director; and (3) the function of the life of the spiritual director in the directing relationship.

9.2.5.1 The Life of the Spiritual Director as the Foundation for Spiritual Direction

The life of the director builds the foundation for effective spiritual direction. If the lifestyle of the director is not worthy of imitation, then no accumulation of

77 We realize at the outset, that divergent opinions and readings of these texts are a fact of life in the corporate body of Christ, and that some stand in contradiction to one another. The need for patient listening to proponents of these divergent perspectives combined with deeper reflection upon the text is vital.

knowledge, no title or mastery of technique can make up for this.[78] When this dimension is in place, however, then lack of technique or knowledge is not an insurmountable barrier to spiritual direction. It is for this reason Barry and Connolly remark that any individual, no matter what formal training, can be involved in spiritual direction.

> By what right does one do this work [of spiritual direction]? There is no office or order of spiritual director in the Church. Some of the most outstanding spiritual directors in Christian history—like Catherine of Siena and Ignatius of Loyola—either never had an office or orders, or did much of their work of direction before they held such an office. Generally speaking, effective spiritual directors are discovered by the Christian community.[79]

Barry and Connolly speak here about the power of the life of the director as the key to effective direction. The magnetism of the God-oriented lives of individuals attracts others to them, who are in search of spiritual direction.

From the examples Barry and Connolly provide, the "office of spiritual direction," came not as a goal they pursued, but as a by-product of a powerful, God-oriented life. Paradoxically, it seems the most effective spiritual directors are not seeking to become spiritual directors. They are solely focused on developing the God-orientation of their lives. They are characterized, as was Paul, by the goal of "wanting to know Christ" and "pressing on to take hold of that for which Christ Jesus took hold of [them]" (Phil 3:10, 12).

When we claim that spiritual direction emerges from the life of the director and that the fundamental priority of the spiritual director needs to be her own gospel-rooted spirituality, an inherent danger arises. The danger is that this focus on one's own life could lead to spiritual narcissism—that is, a spirituality nurtured to feed egotistical desires. This type of spirituality would, however, run counter to the shape of a Pauline spirituality shaped by and focused on the gospel, which, at its core, is missional and servant-oriented.[80] Therefore, the focus of one's life is undertaken as training in how to "walk worthily of the gospel" (Phil 1:27) with an orientation toward more effective service to others.

9.2.5.2 Cultivating the Life of the Spiritual Director

Since the shape of the director's life is the foundation for direction, it is important to cultivate this life with determined intentionality. Historically, the primary means by which the spiritual life (which encompasses all of life) is cultivated is by means of spiritual disciplines. This is not the appropriate place to go into detailed discussion of these disciplines. We note here briefly: (1) the

78 Initially, knowledge, (academic) qualifications, and technique may draw an individual to a director, but it is the authenticity of the director's life that ultimately holds the transformative power for the directee.

79 Barry and Connolly, *Practice*, 122.

80 Cf. 1 Cor 4:1; 9:19-23.

definition and dual intentionality of these disciplines; and (2) the core disciplines that reflect a holistic (Pauline) spirituality.

(1) The definition and dual intentionality of these disciplines. We understand the spiritual disciplines as the means whereby the interior and exterior worlds of an individual are brought into a state of preparation and conditioning for the purpose of achieving specific spiritual goals. These disciplines are concrete bodily activities undertaken for the specific purpose of allowing us to enter more fully into life as Christ intended it to be.[81] This purpose entails a positive as well as a negative dimension: *positively*, it entails undertaking activities that are oriented to strengthening our life with God in Christ; *negatively*, it entails activities that are oriented to removing obstructions that hinder us from entering into the life Christ intended for us.[82] Loosed from the moorings of these purposes, the spiritual disciplines—or other ascetic practices—have little spiritual value and may harbor the potential for physical, mental, spiritual, and emotional damage.[83]

In looking more closely at our role in the growth process, the subtle danger arises of thinking we can effect spiritual change through human effort. Attention paid to our own effort, however, must not be seen in isolation or divorced from the work of the indwelling Spirit, who alone can effect spiritual transformation.[84] What these disciplines can do, however, is put us in a

---

81 Cf. Dallas Willard, *Divine Conspiracy: Rediscovering our Hidden Life in God* (San Francisco: HarperSanFrancisco, 1998), 353-54. Foster understands the purpose of the disciplines as "the total transformation of the person," which "aim at replacing old destructive habits of thought with new life-giving habits" (Richard J. Foster, *Celebration of Discipline: the Path to Spiritual Growth* [San Francisco: HarperSanFrancisco, 1998], 62).

82 Willard defines these purposes as: (1) bringing people "to the point where they dearly love and constantly delight in [the heavenly Father];" and (2) "the breaking of the power of patterns of wrongdoing and evil that govern our lives because of our long habituation to a world alienated from God" (Willard, *Divine Conspiracy*, 321, 341). We misunderstand the intention of these disciplines as evidenced in Scripture when we confuse these two objectives with (1) external conformity, (2) verbal and mental cognition and profession of correct doctrine, (3) faithfulness to church activities or religious routines, or (4) the search for ecstatic experiences (Willard, "Spiritual Disciplines," 320).

83 This can be seen clearly some abstruse practices of the Desert Fathers. One example, among the many that can be found in *The Lausiac History* and *The Historia Monachorum in Aegypto*, will suffice: "Early one morning when [Macarius of Alexandria] was sitting in his cell a gnat stung him on the foot. Feeling the pain, he killed it with his hand, and it was gorged with his blood. He accused himself of acting out of revenge and he condemned himself to sit naked in the marsh of Scete out in the great desert for a period of six months" (Palladius, *Lausiac History* [ACW 34; New York: Paulist Press, 1964], 59).

84 Cf. Willard, "Spiritual Formation in Christ," 256.

position, in which God has "space" to work these responses in us.[85] The disciplines prepare us for and open us to the work of the Spirit.

(2) Core disciplines that reflect a holistic (Pauline) spirituality. What, then, are disciplines that can place us in a position of being transformed by the Spirit? It is significant that there is no list of spiritual disciplines in Scripture. There are hints at various practices undertaken for specific spiritual purposes, but there are no "ten commandments," which everyone is required to perform.[86] This is, however, as it should be:

> Not only is the outcome of our progression . . . not under our control, but we are not told in any systematic way how to do our part in the process. . . . This is because the process is to be a walk with a person [i.e., the person of Jesus Christ]. But it is also because what is needed is very much an individual matter, a response to the particular needs of individual disciples. Perfectly general instructions simply cannot be given.[87]

Since, by definition, a discipline is an activity undertaken for the purposes of enabling us to enter more fully into the life Christ intended for us, then it stands to reason that the number of disciplines is virtually limitless. The aspects that transform an activity into a spiritual discipline are: (1) the intentionality of the activity, (2) the faithful practice of the activity, and (3) the resulting effects this has in the life of the individual. The controlling factor in the choice of the activity is determined by whether the activity allows us to enter more fully into the life of Christ.

Although one need not be bound by a predefined set of disciplines, it is wise to look at the use of the disciplines in history. This provides a point of orientation to determine which disciplines have a proven track-record for aiding people in their growth.[88] The disciplines took on clear shape in the tradition of the Desert Fathers of Egypt and Syria (fourth century A.D.), the earliest systematic treatment of spiritual disciplines appearing to be those of John Cassian in his *Institutes* and *Conferences*. His semi-Pelagian views notwithstanding, Cassian understood himself to be the transmitter of the teachings of the Desert Fathers. In these extremely influential works, he wisely

---

85 The principle encapsulated in Phil 2:12-13 reveals the interplay between our effort and God's working: our part is to expend effort in a certain direction in the knowledge that God is at work in us.

86 We have mentioned above prayer, meditation, memorization, and Scripture reading. Any number of other practices in Scripture could be added to the list.

87 Willard, Divine *Conspiracy*, 350.

88 For a detailed look at various spiritual disciplines, see the three volumes of Jill Raitt, John Meyendorff, and Bernard McGinn, eds., *Christian Spirituality II: High Middle Ages and Reformation* (vol. 17 of *World Spirituality: An Encyclopedic History of the Religious Quest*; 25 vols.; New York: Crossroad, 1987). These volumes trace the history of spirituality from its origins to the modern era.

details how one can combat the eight principal vices by engaging in the practice of specific activities.[89]

Two helpful modern lists, which overlap with one another, but are organized according to different principles, are those suggested by Willard and Foster.

Willard organizes his suggested list based on the principles of *abstinence* and *engagement*. The disciplines of abstinence are "designed to weaken or break the power of life involvements that press against our involvement with the kingdom of God."[90] The disciplines of engagement, conversely, immerse one more fully into the life of the kingdom.[91]

Disciplines of Abstinence	*Disciplines of Engagement*
Solitude	Study
Silence	Worship
Fasting	Celebration
Frugality	Service
Chastity	Prayer
Secrecy	Fellowship
Sacrifice	Confession
Watching	Submission

The structure of this dual list of Willard, though surely unintended, has its negative side: the holistic, communitarian and missional dimensions of life as Christ intended it are not immediately apparent. The structure of Foster's list remedies this and provides a healthy supplement/balance to Willard's:[92]

The Inward Disciplines	*The Outward Disciplines*	*The Corporate Disciplines*
Meditation	Simplicity	Confession
Prayer	Solitude	Worship
Fasting	Submission	Guidance
Study	Service	Celebration

The recent work by Adele Ahlberg Calhoun, *Spiritual Disciplines Handbook: Practices that Transform Us*, takes the discussion of the spiritual

89 John Cassian, *Conferences* (ACW 57; New York: Newman Press, 1997); John Cassian, *Institutes* (ACW 58; New York: Newman Press, 2000). The vices are: gluttony, fornication, avarice, anger, sadness, acedia, vainglory, and pride.

90 Willard, Divine *Conspiracy*, 418.

91 For a detailed discussion of these, see Willard, *Spirit of the Disciplines*, 156-92.

92 For a detailed discussion with practical suggestions, see Foster, *Celebration*. These three dimensions, though not mentioned as spiritual disciplines, dovetail with Elizabeth O'Connor's conception of the Christian life as a *journey inward* and a *journey outward*. The inward journey is marked by the engagement with oneself, with God, and with others in community. The outward journey is marked by the mission of the community beyond itself (Elizabeth O'Connor, *Journey Inward, Journey Outward* [San Francisco: HarperSanFrancisco, 1975]).

disciplines to a whole new level, providing further nuancing in our relationship to God, self, the spiritual community, creation, and those in need:[93]

Worship	*Open Myself to God*	*Relinquishing the False Self*	*Share My Life with Others*
Celebration Gratitude Holy Communion Rule for Life Sabbath Worship	Contemplation Examen Journaling Practicing the Presence Rest Retreat Self-Care Simplicity Slowing Teachability	Confession and Self-Examination Detachment Discernment Secrecy Silence Solitude Spiritual Direction Submission	Accountability Partner Chastity Community Covenant Group Discipling Hospitality Mentoring Service Small Group Spiritual Friendship

The Corporate Disciplines	*Hear God's Word*	*Incarnate the Love Of Christ*	*Pray*
Confession Worship Guidance Celebration	Bible Study Devotional Reading Meditation Memorization	Care of the Earth Compassion Control of the Tongue Humility Justice Stewardship Truth Telling	[Various methods of prayer are listed]

It should be obvious that all such schemes have their shortcomings. No matter which scheme one chooses, the decisive factor is for the individual—through guidance and experimentation—to develop her own set of practices that enables her to live a consistent and unencumbered life in relationship to God and in service to him.

9.2.5.3 Use of the Life of the Spiritual Director in the Direction Relationship

The final subset of implications regarding the shape of the life of the director himself, which we will discuss, is how the spiritual director can use the concept of imitation within the framework of the direction relationship.

The core implication that we see is—simply put—the open, unabashed, humble invitation by the director to the directee, to look at the director's life as a pattern for living a Christocentric life. The paradigm seen in 1 Thess 2:1-12 has relevance here. As we have already seen, Paul invites the recipients of this

93 Adele Ahlberg Calhoun, *Spiritual Disciplines Handbook: Practices That Transform Us* (Downers Grove: InterVarsity, 2005), 7-8.

text to examine his life (in community with the apostolic band) to ensure that it is an authentic representation of a Christocentric life. Implicit in these verses are two aspects that have direct relevance for the direction relationship: (1) these verses contain an open invitation to learn from Paul's life; (2) they at the same time contain controls that keep this relationship from abuse. When Paul calls them to examine his life, he implies that he may be called into question in the case that they find he has not lived up to the standard of which he is speaking. The standard for measuring his actions revolves around the gospel (1 Thess 2:8). Thus, the recipients could legitimately call Paul into question just as Paul himself had called Peter into question (cf., Gal 2:11-21), based on a proper understanding of the gospel.

In the same way today the spiritual direction relationship is an open invitation by the director to the directee to look at and learn from his life, and this relationship can be guarded from abuse by constant reference to and reflection on the gospel.[94] The directee can and must have the right to scrutinize the life of the director.

This call to look at the director's life as a pattern for living is, therefore, a call to transparency and intimacy. This interaction cannot focus on life, spiritual disciplines, and theology as merely abstract entities. The interaction is based on *the director's* entire life (the so-called "private" as well as the "public" life), the disciplines *he* practices, and how *he* embodies the gospel. In authentic direction, nothing is hidden.

The director, according to our findings, would invite the directees to learn whatever they can from the how the director lives her life and to take and apply it to their lives.

How this can be done is perhaps best illustrated by the practice of the Desert Fathers. The Desert Fathers had the practice, when individuals would wish to learn from them, of having the disciples live with them and enter into practicing the same *regula vita* of the abba ("father," director). This was not a command, but an invitation to observe and follow the life of the abba for a time. Lucien Regnault, in a wonderful overview of the shape of the desert father's lives, describes how this occurred. When pilgrims came to a father, the father would shy away from giving instructions. Regnault recounts:

> Such was the case with Cronius, Theodore of Pherme, Sisoes and many others. "Do what you see," Sisoes would say. And Abba Or: "What you see me do, do likewise." Isaac tells of living successfully with Cronius, then with Theodore, and that neither one gave him orders. To a remark by the elders on this subject, Theodore replied, "Am I then a community superior, to order him around? I tell him nothing, but, if he wants, let him do what he sees me doing." . . . It seems that, in the desert, authority was only exercised grudgingly, each being afraid to

94 This use of self as example must have as its focus the Christocentric shape of the director's life as the appropriate control for what one reveals and what one does not (Oden, *Pastoral Theology*, 131).

> impose his will and hinder the freedom of the Spirit. To a brother who asked him what must be done, Poemen says, "Go, live with someone who says, 'What do I want?' and you'll find rest." In other words, go live with someone who doesn't want to impose his will on others. . . . The disciple learned more watching the elder live, and living with him, than listening to drawn-out speeches.[95]

The practicalities of modern day life prohibit most people from this sort of communitarian life with a director. However, whether it be an appointment in an office, ministry together, a retreat setting, or actual living in community with the director, it is imperative that the directee be able to observe up close the concrete shape of the life of the director and learn from that.

In the initial stages it may be, depending on the maturity and needs of the directee, advisable for the directee to orient herself to the actual practices of the director. Then, after learning or practicing the director's rule of life for a time, the directee could develop her own—similar to the practice of the Desert Fathers.

This amounts to nothing less than "spiritual apprenticeship," in which, during the apprenticeship phase, the apprentice adopts the perspective and learns the methods of the master artisan in order to "become like" the artisan.[96] Then, when the period of apprenticeship is completed, the new artisan, having attained sufficient experience, can develop his own *regula vita* and can be one who humbly says to another, "Imitate me as I imitate Christ."

---

95 Lucien Regnault, *The Day-to-Day Life of the Desert Fathers in the Fourth-Century Egypt* (Petersham, Mass.: St. Bede's, 1999), 131-32.

96 For a brilliant discussion of this concept, see Stanley Hauerwas, "Discipleship as a Craft, Church as a Disciplined Community" (originally published in *ChrCent*, October 1, 1991, pp. 881-84)," in Religion Online: http://www.religion-online.org/cgi-bin/relsearchd.dll/showarticle?item_id=110.

Bibliography

Adam, A. K. M. "Walk This Way: Repetition, Difference, and the Imitation of Christ." *Int* 55 (2001): 19-33.

Adsit, Christopher B. *Personal Disciplemaking: A Step-by-step Guide for Leading a Christian from New Birth to Maturity*. San Bernardino, Calif.: Here's Life, 1988.

Agan, James. "The Christological Context of Luke-Acts: Moral Imitation in Early Christian Literature." Unpublished paper. n.d.

——— "The Pauline Epistles." Unpublished paper. n.d.

Aichele, George. Review of Elizabeth A. Castelli, *Imitating Paul: A Discourse of Power*. *ThTo* 50 (1993): 130.

——— Review of Elizabeth A. Castelli, *Imitating Paul: A Discourse on Power*. *Cross Currents* 43 (1993): 130-33.

Alexander, Loveday. "Hellenistic Letter-Forms and the Structure of Philippians." Pages 87-101 in *New Testament Essays in Honour of David Hill*. Edited by Christopher Tuckett. Sheffield: JSOT Press, 1989.

Allen, Ronald J. Review of Elizabeth A. Castelli, *Imitating Paul: A Discourse on Power*. *Encounter* 53 (1992): 292-94.

Anderson, Keith R. and Randy D. Reese. *Spiritual Mentoring: A Guide for Seeking and Giving Direction*. Downers Grove: InterVarsity, 1999.

Bailey, Kenneth E. "Informal Controlled Oral Tradition and the Synoptic Gospels." *Them* 20, no. 2 (1995): 4-11.

Balz, Horst Robert, and Gerhard Schneider, eds. *Exegetisches Wörterbuch zum Neuen Testament*. 3 vols. Stuttgart: Kohlhammer, 1980.

Baird, William R. Review of Elizabeth A. Castelli, *Imitating Paul: A Discourse on Power*. *Mid-Stream* 31 (1992): 272-74.

Barrett, C. K. *A Commentary on the First Epistle to the Corinthians*. BNTC. London: Black, 1968.

Barry, William A. and William J. Connolly. *The Practice of Spiritual Direction*. San Francisco: HarperSanFrancisco, 1982.

Barth, Karl. *The Epistle to the Philippians*. Translated by W. Leitch. London: SCM, 1962.

Bauckham, Richard. "For Whom Were Gospels Written?" Pages 9-48 in *The Gospels for All Christians: Rethinking the Gospel Audiences*. Edited by Richard Bauckham. Edinburgh: T&T Clark, 1998.

Bauckham, Richard, ed. *The Gospels for All Christians: Rethinking the Gospel Audiences*. Edinburgh: T&T Clark, 1998.

Bauer, Walter, Frederick W. Danker, W. F. Arndt, and F. W. Gingrich, eds. *Greek-English Lexicon of the New Testament and Other Early Christian Literature*. Chicago: University of Chicago Press, 2000[3].

Beare, Francis Wright. *A Commentary on the Epistle to the Philippians*. BNTC. London: Black, 1959.

——— "St. Paul as Spiritual Director." Pages 303-14 in *Studia Evangelica II*. Edited by Frank L. Cross. *TUGAL*. Berlin: Akademie Verlag, 1964.

Beck, James R. *Jesus and Personality Theory: Exploring the Five-Factor Model.* Downers Grove: InterVarsity, 1999.

Belleville, Linda. "'Imitate Me, Just as I Imitate Christ': Discipleship in the Corinthian Correspondence." Pages 120-42 in *Patterns of Discipleship in the New Testament.* Edited by Richard N. Longenecker. Grand Rapids: Eerdmans, 1996.

Berger, Peter. *A Far Glory: The Quest for Faith in an Age of Credulity.* New York: Free Press, 1992.

Best, Ernst. *A Commentary on the First and Second Epistles to the Thessalonians.* BNTC. London: Black, 1972.

——— *Paul and His Converts.* Edinburgh: T&T Clark, 1988.

Betz, Hans Dieter: *Nachfolge und Nachahmung Jesu Christi im Neuen Testament.* BHT 37. Tübingen: Mohr Siebeck, 1967.

BibleWorks. CD-ROM, version 7.0.Norfolk, Va.: BibleWorks, LLC, 2006.

Biehl, Bob and Glen Urquhart. *Mentoring: How to Find a Mentor, How to Become One.* Laguna Niguel, Calif.: Masterplanning Group International, 1990.

Black, David Alan. "The Discourse Structure of Philippians: A Study in Text-linguistics." *NovT* 37 (1995): 16-49.

Bloomquist, L. Gregory. *The Function of Suffering in Philippians.* JSNTSup 78. Sheffield: JSOT Press, 1993.

Bockmuehl, Markus. *A Commentary on the Epistle to the Philippians.* BNTC. London: Black, 1997.

Booth, Wayne C. *A Rhetoric of Irony.* Chicago: University of Chicago Press, 1974.

Boyarin, Daniel. *A Radical Jew: Paul and the Politics of Identity.* Contraversions 1. Berkeley, Calif.: University of California Press, 1994.

Boyd, Jeffrey H. "Biblical Psychology: A Creative Way to Apply the Whole Bible to Understanding Human Psychology." *TJ* n.s., 21 (2000): 3-16.

——— "An Insider's Effort to Blow Up Psychiatry." *TJ* n.s., 17 (1996): 223-39.

Bright, William R. *Ten Basic Steps to Christian Maturity.* San Bernardino, Calif.: Here's Life, 1983.

——— *The Transferable Concepts.* San Bernardino, Calif.: Campus Crusade for Christ, 1972.

Brooks, James A. and Carlton L. Winbery. *Syntax of New Testament Greek.* Washington D.C.: University Press of America, 1983.

Brown, Colin, ed. *The New International Dictionary of New Testament Theology.* 4 vols. Grand Rapids: Zondervan, 1975-1985.

Brown, Raymond E. *An Introduction to the New Testament.* Edited by David Noel Freedman, Anchor Bible Reference Library. New York: Doubleday, 1997.

Bruce, F. F. *1 and 2 Corinthians.* NCBC. Grand Rapids: Eerdmans, 1980.

Bultmann, Rudolf. *Jesus and the World.* New York: Scribners, 1921.

Burke, Trevor J. "Pauline Paternity in 1 Thessalonians." *TynBul* 51 (2000): 59-80.

Burns, David D. *Feeling Good: The New Mood Therapy.* New York: New American Library, 1981.

Calhoun, Adele Ahlberg. *Spiritual Disciplines Handbook: Practices That Transform Us.* Downers Grove: InterVarsity, 2005.

Carson, D. A. and Douglas J. Moo. *An Introduction to the New Testament.* Grand Rapids: Zondervan, 2005[2].

Cassian, John. *Conferences.* Translated by Boniface Ramsey. *ACW* 57. New York: Newman Press, 1997.

——— *Institutes*. Edited by Walter J. Burghardt, John Dillon, and Dennis D. McManus. Translated by Boniface Ramsey. *ACW* 58. New York: Newman Press, 2000.

Castelli, Elizabeth A. *Imitating Paul: A Discourse of Power*. LCBI. Louisville, Ky.: Westminster, 1991.

Chan, Simon. *Spiritual Theology: A Systematic Study of the Christian Life*. Downers Grove: InterVarsity, 1998.

Clarke, Andrew D. "'Be Imitators of Me': Paul's Model of Leadership." *TynBul* 49 (1998): 329-60.

——— "Equality or Mutuality? Paul's Use of 'Brother' Language." Pages 152-64 in *The New Testament in Its First Century Setting: Essays on Context and Background in Honour of Bruce W. Winter on His 65th Birthday*. Edited by P. J. Williams, Andrew D Clarke, Peter M. Head, and David Instone-Brewster. Grand Rapids: Eerdmans, 2004.

Clinton, J. Robert and Richard W. Clinton. *The Mentor Handbook: Detailed Guidelines and Helps for Christian Mentors and Mentorees*. Altadena, Calif.: Barnabas, 1991.

Coke, Paul T. Review of Elizabeth A. Castelli, *Imitating Paul: A Discourse of Power*. *AThR* 74 (1992): 520.

Collange, Jean-Francois. *The Epistle of Saint Paul to the Philippians*. Translated by A. W. Heathcote. London: Epworth, 1979.

Collins, Raymond F. *First Corinthians*. SP 7. Collegeville, Minn.: Liturgical Press, 1999.

——— *Studies on the First Letter to the Thessalonians*. BETL 66. Leuven: Leuven University Press, 1984.

Conzelmann, Hans. *1 Corinthians: A Commentary on the First Epistle to the Corinthians*. Translated by James W. Leitch. Hermeneia. Philadelphia: Fortress, 1975.

Court, John M. Review of Elizabeth A. Castelli, *Imitating Paul: A Discourse of Power*. *ExpTim* 104 (1993): 281.

Craig, Clarence Tucker and John Short. *The First Epistle to the Corinthians*. *IB* 10. New York: Abingdon, 1953.

Culpepper, R. Alan. "Co-workers in Suffering: Philippians 2:19-30." *RevExp* 77 (1980): 349-58.

Dalton, William J. "The Integrity of Philippians." *Bib* 60 (1979): 97-102.

Davies, Eryl W. "Walking in God's Ways: The Concept of *Imitatio Dei* in the Old Testament." Pages 99-115 in *In Search of True Wisdom: Essays in Old Testament Interpretation in Honour of Ronald E. Clements*. Edited by Edward Ball. JSOTSup 300. Sheffield: Sheffield Academic Press, 1999.

Davies, W. D. *Paul and Rabbinic Judaism: Some Rabbinic Elements in Pauline Theology*. London: SPCK, 1962.

Davis, Casey Wayne. *Oral Biblical Criticism: The Influence of the Principles on the Literary Structure of Paul's Epistle to the Philippians*. JSNTSup 172. Sheffield: Sheffield University Press, 1999.

Davis, Ron Lee. *Mentoring: The Strategy of the Master*. Nashville: Thomas Nelson, 1991.

de Boer, Willis P. *The Imitation of Paul: An Exegetical Study*. Kampen: Kok, 1962.

——— Review of Elizabeth A. Castelli, *Imitating Paul: A Discourse of Power*. *CTJ* 29 (1994): 236-40.

de Boor, Werner. *Der Brief des Paulus an die Philipper*, WSB. Wuppertal: Brockhaus,

1989.

de Silva, David A. *Honor, Patronage, Kinship & Purity: Unlocking New Testament Culture*. Downers Grove: InterVarsity, 2000.

Design for Discipleship. Colorado Springs, Colo.: NavPress, 1980.

Dibelius, Martin, "Nachfolge Christi: I. im NT." Pages 395-96 in vol. 4 of *RGG*. Tübingen: Mohr Siebeck, 1930².

——— *An die Thessalonicher I-II; an die Philipper*. HNT 11. Tübingen: Mohr Siebeck, 1925².

Driskill, Joseph. "Pastoral Counseling and Spiritual Direction: Where the Twain Meet." *PastPsych* 41 (1993): 217-36.

Duff, Antony. *Intention, Agency, and Criminal Liability: Philosophy of Action and the Criminal Law*, PhInt. Cambridge, Mass.: Blackwell, 1990.

Dumm, Manfred. "'Nachahmung'—Ein vergessenes Thema?" *JETh* 10 (1996): 33-86.

Dunn, James D. G. *The Theology of Paul's Letter to the Galatians*. Edited by James D. G. Dunn, NTT. Cambridge: Cambridge University Press, 1993.

——— *The Theology of Paul the Apostle*. Grand Rapids: Eerdmans, 1998.

——— *Jesus Remembered*. Vol. 1, Christianity in the Making. Grand Rapids: Eerdmans, 2003.

——— *New Perspective on Jesus: What the Quest for the Historical Jesus Missed*. Grand Rapids: Baker Academic, 2005.

——— "Jesus in Oral Memory: The Initial Stages of the Jesus Tradition." www.ntgateway.com/Jesus/dunn.rtf (accessed June 20, 2006).

Edwards, Tilden H. *Spiritual Director, Spiritual Companion: Guide to Tending the Soul*. Mahwah, N.J.: Paulist Press, 2000.

——— *Spiritual Friend: Reclaiming the Gift of Spiritual Direction*. Mahwah, N.J.: Paulist Press, 1980.

Egger, Wilhelm. *Galater, Philipperbrief, Philemonbrief*. NEB 9. Würzburg: Echter, 1985.

Eims, Leroy. *The Lost Art of Disciplemaking*. Colorado Springs, Colo.: NavPress, 1978.

Engstrom, Ted W. *The Fine Art of Mentoring*. Brentwood, Tenn.: Wohlgemuth & Hyatt, 1989.

Evans, Craig A., and Stanley E. Porter, eds. *Dictionary of New Testament Backgrounds*. Downers Grove: InterVarsity, 2000.

Fee, Gordon D. *God's Empowering Presence: The Holy Spirit in the Letters of Paul*. Peabody, Mass.: Hendrickson, 1994.

——— *Paul's Letter to the Philippians*. NICNT. Grand Rapids: Zondervan, 1995.

——— "To What End Exegesis? Reflections on Exegesis and Spirituality in Philippians 4:10-20." *BBR* 8 (1998): 75-88.

——— *The First Epistle to the Corinthians*. NICNT. Grand Rapids: Eerdmans, 1987.

Fiore, Benjamin. "'Covert Allusion' in 1 Corinthians 1-4." *CBQ* 47 (1985): 85-102.

——— *The Function of Personal Example in the Socratic and Pastoral Epistles*. AnBib 105. Rome: Biblical Institute Press, 1986.

Fitzgerald, John T., "Epistle to the Philippians," *ABD on CD-ROM*. Logos Library System Verșion 3.0a, 2006. Print ed.: David Noel Freedman, ed. *ABD*. 6 vols. New York: Doubleday, 1992.

Fortna, Robert T. "Philippians: Paul's Most Egocentric Letter." Pages 220-34 in *The Conversation Continues: Studies in Paul and John in Honor of J. Louis Martyn*. Edited by Robert T. Fortna and Beverly Roberts Gaventa. Nashville: Abingdon,

1990.

Foster, Richard J. *Celebration of Discipline: the Path to Spiritual Growth*. San Francisco: HarperSanFrancisco, 1998.

Fowl, Stephen E. *The Story of Christ in the Ethics of Paul: An Analysis of the Function of the Hymnic Material in the Pauline Corpus*. JSNTSup 36. Sheffield: JSOT Press, 1990.

——— "Christology and Ethics in Philippians 2:5-11." Pages 140-53 in *Where Christology Began: Essays on Philippians 2*. Edited by Ralph P. Martin and Brian J. Dodd. Louisville, Ky.: Westminster John Knox, 1998.

Frame, James Everett. *The Epistles of St. Paul to the Thessalonians*, ICC. Edinburgh: T&T Clark, 1912.

Fraser, John W. "Paul's Knowledge of Jesus: 2 Corinthians v:16 Once More." *NTS* 17 (1971): 293-313.

Freedman, David Noel, ed. *ABD on CD-ROM.* Logos Library System Version 3.0a, 2006. Print ed.: David Noel Freedman, ed. *ABD*. 6 vols. New York: Doubleday, 1992.

Furnish, Victor. *Theology and Ethics in Paul*. Nashville: Abingdon, 1968.

Gadamer, Hans-Georg. *Truth and Method*. Translated by Joel Weinsheimer and Donald Marshall. New York: Crossroad, 1992^2.

Gaines, Jeffrey S. "Spiritual Direction as Choosing Life: Excerpts from an Interview with Jeffrey S. Gaines." http://www.sdiworld.org/html/whatis.htm#distinct (accessed April 12, 2000).

——— "Connections: SDI Newsletter (June 2000)." http://www.sdiworld.org/html /newsletr.html (accessed May 17, 2001).

Ganje-Fling, Marilyn A., and Patricia R. McCarthy. "A Comparative Analysis of Spiritual Direction and Psychotherapy." *JPT* 19 (1991): 103-17.

Garland, David E. "The Composition and Unity of Philippians: Some Neglected Literary Factors." *NovT* 27 (1985): 141-73.

Gathercole, Simon. "The Influence on New Testament Studies of Post-Structuralism with Special Reference to John Dominic Crossan and Elizabeth Castelli (Part II Dissertation submitted for Tripos)." Ph.D. diss., King's College, Cambridge University, 1996.

Gaventa, Beverly Roberts. *First and Second Thessalonians*, IBC. Louisville, Ky.: John Knox, 1998.

——— "The Maternity of Paul: An Exegetical Study of Galatians 4:19." Pages 189-201 in *The Conversation Continues: Studies in Paul and John in Honor of J. Louis Martyn*. Edited by Robert T. Fortna and Beverly Roberts Gaventa. Nashville: Abingdon, 1990.

Gerhardsson, Birger. *Memory and Manuscript: Oral Tradition and Written Transmission in Rabbinic Judaism and Early Christianity*. Lund: Gleerup, 1961.

——— *The Origins of the Gospel Traditions*. Philadelphia: Fortress, 1979.

——— *Tradition and Transmission in Early Christianity*. Lund: Gleerup, 1964.

——— "Der Weg der Evangelientradition." Pages 79-102 in *Das Evangelium und die Evangelien: Vorträge vom Tübinger Symposium 1982*. Edited by Peter Stuhlmacher. WUNT 28. Tübingen: J. C. B. Mohr, 1982.

Gerhart, Mary and Allan Russell. *Metaphoric Process: The Creation of Scientific and Religious Understanding*. Fort Worth, Tex.: Texas Christian University Press, 1984.

Getty, Mary Ann. "The Imitation of Paul in the Letters to the Thessalonians." Pages

277-83 in *The Thessalonian Correspondence*. Edited by Raymond F. Collins and Norbert Baumert. BETL 87. Leuven: Leuven University Press, 1990.

Gnilka, Joachim. *Der Philipperbrief*. HTKNT 10. Vienna: Herder, 1968.

Gorman, Michael J. *Apostle of the Crucified Lord: a Theological Introduction to Paul and his Letters*. Grand Rapids: Eerdmans, 2004.

Gratton, Carolyn. *The Art of Spiritual Guidance: A Contemporary Approach to Growing in the Spirit*. New York: Crossroad, 1992.

Gruenler, Royce Gordon. *New Approaches to Jesus and the Gospels: A Phenomenological and Exegetical Study of Synoptic Christology*. Grand Rapids: Baker, 1982.

Guenther, Margaret. *Holy Listening: The Art of Spiritual Direction*. Boston: Cowley, 1992.

Harris, Murray J. "2 Corinthians." Pages 299-406 in vol. 10 of *EBC*. Grand Rapids: Zondervan, 1976.

Harvey, John D. *Listening to the Text: Oral Patterning in Paul's Letters*. ETSS 1. Grand Rapids: Baker, 1998.

Havelock, E. A. "Oral Composition in the Oedipus Tyrannus of Sophocles." *NLitHist* 16 (1984): 175-97.

Hawthorne, Gerald F. *Philippians*. WBC 43. Waco: Word, 1983.

——— "The Imitation of Christ: Discipleship in Philippians." Pages 163-79 in *Patterns of Discipleship in the New Testament*. Edited by Richard N. Longenecker. Grand Rapids: Eerdmans, 1996.

Hawthorne, Gerald F., and Ralph P. Martin, eds. *Dictionary of Paul and His Letters*. Downers Grove: InterVarsity, 1993.

Hawthorne, Gerald F., Ralph P. Martin, and Daniel G. Reid, eds. *Dictionary of the Later New Testament and its Developments*. 1997.

Hays, Richard B. "Christology and Ethics in Galatians: The Law of Christ." *CBQ* 49 (1987): 268-90.

——— *Echoes of Scripture in the Letters of Paul*. New Haven, Conn.: Yale University Press, 1989.

——— *The Faith of Jesus Christ: the Narrative Substructure of Galatians 3:1-4:11*. Grand Rapids: Eerdmans, 2002[2].

——— *Moral Vision of the New Testament: A Contemporary Introduction to New Testament Ethics*. San Francisco: Harper, 1996.

Heil, Christoph. Review of Elizabeth A. Castelli, *Imitating Paul: A Discourse of Power*. *BZ* n.s., 36 (1992): 279-81.

Hendricks, Howard and William Hendricks. *As Iron Sharpens Iron: Building Character in a Mentoring Relationship*. Chicago: Moody, 1995.

Hendriksen, William. *Philippians*, NTC. London: Banner of Truth Trust, 1962.

Hengel, Martin. *Nachfolge und Charisma: Eine exegetisch-religionsgeschichtliche Studie zu Mt 8,21ff und Jesu Ruf in die Nachfolge*. BZNW 34. Berlin: Töpelmann, 1968.

Hering, Jean. *The First Epistle of Saint Paul to the Corinthians*. London: Epworth Press, 1962.

Hirsch, E. D. *The Aims of Interpretation*. Chicago: University of Chicago Press, 1976.

——— *Validity in Interpretation*. New Haven, Conn.: Yale University Press, 1967.

Holladay, Carl R. *Critical Introduction to the New Testament: Interpreting the Message and Meaning of Jesus Christ*. Nashville: Abingdon, 2005.

Holloway, Paul. *Consolation in Philippians: Philosophical: Sources and Rhetorical Strategy*. SNTSMS 112. New York: Cambridge University Press, 2001.

Holmes, Michael W. *1 & 2 Thessalonians*, NIVAC. Grand Rapids: Zondervan, 1998.

Holtz, Traugott. *Der erste Brief an die Thessalonicher*. EKKNT 13. Zurich: Benzinger, 1986.

Hooker, Morna. "Philippians 2:6-11." in *Jesus und Paulus: Festschrift for W. G. Kümmel*. Edited by Earl E. Ellis and E. Grässer. Tübingen: Mohr Siebeck, 1975.

——— "The Letter to the Philippians." Pages 232-37 in *The New Interpreter's Bible. New Testament Survey*. Edited by Nashville: Abingdon, 2006.

——— "The Letter to the Philippians." Pages 467-549 in *NIB* 11. Nashville: Abingdon, 2000.

Horrell, David. "Theological Principle or Christological Praxis? Pauline Ethics in 1 Corinthians 8.1-11.1." *JSNT* 67 (1997): 83-114.

Horsley, G. H. R., and S. R. Llewelyn, eds. *New Documents Illustrating Early Christianity, Vols 1-4*. Sydney: Macquarrie University, 1981-.

Howard, Nicholas C., Mark R. McMinn, and Leslie D. Bissell. "Spiritual Directors and Clinical Psychologists: A Comparison of Mental Health and Spiritual Values." *JPT* 28 (2000): 308-20.

Howell, David B. Review of Elizabeth A. Castelli, *Imitating Paul: A Discourse on Power*. *PRSt* 20 (1993): 317-20.

Hurtado, Larry. "Jesus as Lordly Example in Philippians 2:5-11." Pages 113-26 in *From Jesus to Paul: Studies in Honour of Francis Wright Beare*. Edited by Peter Richardson and John Coolidge Hurd. Waterloo: Wilfred Laurier University Press, 1984.

——— *How on Earth Did Jesus Become a God? Historical Questions About Earliest Devotion to Jesus*. Grand Rapids: Eerdmans, 2005.

——— *Lord Jesus Christ: Devotion to Jesus in Earliest Christianity*. Grand Rapids: Eerdmans, 2003.

Jeff, Gordon. *Spiritual Direction for Every Christian*. London: SPCK, 1987.

Johnson, John E. "The Prophetic Office as Paradigm for Pastoral Ministry." *TJ* n.s., 21 (2000): 61-81.

Johnson, Luke Timothy and Todd C. Penner. *The Writings of the New Testament: An Interpretation*. Rev. ed. Minneapolis: Fortress, 1999.

Jones, Alan W. *Exploring Spiritual Direction: An Essay on Christian Friendship*. San Francisco: HarperSanFrancisco, 1982.

——— *Soul Making: The Desert Way of Spirituality*. San Fransisco: HarperSan Fransisco, 1985.

Jones, Timothy K. *Mentor and Friend: Building Friendships that Point to God*. Oxford: Lion, 1991.

Joubert, Stephan J. "Managing the Household: Paul as *Paterfamilias* of the Christian Household Group in Corinth." Pages 213-23 in *Modeling Early Christianity: Social-Scientific Studies of the New Testament in its Context*. Edited by Philip F. Esler. London: Routledge, 1995.

Julian, Rachel. "The Practice of Psychotherapy and Spiritual Direction." *JRH* 31 (1992): 309-16.

Kamlah, E. *Die Form der katalogischen Paränese im Neuen Testament*. WUNT 7. Tübingen: Mohr Siebeck, 1964.

Karris, Robert J. "Romans 14:1-15:13 and the Occasion of Romans." Pages 75-99 in

The Romans Debate. Edited by Karl P. Donfried. Minneapolis: Augsburg, 1977.

Käsemann, Ernst. "Kritische Analyse von Phil 2:5-11." *ZTK* 47 (1950): 313-60.

Kelsey, Morton. *Companions on the Inner Way: The Art of Spiritual Guidance*. New York: Crossroad, 1991.

Kent, Homer A., Jr. "Philippians." Pages 93-159 in vol. 11 of *EBC*. Grand Rapids: Zondervan, 1978.

Kim, Seyoon. "Imitatio Christi (1 Cor 11:1)." Paper presented at the annual meeting of the IBR, Toronto, Canada, November 2002.

——— *The Origin of Paul's Gospel*. WUNT 4. Tübingen: J. C. B. Mohr, 1981.

Hawthorne, Gerald F., and Ralph P. Martin, eds. *Dictionary of Paul and His Letters*. Downers Grove: InterVarsity, 1993.

Kittay, Eva Feder. *Metaphor: Its Cognitive Force and Linguistic Structure*. Oxford: Clarendon, 1989.

Kittel, G., and G. Friedrich, *Theologisches Wörterbuch zum Neuen Testament*. 10 Vols. Stuttgart: Kohlhammer, 1933-1979.

Klauck, Hans-Josef. *1. Korintherbrief*. NEB 7. Würzburg: Echter, 1984.

Köster, Helmut. "Apostel und Gemeinde in den Briefen an die Thessalonicher." Pages 287-98 in *Kirche: Festschrift für Günther Bornkamm zum 75. Geburtstag*. Edited by Dieter Lührmann and Georg Strecker. Tübingen: Mohr Siebeck, 1980.

Kraftchick, Steven J. "A Necessary Detour: Paul's Metaphorical Understanding of the Philippian Hymn." *HBT* 15 (1993): 1-37.

Kremer, Jakob. *Der erste Brief an die Korinther*. RNT. Regensburg: Friedrich Pustet, 1997.

Krentz, Edgar M., "First and Second Epistles to the Thessalonians." *ABD on CD-ROM*. Logos Library System Version 3.0a, 2006. Print ed.: David Noel Freedman, ed. *ABD*. 6 vols. New York: Doubleday, 1992.

Kümmel, Werner Georg. *Introduction to the New Testament*. Translated by Howard Clark Kee. Revised ed. Nashville: Abingdon, 1975.

——— "Jesus und Paulus." in *Heilsgeschehen und Geschichte: Gesammelte Aufsätze 1933-1964 von Werner Georg Kümmel*. Edited by Erich Grässer. Marburg: Elwert, 1965.

Kurz, Albert L. *Disciplemaker: Practical Lessons for Maturing Believers (Workbook)*. Chicago: Moody, 1981.

Kurz, William S. "Kenotic Imitation of Paul and of Christ in Philippians 2 and 3." Pages 103-26 in *Discipleship in the New Testament*. Edited by Fernando F. Segovia. Philadelphia: Fortress, 1985.

Lang, Friedrich. *Die Briefe an die Korinther*. NTD 7. Göttingen: Vandenhoeck & Ruprecht, 1994[2].

Lantz, Jim and Jan Lantz. "Franklian Psychotherapy and Spiritual Direction." *JRH* 31 (1992): 297-308.

Larsson, Edvin. *Christus als Vorbild: Eine Untersuchung zu den paulinischen Tauf- und Eikontexten*. Translated by Beatrice Steiner. ASNU 23. Uppsala: Gleerup Lund, 1962[3].

——— "μιμέομαι κτλ." Pages 1053-57 in vol. 2 of *EWNT*. Edited by Horst Balz and Gerhard Schneider. Stuttgart: Kohlhammer, 1992.

Leech, Kenneth. *Soul Friend: The Practice of Christian Spirituality*. San Francisco: Harper & Row, 1977.

Lietzmann, Hans and Werner Georg Kümmel. *An die Korinther I-II*. HNT 9. Tübingen:

J. C. B. Mohr, 1949[4].

Lightfoot, J. B. *Notes on the Epistles of St. Paul*. Grand Rapids: Zondervan, 1957.

——— *St Paul's Epistle to the Philippians*. London: Macmillan, 1868.

Lindbeck, George A. *The Nature of Doctrine: Religion and Theology in a Postliberal Age*. Philadelphia: Westminster, 1984.

Lindemann, Andreas. *Der erste Korintherbrief*. HNT 9/1. Tübingen: Mohr Siebeck, 2000.

Llewelyn, S. R., "Ammonius to Appolonios (*P.Oxy*. XLII 3057): The Earliest Christian Letter on Papyrus?" Pages 169-77 in *NewDocs* vol. 6. Edited by Gregory H. Horsley and S. R. Llewelyn. Macquarie: Ancient History Documentary Research Centre, 1992.

Lohmeyer, Ernst. *Die Briefe an die Philipper, an die Kolosser und an Philemon*, KEK 9. Göttingen: Vandenhoeck & Ruprecht, 1929.

Lohse, Eduard, "Nachfolge Christi: I. im NT." Pages 1286-88 in vol. 4 of *RGG*. Tübingen: Mohr Siebeck, 1960[3].

Longenecker, Bruce W., ed. *Narrative Dynamics in Paul: A Critical Assessment*. Louisville, Ky.: Westminster John Knox, 2002.

Longenecker, Richard N. *The Road from Damascus: the Impact of Paul's conversion on His Life, Thought, and Ministry*. Grand Rapids: Eerdmans, 1997.

Longenecker, Richard N., ed. *Patterns of Discipleship on the New Testament*. Grand Rapids: Eerdmans, 1996.

Louw, Johannes P. and Eugene Nida. *Greek-English Lexicon of the New Testament based on Semantic Domains*. New York: United Bible Societies, 1988.

Lund, N. W. *Chiasmus in the New Testament: A Study in the Form and Function of Chiastic Structures*. Chapel Hill: University of North Carolina, 1942.

Luter, A. Boyd. "Ears to Hear: Pauline Orality and the Structure of Philippians." Paper presented at the annual meeting of the ETS, Nashville, Tenn. November 2000.

Luter, A. Boyd and Michelle V. Lee. "Philippians as Chiasmus: Key to the Structure, Unity and Theme Questions." *NTS* 41 (1995): 89-101.

Lyons, George. *Pauline Autobiography: Toward a New Understanding*. SBLDS 73. Atlanta: Scholars Press, 1985.

MacDonald, Gordon. "Disciple Abuse." *DJ* 30 (1985): 24-28.

Mahoney, Michael J. *Cognition and Behavior Modification*. Cambridge: Ballinger, 1974.

Malherbe, Abraham J. "'Gentle as a Nurse': The Cynic Background to 1 Thess 2." *NovT* 12 (1970): 203-17.

Mangis, Michael W. "Spiritual Formation and Christian Psychology: A Response and Application of Willard's Perspective." *JPT* 28 (2000): 259-62.

Mare, W. Harold. "1 Corinthians." Pages 175-297 in vol. 10 of *EBC*. Grand Rapids: Zondervan, 1976.

Marshall, John W. "Paul's Ethical Appeal in Philippians." Pages 357-74 in *Rhetoric and the New Testament: Essays from the 1992 Heidelberg Conference*. Edited by Stanley E. Porter and Thomas H. Olbricht. JSNTSup 90. Sheffield: JSOT Press, 1993.

Marshall, P. *Enmity at Corinth: Social Conventions in Paul's Relations with the Corinthians*. Tübingen: J. C. B. Mohr, 1987.

Martin, Ralph P. *Carmen Christi: Philippians ii. 5-11 in Recent Interpretation and in the Setting of Early Christian Worship*. New York: Cambridge University Press, 2005.

——— *The Epistle of Paul to the Philippians*. TNTC 11. Grand Rapids: Eerdmans, 1987.

——— *Hymn of Christ: Philippians 2:5-11 in Recent Interpretation & in the Setting of Early Christian Worship*. Downers Grove: InterVarsity, 1997.

——— *Reconciliation: A Study of Paul's Theology*. Grand Rapids: Zondervan, 1990.

Martyn, J. Louis. "Epistemology at the Turn of the Ages: 2 Corinthians 5:16." Pages 269-87 in *Christian History and Interpretation: Studies Presented to John Knox*. Edited by William R. Farmer, Charles F. D. Moule, and Reinhold R. Niebuhr. Cambridge: Cambridge University Press, 1967.

May, Gerald. *Care of Mind/Care of Spirit: Psychiatric Dimensions of Spiritual Direction*. San Francisco: Harper & Row, 1982.

Mayer, Bernhard. *Philipperbrief, Philemonbrief*. SKK 11. Stuttgart: Verlag Katholisches Bibelwerk, 1992.

McFague TeSelle, Sally. *Speaking in Parables: A Study in Metaphor and Theology*. Philadelphia: Fortress, 1975.

Melick, Richard R. *Philippians, Colossians, Philemon*. NAC 32. Nashville, Tenn.: Broadman, 1991.

Merk, Otto. "Nachahmung Christi: Zu ethischen Perspektiven in der paulinischen Theologie." Pages 172-206 in *Neues Testament und Ethik: Für Rudolf Schnackenburg*. Edited by Helmut Merklein. Freiburg: Herder, 1989.

Merklein, Helmut. *Der erste Brief an die Korinther (Kapitel 1-4)*. ÖTKNT 7/1. Gütersloh: Gütersloher, 1992.

——— *Der erste Brief an die Korinther (Kapitel 5,1-11,1)*. ÖTKNT 7/2. Gütersloh: Gütersloher, 2000.

Merton, Thomas. *Spiritual Direction and Meditation*. Collegeville, Minn.: Liturgical Press, 1960.

Metzger, Bruce M. *A Textual Commentary on the Greek New Testament*. London: United Bible Societies, 1975.

Michael, J. Hugh. *The Epistle of Paul to the Philippians*. MNTC. London: Hodder & Stoughton, 1927.

Michaelis, Wilhelm. *Der Brief des Paulus an die Philipper*. THKNT 11. Leipzig: Deichertsche Verlagsbuchhandlung, 1935.

——— "μιμέομαι κτλ." Pages 659-74 in vol. 4 of *TWNT*. Stuttgart: Kohlhammer, 1942.

Mitchell, Margaret M. Review of Elizabeth A. Castelli, *Imitating Paul: A Discourse of Power*. *JR* 72 (1992): 581-82.

Moo, Douglas J. *The Epistle to the Romans*. NICNT. Grand Rapids: Eerdmans, 1996.

Moon, Gary W., D. E. Willis, J. W. Bailey, and J. C. Kwasny. "Self-Reported Use of Christian Spiritual Guidance Techniques by Christian Psychotherapists, Pastoral Counselors, and Spiritual Directors." *JPT* 12 (1993): 24-37.

Moreland, J. P. "Restoring the Substance to the Soul of Psychology." *JPT* 26 (1998): 29-43.

Moreland, J. P. and David M. Ciocchi. *Christian Perspectives on Being Human: A Multidisciplinary Approach to Integration*. Grand Rapids: Baker, 1993.

Moreland, J. P. and Dallas Willard. *Love your God with All Your Mind: The Role of Reason in the Life of the Soul*. Colorado Springs, Colo.: NavPress, 1997.

Morris, Leon. *The First and Second Epistles to the Thessalonians*, NLCNT. London: Marshall Morgan and Scott, 1959.

Murphy, Nancey C. *Anglo-American Postmodernity: Philosophical Perspectives on*

Science, Religion, and Ethics. Boulder, Colo.: Westview, 1997.

Neil, William. *The Epistle of Paul to the Thessalonians*. MNTC. London: Hodder & Stoughton, 1948.

Newbigin, Lesslie. *Foolishness to the Greeks: The Gospel and Western Culture*. Grand Rapids: Eerdmans, 1986.

——— *The Gospel in a Pluralist Society*. London: SPCK, 1989.

O'Brien, Peter T. *Commentary on Philippians*. NIGNT. Grand Rapids: Eerdmans, 1991.

——— *Introductory Thanksgivings in the Letters of Paul*. NTSup 49. Leiden: Brill, 1976.

O'Connor, Elizabeth. *Journey Inward, Journey Outward*. San Francisco: HarperSanFrancisco, 1975.

Oden, Thomas. *Pastoral Theology*. San Francisco: Harper & Row, 1983.

Olbricht, Thomas H. "An Aristotelian Rhetorical Analysis of 1 Thessalonians." Pages 216-36 in *Greeks, Romans, and Christians: Essays in Honor of Abraham J. Malherbe*. Edited by David L. Balch, Everett Ferguson, and Wayne A. Meeks. Minneapolis: Fortress, 1990.

Orr, William and James Arthur Walther. *1 Corinthians*. AB 32. New York: Doubleday, 1976.

Palladius. *Lausiac History*. Edited by Johannes Quasten, Walter J. Burghardt, and Thomas Comerford Lawler. Translated by Robert T. Meyer. *ACW* 34. New York: Paulist Press, 1964.

Palmer, Parker J. *To Know as We are Known: Education as a Spiritual Journey*. San Francisco: HarperSanFrancisco, 1993.

Plummer, Alfred. *Commentary on St. Paul's Epistle to the Philippians*. London: Robert Scott, 1919.

Plummer, Robert L. "Imitation of Paul and the Church's Missionary Role in 1 Corinthians." *JETS* 44 (2001): 219-35.

Pogoloff, S. M. *Logos and Sophia: The Rhetorical Situation of 1 Corinthians*. Atlanta: Scholars Press, 1992.

Pollard, T. Evan. "The Integrity of Philippians." *NTS* 13 (1966): 56-66.

Porter, Stanley E. and Jeffrey T. Reed. "Philippians as a Micro-Chiasm and Its Exegetical Significance." *NTS* 44 (1998): 213-31.

Putt, B. Keith. Review of Elizabeth A. Castelli, *Imitating Paul: A Discourse on Power*. *SwJT* 35 (1992): 61.

Raitt, Jill, John Meyendorff, and Bernard McGinn, eds. *Christian Spirituality II: High Middle Ages and Reformation*. Vol. 17 of World Spirituality: An Encyclopedic History of the Religious Quest. 25 vols. New York: Crossroad, 1987.

Reed, Jeffrey T. *A Discourse Analysis of Philippians: Method and Rhetoric in the Debate over Literary Integrity*. JSNTSup 136. Sheffield: Sheffield University Press, 1997.

——— "Philippians 3:1 and the Epistolary Hesitation Formulas: The Literary Integrity of Philippians, Again." *JBL* 115 (1996): 63-90.

Regnault, Lucien. *The Day-to-Day Life of the Desert Fathers in the Fourth-Century Egypt*. Translated by Etienne Poirier, Jr. Petersham, Mass.: St. Bede's, 1999.

Richard, Earl J. *First and Second Thessalonians*. SP 11. Collegeville, Minn.: Glazier, 1995.

Richards, E. Randolph. *Paul and First-Century Letter Writing: Secretaries, Composition, and Collection*. Downers Grove: InterVarsity, 2004.

Riesenfeld, Harald. "The Gospel Tradition and Its Beginning." Pages 1-29 in *The Gospel Tradition*. Edited by Philadelphia: Fortress, 1970.

Rinehart, Stacy. "Discipleship: Looking Backward, Looking Forward." *DJ* 55 (1990): 8-9.

Roberts, Robert C. "Outline of Pauline Psychotherapy." Pages 134-63 in *Care for the Soul: Exploring the Intersection of Psychology & Theology*. Edited by Mark R. McMinn and Timothy R. Phillips. Downers Grove: InterVarsity, 2001.

Robertson, Archibald and Alfred Plummer. *A Critical and Exegetical Commentary on the First Epistle of St. Paul to the Corinthians*, ICC. New York: C. Scribner's Sons, 1911.

Roetzel, Calvin J. Review of Elizabeth A. Castelli, *Imitating Paul: A Discourse on Power*. *CRBR* 6 (1993): 213-15.

Sanders, Boykin. "Imitating Paul: 1 Cor 4:16." *HTR* 74 (1981): 353-63.

Sanders, Edward P. *Paul and Palestinian Judaism: A Comparison of Patterns of Religion*. Philadelphia: Fortress, 1977.

Satinover, Jeffrey. *Homosexuality and the Politics of Truth*. Grand Rapids: Baker, 1996.

Schlier, Heinrich. *Der Brief an die Galater*. KEK 7. Göttingen: Vandenhoeck & Ruprecht, 1949.

——— *Der Philipperbrief*. Einsiedeln: Johannesverlag, 1980.

Schnelle, Udo. *Apostle Paul: His Life and Theology*. Grand Rapids: Baker Academic, 2005.

Schrage, Wolfgang. *Die konkreten Einzelgebote in der paulinischen Paränese. Ein Beitrag zur neutestamentlichen Ethik*. Gütersloh: Gütersloher, 1961.

——— "Das apostolische Amt des Paulus nach 1 Kor 4,14-17." Pages 103-19 in *L'Apôtre Paul, Personnalité, Style et Conception du Ministère*. Edited by A. Vanhoye. BETL 73. Leuven: Leuven University Press, 1986.

——— *Ethik des Neuen Testaments*. NTDER 4. Göttingen: Vandenhoeck & Ruprecht, 1989.

——— *Der erste Brief an die Korinther, 1. Teilband 1 Kor 1,1-6,11*. EKKNT 7/1. Zurich: Benzinger, 1991.

——— *Der erste Brief an die Korinther, 2 Teilband 1 Kor 6,12-11,16*. EKKNT 7/2. Zurich: Benzinger, 1995.

Schulz, Anselm. *Nachfolgen und Nachahmen: Studien über das Verhältnis der neutestamentlichen Jüngerschaft zur urchristlichen Vorbildethik*. SANT 6. Munich: Kösel, 1962.

Schulz, Siegfried. *Neutestamentliche Ethik*. Zürich: Theologischer Verlag, 1987.

Schütz, John Howard. *Paul and the Anatomy of Apostolic Authority*. SNTSMS 26. Cambridge: University Press, 1976.

Scott, Ernest F. and Robert R. Wicks. *The Epistle to the Philippians*. *IB* 11. New York: Abingdon-Cokesbury, 1955.

Sellner, Edward C. "Soul Friendship in Early Celtic Monasticism--part I." *Aisling Magazine*, Samhain 1995.

Selwyn, Edward Gordon. *The First Epistle of St. Peter: The Greek Text with Introduction, Notes, and Essays*. TAC. Grand Rapids: Baker, 1981.

Sevenster, J. N. *Paul and Seneca*. Leiden: Brill, 1961.

Shalem Institute for Spiritual Formation. "Spiritual Direction: An Online Verson [sic] of the Shalem Pamphlet on Spiritual Direction." http://www.shalem.org/sd.html (accessed May 19, 2001).

Silva, Moises. *Philippians*. BECNT. Grand Rapids: Baker, 1992.

——— *Philippians*. BECNT. Grand Rapids: Baker Academic, 2005².

Sine, Tom. "Right-Side-Up Values in an Upside-Down World: Whole-Life Discipleship in the '90s." *DJ* 55 (1990): 35-38.

Spencer, F. Scott. Review of Elizabeth A. Castelli, *Imitating Paul: A Discourse of Power*." *CBQ* 55 (1993): 573-74.

Spencer, William David. "The Power in Paul's Teaching (1 Cor 4:9-20)." *JETS* 32 (1989): 51-61.

Spiritual Directors International. *What Is Spiritual Direction?* http://www.sdiworld.org/index.pl/what_is_spiritual_direction2.html (accessed May 15, 2001).

Stanley, David M. "'Become Imitators of Me': The Pauline Conception of Apostolic Tradition." *Bib* 40 (1959): 859-77.

Stanley, Paul D. and J. Robert Clinton. *Connecting: The Mentoring Relationships You Need To Succeed in Life*. Colorado Springs, Colo.: NavPress, 1992.

Stowers, S. K. "Friends and Enemies in the Politics of Heaven." in *Pauline Theology: Thessalonians, Philippians, Galatians, Philemon*. Edited by Jouette M. Bassler, David M. Hay, and E. Elizabeth Johnson. Minneapolis: Fortress, 1991.

Stuhlmacher, Peter. "Zum Thema: Das Evangelium und die Evangelien." Pages 1-26 in *Das Evangelium und die Evangelien: Vorträge vom Tübinger Symposium 1982*. Edited by Peter Stuhlmacher. WUNT 28. Tübingen: J. C. B. Mohr, 1982.

Thielman, Frank. *Philippians*, NIVAC. Grand Rapids: Zondervan, 1995.

Thiselton, Anthony C. *Interpreting God and the Postmodern Self: On Meaning, Manipulation, and Promise*. Edinburgh: T&T Clark, 1995.

Thomas, Robert L. "1 Thessalonians." Pages 227-98 in vol. 10 of *EBC*. Grand Rapids: Zondervan, 1978.

Thompson, Michael. *Clothed with Christ: The Example and Teaching of Jesus in Romans 12:1-15.13*. JSNTSup 59. Sheffield: JSOT Press, 1991.

——— "The Holy Internet: Communication Between Churches in the First Christian Generation." Pages 49-70 in *The Gospels for All Christians: Rethinking the Gospel Audiences*. Edited by Richard Bauckham. Edinburgh: T&T Clark, 1998.

Thurston, Bonnie Bowman and Judith Ryan. *Philippians and Philemon*. SP 10. Collegeville, Minn.: Liturgical Press, 2005.

Tinsley, Ernest J. *The Imitation of God in Christ: Essays on the Biblical Basis of Christian Spirituality*. Philadelphia: Westminster, 1960.

Turner, Nigel. *Syntax*. Vol. 3 of *Grammar of New Testament Greek*. 3 vols. Edinburgh: T&T Clark, 1963.

Ulrich, Laurel Artress. "The Relationship between Psychotherapy and Spiritual Direction." Ph.D. diss., Andover Newton Theological School, 1986.

Van Kaam, Adrian L. *Transcendence Therapy*. Vol. 7 of *Formative Spirituality*. 7 vols. New York: Crossroad, 1995.

Vanhoozer, Kevin J. *Is There a Meaning in This Text? The Bible, the Reader, and the Morality of Literary Knowledge*. Grand Rapids: Zondervan, 1998.

Vincent, Marvin R. *A Critical and Exegetical Commentary on Epistles to the Philippians and to Philemon*. ICC. New York: Scribners, 1897.

Vitz, Paul. *Psychology as Religion: The Cult of Self Worship*. Grand Rapids: Eerdmans, 1994².

Vögtle, A. *Die Tugend- und Lasterkataloge im Neuen Testament*. NTAbh 16/4. Münster: Aschendorff, 1936.

von Dobschütz, Ernst. *Die Thessalonicher-Briefe*, KEK. Göttingen: Vandenhoeck & Ruprecht, 1909.

Waetjen, Herman C. "Is the 'Imitation of Christ' Biblical?" *Di* 2 (1963): 118-25.

Wakefield, Gordon S. ed. *Dictionary of Christian Spirituality*. London: SCM Press, 1983.

Walter, Nikolaus. "Der Brief an die Philipper." Pages 11-104 in *Die Briefe an die Philipper, Thessalonicher und an Philemon*. NTD 8/2. Göttingen: Vandenhoeck & Ruprecht, 1998.

Wanamaker, Charles A. *The Epistles to the Thessalonians: A Commentary on the Greek Text*. NIGTC. Grand Rapids: Eerdmans, 1990.

Watson, Duane F. "A Rhetorical Analysis of Philippians and its Implications for the Unity Question." *NovT* 30 (1988): 57-88.

Watson, P. J. "Girard and Integration: Desire, Violence, and the Mimesis of Christ as Foundation for Postmodernity." *JPT* 26 (1998): 311-21.

Weaver, Dorothy Jean. Review of Elizabeth A. Castelli, *Imitating Paul: A Discourse of Power*." *Int* 47 (1993): 313-14.

Wegenast, K. *Das Verständnis der Tradition bei Paulus in und in den Deuteropaulinen*. Neukirchen-Vluyn: Neukirchener, 1962.

Weiss, Johannes. *Der erste Korintherbrief*. KEK 9. Göttingen: Vandenhoeck & Ruprecht, 1910.

Wendland, Hans-Dieter. *Die Briefe an die Korinther*. Edited by Peter Stuhlmacher and Georg Friedrich. NTD 7. Göttingen: Vandenhoeck & Ruprecht, 1980.

Wenham, David. *Paul and Jesus: The True Story*. Grand Rapids: Eerdmans, 2002.

——— *Paul: Follower of Jesus or Founder of Christianity?* Grand Rapids: Eerdmans, 1995.

White, L. Michael. "Morality Between Two Worlds: A Paradigm of Friendship in Philippians." Pages 201-15 in *Greeks, Romans, and Christians: Essays in Honor of Abraham J. Malherbe*. Edited by David L. Balch, Everett Ferguson, and Wayne A. Meeks. Minneapolis: Fortress, 1990.

Wibbing, S. *Die Tugend- und Lasterkataloge im Neuen Testament und ihre Traditionsgeschichte unter besonderer Berücksichtigung der Qumran Texte*. BZNT 25. Berlin: Töpelmann, 1959.

Wick, Peter. *Der Philipperbrief: Der formale Aufbau des Briefs als Schlüssel zum Verständnis seines Inhalts*. BZNT 135. Stuttgart: Kohlhammer, 1994.

Wilkins, Michael J. *Concept of Disciple in Matthew's Gospel as Reflected in the Use of the Term μαθητής*. NTSup 59. Leiden: Brill, 1988.

Willard, Dallas. *Divine Conspiracy: Rediscovering our Hidden Life in God*. San Francisco: HarperSanFrancisco, 1998.

——— *Renovation of the Heart: Putting on the Character of Christ*. Colorado Springs, Colo.: NavPress, 2002.

——— *Spirit of the Disciplines: Understanding How God Changes Lives*. San Francisco: Harper & Row, 1988.

——— "Spiritual Disciplines, Spiritual Formation, and the Restoration of the Soul." *JPT* 26 (1998): 101-09.

——— "Spiritual Formation in Christ: A Perspective on What it is and How it Might be Done." *JPT* 28 (2000): 254-58.

Williams, D. M. "Imitation of Christ in Paul, With Special Reference to Paul as Teacher." Ph. D. diss., Columbia University, 1967.

Williams, David John. *Paul's Metaphors: Their Context and Character.* Peabody, Mass.: Hendrickson, 1999.

Willis, Wendel L. "An Apostolic Apologia? The Form and Function of 1 Corinthians 9." *JSNT* 24 (1985): 33-48.

——— *Idol Meat at Corinth. The Pauline Argument in 1 Corinthians 8 and 9.* Chico, Calif.: Scholars Press, 1985.

Witherington, Ben. *Friendship and Finances in Philippi: The Letter of Paul to the Philippians.* Valley Forge, Pa.: Trinity Press, 1994.

——— *Paul's Narrative Thought World: The Tapestry of Tragedy and Triumph.* Louisville, Ky.: Westminster John Knox, 1994.

——— *The Paul Quest: The Renewed Search for the Jew of Tarsus.* Downers Grove: InterVarsity, 1998.

Wittgenstein, Ludwig. *Philosophical Investigations.* Translated by G. E. M. Anscombe. Oxford: Oxford University Press, 1953.

Wolff, Christian. *Der erste Brief des Paulus an die Korinther.* TKNT 7. Leipzig: Evangelische Verlagsanstalt, 1996.

Wright, N. T. "How Can the Bible be Authoritative?" *VE* 21 (1991): 7-32.

——— *Jesus and the Victory of God.* Minneapolis: Fortress, 1992.

——— *The Last Word: Beyond the Bible Wars to a New Understanding of the Authority of Scripture.* San Francisco: HarperSanFrancisco, 2005.

——— *The New Testament and the People of God.* Minneapolis: Fortress, 1992.

——— *The Resurrection of the Son of God*, London: SPCK, 2003.

Yungblut, John R. *The Gentle Art of Spiritual Guidance.* New York: Continuum, 1995.

General Index

Scripture, Apocrypha, and Early Church Index

2 Corinthians

Colossians

1 Thessalonians

Ancient Writings Index

Paternoster Biblical Monographs

(All titles uniform with this volume)
Dates in bold are of projected publication

Joseph Abraham
Eve: Accused or Acquitted?
A Reconsideration of Feminist Readings of the Creation Narrative Texts in Genesis 1–3

Two contrary views dominate contemporary feminist biblical scholarship. One finds in the Bible an unequivocal equality between the sexes from the very creation of humanity, whilst the other sees the biblical text as irredeemably patriarchal and androcentric. Dr Abraham enters into dialogue with both camps as well as introducing his own method of approach. An invaluable tool for any one who is interested in this contemporary debate.

2002 / 0-85364-971-5 / xxiv + 272pp

Octavian D. Baban
Mimesis and Luke's on the Road Encounters in Luke-Acts
Luke's Theology of the Way and its Literary Representation

The book argues on theological and literary (mimetic) grounds that Luke's on-the-road encounters, especially those belonging to the post-Easter period, are part of his complex theology of the Way. Jesus' teaching and that of the apostles is presented by Luke as a challenging answer to the Hellenistic reader's thirst for adventure, good literature, and existential paradigms.

2005 */ 1-84227-253-5 / approx. 374pp*

Paul Barker
The Triumph of Grace in Deuteronomy

This book is a textual and theological analysis of the interaction between the sin and faithlessness of Israel and the grace of Yahweh in response, looking especially at Deuteronomy chapters 1–3, 8–10 and 29–30. The author argues that the grace of Yahweh is determinative for the ongoing relationship between Yahweh and Israel and that Deuteronomy anticipates and fully expects Israel to be faithless.

2004 / 1-84227-226-8 / xxii + 270pp

Jonathan F. Bayes
The Weakness of the Law
God's Law and the Christian in New Testament Perspective

A study of the four New Testament books which refer to the law as weak (Acts, Romans, Galatians, Hebrews) leads to a defence of the third use in the Reformed debate about the law in the life of the believer.

2000 / 0-85364-957-X / xii + 244pp

Mark Bonnington

The Antioch Episode of Galatians 2:11-14 in Historical and Cultural Context

The Galatians 2 'incident' in Antioch over table-fellowship suggests significant disagreement between the leading apostles. This book analyses the background to the disagreement by locating the incident within the dynamics of social interaction between Jews and Gentiles. It proposes a new way of understanding the relationship between the individuals and issues involved.

***2005** / 1-84227-050-8 / approx. 350pp*

David Bostock

A Portrayal of Trust

The Theme of Faith in the Hezekiah Narratives

This study provides detailed and sensitive readings of the Hezekiah narratives (2 Kings 18–20 and Isaiah 36–39) from a theological perspective. It concentrates on the theme of faith, using narrative criticism as its methodology. Attention is paid especially to setting, plot, point of view and characterization within the narratives. A largely positive portrayal of Hezekiah emerges that underlines the importance and relevance of scripture.

***2005** / 1-84227-314-0 / approx. 300pp*

Mark Bredin

Jesus, Revolutionary of Peace

A Non-violent Christology in the Book of Revelation

This book aims to demonstrate that the figure of Jesus in the Book of Revelation can best be understood as an active non-violent revolutionary.

2003 / 1-84227-153-9 / xviii + 262pp

Robinson Butarbutar

Paul and Conflict Resolution

An Exegetical Study of Paul's Apostolic Paradigm in 1 Corinthians 9

The author sees the apostolic paradigm in 1 Corinthians 9 as part of Paul's unified arguments in 1 Corinthians 8–10 in which he seeks to mediate in the dispute over the issue of food offered to idols. The book also sees its relevance for dispute-resolution today, taking the conflict within the author's church as an example.

***2006** / 1-84227-315-9 / approx. 280pp*

Daniel J-S Chae

Paul as Apostle to the Gentiles

His Apostolic Self-awareness and its Influence on the Soteriological Argument in Romans

Opposing 'the post-Holocaust interpretation of Romans', Daniel Chae competently demonstrates that Paul argues for the equality of Jew and Gentile in Romans. Chae's fresh exegetical interpretation is academically outstanding and spiritually encouraging.

1997 / 0-85364-829-8 / xiv + 378pp

Luke L. Cheung

The Genre, Composition and Hermeneutics of the Epistle of James

The present work examines the employment of the wisdom genre with a certain compositional structure and the interpretation of the law through the Jesus tradition of the double love command by the author of the Epistle of James to serve his purpose in promoting perfection and warning against doubleness among the eschatologically renewed people of God in the Diaspora.

2003 / 1-84227-062-1 / xvi + 372pp

Youngmo Cho

Spirit and Kingdom in the Writings of Luke and Paul

The relationship between Spirit and Kingdom is a relatively unexplored area in Lukan and Pauline studies. This book offers a fresh perspective of two biblical writers on the subject. It explores the difference between Luke's and Paul's understanding of the Spirit by examining the specific question of the relationship of the concept of the Spirit to the concept of the Kingdom of God in each writer.

***2005** / 1-84227-316-7 / approx. 270pp*

Andrew C. Clark

Parallel Lives

The Relation of Paul to the Apostles in the Lucan Perspective

This study of the Peter-Paul parallels in Acts argues that their purpose was to emphasize the themes of continuity in salvation history and the unity of the Jewish and Gentile missions. New light is shed on Luke's literary techniques, partly through a comparison with Plutarch.

2001 / 1-84227-035-4 / xviii + 386pp

Andrew D. Clarke

Secular and Christian Leadership in Corinth

A Socio-Historical and Exegetical Study of 1 Corinthians 1–6

This volume is an investigation into the leadership structures and dynamics of first-century Roman Corinth. These are compared with the practice of leadership in the Corinthian Christian community which are reflected in 1 Corinthians 1–6, and contrasted with Paul's own principles of Christian leadership.

***2005** / 1-84227-229-2 / 200pp*

Stephen Finamore

God, Order and Chaos

René Girard and the Apocalypse

Readers are often disturbed by the images of destruction in the book of Revelation and unsure why they are unleashed after the exaltation of Jesus. This book examines past approaches to these texts and uses René Girard's theories to revive some old ideas and propose some new ones.

***2005** / 1-84227-197-0 / approx. 344pp*

David G. Firth

Surrendering Retribution in the Psalms

Responses to Violence in the Individual Complaints

In *Surrendering Retribution in the Psalms*, David Firth examines the ways in which the book of Psalms inculcates a model response to violence through the repetition of standard patterns of prayer. Rather than seeking justification for retributive violence, Psalms encourages not only a surrender of the right of retribution to Yahweh, but also sets limits on the retribution that can be sought in imprecations. Arising initially from the author's experience in South Africa, the possibilities of this model to a particular context of violence is then briefly explored.

***2005** / 1-84227-337-X / xviii + 154pp*

Scott J. Hafemann

Suffering and Ministry in the Spirit

Paul's Defence of His Ministry in II Corinthians 2:14–3:3

Shedding new light on the way Paul defended his apostleship, the author offers a careful, detailed study of 2 Corinthians 2:14–3:3 linked with other key passages throughout 1 and 2 Corinthians. Demonstrating the unity and coherence of Paul's argument in this passage, the author shows that Paul's suffering served as the vehicle for revealing God's power and glory through the Spirit.

2000 / 0-85364-967-7 / xiv + 262pp

Scott J. Hafemann

Paul, Moses and the History of Israel

The Letter/Spirit Contrast and the Argument from Scripture in 2 Corinthians 3

An exegetical study of the call of Moses, the second giving of the Law (Exodus 32–34), the new covenant, and the prophetic understanding of the history of Israel in 2 Corinthians 3. Hafemann's work demonstrates Paul's contextual use of the Old Testament and the essential unity between the Law and the Gospel within the context of the distinctive ministries of Moses and Paul.

2005 / 1-84227-317-5 / xii + 498pp

Douglas S. McComiskey

Lukan Theology in the Light of the Gospel's Literary Structure

Luke's Gospel was purposefully written with theology embedded in its patterned literary structure. A critical analysis of this cyclical structure provides new windows into Luke's interpretation of the individual pericopes comprising the Gospel and illuminates several of his theological interests.

2004 / 1-84227-148-2 / xviii + 388pp

Stephen Motyer

Your Father the Devil?

A New Approach to John and 'The Jews'

Who are 'the Jews' in John's Gospel? Defending John against the charge of antisemitism, Motyer argues that, far from demonising the Jews, the Gospel seeks to present Jesus as 'Good News for Jews' in a late first century setting.

1997 / 0-85364-832-8 / xiv + 260pp

Esther Ng

Reconstructing Christian Origins?

The Feminist Theology of Elizabeth Schüssler Fiorenza: An Evaluation

In a detailed evaluation, the author challenges Elizabeth Schüssler Fiorenza's reconstruction of early Christian origins and her underlying presuppositions. The author also presents her own views on women's roles both then and now.

2002 / 1-84227-055-9 / xxiv + 468pp

Robin Parry

Old Testament Story and Christian Ethics

The Rape of Dinah as a Case Study

What is the role of story in ethics and, more particularly, what is the role of Old Testament story in Christian ethics? This book, drawing on the work of contemporary philosophers, argues that narrative is crucial in the ethical shaping of people and, drawing on the work of contemporary Old Testament scholars, that story plays a key role in Old Testament ethics. Parry then argues that when situated in canonical context Old Testament stories can be reappropriated by Christian readers in their own ethical formation. The shocking story of the rape of Dinah and the massacre of the Shechemites provides a fascinating case study for exploring the parameters within which Christian ethical appropriations of Old Testament stories can live.

2004 / 1-84227-210-1 / xx + 350pp

Ian Paul

Power to See the World Anew

The Value of Paul Ricoeur's Hermeneutic of Metaphor in Interpreting the Symbolism of Revelation 12 and 13

This book is a study of the hermeneutics of metaphor of Paul Ricoeur, one of the most important writers on hermeneutics and metaphor of the last century. It sets out the key points of his theory, important criticisms of his work, and how his approach, modified in the light of these criticisms, offers a methodological framework for reading apocalyptic texts.

2006 */ 1-84227-056-7 / approx. 350pp*

Robert L. Plummer

Paul's Understanding of the Church's Mission

Did the Apostle Paul Expect the Early Christian Communities to Evangelize?

This book engages in a careful study of Paul's letters to determine if the apostle expected the communities to which he wrote to engage in missionary activity. It helpfully summarizes the discussion on this debated issue, judiciously handling contested texts, and provides a way forward in addressing this critical question. While admitting that Paul rarely explicitly commands the communities he founded to evangelize, Plummer amasses significant incidental data to provide a convincing case that Paul did indeed expect his churches to engage in mission activity. Throughout the study, Plummer progressively builds a theological basis for the church's mission that is both distinctively Pauline and compelling.

2006 */ 1-84227-333-7 / approx. 324pp*

David Powys

'Hell': A Hard Look at a Hard Question

The Fate of the Unrighteous in New Testament Thought

This comprehensive treatment seeks to unlock the original meaning of terms and phrases long thought to support the traditional doctrine of hell. It concludes that there is an alternative—one which is more biblical, and which can positively revive the rationale for Christian mission.

1997 / 0-85364-831-X / xxii + 478pp

Sorin Sabou

Between Horror and Hope

Paul's Metaphorical Language of Death in Romans 6.1-11

This book argues that Paul's metaphorical language of death in Romans 6.1-11 conveys two aspects: horror and hope. The 'horror' aspect is conveyed by the 'crucifixion' language, and the 'hope' aspect by 'burial' language. The life of the Christian believer is understood, as relationship with sin is concerned ('death to sin'), between these two realities: horror and hope.

***2005** / 1-84227-322-1 / approx. 224pp*

Rosalind Selby

The Comical Doctrine

The Epistemology of New Testament Hermeneutics

This book argues that the gospel breaks through postmodernity's critique of truth and the referential possibilities of textuality with its gift of grace. With a rigorous, philosophical challenge to modernist and postmodernist assumptions, Selby offers an alternative epistemology to all who would still read with faith *and* with academic credibility.

***2005** / 1-84227-212-8 / approx. 350pp*

Kiwoong Son

Zion Symbolism in Hebrews

Hebrews 12.18-24 as a Hermeneutical Key to the Epistle

This book challenges the general tendency of understanding the Epistle to the Hebrews against a Hellenistic background and suggests that the Epistle should be understood in the light of the Jewish apocalyptic tradition. The author especially argues for the importance of the theological symbolism of Sinai and Zion (Heb. 12:18-24) as it provides the Epistle's theological background as well as the rhetorical basis of the superiority motif of Jesus throughout the Epistle.

***2005** / 1-84227-368-X / approx. 280pp*

Kevin Walton

Thou Traveller Unknown

The Presence and Absence of God in the Jacob Narrative

The author offers a fresh reading of the story of Jacob in the book of Genesis through the paradox of divine presence and absence. The work also seeks to make a contribution to Pentateuchal studies by bringing together a close reading of the final text with historical critical insights, doing justice to the text's historical depth, final form and canonical status.

2003 / 1-84227-059-1 / xvi + 238pp

George M. Wieland

The Significance of Salvation

A Study of Salvation Language in the Pastoral Epistles

The language and ideas of salvation pervade the three Pastoral Epistles. This study offers a close examination of their soteriological statements. In all three letters the idea of salvation is found to play a vital paraenetic role, but each also exhibits distinctive soteriological emphases. The results challenge common assumptions about the Pastoral Epistles as a corpus.

***2005** / 1-84227-257-8 / approx. 324pp*

Alistair Wilson

When Will These Things Happen?

A Study of Jesus as Judge in Matthew 21–25

This study seeks to allow Matthew's carefully constructed presentation of Jesus to be given full weight in the modern evaluation of Jesus' eschatology. Careful analysis of the text of Matthew 21–25 reveals Jesus to be standing firmly in the Jewish prophetic and wisdom traditions as he proclaims and enacts imminent judgement on the Jewish authorities then boldly claims the central role in the final and universal judgement.

2004 / 1-84227-146-6 / xxii + 272pp

Lindsay Wilson

Joseph Wise and Otherwise

The Intersection of Covenant and Wisdom in Genesis 37–50

This book offers a careful literary reading of Genesis 37–50 that argues that the Joseph story contains both strong covenant themes and many wisdom-like elements. The connections between the two helps to explore how covenant and wisdom might intersect in an integrated biblical theology.

2004 / 1-84227-140-7 / xvi + 340pp

Stephen I. Wright

The Voice of Jesus

Studies in the Interpretation of Six Gospel Parables

This literary study considers how the 'voice' of Jesus has been heard in different periods of parable interpretation, and how the categories of figure and trope may help us towards a sensitive reading of the parables today.

2000 / 0-85364-975-8 / xiv + 280pp

Paternoster
9 Holdom Avenue,
Bletchley,
Milton Keynes MK1 1QR,
United Kingdom
Web: www.authenticmedia.co.uk/paternoster

July 2005

Paternoster Theological Monographs

(All titles uniform with this volume)
Dates in bold are of projected publication

Emil Bartos
Deification in Eastern Orthodox Theology
An Evaluation and Critique of the Theology of Dumitru Staniloae

Bartos studies a fundamental yet neglected aspect of Orthodox theology: deification. By examining the doctrines of anthropology, christology, soteriology and ecclesiology as they relate to deification, he provides an important contribution to contemporary dialogue between Eastern and Western theologians.

1999 / 0-85364-956-1 / xii + 370pp

Graham Buxton
The Trinity, Creation and Pastoral Ministry
Imaging the Perichoretic God

In this book the author proposes a three-way conversation between theology, science and pastoral ministry. His approach draws on a Trinitarian understanding of God as a relational being of love, whose life 'spills over' into all created reality, human and non-human. By locating human meaning and purpose within God's 'creation-community' this book offers the possibility of a transforming engagement between those in pastoral ministry and the scientific community.

2005 */ 1-84227-369-8 / approx. 380 pp*

Iain D. Campbell
Fixing the Indemnity
The Life and Work of George Adam Smith

When Old Testament scholar George Adam Smith (1856–1942) delivered the Lyman Beecher lectures at Yale University in 1899, he confidently declared that 'modern criticism has won its war against traditional theories. It only remains to fix the amount of the indemnity.' In this biography, Iain D. Campbell assesses Smith's critical approach to the Old Testament and evaluates its consequences, showing that Smith's life and work still raises questions about the relationship between biblical scholarship and evangelical faith.

2004 / 1-84227-228-4 / xx + 256pp

Tim Chester
Mission and the Coming of God
Eschatology, the Trinity and Mission in the Theology of Jürgen Moltmann
This book explores the theology and missiology of the influential contemporary theologian, Jürgen Moltmann. It highlights the important contribution Moltmann has made while offering a critique of his thought from an evangelical perspective. In so doing, it touches on pertinent issues for evangelical missiology. The conclusion takes Calvin as a starting point, proposing 'an eschatology of the cross' which offers a critique of the over-realised eschatologies in liberation theology and certain forms of evangelicalism.
***2006** / 1-84227-320-5 / approx. 224pp*

Sylvia Wilkey Collinson
Making Disciples
The Significance of Jesus' Educational Strategy for Today's Church
This study examines the biblical practice of discipling, formulates a definition, and makes comparisons with modern models of education. A recommendation is made for greater attention to its practice today.
2004 / 1-84227-116-4 / xiv + 278pp

Darrell Cosden
A Theology of Work
Work and the New Creation
Through dialogue with Moltmann, Pope John Paul II and others, this book develops a genitive 'theology of work', presenting a theological definition of work and a model for a theological ethics of work that shows work's nature, value and meaning now and eschatologically. Work is shown to be a transformative activity consisting of three dynamically inter-related dimensions: the instrumental, relational and ontological.
2005 / 1-84227-332-9 / xvi + 208pp

Stephen M. Dunning
The Crisis and the Quest
A Kierkegaardian Reading of Charles Williams
Employing Kierkegaardian categories and analysis, this study investigates both the central crisis in Charles Williams's authorship between hermetism and Christianity (Kierkegaard's Religions A and B), and the quest to resolve this crisis, a quest that ultimately presses the bounds of orthodoxy.
2000 / 0-85364-985-5 / xxiv + 254pp

Keith Ferdinando

The Triumph of Christ in African Perspective

A Study of Demonology and Redemption in the African Context

The book explores the implications of the gospel for traditional African fears of occult aggression. It analyses such traditional approaches to suffering and biblical responses to fears of demonic evil, concluding with an evaluation of African beliefs from the perspective of the gospel.

1999 / 0-85364-830-1 / xviii + 450pp

Andrew Goddard

Living the Word, Resisting the World

The Life and Thought of Jacques Ellul

This work offers a definitive study of both the life and thought of the French Reformed thinker Jacques Ellul (1912-1994). It will prove an indispensable resource for those interested in this influential theologian and sociologist and for Christian ethics and political thought generally.

2002 / 1-84227-053-2 / xxiv + 378pp

David Hilborn

The Words of our Lips

Language-Use in Free Church Worship

Studies of liturgical language have tended to focus on the written canons of Roman Catholic and Anglican communities. By contrast, David Hilborn analyses the more extemporary approach of English Nonconformity. Drawing on recent developments in linguistic pragmatics, he explores similarities and differences between 'fixed' and 'free' worship, and argues for the interdependence of each.

***2006** / 0-85364-977-4 / approx. 350pp*

Roger Hitching

The Church and Deaf People

A Study of Identity, Communication and Relationships with Special Reference to the Ecclesiology of Jürgen Moltmann

In *The Church and Deaf People* Roger Hitching sensitively examines the history and present experience of deaf people and finds similarities between aspects of sign language and Moltmann's theological method that 'open up' new ways of understanding theological concepts.

2003 / 1-84227-222-5 / xxii + 236pp

John G. Kelly

One God, One People

The Differentiated Unity of the People of God in the Theology of Jürgen Moltmann

The author expounds and critiques Moltmann's doctrine of God and highlights the systematic connections between it and Moltmann's influential discussion of Israel. He then proposes a fresh approach to Jewish–Christian relations building on Moltmann's work using insights from Habermas and Rawls.

***2005** / 0-85346-969-3 / approx. 350pp*

Mark F.W. Lovatt

Confronting the Will-to-Power

A Reconsideration of the Theology of Reinhold Niebuhr

Confronting the Will-to-Power is an analysis of the theology of Reinhold Niebuhr, arguing that his work is an attempt to identify, and provide a practical theological answer to, the existence and nature of human evil.

2001 / 1-84227-054-0 / xviii + 216pp

Neil B. MacDonald

Karl Barth and the Strange New World within the Bible

Barth, Wittgenstein, and the Metadilemmas of the Enlightenment

Barth's discovery of the strange new world within the Bible is examined in the context of Kant, Hume, Overbeck, and, most importantly, Wittgenstein. MacDonald covers some fundamental issues in theology today: epistemology, the final form of the text and biblical truth-claims.

2000 / 0-85364-970-7 / xxvi + 374pp

Keith A. Mascord

Alvin Plantinga and Christian Apologetics

This book draws together the contributions of the philosopher Alvin Plantinga to the major contemporary challenges to Christian belief, highlighting in particular his ground-breaking work in epistemology and the problem of evil. Plantinga's theory that both theistic and Christian belief is warrantedly basic is explored and critiqued, and an assessment offered as to the significance of his work for apologetic theory and practice.

***2005** / 1-84227-256-X / approx. 304pp*

Gillian McCulloch

The Deconstruction of Dualism in Theology

With Reference to Ecofeminist Theology and New Age Spirituality

This book challenges eco-theological anti-dualism in Christian theology, arguing that dualism has a twofold function in Christian religious discourse. Firstly, it enables us to express the discontinuities and divisions that are part of the process of reality. Secondly, dualistic language allows us to express the mysteries of divine transcendence/immanence and the survival of the soul without collapsing into monism and materialism, both of which are problematic for Christian epistemology.

2002 / 1-84227-044-3 / xii + 282pp

Leslie McCurdy

Attributes and Atonement

The Holy Love of God in the Theology of P.T. Forsyth

Attributes and Atonement is an intriguing full-length study of P.T. Forsyth's doctrine of the cross as it relates particularly to God's holy love. It includes an unparalleled bibliography of both primary and secondary material relating to Forsyth.

1999 / 0-85364-833-6 / xiv + 328pp

Nozomu Miyahira

Towards a Theology of the Concord of God

A Japanese Perspective on the Trinity

This book introduces a new Japanese theology and a unique Trinitarian formula based on the Japanese intellectual climate: three betweennesses and one concord. It also presents a new interpretation of the Trinity, a co-subordinationism, which is in line with orthodox Trinitarianism; each single person of the Trinity is eternally and equally subordinate (or serviceable) to the other persons, so that they retain the mutual dynamic equality.

2000 / 0-85364-863-8 / xiv + 256pp

Eddy José Muskus

The Origins and Early Development of Liberation Theology in Latin America

With Particular Reference to Gustavo Gutiérrez

This work challenges the fundamental premise of Liberation Theology, 'opting for the poor', and its claim that Christ is found in them. It also argues that Liberation Theology emerged as a direct result of the failure of the Roman Catholic Church in Latin America.

2002 / 0-85364-974-X / xiv + 296pp

Jim Purves

The Triune God and the Charismatic Movement

A Critical Appraisal from a Scottish Perspective

All emotion and no theology? Or a fundamental challenge to reappraise and realign our trinitarian theology in the light of Christian experience? This study of charismatic renewal as it found expression within Scotland at the end of the twentieth century evaluates the use of Patristic, Reformed and contemporary models of the Trinity in explaining the workings of the Holy Spirit.

2004 / 1-84227-321-3 / xxiv + 246pp

Anna Robbins

Methods in the Madness

Diversity in Twentieth-Century Christian Social Ethics

The author compares the ethical methods of Walter Rauschenbusch, Reinhold Niebuhr and others. She argues that unless Christians are clear about the ways that theology and philosophy are expressed practically they may lose the ability to discuss social ethics across contexts, let alone reach effective agreements.

2004 / 1-84227-211-X / xx + 294pp

Ed Rybarczyk

Beyond Salvation

Eastern Orthodoxy and Classical Pentecostalism on Becoming Like Christ

At first glance eastern Orthodoxy and classical Pentecostalism seem quite distinct. This ground-breaking study shows they share much in common, especially as it concerns the experiential elements of following Christ. Both traditions assert that authentic Christianity transcends the wooden categories of modernism.

2004 / 1-84227-144-X / xii + 356pp

Signe Sandsmark

Is World View Neutral Education Possible and Desirable?

A Christian Response to Liberal Arguments

(Published jointly with The Stapleford Centre)

This book discusses reasons for belief in world view neutrality, and argues that 'neutral' education will have a hidden, but strong world view influence. It discusses the place for Christian education in the common school.

2000 / 0-85364-973-1 / xiv + 182pp

Hazel Sherman

Reading Zechariah

The Allegorical Tradition of Biblical Interpretation through the Commentary of Didymus the Blind and Theodore of Mopsuestia

A close reading of the commentary on Zechariah by Didymus the Blind alongside that of Theodore of Mopsuestia suggests that popular categorising of Antiochene and Alexandrian biblical exegesis as 'historical' or 'allegorical' is inadequate and misleading.

***2005** / 1-84227-213-6 / approx. 280pp*

Andrew Sloane

On Being a Christian in the Academy

Nicholas Wolterstorff and the Practice of Christian Scholarship

An exposition and critical appraisal of Nicholas Wolterstorff's epistemology in the light of the philosophy of science, and an application of his thought to the practice of Christian scholarship.

2003 / 1-84227-058-3 / xvi + 274pp

Damon W.K. So

Jesus' Revelation of His Father

A Narrative-Conceptual Study of the Trinity with Special Reference to Karl Barth

This book explores the trinitarian dynamics in the context of Jesus' revelation of his Father in his earthly ministry with references to key passages in Matthew's Gospel. It develops from the exegeses of these passages a non-linear concept of revelation which links Jesus' communion with his Father to his revelatory words and actions through a nuanced understanding of the Holy Spirit, with references to K. Barth, G.W.H. Lampe, J.D.G. Dunn and E. Irving.

***2005** / 1-84227-323-X / approx. 380pp*

Daniel Strange

The Possibility of Salvation Among the Unevangelised

An Analysis of Inclusivism in Recent Evangelical Theology

For evangelical theologians the 'fate of the unevangelised' impinges upon fundamental tenets of evangelical identity. The position known as 'inclusivism', defined by the belief that the unevangelised can be ontologically saved by Christ whilst being epistemologically unaware of him, has been defended most vigorously by the Canadian evangelical Clark H. Pinnock. Through a detailed analysis and critique of Pinnock's work, this book examines a cluster of issues surrounding the unevangelised and its implications for christology, soteriology and the doctrine of revelation.

2002 / 1-84227-047-8 / xviii + 362pp

Scott Swain

God According to the Gospel

Biblical Narrative and the Identity of God in the Theology of Robert W. Jenson

Robert W. Jenson is one of the leading voices in contemporary Trinitarian theology. His boldest contribution in this area concerns his use of biblical narrative both to ground and explicate the Christian doctrine of God. *God According to the Gospel* critically examines Jenson's proposal and suggests an alternative way of reading the biblical portrayal of the triune God.

***2006** / 1-84227-258-6 / approx. 180pp*

Justyn Terry

The Justifying Judgement of God

A Reassessment of the Place of Judgement in the Saving Work of Christ

The argument of this book is that judgement, understood as the whole process of bringing justice, is the primary metaphor of atonement, with others, such as victory, redemption and sacrifice, subordinate to it. Judgement also provides the proper context for understanding penal substitution and the call to repentance, baptism, eucharist and holiness.

***2005** / 1-84227-370-1 / approx. 274 pp*

Graham Tomlin

The Power of the Cross

Theology and the Death of Christ in Paul, Luther and Pascal

This book explores the theology of the cross in St Paul, Luther and Pascal. It offers new perspectives on the theology of each, and some implications for the nature of power, apologetics, theology and church life in a postmodern context.

1999 / 0-85364-984-7 / xiv + 344pp

Adonis Vidu

Postliberal Theological Method

A Critical Study

The postliberal theology of Hans Frei, George Lindbeck, Ronald Thiemann, John Milbank and others is one of the more influential contemporary options. This book focuses on several aspects pertaining to its theological method, specifically its understanding of background, hermeneutics, epistemic justification, ontology, the nature of doctrine and, finally, Christological method.

***2005** / 1-84227-395-7 / approx. 324pp*

Graham J. Watts

Revelation and the Spirit

A Comparative Study of the Relationship between the Doctrine of Revelation and Pneumatology in the Theology of Eberhard Jüngel and of Wolfhart Pannenberg

The relationship between revelation and pneumatology is relatively unexplored. This approach offers a fresh angle on two important twentieth century theologians and raises pneumatological questions which are theologically crucial and relevant to mission in a postmodern culture.

2005 */ 1-84227-104-0 / xxii + 232pp*

Nigel G. Wright

Disavowing Constantine

Mission, Church and the Social Order in the Theologies of John Howard Yoder and Jürgen Moltmann

This book is a timely restatement of a radical theology of church and state in the Anabaptist and Baptist tradition. Dr Wright constructs his argument in dialogue and debate with Yoder and Moltmann, major contributors to a free church perspective.

2000 / 0-85364-978-2 / xvi + 252pp

Paternoster
9 Holdom Avenue,
Bletchley,
Milton Keynes MK1 1QR,
United Kingdom
Web: www.authenticmedia.co.uk/paternoster

July 2005

www.ingramcontent.com/pod-product-compliance
Lightning Source LLC
LaVergne TN
LVHW020529100826
845148LV00010B/1396

* 9 7 8 1 5 5 6 3 5 6 6 1 2 *